The Design of
Rural Development

The Design of Rural Development

Lessons from Africa

UMA LELE

With a new postscript by the author

Published for the World Bank

THE JOHNS HOPKINS UNIVERSITY PRESS
Baltimore and London

Originally published, 1975 (cloth and paperback)
Second printing, 1976 (paperback)
Third printing, with new postscript, 1979 (paperback)

Library of Congress Cataloging in Publication Data

Lele, Uma J.
   The design of rural development.
   Bibliography: p.
   Includes index.
   1. Africa—Rural conditions—Case studies. 2. Underdeveloped areas—Economic policy. 3. Underdeveloped areas—Social conditions. I. International Bank for Reconstruction and Development. II. Title.
HN 773.5.L34   309.2'63'096   75-10896
ISBN 0-8018-1756-0
ISBN 0-8018-1769-2 pbk.

Foreword

How to raise productivity among the rural poor in developing countries is one of the two or three most urgent questions confronting the international development community today.

The scale of the problem is immense:

• Of the 2,000 million people in the World Bank's developing member countries, roughly 1,500 million live on the land, and nearly half of those are entrapped in what can only be described as absolute poverty.

• The number of the absolute poor increases and their enforced degradation deepens with every passing year, despite more than two decades of extraordinary worldwide economic growth.

The problem is not merely that the benefits of economic growth have been inequitably distributed, as they have, but that the poor themselves have been unable to contribute to that growth.

The solution, then, lies in raising the productivity of the poor, so that their own incomes can rise as those of others in their societies do.

But how? So far no one has the complete answers, but we in the World Bank are accelerating our efforts to find them, along with many others in governments, international agencies, and academic institutions around the world.

This book represents an important element of our research in this direction. It results from a major study of rural development policies and programs in sub-Saharan Africa. From that experience, it attempts to draw lessons to guide our current and continuing operations in support of government programs to raise the productivity of the rural poor.

ROBERT S. MCNAMARA
President, The World Bank

Table of Contents

I.   **Rural Development Perspectives in Africa**   3

Nature and magnitude of the problem   *3*
Design, timing, and methodology of the study   *6*
Overview of development programs   *12*
The concept of rural development   *19*

II. **Nature of the Production Systems 1:**
     Some Key Influences on the Development of Farming   22

Factors affecting labor flow
    into smallholder agriculture   *23*
The food constraint and specialization
    in agriculture   *27*
Mechanization in smallholder agriculture   *33*
Migration and the development
    of farming systems   *38*
Regional equity in rural development   *45*

III. **Nature of the Production Systems 2:**
     Diversification of Productive Activities   46

Diversification in integrated
    rural development programs   *46*
Development of technological capability
    for diversification   *50*
Farming systems and intraregional equity   *53*
Livestock development in the traditional sector   *56*
Concluding remarks   *60*

IV. **Agricultural Extension and Mass Participation**   62

Different organizational approaches
    to extension services   *64*
Intensity of extension services
    in rural development programs   *66*
Costs implicit in intensity of extension services   *68*
Profitability of technology
    and effectiveness of extension   *69*

Incentives and performance of extension services   *71*
Local participation in extension activities   *73*
Neglect of women in agricultural extension   *76*
Implications of past extension experience
for organization of future extension   *78*

V.   Agricultural Credit   **81**

Some issues related to organization
of agricultural credit   *81*
Potential for saving in the subsistence sector   *82*
Institutional smallholder credit
and formal administrative requirements   *84*
Factors affecting repayment of credit   *93*
Implications of past credit components
for design of future programs   *96*

VI.   Marketing of Agricultural Output   **100**

Factors influencing marketing components   *101*
Effectiveness of marketing components
in the development projects   *102*
Implications for the design
of marketing components   *112*

VII.   Social Services   **116**

Economic justification for social services   *117*
Discrepancies between demand
for social services and resource availability   *120*
Implications for resource mobilization
and increasing participation   *124*

**VIII. Forms of Rural Development Administration 1:
Autonomous Projects**   **127**

Issues related to project authorities   *127*
Africanization of management
in autonomous projects   *130*
Politics, management, and Africanization   *134*
Direction and coordination in the transfer
of functions to the regular administration   *138*
Concluding statement   *140*

**IX.   Forms of Rural Development Administration 2:
Nationally Planned Programs**   **142**

The Special Rural Development Program
in Kenya   *143*
Decentralization and the *ujàmaa* movement
in Tanzania   *151*

X.   Training for Rural Development   162

Training programs and the rural population   *162*
Training of field staff   *170*
Training of managers   *171*

XI.   Summary and Conclusions   175

Some major issues related to designing
   rural development programs   *175*
Effect of national policies on past programs   *178*
Institutional development in past programs   *186*
Implications of the findings of ARDS
   for designing rural development programs   *189*

Glossary   193

Acronyms and non-English terms
   used in the text   *193*
National currencies and exchange rates, 1972   *196*
Equivalents of weights and measures   *196*

Appendix: Project Reviews   197

Cameroon   *197*
Ethiopia   *202*
Kenya   *204*
Malawi   *214*
Mali   *216*
Nigeria   *219*
Tanzania   *221*

Postscript to the Third Printing   227

Rural development objectives and principal findings of
   the previous analysis   *228*
Review of recent World Bank assistance to East African
   rural development   *230*
Expectations and achievements   *236*
The unfinished business: new issues and old   *239*
A concluding remark   *255*

Bibliography   257

Background sources used   *257*
Additional basic reading   *268*

Index   269

Text Tables

1.1   Selected national statistics for the countries containing
        programs reviewed   4
1.2   Major features of the projects reviewed   8

3.1   Comparison of 1966 and 1971 crop production, Chilalo
        Awraja, Ethiopia   47
3.2   Milk purchased, in liters, by CADU, Ethiopia,
        1967/68-1971/72   47
3.3   A comparison of pre-project forecast for year 9
        (maturity) and actual year 2 crop yields in quintals
        per hectare, WADU, Ethiopia   48
3.4   Projected and actual yields of maize and groundnuts in
        quintals per hectare, LLDP, Malawi,
        1969/70-1973/74   49

5.1   Amount of credit and number of loans extended in
        three rural development programs, Ethiopia,
        1967/68-1972/73   86
5.2   Seed and fertilizer distributed on credit in three rural
        development programs, in quintals, Ethiopia,
        1967/68-1972/73   87
5.3   Number and percentage of credit takers and distribu-
        tion of gross benefits, by land tenure and size of hold-
        ing, CADU, Ethiopia, 1968-71   88
5.4   Distribution of inputs on credit by tenancy and sizes of
        farms in nine minimum package areas, Ethiopia,
        1971/72   89
5.5   Distribution of inputs on credit by tenancy of farms in
        the Wolamo Highlands, WADU, Ethiopia, 1971/72   89
5.6   Seasonal credit: amount loaned, number of borrowers,
        and default rates, LLDP, Malawi, 1968/69-1973/74   91
5.7   Total inputs supplied on credit and hectarage covered,
        LLDP, Malawi, 1968/69-1972/73   91

6.1   Grain purchases by the Marketing Division of CADU,
        Ethiopia, and additional benefits received by farmers,
        1967/68-1971/72   103
6.2   Commodities handled by the Marketing, Credit and Co-
        operatives Division of WADU, Ethiopia, 1971/72   104

7.1   Estimated development/recurrent expenditure ratios
        for public services, Kenya, 1966-70   124
7.2   Estimated capital/recurrent expenditure ratios for
        education and health, Tanzania, 1973-80   124

Maps

Cameroon—French technical assistance programs   198
Ethiopia—major rural development programs   201
Kenya—livestock areas   205
Kenya—rural development programs   207
Kenya—agricultural potential and patterns of rural
  migration   211
Malawi—Lilongwe Land Development Program   215
Mali—French technical assistance programs   217
Nigeria—small industrial development   220
Tanzania—tobacco and cotton areas   224

Preface

What explains the very limited impact of past development programs on the low-income rural populations in Africa? Why—despite a great variety of approaches tried by donor and national agencies and despite a great amount of experience generated by these efforts—has the problem of rural poverty remained acute? If future rural development programs are to leave a more long-lasting and positive imprint on rural Africa and the rural world in general, what lessons has this experience to offer for the specification of target groups, the sequencing and phasing of activities, and the choice of policies and institutions?

Concern about these questions and a search for more realistic operational guidelines resulted in intense discussion within the World Bank in 1971. This revealed how little theoretical framework there actually was for guidance in designing and administering programs in rural development and how little systematic, operationally focused analysis actually existed of the practical experience of the past. From this discussion emerged the basis for the present study.

In carrying out a study of this kind, an international agency such as the World Bank is able, of course, to provide an operational focus; but equally important, it is able to draw upon comprehensive evidence developed from a diverse set of experiences in order to examine some of the most important policy and institutional issues of development faced by national governments and donor agencies. To exploit these opportunities, however, analysis of the development issues must go well beyond the use of formal analytical tools if an understanding is to be reached of the many administrative, technological, sociopolitical, and environmental factors that influence the quality of rural planning and that often explain the ineffectiveness of its implementation at the micro level.

To analyze such issues, the present study draws on detailed evidence from seventeen rural development programs in sub-Saharan Africa. In each case existing survey data and analysis have been used in combination with interviews with a number of persons involved in planning, implementation, and evaluation of the programs. From the mass of micro evidence produced, the study identifies the most basic factors that require attention if the gap between the overall objectives of rural development and the actual performance is to be reduced.

Thus, the most important feature of the study lies not so much in a set of definitive solutions as in a way of analyzing the diverse sets of specific constraints and potentials that are encountered in rural areas. There nevertheless emerges from the evidence much practical insight — about an appropriate balance between development of food and export crops, for example, and between productive and social activities, central direction and grass root involvement, and precision in planning and flexibility in implementation. Most important, the study documents the need for, and the nature of, an overall policy and an institutional framework that are conducive to the objectives of rural development.

The field investigations and analyses were carried out by twenty reviewers, whose names, along with salient features of the projects they reviewed, are contained in Table 1.2 (pages 8–11); references to their observations also appear throughout the book. An appendix to the book contains additional description of these programs. The observations in individual studies are supplemented by my extensive field investigations in project areas and by review of a substantial literature on African rural development. There simply would not have been an effective substitute for the highly diversified field investigations and analyses, although administering such a large exercise and synthesizing its findings was not a task without frustrations.

Formulation and completion of a study of this magnitude would not have been possible without the contributions and active support of a large number of individuals and institutions. Members of the Bank's Eastern Africa Region — in particular Shahid Husain, K.G.V. Krishna, and Lyle Hansen — initiated the idea of an operationally oriented study. The governments, research institutions, and the rural people in the countries in which the programs are located, as well as the donor agencies that have financed the programs reviewed, provided much of the information analyzed in individual studies.

Graham Donaldson and Robert Shaw participated in the project reviews and supervised eight project reports. Shirin Velji prepared the substantial bibliography. The final drafts of the manuscript were completed at Cornell University, where I was a senior research fellow at the Center for International Studies and a visiting associate professor in the Department of Agricultural Economics. Milton Esman, Bernard F. Stanton, and Norman Uphoff were instrumental in providing this reflective environment. At Cornell, Arthur Goldsmith assisted me in the writing of the final drafts; his diligence and intellectual curiosity made plodding through thousands of pages of project reviews and related literature a surprisingly manageable task.

Perhaps nothing better indicates the interest in the subject matter than the number of my colleagues at the Bank on whose operational experience I was able to draw and who read and contributed to improvement of the study at various stages. I am much indebted to John Cleave, Andrew Mercer, Bengt Nekby, Peter Nottidge, and Walter Schaefer-Kehnert for their input. Colleagues outside the Bank also took an energetic interest in the study. My many stimulating discussions with John Mellor were responsible for much improvement in the manuscript. Comments by Raj Krishna, Guy Hunter, Jon Moris, Michael Lipton, Carl Eicher, Bruce Johnston, Robert Chambers, Albert Waterston, and Ted Owens helped to broaden the scope of the issues. Of the many African nationals with whom I have had discussions, I am particularly grateful to Paulos Abraham and Philip Mbithi for the indigenous perspective that they provided. Other persons who commented are acknowledged throughout the book, by references to either personal discussions or to their publications.

Alun Morris and Rachel Anderson edited the manuscript and improved its overall presentation; the index was prepared by Annette Braver.

The carrying out of a study such as this, which deals with a diverse set of issues and caters to a broad range of interests, is a rope trick difficult to perform, even for an Indian. I particularly appreciate the unstinting support that I received from Hans Adler, Bernard Bell, Sir John Crawford, Price Gittinger, P.D. Henderson, James Hendry, Nathan Koffsky, Stanley Please, and Alexander Stevenson. Not only have they contributed substantively to the study, but also they have ensured its successful completion in numerous important ways.

Despite these many contributions, I alone am responsible for the views expressed and for those deficiencies which may remain.

UMA LELE

Washington, D.C.
June 1975

The Design of
Rural Development

CHAPTER I

Rural Development Perspectives in Africa

Nature and Magnitude of the Problem

This study of rural development in Africa—the African Rural Development Study, or ARDS—grew out of a substantial interest within the World Bank in finding ways of designing relevant projects that could be accomplished despite limited resources, particularly of money and trained manpower, and that would reach a large proportion of the low-income rural population.

The World Bank's concern was prompted by the fact that between 85 and 95 percent of the nearly 310 million people living in sub-Saharan Africa live in rural areas. Most survive on a meager annual per capita income of less than $100,[1] based largely on low productivity agriculture and livestock (Table 1.1). Their production is oriented mainly towards subsistence. The marketed agricultural production comes largely from a small subsector of large estates, organized ranches, and commercial smallholders. Agriculture constitues the largest sector in the gross national products of most African countries (Table 1.1).

Kenya well illustrates the importance of the rural sector in African economies. Recent estimates indicate that, in 1971, 90 percent of the Kenyan population of approximately 11.7 million lived in the rural sector. Of these, 70 percent consisted of smallholders whose gross annual per capita income was rarely more than $70. Two percent were landless and 12 percent were nomads.

According to recent estimates made by the World Bank, nomads constitute as much as 25 percent of the population in some Sahel countries (Chad, Mali, Mauritania, Niger, Senegal, and Upper Volta). To support their cattle, they depend on vast areas of low-potential land with an unreliable annual rainfall of 250–500 millimeters. Statistics on the levels of living of this traditional pastoral sector are even poorer than those on the subsistence agricultural sector. It is apparent, however, that nomadic living standards are comparable with, if not lower than, those in the subsistence agricultural sector.

---

1. For purposes of comparison, unless otherwise specified, all monetary figures used in this book have been converted into U.S. dollars at official 1972 exchange rates and rounded.

Table 1.1: Selected National Statistics for the Countries Containing Programs Reviewed

Country	Total population mid-1971 (millions) (1)	Population as percentage of total population of sub-Saharan Africa[a] (2)	Rural population as percentage of total (3)	Annual population growth rate 1965–71 (percent) (4)	Per capita agricultural land (hectares) (5)	Per capita GNP, 1971 (US$) (6)	Percent of GDP originating in agriculture, forestry, and fishing (7)	Index of per capita food production in 1972 (base 1961–65 = 100) (8)
Cameroon	5.8	2.4	80	2.1	2.6	200	40	114
Ethiopia	25.3	10.4	91	2.4	2.8	80	54	109
Kenya	11.7	4.8	89	3.3	0.5	160	34	105
Malawi	4.6	1.9	94	2.5[b]	n.a.	90	52	122
Mali	5.1	2.1	88	2.1	7.7	70	43	85
Nigeria	56.5	23.3	76	2.5	0.8	140	50	86
Tanzania	13.2	5.5	92	2.8	4.1	110	40	140[c]

n.a. Not available

a. Excluding South Africa, Rhodesia, Angola, and Mozambique.
b. Recent estimates indicate a more-rapid growth rate in the 1970s, between 3.0 and 3.5 percent per year.
c. Estimates made by the World Bank's Agricultural and Rural Development Sector Survey of Tanzania, conducted in the fall of 1973, indicate a much smaller growth rate of agricultural production than implied in FAO data. According to the survey's estimates, which were based on statistics provided by the government of Tanzania, increases in agricultural production from the 1968–72 period have barely kept pace with the rate of growth of the rural population. The annual growth of agricultural production measured in constant prices declined from 3.9 percent over the period 1964–68 to an annual rate of 2.4 percent during the 1968–72 period. At the same time, the annual rate of growth of total GDP decreased from 6.3 percent to 4.3 percent over comparable periods. These figures indicate that virtually no net per capita gains in agricultural productivity were achieved.

Source: Columns 1, 2, 4, and 6 – World Bank Atlas (Washington, D.C.: World Bank, 1973).
Columns 3, 5, and 7 – USAID, Statistics and Reports Division, AID Economic Data Book for Africa (Washington, D.C.: U.S. Government Printing Office, annual, various years, 1970–74).
Column 8 – Food and Agriculture Organization of the United Nations, FAO Production Yearbook, 1972, vol. 26 (Rome: FAO, 1973).

Per capita cultivable land is higher in Africa compared to the densely populated parts of Asia as, for example, an average of 2.84 hectares in Ethiopia (Table 1.1) compared to 0.28 hectares in India. However, labor input tends to be lower and soils are generally poorer.[2] Hence, average per hectare yields of principal crops may be lower in Africa than those attained in Asia.[3]

The overall per capita food production in sub-Saharan Africa has not shown much increase (Table 1.1). Contrary to much of the conventional wisdom on development, which assumed that growth would lead to greater participation, increases in productivity in the already commercialized rural subsector have had relatively little effect on the living standards of the subsistence population.

With annual population growth rates in the range of 2.5 to 3.5 percent, the population pressure on land has been increasing rapidly with all the consequent effects of poverty: hunger, unstable family life, poor nutrition, ill health, and little or no access to formal education.

Understandably, the attraction of the city lights is considerable. Recent censuses show that between 1962 and 1969 the population of Nairobi grew at the rate of 15.2 percent per year. According to estimates reported by the World Bank, between 1957 and 1967 the migrant population in Dar es Salaam increased at an average rate of 8 percent per year. However, urban employment has not been increasing rapidly enough to absorb the flood of rural migrants, partly because of the particular enclave nature of industrial development.

The manufacturing sector has included a relatively small indigenous entrepreneurial element and few linkages to domestic resources or to rural demand. Industrial production has been capital intensive, based largely on imported inputs, and caters to a small market of relatively high-income domestic urban consumers.[4] In the absence of development of the subsistence rural sector, inadequate effective demand remains a major constraint to development of the manufacturing and the service sector, which otherwise holds considerable potential for increasing employment.[5] Improving living standards of the subsistence rural sector is important, not only as a holding operation until industrialization can advance sufficiently to absorb the rural exodus, but frequently as the only logical way of stimulating overall development. This approach is also essential for purposes of improving the general welfare of an extremely large section of the low-income population.

2. Lawrence Dudley Stamp and W.T.W. Morgan, *Africa: A Study in Tropical Development*, 3rd ed. (New York: Wiley, 1972).

3. See Food and Agriculture Organization of the United Nations, *FAO Production Yearbook, 1971*, vol. 25 (Rome: FAO, 1972), Table 13B. FAO estimates indicate that per capita caloric intake is also generally lower in sub-Saharan Africa than in South Asia, although fat and protein consumption is often higher. See Tables 136–38.

4. See International Labour Organisation, *Employment, Incomes and Equality: A Strategy for Increasing Productive Employment in Kenya*, report of an interagency team financed by the United Nations Development Programme and organized by ILO (Geneva: ILO, 1972).

5. See John W. Mellor and Uma J. Lele, "Growth Linkages of the New Foodgrain Technologies," in *Indian Journal of Agricultural Economics*, vol. 28, no. 1 (January–March 1973), pp. 35–55; also Uma J. Lele and John W. Mellor, "Jobs, Poverty, and the 'Green Revolution'," in *International Affairs*, vol. 48, no. 1 (January 1972).

Design, Timing, and Methodology of the Study

Rural development has, therefore, received a great deal of attention in recent years in development literature, national plans, political platforms, and in the lending programs of most donors.[6] This widespread interest is reflected in the considerable increase in the number of rural development programs being undertaken by the national governments and assisted by external donors. However, the knowledge as to how to bring about development of the subsistence rural sector is still very limited.

The African Rural Development Study was carried out to improve such knowledge and to provide guidelines, based on analysis of past experience, for design and implementation of the World Bank's future rural development programs in Africa. ARDS builds on earlier Bank-initiated research into agricultural development in tropical Africa.[7] However, as distinct from the previous efforts, the present study is marked by three new areas of concern. First, in recent years there has been an explicit interest in promoting participation of the lowest income groups through rural development programs. Second, development has been viewed more broadly from the perspective of improved welfare as well as of increased agricultural productivity. Consequently, there has been a keen interest in identifying ways of establishing priorities and of time-phasing between and among both productive and social service activities. Third, there has been a clear recognition of the financial, manpower, and institutional constraints encountered in rural development. This has identified the need to find ways of making maximum use of these resources and of augmenting the existing rural potential over time.

The focus of the study is, therefore, consciously operational—for example, to examine the factors which influenced the choice of interventions in planning past programs, including the capacity of these programs to identify constraints and potentials in the course of planning and implementation, and to assess the extent to which the programs were able to deal with circumstances not initially forseen. One of the main objectives of ARDS has, thus, been to investigate whether and how the reviewed projects and similar programs should have been designed, had there been more concern with broad participation, overall welfare, and the utilization of local financial and institutional resources. Relatedly, the study also investigates whether there is a need to bring about institutional and procedural changes in planning and implementing rural development programs to increase their effectiveness in realizing the new objectives of development.

For the comparative evaluations on which the major findings presented here are based, seventeen sets of rural development projects and programs involving the participation of a number of multilateral, bilateral, and national agencies were carefully analyzed. These were selected from nearly sixty programs in various parts of sub-Saharan Africa initially listed for perusal. While no limited survey can claim to be exhaustive, the projects

---

6. See, for instance, Robert S. McNamara, *Address to the Board of Governors,* Nairobi, September 24, 1973 (Washington, D.C.: World Bank, 1973).

7. See the Bank-sponsored study by John C. de Wilde, *Experiences with Agricultural Development in Tropical Africa,* 2 vols. (Baltimore: Johns Hopkins Press, 1967).

were selected to represent a very considerable diversity in design and implementation as well as in the environment in which they are situated.[8] The reviews were carried out with a view to raising a consistent set of questions about these programs and projects so as to facilitate comparison and to provide the basis for obtaining operational insights.[9] This work has also drawn on the rural sector surveys conducted by the Bank in Kenya in 1972 and in Tanzania in 1973 as part of the African Rural Development Study. These surveys analyzed development policies to evolve lending strategies for the two countries.

The objectives and the methodology of the study were finalized after considerable discussions among various Bank staff as well as with persons outside the World Bank who had been involved in rural development. From these discussions a consensus emerged that, before collecting additional information, it was necessary to analyze the existing information systematically and comparatively, to review the state of the knowledge on rural development, to improve operational decisions, and to develop insights into the priorities for further operational research.

Given the considerable interest of the operational parts of the Bank in the findings of the study, the evaluations of the programs on which this report is based were completed in sixteen months between July 1972 and December 1973. All the reviews were based on data already collected by a number of agencies. With a few exceptions no field surveys to obtain additional quantitative data were conducted. However, in all cases data analyses were combined with field investigations. These consisted of (a) interviews with persons who had considerable experience in design, implementation, supervision, and evaluation of the specific programs reviewed or similar other programs; (b) interviews with the rural people who were being reached through programs; and (c) searches for additional sources of data related to programs reviewed from other donor, government, and research agencies.

---

8. See Table 1.2 of this study. The following section of this chapter and the Appendix contain additional information and map locations of the programs reviewed. To facilitate comparative analysis in conducting reviews, some of the programs were grouped together. Therefore, although seventeen sets of programs were reviewed, only thirteen project reports were prepared. The last column of Table 1.2 indicates the grouping of the programs, and the Appendix provides their corresponding descriptions.

9. In this report the terms "projects" and "programs" are used interchangeably. However, since the analysis is carried out with the objective of providing guidelines to the Bank Group for designing projects, the distinction between the two is worth noting at this stage. A project is generally understood to mean (a) a well-defined range of activities which lend themselves to rather precise specification of objectives to planning, financing, and implementing within an organized unit and which have a clear beginning; (b) a set of targets by which to judge their performance; and (c) an orderly specified end. A number of activities financed by donor agencies in the rural sector have usually been designed, appraised, implemented, and evaluated within this project concept. On the other hand, the *ujamaa* movement and the Sukumaland cotton development in Tanzania or the spontaneous squatter settlements in Kenya are not projects in this sense. They have been prompted by broader sociopolitical or administrative considerations which do not lend themselves to precise specification of objectives or to a precise set of targets by which to judge their performance. Therefore, although many of the issues in this book are presented in terms of their implications for project design and implementation, the analysis deals with broader questions related to development of the low-income subsistence sector. As will be apparent later in the text, these broader questions have substantial implications for what constitutes a project. It should also be noted that, despite their obvious limitations and for the sake of brevity, the terms "low income" or "subsistence" are used interchangeably in this study to describe the target populations.

Table 1.2: Major Features of the Projects Reviewed

Country	Project	Category	First year of implementation	Project aim
Cameroon	Zones d'Action Prioritaires Intégrées (ZAPI)	Regional integrated rural development	1967	To integrate rural development under independent, nongovernmental companies set up in each of seven selected areas in the East and South Central provinces; involving farmer organizations, extension and credit, and social development
Cameroon	Société de Développement du Nkam (SODENKAM) Land Settlement Scheme	Regional settlement and integrated rural development	1966	To integrate development of pioneer villages in a sparsely populated region of 120,000 hectares in the Littoral province; technical and cooperative marketing support for coffee and cocoa production; social development
Ethiopia	Chilalo Agricultural Development Unit (CADU)	Regional integrated rural development	1967	To provide a wide range of productive and social services, assisting participants to increase net per capita income
Ethiopia	Wolamo Agricultural Development (WADU)	Regional integrated rural development and settlement	1970	As above—and to establish 1,750 settlers in two lowland areas of Wolamo
Ethiopia	Minimum Package Program (MPP)	Miscellaneous	1970	To provide rudimentary facilities, including credit, fertilizer, improved seeds, extension, cooperative development, and feeder roads for 100 areas in the fourteen highland provinces to be reached by 1980
Kenya	Kenya Livestock Development Project (KLDP)	Miscellaneous	1970 (Swynnerton Plan developed in mid-fifties. Kenya Range Development Program began in 1964)	To provide credit for development of individual, commercial, company, and group ranches and grazing blocks to promote rural employment and to increase production and export of livestock products
Kenya	Agricultural Finance Corporation (AFC)	Functional	1963 (Some functions begun under British Land Transfer Program in 1961 and the Land and Agriculture Bank in 1931)	To finance a large number of activities throughout the rural sector, including purchase of land from European owners, livestock raising, procurement of farm equipment, and on-farm development
Kenya	Special Crops Development Authority (SCDA); Kenya Tea Development Authority (KTDA)	Commodity	SCDA: 1960 (to 1964); KDTA: 1964	To increase tea production and exports among smallholders

8

Project cost[a]	Financing agencies	Project population[b]	Average size[c] of holding	Authors of reports prepared under the study
South Central province: $2.48 million (to 1972); *East province:* Initial financial assistance of $0.7 million provided to the project, excluding technical assistance	FAC and government of Cameroon	Population of approximately 175,000 in the seven ZAPIs	Less than 3 hectares for cocoa and 1 hectare for food crops	G. Belloncle D. Gentil
$0.5 million (1972/73)	Government of Cameroon	Settlement of 18,000 to 22,500 inhabitants by 1981	1.0–2.0 hectares	
$19.3 million (to 1975)	SIDA, with government of Ethiopia	Population within Chilalo Awraja of 400,000	3 hectares	T. Tecle
$5.1 million (to 1974)	IDA, United Kingdom, and World Food Program, with government of Ethiopia	Population within Wolamo Awraja of 240,000; 460 old settlements reorganized and about 207 new settlers accommodated by October 1972	0.5 hectares	
$30 million (to 1976)	IDA, SIDA, and FAO, with government of Ethiopia	Approximately 5 million people living in MPP areas in 1974; 19 million people to be reached by 1980s	0.7–2.0 hectares	
$11.3 million (to 1974) [d]	IDA, SIDA, USAID, with government of Kenya	2,500–3,000 ranchers or pastoralists	*Individual ranches:* 600 hectares; *commercial ranches:* 3,250 hectares; *group ranches:* 18,000 hectares; *grazing blocks:* 700,000 hectares	H. Jahnke H. Ruthenberg H. Thim
$33 million (total assets in 1971) [e]	IDA, SIDA, British Land Transfer Program, Federal Republic of Germany, with government of Kenya	Covers the entire country	Not applicable	J.D. von Pischke
$15.6 million (to 1971)	IDA, Commonwealth Development Corporation (CDC), the Federal Republic of Germany, with government of Kenya	66,500 farmers cultivating tea (1972)	2.7 hectares	D. Sullivan

(Table continues on the following page.)

9

Table 1.2 (continued)

Country	Project	Category	First year of implementation	Project aim
Kenya	Special Rural Development Program (SRDP)	Regional integrated rural development	1971	To enable major strategic exercise by the Kenyan government in decentralized and innovative planning, embracing numerous programs for increasing rural incomes, employment and welfare
Kenya	Spontaneous Land Settlement	Spontaneous effort	Not applicable	Substantial local self-help among squatters who have established settlements on land to which they have no title
Malawi	Lilongwe Land Development Program (LLDP)	Regional integrated rural development	1967	To increase production of major crops in a concentrated area of 465,587 hectares through improvements in rural infrastructure, land reorganization, training, credit, extension, marketing, and livestock development
Mali	Compagnie Française pour le Développement des Fibres et Textiles (CFDT)	Commodity	1952	To increase cotton production and exports
Mali	Bureau pour le Développement de Production Agricole (BDPA)— Opération Arachide	Commodity	1967	To improve groundnut production and marketing and to increase exports
Nigeria	Small-scale rural industries: Industrial Development Center (IDC) and Small Industry Credit Schemes (SIC)	Miscellaneous	IDC: 1962; SIC: 1966	To provide finance, investment guidance, training, and other services for new and expanding small industries
Tanzania	Urambo Settlement Scheme; Tumbi Settlement Scheme; World Bank Flue-Cured Tobacco Project	Commodity	Urambo: 1951; Tumbi: 1954; World Bank: 1970	To increase tobacco production through settlement schemes at Urambo and Tumbi linked to farmers' cooperatives and provision of credit and extension and to increase tobacco production for export in 150 *ujàmaa* villages in the Tabora region through a program linked to collective processing
Tanzania	Sukumaland Cotton Development	Commodity	1950	To increase production of cotton for export on existing and new farms in the Sukumaland area of northwest Tanzania through government initiatives in husbandry, credit, extension, research, land clearance, and cooperatives
Tanzania	*Ujàmaa* village development	Regional integrated rural and social development	1967	To create communally organized self-help villages, promoted through decentralized administration and the Tanganyika African National Union (TANU)

a. The cost figures are based on the best available information and converted to U.S. dollars at official 1972 currency exchange rates. In several cases where the project was of an informal and/or broadly defined nature, it was impossible to estimate costs.

b. Except for SODENKAM, KLDP, KTDA, and Smallholder Tobacco Development, the population figures refer to the number of persons living within the project area, many or most of whom are not direct participants in program activities. These nonparticipants may, nonetheless, "benefit" from the project's interventions, though the impact will, of course, be greater on the active participants.

Project cost[a]	Financing agencies	Project population[b]	Average size[c] of holding	Authors of reports prepared under the study
$1.6 million (in 1972/73)	Government of Kenya, with USAID, SIDA, the United Kingdom, NORAD, and the Netherlands	Six districts with population of 826,000 (1971)	Not applicable	N. Bedi
Not applicable	Not applicable	The Kenyan squatter population is approximately 300,000 (1969)	Not applicable	P. Mbithi C. Barnes
$14.6 million (to 1975)	IDA with government of Malawi	Population of 550,000 (1973) within Lilongwe district	2.0–4.0 hectares	B.H. Kinsey
$9.8 million (up to 1971/72)	European Development Fund and FAC	Population of 1.0 million within cotton zone (1971/72)	4.0–5.0 hectares	W. Anderson
$19.7 million (up to 1971/72)	FAC with project support by World Bank	Population of 0.75 million within the groundnut operation (1971/72)	3.83 hectares (1970)	W. Anderson
Not available	USAID with government of Nigeria	IDC: northern and eastern regions; SIC: northern region	Not applicable	H. Turner M. Shah
Urambo: $0.26 million (in 1964/65); Tumbi: $0.10 million (in 1964/65); World Bank: $14.7 million (by 1978)	Urambo: originally Tanganyika Agricultural Corporation; Tumbi: originally British American Tobacco Co.; World Bank: International Development Association (IDA), with government of Tanzania	Urambo: 2,400 farmers cultivating tobacco (1970); Tumbi: 4,600 farmers cultivating tobacco (1970); World Bank: 15,000 to 30,000 farmers cultivating tobacco (by 1978)	Urambo: 2.0 hectares; Tumbi: 1.2 hectares; World Bank: 4.0 hectares[f]	M. Agarwal D. Linsenmeyer
Not available	Government of Tanzania and IDA	Sukumaland population of 2.5 million	3.1 hectares	M. Collinson
Not available	Government of Tanzania with assistance from various agencies for specific projects	2 million ujamaa village residents (1973); expected to cover entire rural population by the end of 1975	Not applicable	F. Robinson P. Abraham

c. These figures should be taken only as approximations, as some refer to family holding and others to cropped area per farm. Figures on a more comparable basis could not be obtained.

d. A second livestock project, costing $59.7 million, will enlarge and extend the project as reviewed in this study.

e. Total cost of AFC could not be obtained. In the 1970/71 period AFC disbursed about $4.3 million.

f. The World Bank tobacco project also called for the settlers to be provided with 12 hectares of timberland and 4 hectares of non-arable land.

Source: Project reviews carried out under ARDS.

11

The availability of data varied considerably between programs. For those programs which either had a substantial data base and/or were reviewed by consultants who had earlier carried out considerable primary research on particular programs (as in the case of the Lilongwe Land Development Program in Malawi; cotton development in Sukumaland, Tanzania; or range development in Kenya), much systematic analysis has been possible through reviews.

In other cases (e.g., *ujàmaa* in Tanzania or the French-assisted cotton and groundnut schemes in Mali), even the benefits which are normally considered to be easily quantifiable, such as increases in agricultural production, could not be estimated reasonably accurately. Cost records were insufficient in many cases. Wherever possible, conventional cost/benefit analyses were conducted. However, the major strength of this study lies in its examination of the broad institutional and participatory questions related to rural development rather than in its conventional evaluations of projects.

The methodological tools available for analysis of such institutional and distributional questions are, of course, rather crude—a problem that is compounded by the need for an interdisciplinary approach to such analyses. There is also a broad range of views on rural development and on the validity of some of the research results. Wherever possible, these various points of view have been presented to provide a balance to the arguments and to broaden the perspective.

Substantial literature on African rural development has also been reviewed to support or oppose the observations made in the study. However, a strong consensus emerges on a surprisingly large number of issues.

Overview of Development Programs

The programs selected for analysis may quite justifiably be classified in several alternative ways as, for instance, by degree of integration, breadth of objectives, size of target population, or by funding agencies. To emphasize their diversity in design and implementation and to point to the gradual shift in objectives, they are classified into the following five categories:

Commodity Programs

The first investments in the development of low-income subsistence agriculture in Africa were prompted by the relatively straightforward objective of increasing production of export crops in the smallholder sector. They were financed by European commercial companies, development corporations, or the governments of former colonies. Four sets of such programs were selected for analysis.

To increase tea production and exports among smallholders, the Kenya Tea Development Authority (KTDA, first known as the Special Crops Development Authority) was established by the Kenyan government in 1960. By 1972 the project had brought 24,900 hectares in ten districts under tea cultivation and produced almost 313,000 quintals of green leaf. The net return from a hectare of tea (1970/71) was approximately $543. To put rural income disparities in Africa in a proper perspective, it is important to note that, even with a substantial improvement, the per capita average annual net cash income from tea production was only about $41, compared to the per capita cash income of $7 in the pre-program era.[10] The smallholder sector presently accounts for 21 percent of Kenya's total tea production. KTDA is known as one of the most successful and profitable rural development projects.

Development of smallholder tobacco was undertaken by the Tanganyika Agricultural Corporation (TAC) in the Urambo region of Tanganyika in 1951. The scheme is now managed by the Urambo Farmers Cooperative Society. A similar scheme, presently managed by the Tabora Tobacco Growers Cooperative Society, was started by the British American Tobacco Company (BAT) in the nearby Tumbi region in 1954. Combined tobacco production in the two schemes grew from about 1,110 quintals in 1960 to nearly 36,300 quintals by 1970. The two schemes produced about a third of Tanzania's flue-cured tobacco (flue-cured tobacco constitutes over 80 percent of Tanzania's tobacco exports). In the mid-1960s the per capita cash income of the tobacco-growing population was estimated to be $21 in Tumbi and $62 in Urambo, compared to $5–$10 for the non-tobacco–farming population in the Tabora region.[11]

In Mali a cotton production operation was undertaken in 1952 with assistance from the Compagnie Française pour le Développement des Fibres et Textiles (CFDT). A similar scheme for groundnuts—Opération Arachide—was started by the Bureau pour le Développement de Production Agricole (BDPA) in 1967. In 1972 the CFDT project produced virtually all of Mali's cotton and the BDPA scheme about half of Mali's groundnuts. From 1961 to 1972 CFDT's cotton production increased from 6,000 to 68,000 metric tons. Between 1967 and 1972 groundnut production under BDPA increased from 18,000 to 75,000 metric tons. Participants in the CFDT project had net per capita cash incomes of approximately $14 in 1972. The figure for participants in BDPA was approximately $2–$5.

In these export crop schemes, the agricultural services of extension, credit, inputs, marketing, and processing have been administered through project authorities or parastatal organizations. The project authorities have considerable autonomy, although technically they may be under the Ministry of Agriculture. Most cash crop schemes initially managed by expatriates are being more rapidly Africanized since independence.

10. The per capita income figures given here and below are only approximations and are not strictly comparable between projects, since some refer to net income and others to net cash income (i.e., excluding the value of subsistence production). More comparable figures could not be obtained. The existing income statistics are useful, however, in indicating levels of living in the program areas. The production and hectarage figures are likewise limited. Though based on the best available information, there are inevitable disparities in the quality and currency of the data. Sources and limitations of various data series are discussed in individual project reviews. Where relevant for analyses, these questions have been discussed in the subsequent chapters. A further difficulty is encountered in estimating the number of persons reached by a specific project activity, which generally refers to a narrow definition of project benefits. References to population covered by a project imply the potential population that may eventually be reached according to the broader criteria.

11. See W. Scheffler, "Tobacco Schemes in the Central Region," in *Smallholder Farming and Smallholder Development in Tanzania,* ed. Hans Ruthenberg, Afrika-Studien no. 24 (Munich: Weltforum Verlag, 1968); and W. Scheffler, *Baüerliche Produktion unter Aufsicht am Beispiel des Tabakanbaus in Tanzania, Eine Social-Ökonomische Studie,* Afrika-Studien no. 27 (Munich: Weltforum Verlag, 1968).

Development of export crops has also occurred through normal administrative efforts. Cotton development in Sukumaland, Tanzania, is such a
case. As a result of the Tanzanian government's extension program, tsetse
fly clearance, and cotton marketing service, average cotton hectarage per
farm in Sukumaland increased from 0.28 hectares in 1950 to 1.54 hectares
in 1966. Total cotton production in the area grew from 40,000 bales in 1950
to 405,000 bales in 1970. The increase in cotton production was facilitated
by the more than doubling of the world market price of cotton, which rose
from $0.09 to $0.21 per kilogram between 1950 and 1962. According to the
detailed farm management surveys carried out by Collinson, the annual
per capita cash income in the region increased from less than $2 to about
$22 between 1950 and 1966.

The major differences between the export crop developments undertaken by the indigenous administrations and those undertaken with commercial or foreign assistance and administered through autonomous project
authorities are the latter's greater administrative coordination and use of
trained manpower and financial resources. For example, while KTDA had
one extension worker for every 120 farmers and CFDT one for every 175
farmers, the ratio in Sukumaland has been 1:1,020. KTDA's total operating
expenses per beneficiary, excluding capital costs for factory construction,
road building, and so forth, were estimated to be $200 by 1971, or $18 per
beneficiary per year. Given the 1.7 million to 2.0 million farm familes in
Kenya, if similar investment were undertaken on a national scale, it would
mean an annual recurrent expenditure of approximately $30–$36 million
for agriculture services alone. The Kenyan government's total recurrent expenditure on agriculture averaged $24.3 million between 1968 and 1971.[12]

Obviously, to apply the intensity of KTDA's extension effort on a national scale, the government would have had to increase its spending on agriculture by only 25 to 50 percent. However, it is not so much the total
resources allocated which determine effectiveness as the way in which the
resources are used. In this regard KTDA has been extraordinarily effective.
The reasons for KTDA's success are analyzed later in this study.

Regional Rural Development Programs

The regional programs reviewed under ARDS may be classified as two
types: (a) integrated rural development programs undertaken mainly on the
initiative of donor agencies and planned and administered by expatriates
and (b) regional development programs undertaken with substantial initiative and participation by national governments. Three sets of integrated
programs of the first type and two sets of the second were selected for analysis in this review.

Programs of the first type include (i) the Chilalo Agricultural Develop-
ment Unit (CADU) and the Wolamo Agricultural Development Unit
(WADU), both in Ethiopia; (ii) the Lilongwe Land Development Program
(LLDP) in Malawi; (iii) the Zones d'Action Prioritaires Intégrées (ZAPI)

---

12. USAID, Statistics and Reports Division, "Central Government Finances: Kenya," in
AID Economic Data Book for Africa, revision no. 286 (Washington, D.C.: U.S. Government
Printing Office, October 1972).

and the Société de Développement du Nkam (SODENKAM) settlement scheme (originally Opération Yabassi-Bafang), both in Cameroon.

These regional programs have been based on the assumption that a critical minimum effort is necessary to make a noticeable impact on the target populations in a relatively short period. The integrated programs have, therefore, simultaneously provided a number of productive and social services, such as soil conservation measures, roads, general agricultural extension, credit, marketing services, livestock development services, training, health clinics, water supply, and nutrition education. As in many agro-industrial enterprises, the integrated programs have involved substantial concentrations of financial and trained manpower resources in relatively small geographical areas (see Table 1.2).

For example, the Lilongwe Land Development Program in Malawi originally covered an area of only 238,460 hectares. During negotiations with IDA the program expanded to include an estimated 465,550 hectares. LLDP was expected to increase the per capita net annual income of participants in the program from approximately $10 to the range of $17–$35, depending on how income was defined and estimated. By the 1972/73 period LLDP had constructed 851 miles of roads, fifteen major bridges, and 340 boreholes. In the same year the program trained 25,000 farmers and distributed 23,000 seasonal credit loans worth a total of approximately $457,000.

In Ethiopia the Chilalo Agricultural Development Unit, located in Chilalo Awraja, covers about one million hectares. The project was extended to assist participants in attaining a net annual per capita income of approximately $33. In the 1972/73 period CADU distributed 13,000 loans totaling about $420,000. The program also carries out substantial staff training as well as developing agricultural technology, marketing cooperatives, feeder roads, and an improved water supply. LLDP and CADU each employed over thirty expatriates during their first few years of program implementation.

Also in Ethiopia the Wolamo Agricultural Development Unit in Wolamo Awraja is more modest in scale. In its first phase the program was expected to raise the per capita cash income of members of 7,750 participating farm families from $11 a year to $18–$24. In 1972 the program disbursed 7,400 loans worth $132,000. WADU has also conducted road and water development programs and has settled or reorganized 600 families in sparsely populated lowland areas. At the time the program was reviewed, WADU had carried out little staff training.

The seven integrated priority action zones, or ZAPIs, located in the South Central and East province of Cameroon, were planned in 1966 by Compagnie d'Etudes Industrielles et d'Aménagement du Territoire (CINAM), a private French firm. Participants in the three East ZAPIs were expected to increase their annual per capita income from $19 to $47. In 1972 the four South Central ZAPIs loaned about $363,000 as working capital for cocoa production. ZAPIs have also involved an intensive extension effort (one advisor per 150 farmers), women's extension programs, and the establishment of farmers' organizations. The programs carried out by ZAPIs in the East province were similar. In 1972 they disbursed approximately $45,700 in loans.

The SODENKAM settlement scheme, located in the Littoral province of Cameroon, was designed by Société Centrale pour les Etudes du Territoire–Coopération (SCET–Coopération) in 1964. By 1972, 1,180 pioneer familes had been settled in the project area. To date SODENKAM has distributed 400,000 coffee seedlings and 300,000 cocoa seedlings and has built ten schools and six health dispensaries. The program also has a cooperative marketing component.

Because the existing indigenous administrative capacity in Malawi, Ethiopia, and Cameroon was inadequate for the implementation of complex rural development programs, the integrated programs were administered through parallel administrative structures established along the line of agro-industrial enterprises. In creating such autonomous administrative units, it was assumed that the improvements in the indigenous administrative systems essential to achieve similar results on a wider scale could often be initiated more effectively by the demonstration effect of the integrated projects than by the alternative of improving the inadequate, uncoordinated, and ill-trained existing administration. In the short run the use of a large number of expatriates in managerial positions made possible by the creation of autonomous project authorities has also substantially increased the capacity of the recipient countries to invest in regional development.

Unlike the integrated programs, the two nationally initiated efforts reviewed in the study, namely, the Special Rural Development Program (SRDP) in Kenya and the *ujàmaa* movement and associated decentralization of administration in Tanzania, have been undertaken largely with the objective of improving the domestic capacity for planning and implementation. It is hoped that with this approach the indigenous administrations will develop the capability to carry out effectively the ultimate objective of increasing the incomes and welfare of the mass of the subsistence rural population.

SRDP, conceived in 1966, was a major administrative effort to improve interministerial and interdepartmental coordination. Implicit in the SRDP concept was the delegation of planning and implementing responsibility to the lower levels of administration so as to reduce the planning and implementation gap and thus improve the effectiveness of rural administration. The program involved the initiation of a variety of rural development schemes, including a master farmer project, the development of hybrid maize and cotton, a cattle development program, youth training, road construction, and home economics extension. These schemes were to be planned and administered by divisional and local-level administrators. In 1971 SRDP covered six districts with 8 percent of Kenya's rural population. Apart from improving administrative effectiveness in the districts, SRDP aimed at producing administrative innovations that would be a step towards greater administrative decentralization on a national scale. Thus, SRDP is essentially an exercise in deconcentration of administrative authority.[13]

In Tanzania, by contrast, there has been an attempt to bring about

13. See David K. Leonard, "Communication and Deconcentration," in *Development Administration: The Kenyan Experience,* eds. Goran Hyden, Robert Jackson, and John Okumu (Nairobi: Oxford University Press, 1970), pp. 102–11; and Chapter IX of this book.

devolution of administrative power by fostering participation of the peasant masses in the planning and implementation of rural development programs. *Ujàmaa* village settlements constitute a major part of the development strategy. It is expected that ultimately all activities in the *ujàmaa* villages will be undertaken on a cooperative basis. Between the Arusha declaration of *ujàmaa* policy in 1967 and the year 1973, more than 5,500 *ujàmaa* villages were formed. The degree of local participation and collective cultivation varies substantially among these villages. Since 1972 primary administrative authority for the planning and implementation of the rural development effort has been vested in the regional offices rather than in central ministries. The village and ward-level committees, which represent smallholder interests, and the Tanganyika African National Union (TANU), which is the national political party, have also been assigned a greater role than they enjoyed previously in the allocation of budgetary resources and the planning and implementation of local programs.

Functional Programs

While the regional programs involve a multifaceted approach to rural development, the functional programs are undertaken to remove a single constraint that is considered to be particularly critical for getting rural development under way. Investment may be directed only to the development of a national network of adaptive agricultural research, to training extension services, to the construction of feeder roads, to the provision of agricultural credit, or to improving the agricultural marketing network. Functional programs are appealing because of their relatively clear and limited objective and their potential for benefiting large numbers of rural people. In one sense functional programs are also somewhat easier to implement than integrated programs, since they involve only the development of a single major institutional structure. Substantial investment in a particular functional program can also be an effective means of emphasizing the program's critical importance, of generating a long-term national commitment to it, and of ensuring that sufficient national resources are allocated for its continuance. Functional programs may also be effective in stimulating other developments—e.g., demand for fertilizer may be stimulated by profitable technologies, and production for market may be prompted by feeder roads.

The agricultural credit administered by Kenya's Agricultural Finance Corporation (AFC) constitutes such a functional program. Though the bulk of AFC's operations have been aimed at large-scale farmers, the agency has had programs for smallholders since 1965. Most significant of these has been the World Bank's smallholder credit project (IDA 105), for which IDA provided $3.6 million in 1967. Aimed to assist 8,100 farmers with per capita cash incomes of approximately $30–$35, by 1972 the project had approved 10,000 loans averaging $470.[14] Nevertheless, during the fiscal year ending in March 1971, only about 30 percent of AFC's total disbursements, or $1.3 million, were classified as small-scale loans (i.e., loans under $1,400).

14. The cotton and tobacco development schemes in Tanzania discussed above have also been assisted through similar credit programs financed by loans from IDA. These funds have been administered through the Tanzanian Rural Development Bank.

AFC's activities cover the entire country and involve financing a large number of activities in the rural sector, including the purchase of land from European owners, livestock raising, and the procurement of farm equipment. AFC's interest rates ranged from 3.5 percent per annum on loans for land purchases to 7.5–8.0 percent for seasonal loans to smallholders. By contrast, the interest rates charged by traditional sources of credit, such as friends, relatives, and local moneylenders, vary substantially. They are, however, generally presumed to be far higher than those charged by credit institutions, such as AFC, and often exceed 100 percent per year.

Miscellaneous Category of Planned Programs

Production of specific commodities may be developed by providing a number of services related to the development of a specific subsector or region. The Kenya Livestock Development Project (KLDP), the Industrial Development Centers (IDC) in Nigeria, and the Minimum Package Program (MPP) in Ethiopia constitute such cases of subsectoral development.

The livestock program undertaken by the government of Kenya involves the development of commercial, company, individual, and group ranches in Kenya's Central, Eastern, and Rift Valley provinces. In addition, USAID has been assisting in the creation of grazing blocks on marginal land in the Northeast province. By 1972 thirty commercial, eight company, thirty-nine individual, and twenty-five group ranches were financed. Loans to commercial ranches averaged $46,000 per ranch. For company, individual, and group ranches, the average loan sizes were $106,000, $5,570, and $4,250, respectively. It was expected that these loans would generate additional employment for 400 persons on commercial ranches and for 422 persons on company ranches. Loans to individual or group ranches were not expected to create additional employment opportunities but only to support the existing pastoral population. The development of grazing blocks involves direct grants rather than loans. Total investment in the blocks is expected to be $1.5 million.

In 1962 Nigeria established an Industrial Development Center in Zaria. Another IDC was initiated in Owerri the following year. The purpose of these centers was to appraise applications of small industries for financing, to provide advice on investment opportunities, and to sponsor training in a wide range of technical and managerial skills. Between 1969 and 1972 loans of $2.7 million were granted to 294 small enterprises (employing less than fifty persons and with fixed assets worth $90,000 or less) in such industries as baking, sawmilling, printing, and motor vehicle repairing.

To spread the benefits of agricultural development more broadly than is possible in the integrated programs, the Minimum Package Program (MPP) was undertaken by the Ethiopian government in 1971 on the initiative of the Swedish technical experts involved in the Chilalo Agricultural Development Unit. The program is being implemented by the Evaluation and Program Implementation Department of the Ministry of Agriculture. As its name suggests, MPP involves the provision of only those services considered to be critical for rural development. In this case they include agricultural extension, credit, cooperative development, and feeder roads. Plans call for the development by 1981 of one hundred MPP areas in the fourteen highland provinces. Some twenty-eight of these areas were in operation in

1974. Each MPP area is intended to contain about 10,000 farming families. If developed according to plan, MPP will cover about half of the geographic area of Ethiopia and will involve the entire agricultural population, excluding the nomadic tribes.

Spontaneous Efforts

Unlike Tanzania, which has adopted an explicit policy of fostering the broad participation of the lowest income groups in development, some countries have not taken adequate steps to encourage participation of the lowest income rural populations. Nevertheless, even in such situations, considerable development effort may be under way through local initiative. It is estimated that in Kenya, as a result of the landlessness, unemployment, and the lack of alternative economic opportunities, 300,000 people of various tribal origins have established squatter settlements on land to which they have no title. These settlements receive few, if any, government services. However, they have displayed a notable degree of self-help in the establishment of schools and health clinics. Three representative squatter settlements, the Kibwezi-Mtito-Chylulu hill zone in southeast Kenya and Ngoliba B and D and the Muka Maku Cooperative Society in central Kenya were reviewed as part of ARDS.

pp. 19-21

The Concept of Rural Development

It is apparent that the programs reviewed together involve a very considerable effort to extend development to low-income subsistence populations, although the intensity of the effort varies widely among them. The diversity in the programs is not confined, however, to the degree of effort. It extends to a variety of other factors. For instance, the programs vary considerably in their emphasis on the realization of specific objectives. They also illustrate the considerable range in potential and constraint that exists among regions and countries in terms of policies, institutions, physical and human resources, and technological possibilities. Consequently, they demonstrate in a concrete way the possible divergence between the objectives of rural development and the physical and institutional potential for their realization.

Further, the programs reflect the varying degrees of knowledge as to the actual potential and the most effective ways of developing it. They, therefore, manifest the desire of the planners to experiment with alternative approaches. Thus, apart from the genuine diversity, the programs reflect the gaps between the facts and the assumptions on which rural development planning is often based. Such gaps frequently explain differences between expected and actual project performance. The past programs also differ in their flexibility in implementation. They, therefore, display varying ability to minimize losses from unanticipated responses and to exploit unforeseen potential. The analysis of these past efforts should provide useful insights into the nature of interactions and conflicts among these numerous and immensely variable factors. It should also illuminate the preconditions necessary for ensuring the effectiveness of alternative approaches and, thus, provide useful lessons for the formation and implementation of future rural development strategies. The thrust of the study is, therefore, positive. It is not meant to be a postmortem undertaken to deliver a verdict on past performance.

But before commencing with the discussion of these issues and particularly in view of the very broad range of objectives, it is essential to outline the new objectives or concept of rural development.

In this study rural development is defined as improving living standards of the mass of the low-income population residing in rural areas and making the process of their development self-sustaining. This simple definition has three important features with substantial implications for how rural development programs are designed and implemented:

1. Improving the living standards of the subsistence population involves mobilization and allocation of resources so as to reach a desirable balance over time between the welfare and productive services available to the subsistence rural sector.

2. Mass participation requires that resources be allocated to low-income regions and classes and that the productive and social services actually reach them.

3. Making the process self-sustaining requires development of the appropriate skills and implementing capacity and the presence of institutions at the local, regional, and national levels to ensure the effective use of existing resources and to foster the mobilization of additional financial and human resources for continued development of the subsistence sector. Self-sustenance thus means involving, as distinct from simply reaching, the subsistence populations through development programs.

The achievement of these aims requires consideration of the interaction of a variety of specific issues which have a profound impact on the design and performance of individual programs. These issues may be classified in three general categories:

1. National policies: i.e., land tenure systems, commodity pricing and marketing systems, wages and interest rate structures, and so forth.

2. Administrative systems: i.e., the degree of centralization-decentralization in the governmental structure.

3. Scope for institutional pluralism: i.e., the distribution of development responsibility among the normal government structure; semi-autonomous government structure; private, commercial, and traditional institutions; and elective bodies.

This study, however, was not meant as an analysis of policies and institutions per se. Nor was it intended with a view to influence changes in policies and institutions in the specific cases under consideration. Subsequent to the conduct of the study, as a result of domestic sociopolitical factors, policy changes have already occurred in some cases, as, for instance, in the case of the land tenure situation in Ethiopia or the collectivization in Tanzania. The purpose of the study has been to analyze, among other things, the effect of such overall policies and institutions on programs and to draw general lessons from these experiences for designing future programs. The chapters are, therefore, organized around the issues faced in planning and implementing programs directed towards the subsistence sector. Chapters II and III discuss development of the farming systems. Chapters IV, V, and VI describe the organization and delivery of agricultural services. Chapter VII examines the issues related to the provision of social services. Chapter VIII analyzes the performance of the parallel administrative structures, and Chapter IX examines the performance of administrative decentralization in Kenya and Tanzania. Chapter X points out the role of training in rural development programs. Chapter XI summarizes the findings of the study and points out their implications for the design and implementation of future rural development programs.

CHAPTER II

Nature of the Production Systems 1: Some Key Influences on the Development of Farming

Numerous interrelated choices have to be made in planning the development of subsistence agriculture. For instance, there are questions related to the appropriate production mix. Should programs involve promotion of a single, obviously profitable crop with an assured export market, as in the earlier export crop schemes; or should they emphasize development of the overall farming system as is being attempted in some of the more recent rural development programs? There are also questions related to an appropriate factor mix. Under what conditions may capital-intensive production processes be promoted? Choices with regard to capital or labor intensity are, of course, closely related to a production mix.

Several other questions with regard to factor proportions also need resolution. For instance, under what circumstances does development of farming necessitate settlement of populations on new land as distinct from intensification of already cultivated land? And further, under what conditions should development of farming be brought about by concentration of financial and administrative resources in a few regions, as is being attempted in the integrated rural development programs; and when may equitable allocation of resources between regions be justified, as in a minimum package program?

This chapter examines some of the factors that influenced choices related to these issues in the programs reviewed, the effectiveness of the interventions adopted on the basis of these choices in fulfilling the pronounced objectives of the programs, and some of the unanticipated consequences of the interventions of past programs.

As a background for discussion of these issues, Section 1 discusses some of the main factors that appear to influence the flow of labor input into traditional African agriculture. Section 2 points out the close interaction between the labor constraint and the food constraint, the effect of the joint food-labor constraint on farm-level efficiency and on rural welfare, and the implications of the joint labor-food constraint for the choice of a production mix. Section 3 discusses implications of the labor constraint for mechanization of agriculture and assesses the effectiveness of past efforts at mechanization. Section 4 discusses the nature of rural migration, its interaction with land policies and labor supply, and the implications of these various factors for regional allocation of resources for agricultural development. Section 5 examines some of the conditions under which geographical concentration or diffusion of resources may be necessary in early stages of development to ensure regional equity.

Factors Affecting Labor Flow into Smallholder Agriculture

Evidence suggests that, compared to Asia, labor availability in Africa is frequently a greater constraint to increasing agricultural productivity than is the availability of land.[1] As a result, technological innovations, which require intense labor input, often may not result in the full realization of potential production increases. At the same time, however, there is some prima facie evidence of surplus labor in African agriculture. On an average, African smallholders devote only about 1,000 man hours per adult per year to agricultural activities, compared to up to 3,000 man hours in several Asian countries.[2] Thus, there is the seeming paradox of a farm labor shortage combined with an apparent labor surplus. The explanation for this contradition lies in the way the labor time is allocated in African agriculture—i.e., *(a)* in the seasonality of labor usage; *(b)* in the allotment of time between farm work, nonfarm activities, and leisure; and *(c)* in the division of labor between the sexes. Because these three factors influence the amount of labor allocated to agricultural work at any given point in time, they frequently pose a constraint to increasing productivity, limiting the effectiveness of interventions introduced through programs. The effect of these three factors on the supply of labor to agriculture, therefore, needs elaboration.

Seasonality of Labor Usage

The seasonality of labor usage is perhaps the most important element in the labor constraint. For example, cotton farmers in Sukumaland, Tanzania, experience heavy demand for labor in January and February when their crops must be weeded and again during the harvest period in June and July. By contrast, little labor is needed from August through November.[3] Norman observes a similar seasonality in labor use in northern Nigeria. Most agricultural work occurs during the wet season with peak labor requirements during June and July. The dry season, November through April, is marked by little farm activity.[4] Due to the variability in

1. See, for example, D.W. Norman, "The Organisational Consequences of Social and Economic Constraints and Policies in Dry-Land Areas," paper presented to the Second International Seminar on Change in Agriculture, Reading, U.K., September 9–19, 1974; and M.I. Kolawale, "The Role of Agricultural Labor in Nigerian Rural Development," paper presented to the Seminar on Rural Development, Ife, Nigeria, November 1973.

2. See John H. Cleave, *African Farmers: Labor Use in the Development of Smallholder Agriculture* (New York: Praeger, 1974), p. 34.

3. Ibid., p. 92.

4. D. W. Norman, "Inter-disciplinary Research on Rural Development: The Reru Experience," paper prepared for a Development from Below Workshop, organized by the Overseas Liaison Committee of the American Council on Education and the Association for the Advancement of Agricultural Sciences in Africa, Addis Ababa, Ethiopia, October 12–20, 1973.

ecological conditions, the seasonal labor usage, of course, varies substantially between regions.[5]

While the peaks and troughs in the demand for agricultural labor are primarily a result of climatic factors, cropping patterns obviously affect the specific profile of the labor schedule. To reduce seasonal labor bottlenecks, new crop mixtures have to be such as to permit flexibility in the timing of labor input and to allow the use of labor to be spread more evenly throughout the year. Such crop mixtures as, for instance, maize, legumes, and cotton in Sukumaland or sorghum, millet, cowpeas, groundnuts, and cotton in northern Nigeria, have proven popular in many parts of Africa.

The response to new crops is, however, substantially influenced by the extent to which the new crops complement or compete with the existing cropping pattern and the seasonal labor use. Norman observes, for example, that farmers in northern Nigeria have responded quite favorably to the introduction of tobacco, because demand for the bulk of labor for tobacco production does not conflict with the seasonal demands of major crops in the area. Best results for tobacco production are obtained when seed beds are prepared in early July and the tobacco seedlings transplanted about six weeks later. Harvest takes place towards the beginning of October. By contrast, there seems to be less scope for fostering tomato production, also being promoted in the same area. The tomato crop is quite demanding of labor time (approximately 296 man hours per hectare). It must be planted between May and June and harvested between August and October. The labor input is, thus, required at a time of traditional peak labor demand, aggravating rather than supplementing the existing demand for labor.

The relatively greater ease in increasing tobacco compared to tomato production in northern Nigeria has, of course, also been a result of the higher returns to the former crop.[6] The question of differing returns to different activities leads to the second important factor that influences the labor available to agricultural production—namely, the allocation of time between farm and off-farm activities and leisure.

Allocation of Time

According to Cleave, adult family members typically work only twenty to forty hours a week on their land, even during peak months. On an annual basis they may spend only three to four hours a day on agricultural work—such as planting, weeding, or harvesting. Of the remaining daylight hours, on a yearly basis, often somewhat less than half are devoted to off-farm activities—e.g., income-generating odd jobs, domestic chores, social obligations, and so forth. Leisure takes up the remainder of the time.[7] It is

5. See John C. de Wilde, *Experiences with Agricultural Development in Tropical Africa*, 2 vols. (Baltimore: Johns Hopkins Press, 1967) for an excellent description of the ecoclimatic conditions and farming systems in Africa.

6. Returns per hectare (excluding labor costs) are $222.30–$259.35 for tobacco and $172.90 for tomatoes. For a further discussion of these points, see D.W. Norman, "The Organisational Consequences of Social and Economic Constraints and Policies in Dry-Land Areas."

7. For instance, as Cleave reports, D. Pudsey found that, among fifteen male farmers in Kakangi, Uganda (1964–65), the typical work day was broken into 3.6 hours of farm work, 3.5 hours of off-farm activities, and 4.9 hours of leisure. Among nine male tea farmers in Kyarusozi, Uganda (1965), the pattern was 4.1 hours of farm work, 3.5 hours of off-farm activities, and 4.1 hours of leisure. It is interesting to note that the tea farmers devoted longer hours to their crops, presumably because the returns to tea production were attractive. It is

clear that some slack time exists in the off-farm activities and leisure periods that can be transferred to agricultural work.

It would be incorrect to assume, however, that the time-use pattern common to smallholder agriculture is inherently wasteful or inefficient. Off-farm activities in subsistence agriculture are frequently of legitimate economic or social value, although the relatively large proportion of time spent on visiting neighbors and on traditional and similar activities may seem incompatible with a highly productive farming system.[8] The large amount of leisure also seems necessary because of the low caloric intake of smallholders and the often arduous nature of manual fieldwork, although systematic evidence is still very limited on this particular constraint.[9] Finally, the seemingly short period devoted to farm work is frequently justified by the marginal disutility of labor in technologically underdeveloped agriculture in which returns from labor are frequently too low to prompt further substitution of labor from nonfarm to farm activities.[10]

The allocation of time between various daily activities is, however, quite flexible and, therefore, amenable to change, provided appropriate interventions are introduced. With men, an increase in agricultural activity tends to be at the expense of various off-farm activities, while with women the tendency is to sacrifice leisure time.[11] One explanation for this pattern may be that in some cases women's chores and duties are less strenuous than the men's; hence, women require shorter recuperative periods. However, an equally if not more important reason seems to be that male nonagricultural work is frequently less critical than are the typical female household responsibilities, allowing men to transfer their time from off-farm to farm work more easily than the women.[12] The important fact is that there is considerable scope for increasing the labor input to agriculture, though "the existence of a range of [competing] demands on time. . .raises the opportunity cost of agricultural work and reduces the readiness with which the flow of labor into agriculture can be increased."[13]

Significant shifts in the daily work pattern can, therefore, be brought about only where profitable innovations are available that increase the marginal productivity of agricultural labor sufficiently to offset the attraction of other household, social, or income-earning activities. There are numerous examples that support this assertion. For example, farmers in Shinyanga district in Sukumaland, where farm income is about $99 per hectare, devote approximately 160 hours to their crops during the busiest month of the season. Farmers in nearby Ukerewe district, where income per hectare is only about $52, devote a mere 45 hours to farm activities during the peak month.[14] Cleave's summary of labor use patterns in a number

also noteworthy that the tea farmers seem to require less leisure time. See Cleave, *African Farmers: Labor Use in the Development of Smallholder Agriculture,* pp. 152–56.

8. Cleave points out that ceremonial duties, often considered an important drain on productive activities, are scheduled for periods of low labor demand. See ibid., p. 180.

9. Ibid., pp. 178–79.

10. John Mellor, "The Use and Productivity of Farm Family Labor in Early Stages of Agricultural Development," in *Journal of Farm Economics,* vol. 45, no. 3 (August 1973), pp. 517–34.

11. Cleave, *African Farmers: Labor Use in the Development of Smallholder Agriculture,* p. 180.

12. Belloncle and Gentil point out the many competing demands on the women's time arising from their household and productive chores.

13. Cleave, *African Farmers: Labor Use in the Development of Smallholder Agriculture,* p. 180.

14. Ibid., p. 20, Table 2.2 and p. 124, Table 5.2. The figures are for the late 1960s.

of areas in Africa also indicates that the labor input to agriculture tends to be higher in areas where commercial crops make up a large proportion of the crops grown.[15]

Agricultural innovations must, of course, also be profitable relative to income-earning nonfarm activities if they are to lead to a greater labor input to agriculture. For example, although the introduction of tractors among maize farmers surveyed in western Nigeria resulted in a net saving of 12.4 man days per hectare, almost all of the time saved was spent on nonfarm activities like trading, carpentry, and tailoring.[16] Evidently, the marginal return to farm labor was less than the return to other kinds of labor.

Sexual Division of Labor

The division of labor between men and women is the third major factor that influences labor availability in smallholder farming. In traditional African agriculture there frequently tends to be a marked distinction in the roles of the sexes, although this division is bewilderingly variable in various parts of Africa. Cash crops and heavy work such as plowing have tended to be a male responsibility. Food crops and lighter work like weeding are more often the women's charge. Women are also responsible for the bulk of the domestic work—such as food preparation, wood and water gathering, and child rearing. The total amount of labor input by sexes is often quite disproportionate. A recent article by the United Nations Economic Commission for Africa observes that women provide 60 to 80 percent of the agricultural labor used in parts of Africa. According to ECA, the case of the West Lake region in Tanzania is typical: men spend about 1,800 hours annually on agriculture while women spend about 2,600 hours.[17] Cleave cites numerous similar examples which suggest that, compared to men, African women often work longer both in farm and nonfarm activities.[18] This observation is also strongly supported by Belloncle and Gentil in their review of the ZAPI and SODENKAM programs in Cameroon. A rigid division of labor on a sexual basis in which men refuse to perform "women's work" therefore places a limitation on the amount of labor available for agricultural production.

There is a good deal of evidence, however, that the sexual division of labor is flexible and may be breaking down in many areas. Where new technologies have been introduced, it is not uncommon to find men and women

15. For example, in southwest Nigeria (c. 1967) male farmers in the Alade area, where commercial crops account for 74 percent of the crops grown, spend about 1,610 hours per year on agricultural work. By contrast in the Akumazi area, with 39 percent commercial crops, males spend only about 730 hours a year on farm work. Of course, the trend towards increased labor in response to commercialization is only general in nature; and there are many exceptions. For instance, in the same part of Nigeria, male farmers in Iloffa devote 2,135 hours a year to agricultural work, though only 32 percent of their crops are commercial. Obviously, other factors, such as soil and climatic conditions, are also important determinants of the amount of labor time that is devoted to farming. See ibid., p. 32, Table 3.1.

16. M.I. Kolawole, "An Economic Study of Tractor Contracting Operations in Western Nigeria," Ph.D. dissertation, Cornell University, 1972.

17. See United Nations Economic Commission for Africa, Human Resources Development Division, "Women: The Neglected Human Resources for African Development," in *Canadian Journal of African Studies,* vol. 6, no. 2 (1972), pp. 359–70.

18. Cleave, *African Farmers: Labor Use in the Development of Smallholder Agriculture,* pp. 171–73.

performing the same tasks during periods of intense labor requirements. For instance, the review of KTDA points out that much of the hired labor in smallholder tea cultivation in Kenya is female. In areas where a market exists for food crops, men seem to be willing to assist in food production. Nevertheless, as indicated by ZAPI and SODENKAM, when women are expected to do a disproportionate share of the agricultural work, improvements in farm technology may have the unforseen consequence of increasing the already heavy labor burden on women.[19] Steps that lighten the household tasks of women should, therefore, facilitate labor availability for farm work. For example, innovations, such as improved food preparation techniques or the introduction of wheelbarrows for more efficient water carrying, can reduce the time required for domestic tasks significantly.[20] These questions are discussed further in Chapters IV and VII of this study.

To summarize, the labor problem in African smallholder farming is largely an allocative problem. New cropping patterns and labor-saving innovations can facilitate reallocation and more efficient use of labor, provided such interventions are based on an adequate understanding of the complex economic, sociocultural, and physiological factors that determine the labor utilization pattern in traditional agriculture.

The Food Constraint and Specialization in Agriculture

To what extent were these and other factors that influence labor availability taken into account in planning the commodity projects? This section will illustrate that labor availability in smallholder agriculture is also closely related to the desire of subsistence producers to ensure domestic food needs. The food constraint can be attributed to two factors frequently noted in the traditional African agriculture: (a) the generally high risk and low profitability of food technology, which ties up a substantial amount of labor in food crop production; and (b) the fragmented market systems for food crops which necessitate priority on food production to ensure supply for domestic consumption. The export crop projects reviewed under ARDS illustrate how these two factors can restrict the amount of scarce labor that can be released for the production of more profitable export crops, affecting efficiency in resource use at the farm level. Relatedly, the reviews also indicate how promotion of export crops in the absence of a more profitable food technology may reduce the supplies available for domestic consumption, thus affecting rural welfare.

19. Also see Ester Boserup, *Women's Role in Economic Development* (New York: St. Martin's Press, 1970), p. 21, Table 1. Alternatively, some technological innovations may decrease the role of women in agriculture and, hence, their participation in economic development.

20. Vail estimates that traditional head portage of family water in Tanzania typically requires a labor-time input of 312 hours per year. The introduction of a $10 wheelbarrow, which can carry a much larger quantity of water, results in the reduction of labor time of 208 hours per year. If the time saved were transferred to farm tasks, the resulting net increase in agricultural production of perhaps $20 would more than cover the cost of the wheelbarrow. See David J. Vail, "Technology for Socialist Development in Rural Tanzania," mimeographed, n.d., background paper for the Seventeenth Annual Meeting of the African Studies Association, Chicago, November 1974.

Export Crop Projects
and the Labor-Food Constraint

The commodity projects have frequently had a rather limited objective. Apart from aiming to increase export earnings of specific export crops, the narrow focus of the projects was prompted by a variety of other considerations. In addition to assured markets, profitable technologies existed for export crops due to the substantial early investment in research.[21] Innovations related to export crops were, thus, frequently far easier to promote than those related to food crops.

Further, as will be illustrated in Chapters IV through VI, organization of effective delivery of extension, inputs, and credit has been relatively less difficult, both administratively and financially, in the case of export crops. Not only was it easier to recover costs of delivery of services provided for export crop production, but it was also easier to mobilize substantial additional resources through a combination of pricing and marketing policies. It must be emphasized, therefore, that the deficiency of an export crop approach may frequently lie in its failure to evolve adequately over time to meet the needs of the smallholder producer effectively and not in its initial concentration on highly profitable export crops.

The diverse needs of the small farmers and the necessity to broaden the scope of services to meet such needs is quite evident in the commodity project areas. For example, in the tea-growing districts of Kisii and Kericho, where the Kenya Tea Development Authority has been in charge of promoting production of tea in the smallholder sector since the early 1960s, the increased incomes from tea production have stimulated considerable interest among the smallholder tea farmers in maintaining dairy cows. Although a high-grade cow cost as much as KSh1,800 in 1973, purchases of dairy cows constituted an important item of expenditure among tea growers. However, institutional credit for dairy cows became available through the Department of Agriculture only in 1967 under the IDA credit program. By September 1972, of the KSh26.7 million in total loans disbursed, dairy cattle alone accounted for 40 percent; livestock and complementary facilities comprised 75 percent. In recent years KTDA has also provided extension for maize. However, the multiplicity of administrative channels has led to a number of difficulties in effective implementation of extension for activities other than tea. These are discussed in Chapter IV. ZAPI in Cameroon provides a similar example of the diverse needs of small farmers. Belloncle and Gentil observe that the very careful analysis of the farming system in the south central ZAPI by agronomists of the Institut de Recherches pour l'Agronomie Tropicale (IRAT) has consistently pointed out the steps necessary to improve productivity of the food and livestock activities. Despite a few minor efforts in this direction discussed in later chapters, the main emphasis of the projects, however, continues to remain on the production and export of cocoa.

21. According to figures compiled by the Organization for Economic Cooperation and Development, 81 percent of agricultural research expenditures in Africa went to export crops and only 14 percent to food crops in 1961. By 1971 the proportions had become approximately equal with 45 percent of research expenditures on export crops and 47 percent on food products. Samuel Kassapu, "Dépenses de Recherche Agricole en Afrique," unpublished memorandum (Paris: Organisation pour Coopération et Développement Economique, September 14, 1973), p. 46, Table 1.

The earlier agricultural policy measures in Sukumaland, Tanzania, were also oriented mainly to production of an export crop (in this case, cotton). Since late 1940s there has been tsetse fly clearance, provision of domestic water points, establishment of a cotton research center and a cotton-marketing infrastructure, and provision of extension services to encourage adoption of improved techniques in cotton production. During the period of cotton expansion, there occured a considerable shift in food production from sorghum to maize and, more recently, from maize to rice. For instance, between 1950 and 1960 production of maize per family had increased from 0.96 quintals to 5.62 quintals, while that of sorghum had declined from 8.85 quintals to 1.2 quintals. However, the total production of foodgrains per family declined from 15.81 quintals to 9.18 quintals during the same ten-year period.

If innovations are profitable and involve low risk, participants in the export crop projects respond as favorably to the introduction of services for food crops as they have to livestock development in the tea areas of Kenya. This is indicated by the experiences of the tobacco schemes in Urambo and Tumbi in Tanzania. Though initiated in the early 1950s, it was not until 1964 that the schemes provided services for food production. Since then, credit has been made available to smallholders for purchase of seed and ammonium sulphate for maize and paddy. According to the Urambo Farmers Cooperative Society's annual crop realization accounts, from the 1966/67 period to the 1969/70 period, hectarage under paddy and maize in Urambo increased from 132 hectares to 896 hectares and from 931 to 1,058 hectares, respectively. In the Tumbi tobacco scheme between 1965 and 1970, marketing of paddy increased from 5,440 quintals to 78,930 quintals. Marketing of maize grew from 480 quintals to 2,340 quintals during the same period.

The Food Constraint, Farm-level Efficiency, and Rural Welfare

Such interest in food and livestock development among participants in export crop projects may often be explained by their need to ensure minimum supplies of food for domestic consumption and the consequent restriction on increasing overall agricultural production that is often imposed by their traditional labor allocation pattern. Collinson's analysis of the Sukumaland experience, however, highlights the complex interactions between labor allocation and risk minimization that frequently influence the adoption of new innovations. To maximize yields, the extension service recommends that cotton be planted in December and maize in January. The early planting of cotton results in higher yields, while late-planted maize responds favorably to fertilizer. Further, since maize is often a host for cotton pests, it is advantageous to plant cotton before maize. However, farmers have generally preferred to spread the planting of both crops over a five-month period from October to February. While this does not lead to the full realization of potential increases in per hectare yields, especially of cotton, staggered planting (a) allows greater flexibility in the use of labor time, (b) assures a continuous supply of maize over a longer time period, and (c) reduces the risk of a total failure of the maize crop due to temporary emergencies such as drought or disease. For these various reasons, von

Rotenhan observed that the Sukuma "prefer lower but more secure returns instead of maximum yields."[22]

A similar emphasis on securing domestic food needs is observed by Belloncle and Gentil in the SODENKAM settlements in Cameroon. They point out the inordinate amount of labor time spent by women in the production of food crops. Because productivity of food plots tends to be very low, women frequently have to cultivate several distant plots to ensure adequate food supplies for domestic consumption. Obviously, a low-risk technology that will increase productivity of food crops is critical, not only for increasing welfare but also for releasing labor from food crop production for allocation to production of high-value export crops. Belloncle and Gentil also note that, because of the extractive history of export crop production, attention to food crop development is critical if rural development administrators are to gain the confidence of the populations being reached through programs.

A different manifestation of the food constraint is noted in the tendency among smallholders to sell inputs provided for cash crop production, as has occurred in the tobacco schemes in Tanzania. Smallholders in the tobacco areas shifted a large portion of their land and scarce labor from food crops to tobacco production.[23] As a result, small farmers producing tobacco in Urambo began to experience a deficit in food supplies in the off-season. They, therefore, sold the inputs purchased from the Urambo Cooperative Society (in particular, the fertilizer they received for tobacco production) to large farmers in return for the much-needed food. The fertilizer sales affected not only yields of tobacco on small farms but also the repayment of credit borrowed for the purchase of inputs.

Apart from its adverse effect on allocative efficiency, the neglect of food crop production may also have an adverse effect on nutrition of the rural population, as is suggested in some export crop schemes. For instance, as pointed out earlier, despite the substitution of high-yielding maize for sorghum, the overall production of food crops in Sukumaland declined substantially. Consequently, purchases of food crops increased.

However, field investigations carried out in Sukumaland and evidence

22. D. von Rotenhan, "Cotton Farming in Sukumaland," in *Smallholder Farming and Smallholder Development in Tanzania*, ed. Hans Ruthenberg, Afrika-Studien no. 24 (Munich: Weltforum Verlag, 1968), p. 60. According to von Rotenhan, cotton planted in January (about 30 percent of all cotton hectarage in Sukumaland) may have yields only one-third as large as cotton planted in December. (See pp. 62 and 82.) Norman has suggested that in northern Nigeria, where a similar food-labor constraint limits cotton production, efforts be made to develop a late cotton that can be planted after food crops and still produce maximum yields. See Norman, "The Organisational Consequences of Social and Economic Constraints and Policies in Dry-Land Areas."

23. Although tobacco hectarage varied fairly substantially from one year to another, it reflected a general upward trend.

Tobacco Hectarage Per Farmer
(Urambo Settlement Scheme, Tanzania, 1956–70)

				Year				
	1956	*1958*	*1960*	*1962*	*1964*	*1966*	*1968*	*1970*
Hectarage	0.40	1.40	1.64	0.91	1.10	1.34	1.22	1.18

Source: Data for 1956 and 1964 are based on Linsenmeyer's interviews with Walter Scheffler; for 1956–62, see government of Tanzania, "Urambo Annual Report for 1962–63," Tanganyika Agricultural Corporation, n.d.; and for 1966–70, see government of Tanzania, "Urambo Production Report," unpublished, Ministry of Agriculture and Cooperatives, 1970.

from marketing studies elsewhere suggest that the rural food market is frequently fragmented.[24] Despite the very considerable spontaneous increase in exchange between rural households reflected in the houshold budget data analyzed by Collinson, there is also evidence to indicate that there are pockets of deficit-food regions which do not always receive adequate and timely supplies of food from surplus regions.[25]

The adverse effect of early specialization on rural food supplies is often reinforced by variations in climatic conditions that lead to considerable year-to-year variability in domestic food availability. This is because greater profitability of export crops frequently leads to only the minimum allocation of domestic resources for the production of food crops. Von Rotenhan's study suggests that the shift of hectarage to cotton, combined with the substitution of maize that is considerably more susceptible to rainfall than the hardy millet and the sorghum grown earlier, may have had such an adverse effect on domestic food supplies in Sukumaland.[26] This is supported by Collinson, who observed that poor weather in the late 1960s brought a revival of sorghum and millet as well as a plateau in the upward trend in cotton production.

Anderson, like Collinson, in his review of the CFDT cotton development scheme in Fana, Mali, also observed an adverse effect of export crop specialization on food availability in the program area and the consequent readjustment of the farming system to ensure domestic food supplies. As a result of cotton promotion, the ratio of food crop area to cotton area was less than 2:1 in 1971. With the failure in rainfall during the 1971/72 season, food crop production declined considerably. Farmers discovered that they did not have enough food to carry their families and the migrant seasonal labor through the off season. In the 1972/73 period the ratio of the food crop area to the cotton area increased 3:1. To maintain an adequate supply of food, the project's extension services also began to advocate that every hired laborer grow at least one-half hectare of millet for every one and a half hectares allotted to cotton.

The problem of ensuring food supplies in rural areas is frequently exacerbated by the pricing and marketing policies followed by governments towards food crops. Food crop pricing is particularly susceptible to sociopolitical influences that are often not conducive to domestic food production. The adverse effect of government policy on the diversification of agricultural production and, in particular, on food crops is evident in BDPA's groundnut scheme in Mali.

Mali has been experiencing cereal deficits in the urban areas. During 1972 and 1973 the government imported large quantities of American grain. Office des Produits Agricoles du Mali (OPAM), the government agency charged with buying cereals to supply the cities, was unable to fulfill its annual domestic procurement target of 40,000 metric tons.

24. See the discussion on marketing and distribution problems in P.L. Raikes, P.R. Lawrence, and L.G. Saylor, D. Warner, "Regional Planning in Tanzania: An Economic View from the Field," Economic Research Bureau Paper 68:8 (Dar es Salaam: University College, 1968).

25. Also see Chapter VI of this study for further discussion on this question.

26. See von Rotenhan, "Cotton Farming in Sukumaland," p. 57. The Sukuma apparently prefer the taste of maize to cassava or millet. Thus, despite the greater reliability of the latter crops, they emphasize production of maize.

Since the government is sensitive to urban demands for stable food prices, it has seemed to be reluctant to raise the price of cereals. The wide gap between the cereal price and the prices of groundnuts and cotton reduces the incentive for farmers to grow more food crops than they need locally. Besides, neighboring countries offer much higher prices for cereals, attracting the surpluses that exist in the rural areas and promoting "illegal" channels of marketing.

Further, the weakness of OPAM as a marketing organization makes it difficult to implement a price policy, even if an effective policy were devised. OPAM lacks the personnel and funds to enter the cereals market early. Private merchants buy up the stocks of cereals at low prices and resell their stocks in July and August as the prices rise. An analysis by the Ministry of Production estimated that in 1970 such a "black market" carried on 58 percent of cereal sales and 67 percent of cereal purchases.

To summarize, the initial concentration of administrative and financial resources on a single export crop may have been justified in many of the past commodity projects, given the limited resources available for investment, the often low level of technology available for food production, and the frequent lack of price incentives necessary to increase cereal production. However, past experience also indicates that, in the long run, such concentration may be detrimental to equity as well as to allocative efficiency. Rural development projects need to devote increasing attention to diversified farming and especially to food crop production.

It is important to stress, however, that development of farming systems may not necessarily mean promotion of farm-level self-sufficiency in food production. Nor must it mean generation of massive food surpluses through promoting early regional specialization in food production. The latter strategy may have to be resisted in early stages of development, since both low effective demand and inadequate marketing systems frequently pose a constraint to disposal of surpluses, an issue discussed in detail in Chapter VI. What is often needed is the development of technology and the provision of generalized delivery systems—in particular, extension and inputs for food and export crops as distinct from specialized delivery systems for export crops alone.

The need for the improvement of marketing facilities, including the development of feeder roads and communications between rural habitats, also cannot be overemphasized. As pointed out by the example of Sukumaland, spontaneous exchange of food in rural areas is quite substantial as rural communications and food surpluses increase. The project management of LLDP in Malawi also observed that, in the absence of traditional trading channels, the project would have been burdened with large surpluses of maize and groundnuts not procured by the Agriculture Development and Marketing Corporation (ADMARC). Kinsey's estimates show that as much as 60 percent of the maize traded in the Lilongwe project area may have been handled through traditional channels.

However, because the capacity of the traditional marketing systems and the effective rural demand for food are limited in the early stages, services for food crop development, in many instances, have to be provided over a wide geographical area and their intensity increased gradually to ensure regional equity. The geographical spread of agricultural services needs to be accompanied by the development of an infrastructure to link markets among regions so as to keep pace with the gradual increase in effective demand for food from within the rural areas and from surrounding regions. Such an approach has been adopted in the Minimum Package Program in Ethiopia. However, even in this there has been a considerable adverse effect on prices in the initial years of implementation, particularly in the areas where marketable surpluses are increasing rapidly. This is because construction of feeder roads has not made the anticipated progress.

The regional dispersion or concentration of resources must also depend on the relative agricultural potential between regions and on the scope for population migration between regions. These questions of regional allocation of resources will be discussed after examining the scope in subsistence agriculture for removal of labor bottlenecks through mechanization.

Mechanization in Smallholder Agriculture

One of the frequent solutions to the joint food-labor constraint has been the introduction of mechanical implements to increase the output per unit of labor. These implements vary from simple hand-powered devices to sophisticated engine machinery. The discussion below is focused on effectiveness of two important mechanized innovations, tractors and ox plows, that are linked to modern multicultivators and weeders and are frequently introduced through programs. It illustrates the nature of interactions between mechanization and labor bottlenecks on the one hand and between mechanization and complementary innovations on the other. It is the inadequate understanding of these interactions which frequently explains the failure of the attempts to mechanize traditional agriculture.

Tractors

Tractors have often been viewed as a symbol of modern agriculture in Africa and, consequently, have been promoted through many rural development programs. Though tractors have generally proven well adapted to large-scale Western-style commercial farming, their role in development of smallholder agriculture has been less clear for a variety of reasons. First, since the labor bottleneck in peasant farming is largely seasonal, tractor services are needed at only the few critical periods of peak labor demand. Second, tractors are most useful in field preparation but often are of little utility in weeding or harvesting. Tractors may, therefore, only postpone rather than break the labor bottleneck while doing little to alleviate the problem of underutilization of farm labor at periods of slack agricultural activity.

Under some circumstances tractorization has aggravated labor bottlenecks rather than relieving them. For example, mid-season weeding tends to be a highly labor-demanding activity in much of peasant agriculture.[27] When tractors are used for land preparation but not for weeding, as

---

27. For example, in the Zaria area of northern Nigeria, Norman reports that 26 percent of total agricultural labor time is devoted to weeding, the bulk of which occurs during June and July. Similarly, Ruthenberg indicates that in Sukumaland in 1963 weeding made up 26 percent of the labor input for maize and sorghum production and 29 to 48 percent for cotton. See Norman, "The Organisational Consequences of Social and Economic Constraints and Policies in Dry-Land Areas"; and Hans Ruthenberg, *Farming Systems in The Tropics* (Oxford: Clarendon Press, 1971), p. 71, Table 4.4.

frequently tends to be the case, tractorization increases weeding requirements. This is because tractorization allows expansion of cultivated hectarage and, hence, of the area to be weeded. Since the mid-season weeding period is already a time of peak labor demand, an even tighter labor bottleneck may be created. Similarly, if land is prepared in advance of standard planting dates to make greater use of available tractor time, frequently weed growth becomes well established by the time crops are sown. This, too, creates additional weeding requirements.[28]

Tractorization can, therefore, be successful only if the necessary complementary innovations are introduced to alleviate the labor constraint, especially for weeding. These may take the form of additional capital input—e.g., herbicides or mechanical weeders. Or they may be new planting techniques which reduce weed growth or facilitate weed removal as, for example, the close planting of groundnuts in Opération Arachide or the ridging of cotton in Sukumaland. However, perhaps the most useful step in this regard is to alter cropping patterns to spread the need for labor more evenly through the season. As pointed out earlier, the shortage of labor available to farming activities is largely allocative in nature. New crop mixes and restructured labor patterns can, therefore, provide farmers with the necessary extra labor availability to cope with the possible labor bottlenecks created by tractor use.

Several other problems are frequently encountered in the use of tractors in smallholder farming, including (a) the high capital costs of the equipment and herbicides,[29] (b) the high overhead involved in maintaining and servicing the underutilized machinery,[30] (c) the administrative problems in sharing a limited number of machines among a large number of diverse users, and (d) the technical difficulties of employing tractors under certain topographical and soil conditions.

Of course, none of the above problems is insurmountable. If tractorization is accompanied by substantial increases in productivity, the high capital and recurrent costs of mechanized farming can be justified. Maintenance problems can be partly alleviated by training local people in proper machine use and repair. Administrative problems as well as the need for scale may be corrected by the introduction of effective group or cooperative farming or through the use of cooperative or commercial tractor-hire services. And lastly, research can single out the areas most amenable to tractor usage in addition to providing insights into new ways of adapting mechanization to divergent physical conditions.

Much of the past evidence, however, suggests that successful introduc-

---

28. Of course, tractors may permit an expansion of hectarage sufficient to outweigh the potential decline in per hectare yields resulting from inadequate weeding. This appears to have occurred in some of the sparsely populated areas of Sukumaland, where extensive tractor-assisted cotton farming has resulted in yields that are low on a per hectare basis but high relative to the labor input. See de Wilde, *Experiences with Agricultural Development in Tropical Africa,* vol. 2, p. 430.

29. According to de Wilde, a tractor and a minimum number of accessories would have cost $4,000 to $5,000 in mid-1960 prices. Investment in a large number of such machines can place a severe strain on the limited foreign exchange reserves of a developing nation. See ibid., vol. 1, pp. 113–19.

30. Cleave estimates that tractors may require 1,200 revenue earning hours per year to break even. Tractors are frequently used only half as many hours. See Cleave, *African Farmers: Labor Use in the Development of Smallholder Agriculture,* p. 201.

tion of tractors is difficult in smallholder agriculture. The experience with mechanized farming in Sukumaland illustrates the problems. In 1964 the Tanzanian government introduced a cotton block scheme which was hinged on the use of centralized tractor facilities. The Sukumaland region seemed suitable for mechanization since much of the land is flat, the growing season is short, and the peak labor requirements are high. Many farmers in the early 1960s were already hiring tractor services.[31] Under the scheme, blocks of between 121.5 and 202.4 hectares were to be cultivated by tractors. Individual plots of 1.62 hectares would then be allocated to farmers for cotton production. The farmers were to raise the crop under close supervision but would retain ultimate responsibility for field maintenance and harvest activities.

The scheme never achieved the scale envisaged. Rather than the proposed ratio of 121.5 hectares per tractor, in the 1964/65 period each tractor worked an average of only 27.1 hectares. The success of the cotton blocks was linked to the assumption that intensive farming on the blocks would lead to an increase in yield per hectare more than sufficient to cover the high cost of the program. Yet, rather than the expected 540 kilograms of cotton per hectare in the 1964/65 period, yields averaged only 180 kilograms per hectare during that period. These yield levels were similar to those achieved by farmers not participating in the program. However, the cost per hectare was approximately six times as high as the cost of production of nonparticipants.[32] By the end of the cotton block scheme's first season, costs of mechanical cultivation, fertilizer, and spraying (mostly aerial) amounted to TSh1.13 million. Only about one-fifth of these expenses were recovered.[33]

The Sukuma experience indicates that careful attention has to be paid to ensure that in practice the increases in production resulting from the introduction of tractors will justify their high cost. Where labor is inexpensive, tractorization may only mean substituting high-cost capital for low-cost labor.[34] Though there often is scope for mechanized input to farming, the introduction of manual or animal-powered equipment may be a more feasible alternative than tractors. The recognition of this fact is reflected in Tanzania's *ujàmaa* policy, which emphasizes self-reliance among smallholders and "less spectacular forms of mechanization" that are consistent with local resources.[35]

Despite such a recognition in principle, Vail's study notes that in practice the promise of tractor services is frequently used as an inducement for peo-

31. In the Maswa district 50 percent of the cotton farmers surveyed by Collinson in 1963 used ox plows on their farms, and 50 percent used tractor-hire services. See M.P. Collinson, "Farm Management Survey No. 3, Luguru Ginnery Zone, Maswa District," unpublished background paper, Ukiriguru, Tanzania, 1963.
32. According to Collinson, the low yields on the Cotton Block Scheme were partly the result of substitution of labor from cotton to food production.
33. In the Cotton Block Scheme's first year, less than 5,670 hectares were cleared, of which only about 3,240 hectares were planted. For a further discussion of this project, see de Wilde, *Experiences with Agricultural Development in Tropical Africa*, vol. 2, pp. 437–41.
34. Collinson estimates that a Sukuma cotton farmer could increase his net cash income 14 percent through an additional outlay of TSh11.5 on tractor and labor costs. Yet the same additional outlay, if spent only on labor, could increase net cash income by 26 percent.
35. See government of Tanzania, *Second Five Year Plan, July 1969–June 1974*, vol. 1, General Analysis (Dar es Salaam: Government Printers Office, 1969), pp. 37–38.

ple to form *ujàmaa* villages.[36] Vail attributes this partly to the identification of tractor use with modernity, both by administrators and policymakers in Tanzania and partly to the government's desire to promote its *ujàmaa* program rapidly among a sometimes-reluctant rural population. The alternative of fostering intermediate technology of the kind discussed below also seems to be creating a new rural elite of artisans and craftsmen, many of whom seem to use their spare time and the government-provided equipment to produce and service farm implements for private profit.[37] Such a development conflicts with the egalitarian principles underlying *ujàmaa*. Thus, though there may often be strong economic arguments for limiting the introduction of advanced technology such as tractors, compelling political considerations may constrain the use of alternate strategies. Particularly given that several difficulties are encountered in getting production under way in newly formed *ujàmaa* villages, there is a real danger that such political considerations may lead to a repetition of past mistakes with regard to tractorization.

Ox Plows

The introduction of ox plows to increase labor productivity often seems an attractive alternative to tractorization. Since much of the necessary equipment can be produced and the oxen raised locally, this type of mechanization avoids strain on foreign exchange. The cost of investment in a pair of oxen and a plow is, of course, much lower than that of a tractor. This lessens the need for scale and alleviates the administrative difficulties frequently associated with tractorization. There are also significantly fewer maintenance problems in the case of ox plows.

However, the use of ox plows faces several of the same difficulties encountered with tractors. The first is the fact that, as with tractor use, ox-plow cultivation may aggravate the seasonal labor bottleneck. Von Rotenhan reports that farmers in Sukumaland using hoe cultivation devoted about 1,490 hours a year per hectare of cotton, of which 370 hours and 430 hours, respectively, were spent on land preparation and weeding. Farmers using ox-plow cultivation spent about the same amount of time per hectare (i.e., about 1,520 hours). However, among the ox-plow–using farmers, land preparation accounted for only 120 hours, while labor input for weeding increased to 700 hours. The time saved in the early part of the season as a result of ox plowing was, thus, more than compensated by the increased labor required for weeding later.[38] Because of the heightened weeding bottleneck that may result from using draft animals for field preparation, yields per hectare are sometimes no higher for ox-plow cultivation than for hoe cultivation.[39] The major gain arises from expanded area under cultivation.

36. Vail, "Technology for Socialist Development in Rural Tanzania." For a further discussion of the problems encountered in forming *ujàmaa* villages, see Chapter IX of this study.

37. Vail, "Technology for Socialist Development in Rural Tanzania."

38. The explanation for this fact is that Sukuma farmers do not use an ox-drawn weeder or row cropping in conjunction with ox plows. See von Rotenhan, "Cotton Farming in Sukumaland," p. 75, Table 6.

39. See Hans Ruthenberg, *Agricultural Development in Tanganyika* (Berlin: Springer-Verlag, 1964), p. 185.

Thus, there may be a need, as in the case of tractors, to introduce new crops or crop mixtures that can increase productivity through inserting flexibility in the timing of farm operations. The replacement of broadcast sowing with row planting can also reduce labor bottlenecks. And, of course, there is a wide scope for the employment of low-cost implements that complement ox plows. For example, in the BDPA groundnut scheme in Mali, farmers using traditional methods devote 194 man days per crop of groundnuts and millet. The introduction of ox-drawn multicultivators and seeders can result in a reduction of fifty man days in the labor time per crop. The additional use of a 100-kilogram ox-drawn cart can result in a further saving of twelve man days. Such an ox cart increases costs of mechanization by only 19 percent. Ox-drawn seeders are another potentially effective complement to ox plows. The Tanzania Agricultural Machinery Testing Unit in Arusha has developed an effective inter-row weeder that can be produced at a cost of $7 to $15. This instrument can result in a two-thirds to three-quarters reduction in weeding time for cotton.[40]

Demand for such relatively simple farm implements is frequently substantial in rural areas, particularly when the introduction of such implements is accompanied by other yield-increasing agricultural technologies. In the BDPA groundnut scheme, the number of multicultivators in service increased from 89 to 466 between the 1970/71 period and the 1971/72 period. The number of seeders and carts also increased substantially. Anderson observes that an increasing number of farmers are attempting to obtain several sets of oxen and implements with the goal of expanding their cultivated hectarage. In Tanzania also, as Vail points out, ox plows and seeders are greatly in demand among farmers exposed to the new implements.

The demand for such intermediate technology indicates a strong potential growth linkage between the agricultural sector and the small-industry and service sectors of the rural economy. Promoting use of oxen, plows, weeders, and carts can create employment for craftsmen, mechanics, and cattle producers through the multiplier effects arising from increased agricultural productivity and incomes as well as from increased rural industrial employment and incomes. However, as noted above, political and other considerations may limit the promotion of intermediate technology and thereby restrict these growth linkages.

The promotion of draft equipment is, however, also limited by its cost, which, though far lower than motorized equipment on a per unit basis, still represents a considerable investment for farmers. Anderson estimates that the average cost of animal traction in the BDPA groundnut scheme is about $48 per year, including the purchase of the equipment, feed costs, and depreciation. The true costs are probably somewhat higher, since the implements are subsidized, the amortization periods are quite long, and it is assumed that farmers will use young oxen that can be sold as beef cattle for more than their purchase price.[41] Because the maximum projected revenue

40. See Vail, "Technology for Socialist Development in Rural Tanzania."
41. According to Anderson, a pair of oxen cost about $117. A multicultivator, seeder, and cart represent a combined cost of $160. Feed, upkeep, and taxes amount to about $23 per year. Because the oxen can presumably be resold at a higher price and because the equipment is amortized over a period of five to seven years, the annual cost for introducing animal traction is quite low compared to the initial capital investment.

per hectare of groundnuts for farmers following BDPA–sponsored techniques (early sowing, fungicides, fertilizer, and so forth) is about $70, the average farmer must grow at least an extra two-thirds of a hectare of groundnuts to cover the cost of the animal-drawn equipment. This should be possible because the equipment allows a reduction of about one-third in the man days required to cultivate a hectare of groundnuts. However, the revenue figures assume yields of 12 quintals per hectare. In the 1971/72 period average groundnut yields in the BDPA operation were only 8.1 quintals per hectare. At lower yields the economic viability of introducing animal traction becomes progressively more questionable.[42] This is why even an intermediate level of agricultural mechanization and the related rural industrialization frequently cannot be successful without yield-increasing agricultural technologies.

In summary, it seems that both tractorization and ox-plow cultivation have a potential to increase productivity of smallholder agriculture, provided the appropriate associated inputs and innovations are introduced simultaneously. However, in most conditions ox-plow cultivation may be preferable because of its relatively greater flexibility, lower cost, and greater growth linkages with other sectors of the rural economy.

Migration and the Development of Farming Systems

The availability of labor in smallholder agriculture is also strongly influenced by demographic patterns and intra-rural migration which, in turn, are related to the relative return to investment in agriculture in various regions. Surplus and underemployed labor may be attracted to areas with profitable agriculture and obvious labor bottlenecks. An influx of population to such areas may lead to a rapid increase in production and employment. Conversely, areas with unattractive income and employment opportunities may suffer a net outflow of population, creating labor shortages and economic stagnation. Migration may be temporary or permanent and, in either case, may frequently add substantially to the income of the migrants. On the other hand, a rapid population influx may also lead to a decline in wages and aggravate servitude, rural poverty, and social tensions in the regions of immigration.

Intra-rural migration, therefore, poses yet another set of difficult questions for rural development policy: Should programs be concentrated in areas of high potential to promote employment and attract migrants; or, alternatively, should resources be spread more equitably between regions to reduce inter-regional disparities and discourage migration? There can be no simple solution. In each case, the choice of policy must depend largely upon social and political realities, in particular upon the distribution of land rights among tribes and different economic classes and upon the government's

42. There is additional evidence to indicate that the cost of animal-drawn cultivation is often high, relative to return. Collinson estimates that at Usmao, Sukumaland, the relative cost of ox-plow cultivation is 17 percent greater than for hoe cultivation by hired labor. Besides, the quality of the work performed by ox plows is usually lower. However, relative costs for ox-plow cultivation were still 45 percent lower than for hired tractor services. Cited in Ruthenberg, *Agricultural Development in Tanganyika,* p. 184.

willingness to correct inequities.[43] Existing patterns of migration are, of course, also of considerable importance in determining policy. For example, does migration involve settlers or transient laborers; is it into areas of high or low population density; and is it spontaneous or the result of conscious government policies? Finally and importantly, it is necessary to consider the relative cost of developing various areas. Is an area underpopulated because the land is of low potential or merely as a result of historical accident? Can it be opened up to increased migration through relatively simple steps, like the elimination of trypanosomiasis and malaria; or would there have to be heavy additional investments in physical infrastructure such as roads, irrigation, and soil conservation measures? The experiences related to migration in five countries illustrate the immense complexity of the issues and the difficulty in arriving at a few straightforward guidelines for planning rural development programs. These experiences, however, do provide useful insights as to the type of information needed for assessing the possible choice of interventions.

Tanzania

Population movement in Sukumaland, Tanzania, over the last twenty years illustrates the ease in improving rural living standards when migration involves movement to underpopulated areas of high potential. Traditionally, the Sukuma were organized into independent chiefdoms. Internecine warfare led to demographic concentration, as large border areas separating chiefdoms were too insecure to be farmed and, therefore, left unpopulated. The continued abandonment of these "no man's lands" was reinforced by the prevalence of the tsetse fly. These restraints on territorial expansion were largely removed during the colonial period. The government's tsetse fly clearance effort, combined with a decrease in particularist sentiment, encouraged the spontaneous settlement of many new areas. As a result, despite rapid population growth, the average farm holding in Sukumaland remained fairly constant between 1950 and 1970.[44]

The Sukuma were fortunate in that the underpopulated areas to which they moved tended to be of relatively high potential. Between 1955 and 1970 farmers in the newly settled areas were able to increase their cotton yields per square kilometer by 346 percent as opposed to an increase of 113 percent in the older settled areas.[45]

Out-migration is, of course, limited by the availability of empty land. Besides, population pressure may soon lead to a decline in productivity and living standards. The situation in the Ukerewe district in Tanzania is ex-

43. One of the important factors explaining the Tanzanian government's emphasis on regional equity in the allocation of resources and on the discouragement of private enterprise in the cash crop sector is a dislike of the social implications of the employee-employer relationship in the agricultural sector.

44. Tanzanian census figures bear out the magnitude of out-migration in Sukumaland. Between 1948 and 1967 population in the older settled areas increased by only 1.3 to 1.5 percent per year. By contrast in newly settled areas, population growth rates averaged 3.2 percent and ranged as high as 5.4 percent. See government of Tanzania, *Recorded Population Changes, 1948–1967* (Dar es Salaam: Central Statistical Bureau, n.d.).

45. According to Collinson's evaluation of the available data on Sukumaland cotton production, it should be noted that cotton yields were still 2.5 times greater in the older areas (9.12 bales versus 3.62 bales per square kilometer), probably the result of more intensive cultivation.

emplary. With 178 persons per square kilometer, it is by far the most densely populated area in Sukumaland (average 29.3 persons per square
kilometer). Though its population increased relatively little between 1955
and 1970, cotton yields fell from 8.44 bales to 6.41 bales per square
kilometer. In 1967 per capita net value of production was only TSh99, compared to TSh378 in the more sparsely settled Shinyanga district.[46] Collinson
observes that Ukerewe may be a harbinger of future trends in Sukumaland.

Kenya

Although population movement in Kenya has also been marked by outflow into sparsely settled areas, intra-rural migration in Kenya presents a
sharp contrast to the pattern experienced in Sukumaland. It illustrates the
overriding importance of tribal and political factors which must receive attention in planning rural development programs. Whereas the Tanzanian
government's land policies have encouraged population movement in
Sukumaland, Kenyan policies have frequently tended to discourage a high
rate of out-migration. Consequently, much illegal migration and settlement
has occurred in Kenya with antecedent social, economic, and political
effects.

Like Tanzania, Kenya's pre-colonial period was marked by communal
territorial claims and fluid boundaries between tribal homelands. Fixed
property rights of the European type were first introduced during the colonial era, when supposedly unoccupied areas were classified as Crown
lands. Much of this land, the so-called scheduled areas, was distributed to
white settlers. The remaining land was set aside as native reserves and allocated to various tribes. According to Mbithi and Barnes, these policies
resulted in the loss of much of the best land to Europeans and in the dis-
placement of many indigenous communities.[47] Further, traditional flexibility with respect to land usage was disrupted, threatening the ecological
balance between man and his natural environment.

As a consequence, Kenya's demographic pattern is marked by pockets of
concentration which are unrelated to the carrying capacity of the land.
Much of the high-potential land, particularly in the former White Highlands in Rift Valley province, is relatively unpopulated.[48] Large portions of
the former native reserves, which are often of low potential, are too

46. These problems seem to be connected to three factors: (a) Though holding size has remained constant, the number of persons supported on each holding has increased. (b)
Pressure on the land means that a smaller proportion of the holding can be left fallow. In low-
density Shinyanga an average of 65 percent of each holding was left fallow (1967); in high-den-
sity Ukerewe the proportion was only 49 percent. (c) Similarly, a large share of the holding
must be devoted to food crops—e.g., 32 percent in Ukerewe as opposed to 18 percent in Shinyanga (1967). Figures are based on Collinson's evaluation of available data.

47. According to Ruthenberg, however, "the greater part of the high-potential land—the
estimates vary between two-thirds and more than four-fifths—and definitely almost all the
best land remained available for the African peasants and herdsmen." See Hans Ruthenberg,
African Agricultural Development Policy in Kenya, 1952–1965 (Berlin: Springer-Verlag, 1966),
p.3.

48. High-potential land is defined as those areas receiving more than 86.4 centimeters of
rain per year, medium-potential as areas receiving 61 to 86.4 centimeters, and low-potential as
areas receiving less than 61 centimeters. According to Mbithi and Barnes, the first two categories make up 11.5 percent and 5.5 percent of Kenya's land area, respectively. Von Pischke reports that about half of the former scheduled areas receive more than 101.6 centimeters of
rain per year.

crowded in terms of the land's supportive capacity. This is particularly true in the areas surrounding the Highlands, such as the districts of Kakamega, Kisii, and Murang'a. Still other reserve areas, such as Naruk and Samburu districts, are underpopulated, largely because tribal animosities constrain the settlement of outsiders. And, of course, many people whose ancestral homelands were expropriated are without legal claim to any land. Population pressures in crowded areas squeeze additional people into landlessness.

Except for removing white hegemony in the former scheduled areas, the present Kenyan government, which inherited this inequitable system of land distribution, has not made a significant effort to correct the imbalance through a systematic land distribution policy.[49] Indeed, the government's policies in the agricultural sector may be exacerbating the rate of landlessness. In achieving rural development, unlike Tanzania, Kenya has explicitly opted for the Western model of private capitalism and individual entrepreneurship. According to Mbithi and Barnes, land registration programs and progressive farmer schemes have hastened the decline of communal property and other traditional social arrangements. Unequal access to land through these policies has been accompanied by unequal access to new inputs and, in particular, to credit.[50] Consequently, a new rural elite has emerged that has been able to expand its holdings and increase its incomes. At least partially the growth of this rural elite occurs at the expense of the remaining "less progressive farmers," many of whom join the growing ranks of the landless.

In response to these realities, large numbers of land-hungry peasants have established illegal residence in unoccupied areas, especially in the central and coastal regions. Unlike the formal settlement schemes frequently tried in Africa, such spontaneous squatting is, of course, a relatively inexpensive ad hoc solution to the problem of malallocated land.[51] Its viability, however, seems questionable. Though the land occupied by squatters is sometimes of good quality—such as in the Chylulu Hills bordering on Tsavo National Park—the squatters generally have limited technical knowledge of agricultural practices. This results in low productivity. Frequently, bush burning, charcoal making, poaching, and other exploitative practices are followed, thereby reducing the carrying capacity of the land. Where squatters are of different ethnic stock from the surrounding community, tribal tensions and conflicts are not infrequent. Finally, because the settlements are illegal, the settlers do not have recourse to government services which could assist in their economic development.

49. The order preventing natives from owning land in the scheduled areas was revoked in 1961. Efforts to transfer land from European to African ownership were started shortly thereafter. Most important among these were (a) the Million Acre Scheme, (b) the British Land Transfer Assisted Owner's Scheme, and (c) the Stamp Purchase Plan.

50. The bulk of the credit extended by Kenya's Agricultural Finance Corporation has gone to land purchases and other large-scale uses. According to von Pischke, as of March 31, 1971, loans outstanding for land purchase and large-scale farming and ranching amounted to $25 million or about 88 percent of the loans outstanding. Though AFC has recently attempted to reach more small farmers, in financial year 1970 land purchase and development loans still amounted to 61 percent of the credit extended. See Chapter VI for further points on AFC's credit program.

51. For example, Kenya's Million Acre Scheme cost about $70 million between 1962 and 1970 or over $2,000 for each of the 34,000 families that were settled. According to Mbithi and Barnes, most of these settlers have not achieved their target incomes of $196–$280 per farm per year.

Mbithi and Barnes point out that, quite to the contrary, squatters are often harassed as trespassers and that, on occasion, their huts are burned by government agents attempting to drive off illegal residents. Thus, in the absence of an overall land policy, the squatters remain a smoldering—and perhaps an explosive—problem in Kenya.[52]

Ethiopia

The crucial importance of land policy for rural development strategy is even more strongly evinced in Ethiopia where, until the recent political upheaval, feudalistic land ownership patterns and insecurity of tenure constrained production increases and employment generation. Outside of the northern provinces—where communal land rights have prevailed—land ownership has been highly concentrated in the landed gentry, the Ethiopian Orthodox Church, and the central government.[53] Although statistics on land ownership have not been very reliable, existing estimates indicate that until recently in these areas approximately 50 percent of the farmers were tenants, while perhaps 35 percent of the land area was owned by absentee landlords.[54] The tenants were subject to arbitrary eviction, and in many instances the introduction of profitable farming techniques had led landlords to revoke tenant leases. For example, in CADU the introduction of tractor services, which increased the economies of scale in farming, allowed landowners to expand their own hectarage, forcing large numbers of tenants off the land. Cohen estimates that in Chilalo alone, some 6,500 tenant households may have been evicted between 1966 and 1972 as a result of tractorization.[55] By contrast, the tenants have had little incentive to adopt innovations themselves because their rents were uncontrolled and any increase in productivity frequently led to a corresponding increase in rent. Similarly, there have been no rules concerning compensation for improvements made on rented land; so there has been little inducement for tenants to make capital investments in their holdings. Land policies and the associated rural social organization have also affected access to agricultural services, including credit and extension. These questions are discussed further in Chapters IV and V.

Despite frequent government policy statements concerning the need for tenancy reform, the landowner-dominated Parliament[56] had been able to forestall effective remedial legislation. As recently as 1973 Parliament blocked enactment of a bill which would have restricted rents and secured

---

52. However, as Mbithi and Barnes point out, even a thorough land reform could not supply enough land to support all those who want it. For example, they estimate that if the Rift Valley province were developed to its maximum capacity, it would be able to absorb only about 1.4 million immigrants by the year 2000. Yet, within the same time frame, there is expected to be an overspill of 12.5 million persons from the crowded Central, Western, and Nyangira provinces.

53. Approximately 70 percent of Ethiopia is considered arable. In 1972 the Church owned perhaps 20 percent of this arable land and the government perhaps 12 percent. See John M. Cohen, "Ethiopia After Haile Selassie," in *African Affairs*, vol. 72, no. 289 (October 1973), pp. 369 and 373.

54. Ibid., p. 370.

55. See John M. Cohen, "Effects of Green Revolution Strategies on Tenants and Small-Scale Landowners in the Chilalo Region of Ethiopia," in *Journal of Developing Areas*, vol. 9, no. 3 (April 1975).

56. This section was written before the political changes that occurred in Ethiopia in early 1975.

limited tenant rights to land and improvements.[57] Because of the political difficulties in alleviating the plight of tenants on privately owned land, in recent years increasing attention had been given to settling smallholders on unoccupied government land. However, powerful interest groups constrained this alternative as well. In the past the government's vast holdings—perhaps half of the land area in Ethiopia—had been distributed on a patronage basis. An estimate indicates that between 1942 and 1970 the government may have made land grants to private individuals totaling almost 5 million hectares. However, 80 percent of this land went to civil servants, military and police officials, and other elite, while only about 20 percent went to landless peasants or unemployed persons.[58] Under the political structure that existed until recently, there was little impetus to change this system of land distribution. Thus, for instance, CADU, in attempting to relocate the large number of evicted tenants in Chilalo, was unable to find available government land, despite an estimated 40,000 hectares held by the government in the area.[59]

Nevertheless, there were a number of experiments to establish settlements on unoccupied government land. Many of these were in relatively marginal areas, however. For instance, the WADU settlements located in the lowlands of Abela and Bele are subject to drought, extreme heat, and periodic flooding.[60] Though the WADU settlements are potentially productive, a large capital investment is required for land clearance, drainage ditch construction, development of the infrastructure, and so forth; and the project must also provide food to the farmers during the initial period of settlement. These costs raise questions as to the establishment of such settlement schemes on a wide scale.[61] Where settlement of unoccupied areas is an expensive proposition, the improvement of tenancy rights in previously settled areas is clearly a better economic alternative. In the absence of such land reform, minimization of settlement costs may warrant development of areas which, like the Kenyan squatter settlements, are already undergoing

---

57. Cohen, "Effects of Green Revolution Strategies on Tenants and Small-Scale Landowners in the Chilalo Region of Ethiopia." The political situation has, of course, changed dramatically subsequent to the mutiny and coup d'etat of 1974.

58. See Cohen, "Ethiopia After Haile Selassie." The bulk of the government land is located in the southern part of the country and was acquired during the territorial expansion of the empire in the latter part of the nineteenth century.

59. CADU was successful in relocating ninety-five tenants from Gobe to government land in Assassa. The move was required to make room for a livestock multiplication center. See J.D. MacArthur, *The Development of Policy and Planning for Land Resettlement in Ethiopia,* mimeographed (Bradford, U.K.: Project Planning Centre, University of Bradford, September 1972), p. 106.

60. Tecle notes that the prevalence of malaria was one of the primary reasons why these lowlands were unpopulated. After this disease was eliminated in the late 1950s and early 1960s, Wolamo tribesmen remained reluctant to migrate there, presumably because of their attachment to their traditional homeland.

61. According to the data collected by Tecle, preparation of the plots alone costs about $335 per farm family. Total Phase I costs for the settlement scheme amount to between $1,125 and $1,475 per farm family, depending on how many settlers are established. Only about half of these costs are considered recoverable.

Other dry-land settlement schemes also seem to involve high establishment costs. MacArthur provides figures for settlements at Assassa, Bako, and Leka. On a per farmer basis, establishment costs are $280, $355, and $800, respectively. The Assassa figure is probably too low, since the cost figures do not include surveying, land preparation, the construction of roads, or the provision of water supply. See MacArthur, *The Development of Policy and Planning for Land Resettlement in Ethiopia,* p. 111, Table 4.1.

spontaneous settlement. However, even though this alternative is economically desirable, it is frequently unpalatable politically.

Malawi

Population movement in Malawi is somewhat different from the previous examples in that it often represents migration into areas that are already heavily populated. Malawi has traditionally had a highly mobile population. Kinsey reports that perhaps 13 percent of the Malawian population resides outside the country. Many Malawians have provided labor to mines in neighboring countries. Internal migration is also substantial. In 1966 the average district in Malawi was experiencing net out-migration of 1.1 percent, and much of this movement was to districts containing major rural development programs. Lilongwe—site of LLDP—is typical of these districts, experiencing net annual immigration at the rate of 6.7 percent.[62] According to estimates, in 1973 the population density in Lilongwe was over twice as great as the national average (119 persons versus 53 persons per square kilometer).

Much of the available data suggest that Lilongwe offers favorable economic opportunities. The district is marked by moderately rich soil and ample water supplies. Kinsey reports that, even prior to LLDP, 58 percent of the population derived cash income from the sale of their own produce as opposed to the national average of 36 percent. Similarly, the proportion of persons with no cash income is significantly lower (28 percent) than the national average (37 percent). The presence of LLDP has certainly added to the attractiveness of the area.

A great deal of the recent population growth, however, seems most attributable to the construction of the new national capital at Lilongwe City. Recent estimates indicate that the population of the city is growing by 16 percent per annum with a projected population of 180,000 by 1980.[63] The attraction of this massive construction project can be explained partly by the fact that an unskilled worker in Lilongwe City can earn an annual income that is about three-fourths the average annual farm income in the area. However, many of these employment opportunities are temporary. If additional employment opportunities do not develop in the area, large numbers of people may find themselves unemployed when the construction boom is over. There is also the danger of an impending food shortage. Kinsey estimates that the Lilongwe area must increase food production by 9 percent per year if adequate food supplies are to be produced locally for the growing urban population. Whether resources are concentrated in a few regions or spread more evenly must, thus, depend on the complex interaction of these and other factors discussed in later parts of this book.

Mali

The preceding discussion has concerned semi-permanent migration and settlement. Seasonal population movement is also common in Africa and

---

62. See government of Malawi, Department of Census and Statistics, *Malawi Population Census, 1966,* n.p., n.d.

63. See government of Malawi, Capital City Development Corporation, *Industrial Lilongwe,* n.p., n.d.

poses an entirely different set of problems in administering rural development programs, as illustrated by the example of the CFDT cotton zone in Mali in which the number of transient laborers has increased dramatically in recent years. Though this population influx reflects a measure of success for the program, it has created complex problems in ensuring high productivity and a steady food supply for the rural population.

According to Anderson, the itinerant workers typically devote three to four days a week to a farmer's land. In return they are fed and given access to plots on which they cultivate cotton. At first this increases crop revenues in the program area; however, because the migrants tend to be inadequate farmers, their yields are low. Reaching these individuals through extension is also more difficult, since migrants usually leave the area within one to three years. Repeated cotton growing on the same land exhausts the soil, compounding the productivity problem. As noted earlier, the presence of seasonal workers in the project area also causes food shortages. In the Fana sector in the 1971/72 period, shortages were so severe that millet prices doubled. Such problems will continue as long as the influx of transient labor remains high and policies related to food production continue to be neglected.

Regional Equity in Rural Development

As the experiences in Tanzania, Kenya, Ethiopia, Malawi, and Mali indicate, the interdependent factors influencing population movement in Africa make policy decisions regarding rural development complex. Where the income-earning opportunities in an area are substantial and the political roadblocks are limited, efforts to stimulate population influx in specific regions through further investment of resources may be warranted. However, as illustrated by the spontaneous settlements in Kenya, too great an influx may also prove counterproductive. Therefore, care needs to be exercised not to exceed the supportive capability of the local natural resources. In regions or localities where this has already occurred, it may be prudent to stimulate out-migration by investing resources in the development of areas with declining or stagnant populations. In all cases adequate attention to land use and land rights is essential for success. Each of these interdependent factors has to be considered in weighing the costs and benefits of investment in different geographic areas. Additional considerations related to regional equity are discussed in Chapters VII and VIII.

CHAPTER III

Nature of the Production Systems 2: Diversification of Production Activities

In this chapter some of the additional issues faced in planning the development of the traditional farming systems are discussed. For instance, were the more recent rural development programs, such as CADU, WADU, LLDP, and SRDP, effective in achieving the goal of increasing overall agricultural productivity of the target population? To what extent are these programs developing the technological capability necessary to identify and remove the diverse set of constraints arising from the complex interactions between the physical, demographic, and social variables that affect improvement of the farming system? Alternatively, if the programs do not have a technological component, to what extent have they benefited from the research capacity being developed elsewhere? Lastly, to what extent have the areas had the benefit of profitable technological packages suited to diverse farming systems within program areas so as to promote equity between various classes and regions and among farmers within a region? In addition to these various questions related to development of the farming systems, this chapter also discusses the problems faced in planning the development of the traditional livestock sector.

Diversification in Integrated Rural Development Programs

Table 3.1 shows the estimated increase in yields, hectarages, and production of the principal crops in Chilalo Awraja, Ethiopia, prior and subsequent to the establishment of CADU. CADU has a relatively well-developed research unit carrying out adaptive research on a broad range of problems, including the adaptation of improved seeds and such simple labor-intensive farm implements as an improved plow, an animal-drawn harrow, a new hand hoe, and a stationary thresher. CADU is also conducting research on upgrading milch cattle. CADU's research unit has adapted three improved wheat varieties to suit ecological conditions in the Chilalo area. According to the data collected by CADU's evaluation unit, wheat yields in Chilalo Awraja increased from 1.33 to 2.0 metric tons per hectare from 1966 to 1971. Average yields of beans have also increased to some extent. However, in the first few years, despite efforts at diversification, CADU's major impact has been on wheat production. This has led to considerable wheat surpluses in the Chilalo area within three to four years after the project got under way. As a result, CADU has faced several problems related to marketing and pricing of wheat. The effect of these on adoption of innovations is discussed in Chapters V and VI. There appears to have been a decline in the production of milk in Chilalo in the 1971/72 period as shown by the rather sharp decline in the milk received at CADU's purchase centers (Table 3.2). The decline has been attributed to the substitution of pastureland to cultivation of more profitable wheat. However, CADU has also attempted to improve the quality of local dairy cattle. According to Cohen, in the 1972/73 period the purchases of milk had increased by 70 percent over the previous year. He attributes this to CADU's sustained efforts on the dairy front.[1]

Table 3.1: Comparison of 1966 and 1971 Crop Production, Chilalo Awraja, Ethiopia

	1966 Crop			1971 Crop		
	Area (hectares)	Volume (metric tons)	Yield (metric tons per hectare)	Area (hectares)	Volume (metric tons)	Yield (metric tons per hectare)
Barley	67,900	108,565	1.60	79,300	126,880	1.60
Wheat	23,650	31,457	1.33	51,000	102,000	2.00
Flax	18,950	11,932	0.63	25,300	15,939	0.63
Peas	8,950	11,734	1.31	6,400	8,320	1.30
Corn	4,900	14,863	3.05	17,700	53,985	3.05
Beans	3,900	10,591	2.71	7,800	25,136	3.22
Teff	1,500	1,895	1.25	7,600	9,500	1.25

Source: G. Bergman and H. Lindqvist, *Credit Situation in Chilalo Awraja*, CADU Minor Research Task no. 3 (Asella, Ethiopia: Chilalo Agricultural Development Unit, July 1969); and CADU Crop Sampling Surveys.

Table 3.2: Milk Purchased, in Liters, by CADU, Ethiopia, 1967/68–1971/72

Year	Milk purchased
1967/68	4,000
1968/69	136,000
1969/70	318,000
1970/71	159,000
1971/72	147,113

Source: Government of Ethiopia, Chilalo Agricultural Development Unit, Marketing Divisional Files; and *Cost/Benefit Analysis of CADU for the Period 1967/68–1973/74* (Asella: CADU, 1971).

WADU appears to have been somewhat more successful than CADU in increasing crop yields. The highlands of Wolamo in Ethiopia are suited to grow a range of crops, including maize, wheat, and teff. Two years after the establishment of WADU (i.e., in the 1970/71 period), maize yields per hectare in the highlands are estimated to have increased from 12 quintals to 24

1. Based on personal discussions with John Cohen.

quintals. The project appraisal team of the World Bank had predicted an increase of only up to 13 quintals per hectare in the highlands and up to 18 quintals per hectare in lowland settlement areas by the ninth year of operation. Table 3.3 shows yields of the major crops in WADU. The number of farmers receiving production credit increased to 7,070 by the 1972/73 period, whereas the appraisal had predicted that the number would be 4,000 in that year. The existing data thus indicate that, in the first few years of implementation, the actual rate of return on investment in WADU may have been significantly higher than that expected.

The rapid surpassing of the projected targets in Wolamo has been attributed by the observers of WADU to a combination of the very fertile Wolamo soils, the meticulousness of the Wolamo farmers, and the effectiveness of the extension system. Unfortunately, compared to CADU, WADU's technological research component has been modest and confined mainly to fertilizer trials. Therefore, how effectively WADU will tackle the problems arising from the introduction of more complex innovations in the future still remains to be seen.

Table 3.3: A Comparison of Pre-project Forecast for Year 9 (Maturity) and Actual Year 2 Crop Yields in Quintals per Hectare, WADU, Ethiopia

		Yield	
Crop	Pre-project	Forecast at maturity (year 9)	Actual average (year 2)
Highland			
Maize	8.0	13.0	20.0
Wheat	9.0	12.0	17.0
Teff	5.5	8.5	7.0
Lowland			
Maize	12.0	18.0	24.0
Cotton	1.4	5.6	10.0
Chilies	1.0	5.0	9.0

Source: Government of Ethiopia, Wolamo Agricultural Development Unit, *Annual Report for Year 2 Programs* (Soddo: Ministry of Agriculture, May 1972).

The Lilongwe Land Development Program in Malawi is aimed at increasing productivity of all the major crops grown in the area: namely, maize, groundnuts, and tobacco. During the first phase of program activities, maize production was expected to increase from 66,200 metric tons to 184,-000 metric tons through increase in yields as well as in the area under cultivation. However, the major economic return was to be realized through an increase in the yields and the production of high-value groundnuts. Because of the restriction on exports of tobacco, the project did not provide for an increase in tobacco production. Rather, the aim was to increase tobacco yields so as to permit diversification of hectarage to other crops. The project also aimed at increasing productivity of livestock. Data collected by LLDP's evaluation unit suggest that average maize yields during the first five years of the program, 1969/70 to 1973/74, conformed roughly to projected yields, although there has been substantial annual variability (Table 3.4). The hectarage under improved maize increased from approximately 8,620 (1969/70) to 20,650 (1971/72). Highlighting the inadequacy of the production data, Kinsey points out that during this period total maize production may have been anywhere from 46,300 metric tons to 136,000 metric tons a year, depending on which of the available estimates of farm size, proportion of hectarage under maize, and yields per hectare are used in the calculations.[2]

However, LLDP's main shortfall seems to have been in groundnut production. Both the original and the second World Bank appraisal team envisaged a far greater increase in the yield and the hectarage of groundnuts than seems to have been realized in the first six years. The available data suggest that during the 1972/73 period groundnut yields in the project area declined for the fourth consecutive year and were substantially lower than the yields outside the project area. If the shortfall in groundnut yields is accepted and given the problems encountered in development of the livestock discussed later in this chapter, the rate of return on LLDP during the first six years may have been somewhat lower than projected.

Table 3.4: Projected and Actual Yields of Maize and Groundnuts in Quintals per Hectare, LLDP, Malawi, 1969/70–1973/74

	Maize		Groundnuts	
Season	Projected	Actual	Projected	Actual
1969/70	14.1	11.5	5.9	6.2
1970/71	14.8	13.4	6.0	5.5
1971/72	15.5	15.0	6.2	5.2
1972/73	16.2	13.0	6.3	2.7
1973/74	17.0	13.1*	6.4	4.5*

*Preliminary results.
Source: Based on the Phase I Appraisal of LLDP and the data collected by LLDP's evaluation unit.

More important, however, is the fact that, despite the attempt at diversification, LLDP's major success so far lies in increasing maize production leading to substantial increases in marketable surpluses. Consequently, LLDP, like CADU, has encountered many problems in marketing maize and in maintaining the necessary price incentive. Unless the pricing and

2. Kinsey notes that estimates of the total hectarage cultivated in LLDP vary by as much as 26 percent, while estimates of the proportion planted with maize differ by up to 21 percent. Depending on which estimates are used and in what combination, maize hectarage can vary by as much as 78 percent. Estimates of mean maize yield per hectare range between 11.2 quintals and 19.1 quintals. Thus, the available data provide estimates of total production that vary by 120 percent. LLDP's example is instructive in an important respect, especially as substantial data have been collected in this project. For most other programs the data for baseline and subsequent years are usually very much poorer. In such cases, judging the program mainly on the basis of precise realization of targets has the danger of diverting attention away from the more basic questions related to the project design, implementation, and reliability discussed in this study. There is no question that far greater attention needs to be devoted to collection of reliable data for the baseline and subsequent years to be able to judge project performance objectively. At the same time, in assessing performance, the weight attached to the realization of short-run production targets that are frequently based on the poor initial estimates also needs to be reduced so as to examine the overall program performance in a proper perspective. This and the subsequent chapters outline in considerable detail a point of view as to what such a perspective may be.

marketing problems are tackled, it seems that it will be difficult for these integrated projects to be able to continue the rate of expansion of cereal production that they realized in the first few years. The integrated programs, therefore, raise a dual question as to the efficacy of the marketing components and the prudence of generating massive supluses in small regions in a short period without regard to effective demand. These questions are discussed later. However, to summarize, during the first short period of five years in which the integrated programs had been under way, the goal of diversification had not yet been fully realized.

Development of Technological Capability for Diversification

The difficulties encountered in achieving diversification are, of course, closely related to the efforts to develop suitable technologies. Although, in principle, the role of a profitable technological package is generally well recognized, in practice most programs reviewed seem rather poorly equipped to develop an understanding of the interactions in the existing farming systems and the changes that are generated in the overall system by introduction of one or more innovations.

An effective link of research units with rural development programs is one of the critical steps in adapting research results to particular farming systems. Where such effective research capability does not exist, it is necessary to allocate finances and manpower for developing appropriate technological packages. Such research needs to be distinguished from the agronomic trials conducted on individual crops that frequently fail to take account of the system effects.

Further, it is essential that there be a close link between adaptive research and extension. Far too often there is either not a profitable technological package that takes account of specific local constraints faced in applying research results to farming systems; or there is not effective training of extension agents, making much of the extension effort ineffective. Often the extension service also fails to appreciate its role in identifying the farm-level constraints which can be removed through research. There is, therefore, little emphasis on an adaptive approach to research so as to make the necessary improvements in the package with which the extension service is equipped. Apart from helping to create technological packages, local research stations need to facilitate a two-way flow between research and extension.

Admittedly, such research on multiple-cropping systems is complex; and the task of establishing an effective research-extension link is demanding, both in time and effort. However, its importance cannot be overstated, as is best illustrated by the evidence from the programs reviewed.

The decline in groundnut yields in LLDP exemplifies the paucity of knowledge of the complex interactions involving agronomic and economic factors. Analysis of LLDP highlights two points. The ongoing research effort, conducted outside the purview of the program at the Chitedze governmental station, seems to have been inadequate in developing adaptive technological packages and in identifying and dealing with the constraints introduced by the program's other activities. Further, because of the emphasis on early realization of production targets, far too little attention could be given to developing the right package prior to its dissemination.

According to Kinsey, based on a limited number of research trials, it was decided to issue 4.5 kilograms of sulphur dust to all farmers receiving credit for groundnuts in the 1970/71 season. The sulphur was intended to control leafspot. Before the results of this season were known, the appraisal report had opted in favor of supplying sulphur to growers who were expected to achieve yields of 147 kilograms per hectare. This recommendation was made, although evidence existed to suggest that such a recommendation was premature and probably inappropriate.

The premature introduction of sulphur and the low rate of application stemmed from technical interrelationships which created a conflict of objectives. On the one hand, sulphur was introduced because sulphate of ammonia fertilizer had been phased out and because it was expected that sulphur deficiency in maize would become a problem. On the other hand, the rate of application was kept low because the relationship between soil pH and the use of sulphur was unknown and because it was assumed that heavy applications of sulphur would lower the pH. These technical problems dominated all other considerations, including the effect on the program's credibility of promoting an innovation that may prove to be inappropriate.

In the 1971/72 period the groundnut credit package included 22.4 kilograms of sulphur for one hectare. The amount of sulphur was raised to 89.6 kilograms per hectare in the 1972/73 period. Kinsey observes that the effect of these rates of application on soil pH in the program area is still an open question and may explain the declining yields of groundnuts.

It is also true, however, that a number of central African countries appear to be suffering from a similar decline in groundnut yields, in particular in areas where new maize varieties have been introduced. It has been observed that, given the very considerable labor required for weeding, harvesting, and shelling of groundnuts, the limited labor is probably being allocated to the production of high-yielding maize. Although these two explanations of declining groundnut yields have been put forward, the precise agronomic or economic factors that explain the decline are not known. And yet the knowledge as to whether the pH factor, the labor constraint, the relative prices, or some other factor is affecting groundnut yields is critical in determining whether to undertake agronomic research; whether to avert labor constraint through a different crop rotation, mechanization, or both; or whether to change price relationships. Such problems are faced all too frequently in rural development programs. And yet, they have received relatively little attention in agricultural research.

On the basis of evidence from their own and various other studies of agricultural research in Kenya, Mbithi and Barnes make a similar point in their review of the Kenyan squatter settlements. In Kenya the government research stations serve as the main source of information on maize technology. These stations are usually self-contained institutions which have few or no links with the extension service. Research carried out on farms near Embu and Katumani research stations shows that adoption rates are even lower on these farms than those studied 2 to 100 miles away. The farmers feel that the research station is for the *wazungu* (Europeans); that the stations use *wazungu dawa* (fertilizers), tractors, and aerial irrigation; keep too many books and records; and employ many people in their fields.

Such an attitude implies that the farmers do not perceive the work on the research stations as being suited to their situation. A follow-up on some of the farmers who had attended a field day at one of the stations indicated once again how keenly they felt the lack of relevance of the large-scale operations at the research station to their small farms. The programs are not divisible or adaptable, and the emphasis is on optimal combinations of resources to maximize output without consideration of the scarcity of some of these resources at the small-farm level. Physical science research has been conducted on a very limited scale—e.g., exhaustive soil surveys and full-scale fertilizer trials have been carried out on only two soil types in Trans Nzoia.

Mbithi and Barnes point out that, in addition to these gaps, research is lacking in a strong subsistence or a small-crop base. Little attention has been given to major food crops (such as pigeon peas and bullrush millet) and to small-scale cash crops (such as coriander, green grams, and castor). Development of food crop mixes for different ecological regions has also been neglected in agricultural research.

A similar situation exists in the SODENKAM land settlement in Cameroon. According to Belloncle and Gentil, to ensure that the results achieved on the Nkondjok research farm are suitable for practical adoption, the experimental conditions should faithfully reproduce the conditions under which the technical innovations developed are to be applied in the future. The Nkondjok farm is situated on a fine basaltic plateau, completely cleared, whereas the pioneers' farms are usually in the middle of a forest on fairly steep slopes and have very poor soils. Regardless of the results achieved on the program's Technical Support Center, one may well question how they can be adopted by the pioneers, considering the different and largely artificial conditions under which they have been obtained.

The review further notes that usually there is no direct link between the Nkondjok experiements and SODENKAM's extension programs in the villages. Nor has much attention been given to seeking solutions to the problems faced by the pioneer villages. Rather than developing a coherent applied research program, there has been a series of attempts entrusted to different research institutes with neither a clear definition of the objectives pursued nor an examination of their connection with SODENKAM's policy. This is particularly obvious in the testing of food crops, which have a fundamental bearing on the operation. The effort should obviously have been directed toward research into the types of rotation possible in the area so that the results could be made available to pioneers.

In stock raising, too, the "experimental" program should have been initiated on the basis of the actual conditions in which the cattle would live in the villages; and the desired objective should have been clearly defined. It is certainly a pleasant sight to see the Ndama herd on the farm peaceably grazing on 12 hectares of pasture, but that does not seem to be a sufficient reason to continue on the course adopted by the program in the field of livestock development.

The failure of research to be oriented towards removing or adapting to critical constraints and, hence, to improving performance of the agricultural systems has been observed repeatedly in the reviews of the *ujàmaa,* SRDP, the Sukumaland cotton development, and several others, It has also been emphasized in the previous agroeconomic research on Africa, most notably by de Wilde in his earlier work commissioned by the World Bank.[3] And yet development of effective national research systems remains one of the critical gaps in realizing the objectives of rural development in Africa.

Several steps need particular attention in future rural development programs. There is a substantial need for an explicit commitment among national policymakers and donors to the task of developing agricultural research systems. This commitment needs to be translated into action by allocation of substantially more finances and experienced manpower than in the past to carry out research and, in particular, to train the indigenous manpower in the various disciplines. Such effort is already under way at the international level in the form of the various international research institutes.[4]

However, particularly because the ecological variability is so overwhelming in Africa, there is a need to make a conscious effort to develop a network of national, regional, and local research systems and to create an indigenous manpower capability to operate such systems. Only then will the international effort be able to emphasize adaptive agricultural research. This is where a major gap now exists, despite the fact that a plethora of research institutions and experimental stations already exists in many African countries. Frequently these institutions are ill-staffed, ill-financed, and their efforts poorly coordinated with each other to deal with the many problems that extend across regional and national boundaries. Finally, the linking of agricultural research with action programs cannot be overemphasized. It is only when an effective two-way dialogue between research and extension is established that the current rural development effort will have a noticeable impact.[5]

Farming Systems and Intraregional Equity

As evident from the preceding discussion, the objective of rural development programs may not be only to increase overall productivity in a region but also to increase participation of low-income farmers in agricultural production and incomes and thus to reduce income disparities between classes of farmers. To realize the latter objective, interventions have to be based on the knowledge of the variation in the resources within regions and between

3. See John C. de Wilde, *Experiences with Agricultural Development in Tropical Africa,* 2 vols. (Baltimore: Johns Hopkins Press, 1967).

4. In 1974 the World Bank allocated $34 million for support of international agricultural research, an increase from $15 million in 1972 and $23 million in 1973. In 1975 the World Bank hopes to spend $45 million for this purpose. For a summary of the activities of the institutions supported by the World Bank, see Consultive Group on International Agricultural Research, *International Research in Agriculture* (New York: World Bank/FAO/UNDP, 1974).

5. For a general discussion of some of the problems faced in African agricultural research, see St. George C. Cooper, *Agricultural Research in Tropical Africa* (Nairobi: East African Literature Bureau, 1970). Concerning the role of interdisciplinary research, see D. W. Norman, "Interdisciplinary Research on Rural Development: The Reru Experience." Paper prepared for a Development from Below Workshop, organized by the Overseas Liaison Committee of the American Council on Education and the Association for the Advancement of Agricultural Sciences in Africa, Addis Ababa, October 12–20, 1973.

classes and on the factors that explain the existing allocation of resources, levels of productivity, and variations in it.

How incomes may vary substantially within a target area by crops is illustrated well by the Lilongwe Land Development Program. A study[6] of the Tsabango, Chinyama, and Kabuthu areas in the Lilongwe district shows that the gross return per hectare of groundnuts and tobacco is, respectively, twice and three times that of maize. Given that tobacco growers tend to have holdings that are far above average in size, these returns result in disparities in incomes of up to 300 percent between tobacco growers and non-tobacco growers. This observation holds, irrespective of whether income variation is considered on the basis of a holding or on a per capita basis. Only 30 percent of the farmers in the current program area sell tobacco from 11 percent of the cropped hectarage. The distribution of income is, therefore, highly skewed in favor of this group.

According to Kinsey's estimates for more recent years, there has not been a significant change in relative incomes of tobacco and non-tobacco growers subsequent to the establishment of the program. The variation in income is a result of differences, not only in crops grown, but in soil fertility within program areas. There is, of course, a close relation between soil characteristics and cropping patterns. In Lilongwe the fertile soils existing in some units are also the most suited to tobacco cultivation. These variations lead to the difficult conflicts in achieving the program's objectives of growth and distribution. Kinsey's analysis illustrates the point.

The mean cash value of production in the area covered by the program's extension service is some 22 percent less than in other areas planned for the program but as yet outside the current program area. In 1971 the geographical variation in value of production was 94 percent. One area was 58 percent below the mean value, while another was 23 percent above. LLDP must raise the value of production by more than 50 percent in the less productive areas if the geographical imbalance in value of production is to be eliminated.

The geographical imbalance in income also has important implications for the program's objective of raising the average farm family's net cash income by 70 percent. It is far easier to reach this target by concentrating inputs and extension in the high-value production areas rather than in the low-value production areas.

To a large degree the amelioration of these income differentials between tobacco and non-tobacco growers and, hence, between those areas well suited and ill suited to tobacco production is beyond the project's direct control, since the granting of quotas to grow tobacco is administered by ADMARC, the government marketing agency. Moreover, the principal tobacco production occurs in areas where farm size is above average, thus permitting the growing of both food crops and tobacco. In areas where high population pressures have reduced the average size of holding, tobacco production has declined and is limited by the hectarage available, once food crop needs have been satisfied.

---

6. H.K.F. Hoffman, "Case Studies of Progressive Farming in Central Malawi. Report on a Socio-Economic Survery Conducted in Selected Areas of the Lilongwe Plateau" (n.p.: government of Malawi, July 1967).

If balanced, broad-based growth is an objective of rural development, the question arises as to whether, in parts of Lilongwe where farms are subdivided and submarginal, the provision of agricultural credit and extension is the right strategy or whether an entirely different approach, such as the consolidation of holdings and/or the creation of off-farm employment, should be followed.

Data on intraregional income disparities arising from differences in quality of physical resources[7] are, however, too limited in most cases to permit such judgments in the course of planning. Often, even if the data were available, the programs are ill-equipped to incorporate such information in planning the strategy or in modifying it as new information becomes available during the course of implementation. This is illustrated by the evaluation of SRDP's Vihiga Maize Credit Program carried out by Hay and Heyer of the Institute of Development Studies (IDS) in Nairobi.[8] They point out the diversity in the Vihiga district in ecological conditions, in cropping patterns, and in population density. According to Hay and Heyer, the neglect of the diversity in physical conditions has led to an almost exclusive emphasis on credit for maize. For example, there is substantial migration of male members as a result of availability of off-farm employment. Survey data show that 30 percent of the family heads were absent during the survey period. Consequently, despite the apparent high density of population, there is often considerable shortage rather than surplus of labor, affecting labor availability at peak periods of farming. The planning of the Vihiga Maize Program did not take into account this constraint and its effect on adoption. The amount of maize grown also varies substantially between farms. In fact, a considerable proportion of the land is allocated to crops other than maize, including coffee, tea, certified potatoes, sweet potatoes, beans, sorghum, and millets.

The question, therefore, arises whether excessive emphasis on maize self-sufficiency is the appropriate strategy for either specialization or improvement of income distribution and nutrition in Vihiga. The implications of the objective of maize self-sufficiency have also not been spelled out clearly in the strategy adopted. For example, it is not clear whether maize is to be promoted on each farm or whether self-sufficiency is to be realized in each area in the division or in the division as a whole. These various alternative objectives and the way they affect strategy have substantial implications for distribution of benefits among target populations within a program area. Hay and Heyer emphasize that, though considerable information became available on the Vihiga area, it was not utilized by the American planners who modified the initial plans after USAID decided to fund the Vihiga Maize Program.[9]

The constraints imposed by limited technology, manpower, and information currently available for planning rural development programs are real.

7. The disparities in distribution of benefits arising from institutional constraints (such as land tenure or access to inputs) as distinct from physical constraints (such as soil fertility or rainfall) are discussed in Chapters V, VI, and VII.

8. F.G. Hay and J. Heyer, "The Vihiga Maize Credit Package," in *An Overall Evaluation of the Special Rural Development Programme, 1972,* Institute for Development Studies Occasional Paper no. 8 (Nairobi: University of Nairobi, 1973), Appendix F, p. 5.

9. Ibid., p. F-17. Also see Chapter IX of this study for further discussion of effect of plan modifications on the program's performance.

Given these constraints, a very difficult dilemma is frequently encountered. Should rural development programs involve use of substantial planning resources at the outset to develop different development strategies so as to fulfill the objective of equity in a region, but probably at the cost of depriving other regions of the country of these limited resources? Or, alternatively, should initial efforts be concentrated on simple innovations, such as the use of improved seeds, fertilizer, row planting, and weeding, which can be introduced across the program area with a reasonable degree of modification? Considerations of equity on a larger scale may often necessitate the latter. It is apparent, however, that the program administrators ought to be cognizant of the likelihood of intra-program disparities, begin to collect the necessary information from the very initial stages of implementation, and maintain enough flexibility to deal with the problem of disparities during the course of implementation. In subsequent phases of program implementation, the program may then develop more specific technological packages for the groups that are otherwise likely to be bypassed by general programs.

Livestock Development
in the Traditional Sector

Development of livestock may be as critical for improving rural productivity and welfare as is improvement of the crop-farming system. In pastoral areas cattle raising has traditionally been a major activity, since limited rainfall has precluded crop production. Therefore, in many of these areas, livestock development is the only means of raising living standards. In non-pastoral areas stock raising is an effective complement to crop raising. Improved planting techniques can provide increased supplies of fodder for livestock, which in turn can increase the dairy and meat products available for domestic consumption. In addition, the animals provide manure for enriching the soil and can also be sold for cash.[10]

The program reviews indicate, however, that improvement of the production of livestock is beset with many difficulties, both in pastoral and non-pastoral areas. Livestock development involves a complex interaction of technical, economic, and sociocultural factors, leading to considerable uncertainty as to the response to innovations, a phenomenon best illustrated by performance of the livestock components in the programs reviewed.

In Malawi the increase in the domestic production of beef has not kept pace with the rapidly rising domestic demand.[11] Introducing a livestock

10. Marticou, an agronomist working for ZAPI in Cameroon, pointed out that the "pigs, sheep, and goats which presently cause more damage than they bring in profits, could be the prime agents in agricultural progress. Instead of wandering around all day tearing up fields and plantations, they could be corralled under supervision, given food which, in any case, they would have taken in the fields, and the planters could take advantage of this domestication to gather the dung which is now lost. This would provide work for idle farm labor, would use the cassava which is at present frequently far beyond the farmer's needs, . . . and would constitute a new source of income." H. Marticou, *Les Structures Agricoles dans le Centre Cameroun* (Yaoundé: Ministre de l'Agriculture, Direction des Statistiques, 1961).

11. Between 1966 and 1971, domestic consumption of beef increased by 152 percent, while domestic production increased by only 41 percent. Government of Malawi, *Economic Report, 1972*, Budget Document no. 4 (n.p.: Office of the President and Cabinet, Economic Planning Division, n.d.).

component in LLDP, therefore, seemed to be a step towards improving domestic production of livestock as well as a means of increasing the cash incomes of smallholders. The World Bank's Phase II appraisal of LLDP noted that eighty animals per year were being stall-fed successfully in the program area and urged the creation of a ranch to increase the supply of feeder steers available to program farmers. Stall-feeding is a highly profitable enterprise; gross returns per steer compare favorably with the returns per hectare of maize, groundnuts, or tobacco. Further, because stall-feeding is nonseasonal, farmers can earn income at times of the year when no alternative employment is possible.[12]

LLDP started the Dzalanyama Ranch in 1970 to produce cattle for sale to non-cattle–owning farmers interested in stall-feeding. In addition, it was hoped that the existing cattle owners would be attracted to the new technique of stall-feeding. The ranch, which covers an area of 65,182 hectares, was to acquire 2,500 head of cattle for each of the four years of its development. By 1974 it was intended to produce annually (a) 1,800 high-quality steers for fattening, (b) 700 improved heifers for either milk production or fattening, and (c) some 1,000 additional animals to be sold for slaughter.

The ranch has not performed as expected. By the end of 1972, the cattle population was only 2,250 head, or less than half the projected number. The quality of the animals was poorer than expected. The rate of return has ranged between 4.5 and 5.0 percent. The ranch has been unable to provide many animals for stall-feeding. From October of 1971 to the end of 1972, less than 400 steers were sold or issued on credit. These shortcomings are explained by the ranch's inability to purchase the number of cattle anticipated from local sources. Only 1,800 head were acquired during the first two years of operation, and these were more expensive than foreseen. The average price paid for cows in the local markets has been K43, 20 percent above the expected price of K36.

The stringent cattle supply is largely explained by the complex interaction of the physical, economic, and sociocultural factors that influence the nature of the market in the traditional sector. When the World Bank's approval team estimated the number of cattle that could be obtained from local auction sales, the project area had experienced a series of poor crop years. Farmers were selling off large numbers of stock to compensate for lost income. Based on this high sales volume, it was assumed that sufficient cattle would be available. After the ranch was established, however, there was a series of favorable seasons. Consequently, farmers have been reluctant to market cattle, preferring instead to build their own depleted stock. Further, LLDP competes for the existing cattle, not only with private buyers, but also with the West German project in Salima, which was established subsequent to the planning of the ranch.

Cattle prices have been rising as a result of the shortage of available cattle and the competitive bidding between buyers. LLDP has been reluctant to pay the price commanded by the top-grade stock. Consequently, the limited number of cattle that the ranch has been able to purchase tends to be older

12. Gross margins for 320 of the credit steers issued by LLDP averaged K42 per head. Average cash receipts per grower in the project area from the sale of maize, groundnuts, and tobacco combined was K44 in the 1971/72 period. Thus, a smallholder who fattened only one steer a year could potentially double his annual cash income.

and less productive. Apart from the desire to keep procurement costs low, according to the project management, maintenance of low prices is justified by the backward-sloping supply curve of herders.

The available evidence suggests that Lilongwe farmers are reluctant to part with cattle except in times of economic hardship. Kinsey notes that most farmers sell or slaughter their animals only when they need immediate cash. A 1972 survey conducted by LLDP's Livestock Section indicated that 60 percent of the program's cattle owners considered their stock to be primarily a form of insurance. Only 19 percent viewed cattle as an important source of income. Not surprisingly, the same survey found that, despite its profitability, only one percent of the 2,400 potential stall-feeders in the program area were actually being fattened.[13] The program management has proposed further investigations to improve understanding of the supply response of Lilongwe farmers.

The attitude toward cattle similar to that noted in LLDP is observed elsewhere in Africa, especially among nomadic tribesmen.[14] To rural people cattle is often not only an economic investment but a source of status and an important feature of the community's sociocultural activities. In the light of the economic and social significance of cattle and considering the high mortality rate in the herds, a desire to hold rather than to sell cattle may be natural in some circumstances.[15] It is, therefore, believed by LLDP management that, if prices of cattle rise, herders may be able to obtain cash with fewer sales or with sale of lower grade cattle. However, there is considerable conflict in the existing evidence as to the nature of the price responsiveness of cattle herders. Some evidence indicates that, when incentive prices are offered for cattle, nomadic herdsmen behave like economic men.[16] A case, therefore, may be made for experimenting with higher prices to examine the extent to which farmers are willing to offer their cattle for higher prices.

Further, since the project is a public sector investment, it is not clear whether the reduced benefits to LLDP as a result of the higher domestic cattle prices necessarily mean a net social loss. The higher prices will, after all, be received by local producers. The overall social benefit to the local population from higher prices may outweigh somewhat the disadvantages

---

13. Cossins noted similar attitudes toward cattle in the Shire Lowlands. The rural people kept stock *(a)* as a form of insurance to be sold in years when crops fail, *(b)* as a form of savings to be drawn upon for special occasions, and *(c)* for the breeding of draft animals so a man could maintain or expand his holdings. Cattle were only of minor consideration as a source of food, and then usually for dairy rather than meat products. The only steady cash income received from cattle came from the sale of butter. See Noel J. Cossins, "A Study of People and Their Cattle in the Shire Lowlands," mimeographed study prepared for the World Bank on behalf of the Ethiopian Livestock and Meat Board, 1973, p. 79.

14. The Fulani in sub-Saharan Africa have a saying: "When my wife dies I am sad, but when my cow dies I cry." Ibid.

15. In the Shire Lowlands, for instance, mature females constitute 41 percent of the cattle population. About half of these cows give birth annually, and approximately one-third of the calves die. Taking into consideration the herd mortality rate of 12 percent, yearly increases will average only 2 percent. Of course, epidemics and drought threaten even this negligible growth. As Cossions observes: "One can understand the reasons why an owner of 40 animals, with an expected annual increase of only one animal, sells only when he is forced to." Ibid., p. 62.

16. See, for example, Polly Hill, *Studies in Rural Capitalism in West Africa* (Cambridge: Cambridge University Press, 1970).

of lower return to LLDP. However, it has been proposed that the ranch be stocked by imported cattle. Given the shortage of cattle in Kenya, a major exporter in Africa, it is not clear as to how this alternative compares with increased procurement of domestic cattle. Alternatively, it may mean procuring cattle from other exporters.

The inadequate knowledge of the factors that affect the cattle market lends considerable uncertainty to the future of livestock development in Lilongwe. As the survey data indicate, if individual farmers are attempting to minimize their own risk by enlarging their herds, overgrazing and reduced carrying capacity on the land may result. Under such conditions initial improvements in the quality of cattle through use of high-priced imported cattle may prove self-defeating in the long run unless there is simultaneous increase in stall-feeding and marketing of indigenous cattle.

While promoting livestock production in non-pastoral areas like Lilongwe is difficult, the problems seem even more intractable in the traditional pastoral sector where stock raising is the primary livelihood. The Kenya Livestock Development Project is a case in point. The pastoral areas covered by the project already suffer from serious overgrazing. The Masai are traditionally a herding people, and their herds have been built up to the point where the ecological balance of the area is endangered. The need for destocking is, therefore, urgent. The Masai tradition of common land, private cattle, however, constrains attempts to cut down the population of the herds. As long as the range is open, it is to each cattle owner's individual advantage to enlarge his herd and get the maximum use of the public lands. This, of course, works to the disadvantage of the community as a whole, for the land is incapable of supporting great numbers of cattle.[17]

Destocking means reducing the human population in this region as well. Stock raising is capital intensive rather than labor intensive; it is most productive when undertaken on a large scale. There are already more Masai living on the range than can be supported by stock raising. Even if employment opportunities were created in dairying, slaughtering, tanning, and other related enterprises, the potential for maintaining a large number of people in the pastoral sector is minimal. Range development must eventually involve relocation of a majority of the population and, hence, a disruption of tribal life. Such change can only be brought about gradually as the attitudes of the Masai change with increased education.[18] Many of the past initiatives of the government have been received with considerable suspicion by the Masai.

Since production problems in Masai land are related to the common land, private cattle-grazing system, two general solutions present themselves: to divide the rangeland in individual private holdings or to introduce collective grazing. The overgrazing, overstocking cycle would then be halted. KLDP's efforts have concentrated on the former solution, largely through the encouragement of individual and group ranches.

17. Such problems have, of course, been compounded by the recent series of droughts in the Sahel region and the consequent, if temporary, southern expansion of the Sahara.

18. For a discussion of changes being wrought in Masai society, see Hans G. G. Hedlund, "The Impact of Group Ranches on a Pastoral Society," Institute for Development Studies Staff Paper no. 100 (Nairobi: University of Nairobi, June 1971).

Individual ranches are advantageous in that the owner's limited grazing land dictates a reduction in the size of his herd. The land can, thereby, be given a chance to regain productivity; and the quality of the cattle can be upgraded. The major drawback of these ranches is their size, for in pastoral areas ranches must be very large to take advantage of the erratic rainfall. The individual ranches assisted by KLDP average 600 hectares, which is too small to permit flexible use of the dry grazing land. This size limitation largely accounts for the low 6 percent rate of return on the investment realized on individual ranches.[19]

Group ranches, on the other hand, are of a more efficient size, averaging 18,000 hectares.[20] However, since only the land and not the cattle is group property in these ranches, the common land, private cattle problem persists. Setting individual grazing quotas has been an ineffective means of limiting herd size. Required culling offers a potential solution but remains largely untried to date. The long-range prognosis for these ranches is unclear, for it seems difficult for pastoral people to accept that livestock numbers should be kept fixed, irrespective of year-to-year fluctuation in rainfall and grazing conditions.

The possibility does exist that cooperative group ranches could be established in which most livestock is in a communal herd. This would probably encourage destocking, but it is unlikely that pastoralists would willingly give up their right of free disposal over their cattle. In any event, this particular form of ranching remains largely unexplored by KLDP.

To summarize, it appears that, despite the numerous trials and errors in development of livestock involving traditional nomadic herdsmen, far too little is known about the precise response to such steps as development of a livestock market, provision of water dips, veterinary services, and controlled grazing through grazing blocks that may be undertaken for development of the traditional livestock sector. The knowledge is even poorer and uncertainty even greater than is the case with smallholder agriculture. Though investigation of and experimentation with such interventions must be expanded, the review of the livestock development programs suggests that the only long-term solution to the problem of range development in pastoral areas in Kenya may be for many of the pastoralists to be absorbed by the non-nomadic sector of the society.

Concluding Remarks

The analyses of these various problems related to the development of agricultural and livestock systems indicate that the objectives of raising productivity in the subsistence sector and of ensuring a reasonable degree of

19. KLDP has also been granting loans to company and commercial ranches. The eight company ranches assisted by the program in Taita district averaged 23,000 hectares and were expected to generate a 20 percent rate of return on investment. The thirty commercial ranches receiving loans averaged 3,250 hectares, excluding the special case of the 300,000-hectare Galana Ranch. Their rate of return was expected to be 23 percent. Though they are relatively small in size, most of these latter are heavily involved in feedlot operations, which is a highly profitable enterprise, as in the case of the LLDP stall-feeder program. The internal rate of return from feedlot operations alone on these ranches was estimated at 25 percent.

20. Ecologists still feel that many of these ranches are too small. The rate of return from group ranches is 13 percent.

participation in growth have many dimensions. The programs reviewed have generally been remiss, not so much because they have failed to take into account these various dimensions at the outset, but because over time they have not improved the knowledge of these dimensions and of the interactions among them and, therefore, not developed the capability to tackle the equity problem through improved planning and implementation of programs.

CHAPTER IV

Agricultural Extension
and Mass Participation

Many of the projects reviewed are designed to ameliorate the problems that are so familiar to those acquainted with the traditional approach to extension in Africa. Extension agents are few and far between, ill-paid, ill-trained, ill-equipped with a technical package, and consequently very poor in quality. That the farmer often knows more, at least about what is wrong with the new innovations, and that extension agents often do not follow their own advice have become parts of a folklore of extension in developing countries, Africa being no exception.[1]

To counter the problems faced in traditional extension services, the primary emphasis in virtually all the rural development programs reviewed is on higher intensity of extension—i.e., on increasing the number of extension agents in a limited geographical area so as to increase the agent/farmer ratio. Many, although not all, new rural development programs also provide additional training to its staff and pay higher salaries. There are also considerable differences between the various programs in the organization of the extension system and in the approach to dissemination of innovations.

Has the increase in the intensity of extension in these various programs been effective in alleviating the problems of the traditional extension approach? In this chapter the effectiveness of various extension systems is assessed, not only in terms of their effect on increased production, but also in terms of their ability to disseminate a range of profitable innovations to a mass of the rural population, in particular to the relatively poorer sections of the farming population.

1. For an excellent discussion on problems of traditional extension, see J. Katorobo, *Agricultural Extension in Nyahashenyi*, mimeographed (Kampala: Makerere University College, 1966); J. Katorobo, "Agricultural Modernization: Kahoho Parish—Kigezi District," mimeographed (Kampala: Makerere University College, 1968); David K. Leonard, "The Administration of Kenyan Agricultural Extension Services," Institute for Development Studies (Nairobi: University of Nairobi, 1972); David K. Leonard, "Some Hypotheses Concerning the Impact of Kenya Government Agricultural Extension on Small Farmers," Institute for Development Studies Staff Paper no. 71 (Nairobi: University of Nairobi, 1970); David K. Leonard, W. Opindi, E.A. Lucheme, and J.K. Tumwa, "The Work Performance of Junior Agricultural Extension Staff in Western Province, Basic Tables," Institute for Development Studies Discussion Paper no. 109 (Nairobi: University of Nairobi, 1971); Jon Moris, "Farmer Training as a Strategy of Rural Development," in *Education, Employment and Rural Development: The Proceedings of a Conference held at Kericho, Kenya, in September 1966*, ed. J.R. Sheffield (Nairobi: East African Publishing House, 1967), pp. 322–65; M. Okai, "The Adequacy of the Technical Base for the Agricultural Extension Service in Uganda: A Case Study in Lango District," Rural Development Research Paper no. 6 (Kampala: Makerere University College Department of Agriculture, 1965); M. Okai, "Field Administration and Agricultural Development," mimeographed (Kampala: Makerere University College, 1966); T.M. Othieno

Evaluation of the effectiveness of extension is by no means easy. It raises many methodological problems, some of which arise from the interactions of the extension service with other services such as credit and marketing, while others arise from the very considerable variability between farms in resource endowment and in climatic factors. Such variability may often be far more important in explaining yield differences than is the effectiveness of any particular intervention, including extension. Another important factor is the social organization which, of course, has a profound influence on communications and, therefore, has implications for how extension programs should be organized and administered. For example, under certain circumstances members of the farming population may be far more effective as disseminators of new innovations than are the relatively more urban extension workers. Only to the extent that these various interactions are understood and their variability taken into account can extension services be improved. The methodological problems are not discussed in this chapter. It is important to stress, however, that, given the complexity of the interactions and the overwhelming diversity in the constraints, regular but modest studies of the type used in the analyses presented below seem far more desirable for improving performance of the extension services than do methodologically sophisticated quantitative assessments, which require a substantial amount of data and are demanding of scarce trained manpower.

Assessment of the extension systems in the various programs reviewed suggests that merely intensifying the extension service may often be futile, unless conscious simultaneous effort is made to:

1. Impart a technological package that is sufficiently profitable at the farm level to provide an incentive for the farmer to adopt innovations;
2. Train the extension staff to solve the specific but diverse farm-level constraints faced by the cultivator;
3. Develop an incentive system to encourage the extension service to perform its task efficiently, meaning not only rapid growth in production but also broad participation in the adoption of innovations;
4. Relieve extension of the heavy burden of delivering inputs, writing credit applications, chasing credit defaulters, and so forth; and
5. Enlist the active support and participation of the farmers themselves.

and D.G.R. Belshaw, "Technical Innovation in Two Systems of Peasant Agriculture in Bukedi District: Uganda," paper presented at the East African Institute of Social Research Conference (Kampala: Makerere University College, 1965); R.G. Saylor, "The Administration of Innovations," Economic Research Bureau Paper (Dar es Salaam: University College, 1969); R.G. Saylor, "An Economic Evaluation of Agricultural Extension in Tanzania," Economic Research Bureau Paper (Dar es Salaam: University of Dar es Salaam, n.d.); R.G. Saylor, "A Social/Benefit Analysis of the Agricultural Extension and Research Services in Selected Cotton Growing Areas of Western Tanzania," Economic Research Bureau Service Paper 70.2 (Dar es Salaam: University of Dar es Salaam, 1970); R.G. Saylor, "Studies on the Cost/Benefit Analysis of the Agricultural Research Services in Selected Cotton and Coffee Growing Areas of Tanzania," Economic Research Bureau Paper (Dar es Salaam: University of Dar es Salaam, n.d.); R.G. Saylor, "Variations in Sukumaland Cotton Yields and the Extension Service," Economic Research Bureau Paper 70.5 (Dar es Salaam: University of Dar es Salaam, 1970); E.R. Watts, "Agricultural Extension in Embu District of Kenya," in East African Journal of Rural Development, vol. 2, no. 1 (1969), pp. 63–77; S.K. Taiwo Williams, "The Confluence of Extension Education, Agricultural Extension and Community Development," in Bulletin of Rural Economics and Sociology, vol. 2, no. 3 (1967), pp. 184–93; M. Crawford Young, "Agricultural Policy in Uganda: Capability and Choice," in The State of the Nations: Constraints on Development in Independent Africa, ed. M.F. Lofchie (Berkeley: University of California Press, 1971), pp. 141–64.

Different Organizational Approaches to Extension Services

The extension services in the rural development projects reviewed under ARDS may be classified under two different types. Ruthenberg has described these as the "take it or leave it" approach and the contract farming method.[2] In the former, peasants are brought innovations and information which they are free to accept or reject. In the latter, farmers who volunteer to receive innovations are granted a license; those who fail to follow project guidelines may have their licenses revoked. Take it or leave it extension has been most common in programs involving development of both subsistence and cash crop—e.g., CADU, WADU, and LLDP. Contract farming is usually found in projects specializing in export crop production—e.g., KTDA and the Urambo and Tumbi tobacco schemes. KTDA even has legal authority—granted under the Tea Cultivation Order—to prosecute negligent growers.

With take it or leave it extension, it is evident that innovations must be highly profitable if they are to gain wide acceptance (see Section 4 of this chapter). Profitability is also a prerequisite for successful contract farming—one of the "carrots" that project agencies use to enroll farmer participation. However, the contract farming extension services have the additional benefit of a "stick" to ensure that farmers follow all the rules of proper husbandry. At times, recommended practices may be unpopular, not because of their ultimate unprofitability, but because to the cultivator they seem to involve hardship or sacrifice as, for example, required culling of cattle or the necessity to destroy a crop which has been infected with disease. Recommended practices may also not have an obvious immediate payoff as, for instance, measures to prevent soil erosion. In these situations voluntary cooperation of cultivators may be difficult to obtain without a very substantial effort to convince them of the return to the practice. Such effective communication may be lacking even in contract farming, thus frequently necessitating use of the "stick."

Why have projects adopted such diverse approaches to extension? The export crops have traditionally yielded the high profit margins that are necessary to cover the considerable expense of extension in closely supervised contract farming. Further, export crops frequently involve sophisticated production techniques and high production standards; hence, often they cannot be left to independent field-level control.[3] By contrast, diversified farming, and especially food crop production, has frequently tended to be less profitable and has, therefore, not justified heavy investment in extension personnel. Also, food crops are generally assumed to be less demanding of quality control requirements and, hence, of technical expertise.

---

2. Hans Ruthenberg, "Types of Organisation in Agricultural Production Development," in *Zeitschrift für Auslandische Landwirtschaft,* Jahragang 12, Heft ¾ (July–December 1973), pp. 234–44.

3. For example, fine plucking—that is, the picking of only the tea bud and two leaves—is one of the most important factors in quality tea production. Less precise plucking, which includes older leaves, tends to have an adverse affect on the fermentation process, resulting in poor flavor and color in the finished product. Plucking at too infrequent intervals tends to make the bud hard and the leaves leggy with too much stalk. Careless plucking can damage the plant.

It must be stressed, however, that the differences between the sophistication of technology for export crops and food crops are far less pronounced than generally believed. Nor for that matter is there reason to believe that food production is always less profitable than is the production of tea, tobacco, or similar products. Rather, in many respects the adoption of the take it or leave it approach with regard to innovations for subsistence crops is merely another reflection of the common tendency to neglect the importance of food crop production for rural development (see Chapters II and III). While a coercive extension service may not be warranted, emphasis on suitable technology and effective extension of farm-level practices, the two elements frequently observed in contract farming of export crops, would seem critical in all cases for augmenting production.

Similar to the advice/coerce dilemma in agricultural extension is the question of whether extension workers should be trained as generalists or specialists. Specialization has obvious benefits, particularly given the generally low level of knowledge displayed by many extension workers. It may well be easier to imbue field agents with an effective package of specific recommendations for a particular crop than to train them in a wide variety of farming techniques. By the same token, a specialist may be more effective in communicating his narrow but concrete expertise to the farming population. A survey in Kenya indicates that extension specialists tend to have more command over their technical areas than do agents with more general training.[4]

However, as pointed out earlier, even a smallholder producing an export crop needs assistance with respect to food and livestock activities. Consequently, the farmer tends to demand wide-ranging advice from the extension staff that he is able to see.[5] Therefore, a relatively general extension service is frequently essential if it is to be relevant to the needs of the farmer. Further, specialization may lead to bureaucratic skirmishes in the field with various "experts" pushing contradictory advice at the expense of an overall development effort. McLoughlin observed that frequently "two men give the farmer, not slightly, but radically different advice, plant your cotton early in the year versus plant your cotton in October."[6] Particularly given the frequent need to develop the overall farming system outlined in Chapter II, a generalized extension designed to meet the needs of the farmer seems warranted from the outset, although effective delivery of such a generalized service is by no means easy to introduce for the reasons discussed later in this chapter.

Tobacco production requires similar critical and painstaking harvesting techniques. The leaves of a tobacco plant differ chemically according to their position on the plant. Since the lower leaves ripen earlier than the higher ones, several harvests may be required. Complicating matters further, the signs of ripeness are quite different in leaves of different stalk position.

4. The differential between specialists and generalists is largely accounted for by the greater intensity of rebriefing given to the former. See Leonard et al., "The Work Performance of Junior Agricultural Extension Staff," Table 6.E, 15.E, and 20.E; and Leonard, "Organizational Structures for Productivity in Kenyan Agricultural Extension," in *Rural Administration in Kenya*, ed. David K. Leonard (Nairobi: East African Literature Bureau, 1973), p. 141.

5. Ibid.

6. Peter F.M. McLoughlin, "The Farmer, the Politician and the Bureaucrat: Local Government and Agricultural Development in Independent Africa," notes and papers in *Development* no. 4 (Fredericton, New Brunswick: Peter McLoughlin Associates, n.d.). Other problems may also arise from multiplicity of extension services. In his survey in the Vihiga district, Kenya,

Another important question concerns whether or not extension services should be organized within the existing government bureaucracy or alternatively as an autonomous or semi-autonomous body. Departments of agriculture are frequently ill-equipped to run extension services because of their lack of entrepreneurial ability, their lethargic attitude towards decision making, and their inability to respond to incoming information. Establishment of the extension service as a separate body, run by technical experts and farmer representatives, is, therefore, frequently considered necessary.[7] However, as will be illustrated in Chapters VIII and IX, there is no organizational panacea.[8] The effective organization of agricultural extension has to be viewed as part of the broader and unquestionably urgent problem of improving overall administrative performance. The final choice of specific policy in this matter must, however, depend on the time frame involved and the nature and sophistication of the government bureaucracy.

There are several other considerations that have entered organization and delivery of extension services and affected effectiveness of the programs reviewed. Of these the greatest emphasis has been on increasing the intensity of extension services.

Intensity of Extension Services in Rural Development Programs

Investment in extension services has usually been assessed in terms of extension worker/farmer ratios. In LLDP in Malawi during the first two and a half years after development of each unit, there was to be one extension worker to every 200 farm families. Over the next two and a half years, this ratio was to be reduced to one worker to every 400 families.[9] By contrast in the non-program area, the regional agricultural officer's jurisdiction has had one extension agent per 1,200 to 1,300 holdings.

However, even in the limited program area, the planned ratio of extension workers to farm families had not been reached during Phase I of the program. According to the program review, this was primarily due to the

---

Leonard reported that three agents from the Ministry of Agriculture together spent four days visiting tea growers. Unfortunately, tea growing was the responsibility of the Kenya Tea Development Authority. To compound matters, in recent years KTDA has also taken on the responsibility for the dissemination of information on hybrid maize. Such overlap in extension service suggests "that the pressures in favor of a generalized extension service in peasant areas are quire strong." See D.K. Leonard, "Some Hypotheses Concerning the Organization of Communication in Agricultural Extension," Institute for Development Studies Staff Paper no. 72 (Nairobi: University of Nairobi, 1970), p. 21.

7. Hans Ruthenberg, "Adaption of Extension Projects to Changing Circumstances," paper delivered at the International Seminar on Extension and Other Services Supporting the Small Farmer in Asia by the German Foundation for Developing Countries, Berlin, October 31–November 21, 1972.

8. See John C. de Wilde, *Experiences with Agricultural Development in Tropical Africa*, vol. 1 (Baltimore: Johns Hopkins Press, 1967), p. 180.

9. It has been proposed that, subsequent to the program's development period, the regional extension staff be augmented by the output of the training section included in the program until the ratio of extension agents to farm families in the program area is ultimately stabilized at about one extension agent to 600 to 800 farm families. See World Bank, *Lilongwe Land Development Project, Malawi*, appraisal report no. TO-610a, restricted circulation (Washington, D.C., January 1968).

shortage of trained extension staff, although the initial concentration of administrative effort on infrastructural development may also have affected the attention that could be devoted to the development of extension services. It was anticipated that the desired ratios would be attained during Phase II. In this period extension coverage was also to be extended to an additional 24,000 farming families—i.e., a total of 52,000 program families.

In the Urambo tobacco scheme, the extension worker/farmer ratio declined from 1:323 to 1:802 between 1965 and 1970, while in the Tumbi scheme the ratio dropped from 1:116 to 1:575. Even then, the two schemes had far greater intensity of extension than average. The average extension worker/farmer ratio for Tanzania as a whole has been 1:1,500; while in the Sukumaland cotton-growing areas, it has been 1:1,020. In Kenya KTDA has had an extension agent/farmer ratio of 1:120, compared to 1:500 in Kenya as a whole.

These ratios, of course, provide only rough estimates of the magnitude of intensity. They do not indicate whether a greater number of agents in proportion to farmer population means that more farmers are being reached. They also fail to indicate what reaching a farmer signifies.

Such difficulties in gauging intensity are illustrated by comparison of innovations related to agro-industrial enterprises with those related to food crops. In the former, as, for instance, in KTDA, adoption of innovations is frequently tied to use of other services provided by the program. Participation is, therefore, fairly easy to measure. In the case of food and some export crops, on the other hand, farmers may adopt innovations, such as early planting or close weeding, without necessarily accepting the services provided by the program. Estimation of the number of adopters or of the increase in their productivity is, therefore, difficult in the absence of detailed information on the spread of various types of innovations. These data have been lacking in many of the programs reviewed.

Lacking such information, Tecle estimated effective field staff/farmer ratio for CADU and WADU in Ethiopia by assuming that only those farmers who borrowed credit from the programs were reached by the extension services. Calculated in this manner, in the 1972/73 period CADU had an extension agent/farmer ratio of 1:470 compared to 1:335 in WADU. These are particularly high ratios for Ethiopia, given that prior to CADU or WADU there had been hardly any development of agricultural extension in Ethiopia, compared to Kenya or Tanzania.[10]

In considering intensity of extension, another factor which must be taken into account is the investment in training of extension agents. There are significant variations between countries. In Kenya, for example, most of the junior agricultural assistants have undergone only a one-week course at a farmer training center.[11] Junior staff in the LLDP areas in Malawi, on

10. In 1968 Kenya, with a rural population of 10 million, employed 5,277 extension workers. For Tanzania the figures were 11.5 million and 2,455, respectively. Ethiopia, with a rural population of 22 million, by contrast had only 124 extension agents. See Robert Evenson and Yoav Kislev, *Agricultural Research Productivity* (New Haven, Conn.: Yale University Press, 1975), Appendix Table 2A, Chapter 2.

11. David K. Leonard, "Organizational Structures for Productivity in Kenyan Agricultural Extension," p. 133.

the other hand, are given a period of pre-training and practical experience as well as an intensive course in technical agriculture at Colby College, located within the program area at Chitedze Research Station.[12]

The services available in terms of means of transportation to extension agents may also vary considerably between programs. These have an important bearing on intensity, since significant constraints are often imposed on extension services by transportation problems. For example, in ZAPI in Cameroon, although agents do have bicycles, the brush country in which they work can often be covered only on foot. Consequently, a great deal of time is expended in traveling. A similar situation exists in the Vihiga district of Kenya, where merely attending a staff meeting may involve a four- to six-hour bicycle ride.[13]

In contrast, the LLDP field staff interviewed in Malawi proudly emphasized that they had easier access to vehicles and better roads than did their counterparts in the regional agricultural office. Of course, improving transportation facilities increases costs. However, it also increases the mobility and the initiative of the extension staff. An agent is able to reach more farmers, or reach the same farmers more often, and can become more motivated to get his message across.

Costs Implicit in Intensity of Extension Services

Particularly because costs of extension vary significantly, depending on training, facilities, salaries, and numbers of farmers reached, it is essential to examine intensity of extension in terms of its implications for recurrent budgetary expenditures relative to the return likely to be derived from the extension service and compared to other alternative expenditures. This is necessary even though assessment of effectiveness of extension as compared to that of other investments may be based only on qualitative judgments and substantially influenced by social preferences.[14]

In LLDP in Malawi the cost of extension services is relatively low. Estimates called for $0.90 to be spent per family per year over a period of thirteen years of program development. Over $1.2 million, or about 8.5 percent of the LLDP budget, will be spent on extension by 1975. From other indications of progress on adoption of innovations in LLDP (discussed below), to date the rate of dissemination of innovations implicit in these per family costs appears to have been overestimated. The above figures also exclude the cost of training. However, if LLDP's rather low cost estimates are ac-

12. For a more detailed discussion of the training of extension agents, see Chapter X.

13. David K. Leonard, "Some Hypotheses Concerning the Organization of Communication in Agricultural Extension," p. 20.

14. In Kenya, for example, the expenditure on extension services in 1968 was $4.5 million (see Evanson and Kislev, *Agricultural Research Productivity*). In comparison, the central government's current expenditure on education was only $2.2 million. See USAID, Statistics and Reports Division, "Central Government Finances: Kenya," in *AID Economic Data Book for Africa*, revision no. 286 (Washington, D.C.: U.S. Government Printing Office, October 1972). As will be illustrated in Chapters VII and IX, these proportions are almost the reverse in Tanzania.

cepted, for the intensity of its extension program to be replicated on a nationwide scale, they imply an annual expenditure of nearly $0.9 million or
about 11 percent of the government's estimated expenditure on agricultural
development for the 1972/73 period.[15] Actual expenditures on extension
and training, excluding commercial export crops such as tea and cotton,
amounted to approximately 6 percent of the total expenditure on agricultural development.

Smallholder tea development in Kenya, on the other hand, involved a
much higher investment. KTDA's extension effort has cost a total of more
than $18 per farmer per year, including the cost of the executive and field
staff plus the cost of the input package. If this investment were to be made
on a nationwide basis, it would cost approximately $35 million, or more
than the current annual expenditures on agriculture of the central government in the late 1960s.[16] It is apparent that, without a very major commitment of resources by national governments to rural development and,
equally important, to suitable training of the manpower necessary for expansion of these services, intensity of most of these programs cannot be
replicated on a large-enough scale to reach a mass of the rural population in
the foreseeable future.

Particularly, because of the resources implicit in these programs, three
questions concerning their efficacy need consideration: To what extent are
the extension services equipped with profitable technology? Have they developed ways of tackling the numerous specific problems faced by individual small farmers in adopting innovations? Have they acquired effective means of disseminating new innovations and ideas to the mass of the
rural people rather than to a privileged few?

Profitability of Technology
and Effectiveness of Extension

The lower yields of tobacco in Urambo in comparison with those of
Tumbi in Tanzania are often attributed to a shortage of extension staff at
Urambo. Reports by officials in Urambo argue that the staffing constraint
made it difficult to supervise new farmers and to continue to encourage and
help the old farmers in maintaining the improved methods of production.
However, Agarwal and Linsenmeyer observe that inadequate attention to
the technological problems faced by farmers may be the major cause of the
poorer yield performance of the Urambo scheme. The depletion of the field
staff had been occurring at both places, but productivity at Tumbi had been
increasing while that at Urambo had been decreasing.

The reviews of ZAPI and SODENKAM in Cameroon indicate that,
although closer contact with the population is usually considered to be essential for a successful extension program, it is by no means sufficient if the

---

15. Assuming one million farm families in Malawi. According to estimates made by the
World Bank, expenditures by the Malawian government for agricultural development were
$8.3 million in the 1972/73 period.
16. USAID, Statistics and Reports Division, "Central Government Finances: Kenya."

extension system is not equipped to tackle specific farm-level constraints faced by the cultivators. These programs use close-up teams,[17] founded on the implicit assumptions that: *(a)* the main cause of resistance to new techniques is psychological; and *(b)* the peasant must be convinced of the value of the new techniques, which can occur only through personal contact with the *vulgarisateur* (extension worker). Thus, by emphasizing subjective reasons almost exclusively, planners have neglected to analyze the objective factors which frequently militate against the adoption of new techniques. This point is illustrated by the research carried by Société d'Etudes du Développement Economique et Social (SEDES) in ZAPI, which discovered that individual farmers faced a variety of obstacles in the adoption of copper spray to combat brown rot in cacao buds, even after they were convinced of the importance of using the spray. One planter in four did not have treatment equipment, two planters in four who had the equipment met operating problems, one planter in three had difficulties in finding the water necessary, one planter in three had manpower difficulties, and one planter in two received the treatment too late for the time he would have liked to begin the treatments. Thus, supposedly irrational farmer resistance to new techniques may be far less a constraint than is the unavailability of the necessary inputs.

Other objective factors may induce cultivators to resist recommended practices. For example, despite considerable intensity of extension, the BDPA groundnut operation in Mali has been less successful than anticipated in promoting the use of a fungicide-insecticide for treating millet and groundnut seeds. The area actually treated for the two crops has consistently fallen short of projections by as much as 50 or 60 percent. The slow rate of adoption is explained by the low net return to the insecticide.

Early sowing of groundnuts, another BDPA–sponsored innovation, has also met with resistance. In the period 1970/71 (three years after the program got under way), only 23 percent of the project area had been sown before June 15. The percentage increased to 50 percent the next year. Significantly, about 37 percent of the farmers had not planted their groundnuts as late as July 15 in the period 1970/71. By the period 1971/72 this figure had dropped to only 18 percent. The relatively slow progress in promoting early planting of groundnuts in BDPA may have been a result of a labor constraint similar to that encountered by cotton farmers in Sukumaland.[18]

LLDP's extension program has also had mixed results. The program has promoted the use of fertilizer and the increase of plant population per hectare, both of which have a substantial positive effect on yields of maize and groundnuts. Kinsey's analysis of LLDP Evaluation Unit's survey data for the period 1970/71 indicates that extension visits are significantly, positively associated with higher maize yields. Extension has been less

---

17. The head of the close-up team is a *moniteur* (team head) or *vulgarisateur* (extension worker), who is generally 20 to 30 years old with an elementary education and trained in the project itself over a period of several months at the outset and in short review sessions thereafter. Team numbers may vary, often according to financing possibilities; but it seems to be accepted that the denser the staffing, the better the results. Mediocre results are usually blamed on not enough staff. Staff density varies from one *vulgarisateur* to every 200 planters in the case of ZAPI to one for 50 planters in SODENKAM.

18. See Chapter II of this study.

effective in increasing groundnut production, however, reflecting the futility of the extension effort when the technology is not profitable. Farmers receiving no extension visits during the year had mean yields of 4.93 quintals per hectare, while those receiving five visits averaged only 4.09 quintals. Farmers visited between eleven and twenty times experienced even lower yields, 3.50 quintals per hectare. Only when more than twenty visits were made was there a positive correlation between intensity of extension and groundnut yield; these farmers averaged 5.94 quintals per hectare. Though these findings appear to be somewhat anomalous, a partial explanation for the curious relationship between groundnut yields and extension visits may lie in the various constraints related to groundnut production discussed in Chapter III.[19]

Incentives and Performance of Extension Services

The preceding discussion implies that the absolute number of extension workers in a program area is less important than their individual performance. Programs cannot be very successful without energetic, motivated staff. Staff incentives are, thus, a crucial factor in the success of extension programs. Yet, while there is little disagreement on this point, there seems to be considerable difference of opinion in the project reviews as to what specific type of incentives are most effective.

The two incentives conventionally considered cruicial to staff performance are salaries and promotion. Leonard's study of SRDP's extension workers in the Vihiga district in Kenya points out the effect of the absence of these incentives. His interviews indicated that dissatisfaction among extension agents was widespread. Virtually all of the junior staff complained about their pay. About half were unhappy about the poor prospects for promotion—only a quarter of them had received any promotions in the previous four years; more than half had been in the same position for ten years or more. Compounding the problem, advancement did not even appear to be geared to performance.[20] Chambers and Belshaw point out that unpleasant working conditions and erratic administrative supervision also contribute to the sense of frustration among extension workers.[21]

Increasing pay, rationalizing promotional opportunities, and restructuring the supervisory system would, thus, seem to be an obvious means of improving staff morale and performance in national administrative structures. However, when such simple steps as increasing pay scales and open-

---

19. On the whole, the follow-up study of LLDP, involving much more detailed analysis, indicates a strong correlation between extension visits and adoption of various practices and inputs.

20. Leonard, "Some Hypotheses Concerning the Organization of Communication in Agricultural Extension," pp. 23–24.

21. Robert Chambers and Deryke Belshaw, *Managing Rural Development: Lessons and Methods from Eastern Africa,* Institute for Development Studies Discussion Paper no. 15 (Brighton, U.K.: University of Sussex, June 1973). Chambers and Belshaw feel that improved supervision of the staff, work planning, reporting, and staff evaluation are critical for increasing the effectiveness of extension. Also see references to the PIM management system in Chapter X of this study.

ing opportunities for advancement are taken on a piecemeal basis in isolated programs, they frequently lure staff away from other worthwhile programs.[22] Favorable incentives in one program also cause resentment and envy in staff working elsewhere under less desirable conditions. These factors are discussed in detail in Chapter VIII. Improvement of the extension system, thus, has to be examined in the context of improvement of the overall administrative system rather than in terms of a few small programs.

In improving staff salaries and fringe benefits, another real danger exists—namely, the development of a self-conscious elitism among the staff, causing friction with the local population. Belloncle and Gentil have repeatedly observed this phenomenon in their review of the French technical assistance projects in Cameroon. According to them, to improve staff-farmer relations, it may, in fact, be desirable to keep salaries low, or at least at a point where living standards of the staff do not differ substantially from those of the average farmer. The extent to which low salaries will improve rapport of the extension worker with the rural people may, however, also depend greatly on whether the workers came from rural or urban backgrounds, an issue which will be discussed at the end of this chapter.

A related point is made by Leonard, who observed that formal education of extension workers does not necessarily increase their effectiveness. In Kenya agents with a secondary education had a lower degree of agricultural knowledge than those with an upper primary education. More important, the more educated agents were less persuasive in promoting innovations.[23] There appear to be two explanations for this phenomenon: *(a)* the secondary school finishers tend to come from urban backgrounds and are less committed to extension work, and *(b)* through formal education such individuals may have developed a value system that regards farming as an inferior occupation. However, Leonard also found that the performance of secondary school finishers can be improved through practical training courses.[24]

It is obviously important that field workers be able to work closely with the rural people. Indeed, the development of a personal involvement with the people of a particular community is in itself a strong incentive. As noted earlier, in Tanzania the extension effort has been more effective in the Tumbi region than in Urambo. Linsenmeyer and Agarwal argue that this is largely attributable to the fact that in Urambo the staff live at headquarters and make periodic trips to supervise and advise the farmers; whereas in Tumbi, since 1960, extension staff live in the areas where they work. This puts them in closer contact with the farmers and reduces their travel time. This closer contact seems to have a favorable effect, as there has been a fairly steady increase in productivity per hectare in Tumbi since 1964.

---

22. The Department of Agriculture in Kenya has lost much of its most competent staff to KTDA, as has the Department of Agriculture in Tanzania lost its best staff to BAT, affecting the development of the regular administrative structure in the two countries.

23. Leonard, "Organizational Structures for Productivity in Kenyan Agricultural Extension," pp. 135–38. Leonard notes that R.K. Harrison has observed a similar phenomenon in western Nigeria.

24. It should not be inferred, however, that extension workers require no formal education. The degree of fluency in Swahili was an important factor in determining the agents' effectiveness. Ibid. See also Chapter X for a discussion of the training of extension workers.

Oddly enough, Leonard's analysis of extension in the Vihiga district arrives at an opposite conclusion. His investigations indicated that nonresident agents averaged more farm visits and saw more individuals than did those who worked near their home.[25] This may be explained by the fact that an agent working in his home area finds it easier to shirk his duties. Also, it seems likely that when an agent's constituency consists of his friends and relatives, they are either less persistent in asking for his assistance or know him too well to want his advice. Family and tribal duties may play an additional role in diverting a resident extension agent from his work.

Local Participation
in Extension Activities

The contradictory observations of Linsenmeyer and Agarwal on the one hand and of Leonard on the other lead to perhaps the most crucial factor in the success of an extension program—the extent of popular interest. Whether an agent lives in a community or not is of little importance if the residents of the community genuinely want his services. As pointed out earlier, the profitability of the innovations is of paramount importance in this regard. However, many programs reviewed have also taken other steps to mobilize popular support.

In Kenya KTDA has been remarkably successful in spreading technical innovations. By 1972, 61,000 small farmers were growing tea. Several factors explain this success: As pointed out in Chapter II, *(a)* KTDA has had an exceptionally profitable technology at its disposal; *(b)* KTDA has a rather authoritarian extension system which enforces correct management practices strictly; and *(c)* the project has identified the most important farm-level constraint posed in tea cultivation—namely, the labor requirements of tea production—and has limited the area under tea production to 0.4 hectares per farm. All of these factors have obviously worked in KTDA's favor and contributed to the rapid increase in the number of beneficiaries of the program. In addition, however, KTDA has also enlisted considerable local participation through tea growers' committees, which assist in the administration of the program.

The growers' committees exist at the divisional, district, and provincial levels and consist primarily of representatives chosen by the growers, although there are some ex officio members such as agricultural officers and tea company officials. Serving a dual function, the committees are both a forum for making recommendations from below and a conduit for disseminating policy from above. The tea committees usually attract the more successful, respected, and articulate members of the local communities. Therefore, these representatives exert considerable influence over the other growers.

Tanzania's *ujàmaa* movement has also used a local committee system to enlist popular support for its extension effort. In most of the *ujàmaa* vil-

25. Leonard, "Some Hypotheses Concerning the Organization of Communication in Agricultural Extension," pp. 22–23.

lages, an agricultural committee is responsible for ensuring that villagers follow the advice of the *bwana shamba* (agricultural field agent). However, because of the low level of training of these field agents and the deficiency in research support, the innovations have often been of dubious quality and relevance. These problems are compounded by the national extension strategy, which is directed towards sociopolitical as well as productive goals.[26] Ideological considerations impinge on extension effectiveness by leaning towards exclusive concentration on cooperative agricultural production and by causing extension agents to spend more time raising political consciousness and less time spreading technical advice.

How have the *wajàmaa* (*ujàmaa* villagers) responded to these efforts? The review carried out under ARDS noted that many individuals voiced agreement with cooperative production and generally supported the goals of the national leadership. The villagers' behavior, on the other hand, told a somewhat different story. Many of them continued to give priority to their private plots, making only minimal contributions to community projects. Where farmers were permitted to grow their own cash crops, they devoted as little as eight hours a week to communal farming.[27] Even where mechanization has been used as an incentive for villagization, the popular attitude has been to neglect the communal plot. As the villagers in one village put it: "the tractors do the work for us; the tractor gives us freedom to work on our own *shambas.*"[28] Such attitudes, of course, lead to disparities in the returns from private versus communal farming, thereby reinforcing preferences for the former. In response the central government has granted village committees increasing latitude to enforce the cooperation of village residents.[29] While it is unclear how effective such sanctions will be, forced cooperation obviously conflicts with the democratic principles underlying the *ujàmaa* movement and casts doubt on the government's ability to enlist widespread voluntary support for its program. (For a further discussion of some of the problems faced by *ujàmaa,* see Chapter IX).

While KTDA and the *ujàmaa* movement have attempted to involve local people through direct participation in project administration, CADU in Ethiopia attempts to encourage participation through use of model farmers. Under this approach, certain selected farmers work in close conjunction with extension agents to adopt a wide range of new farming techniques. The increased yields produced by these model farmers are expected to popularize the program and encourage other farmers to adopt innovations. ZAPI in Cameroon has followed a similar course.

26. For a generally sympathetic discussion of this strategy, see William L. Luttrell, "Villagization, Cooperative Production, and Rural Cadres: Strategies and Tactics in Tanzanian Socialist Rural Development," Economic Research Bureau Paper 71.11 (Dar es Salaam: University of Dar es Salaam, 1971).

27. See P.B. Ngeze, "Some Aspects of Agricultural Development in Ujamaa Villages," paper presented to the East African Agricultural Economics Society Conference, Dar es Salaam, 1973, pp. 10–11.

28. Comments recorded by Vail at an *ujàmaa* village in Arusha. See David J. Vail, "Technology for Socialist Development in Rural Tanzania," mimeographed, n.d., background paper for the Seventeenth Annual Meeting of the African Studies Association, Chicago, November 1974.

29. Clyde R. Ingle, "Compulsion and Rural Development in Tanzania," in *Canadian Journal of African Studies,* vol. 4, no. 1, Winter 1970, pp. 77–100. The anti-communal attitudes of many *ujàmaa* villagers is further revealed by the widespread theft from communal plots.

The use of opinion leaders and progressive farmers as the vehicle for generating mass support seems to result in undue concentration of extension effort on the relatively better-off members of the community. It should be emphasized that the concern is not so much that the innovations spread to the better-off farmers first but that, through such an approach, the neediest members of the community may be frequently overlooked in many programs. A study made by CADU's Evaluation Unit suggests that there is a marked difference between adopters and non-adopters.[30] The non-adopters have smaller cultivated areas than do the adopters. They have fewer numbers of cows and oxen; they are less often members of groups and associations; they have a lesser ability to read and write; and most of them are tenants (only 10 percent of adopters were tenants). Even among the adopters, the model farmers were younger, more literate, and more likely to be the members of groups, according to the study.

A similar situation exists in ZAPI, where a study observed that farmer leaders differed greatly from the average planter. The leaders were young—almost half of them between 30 and 40 years of age. All of them were literate, as compared with a literacy rate of 57 percent for the male population at large. Forty-eight percent of the leaders qualified as large-scale planters, whereas only 17 percent of other farmers fell under the same category.

Leonard's survey in Kenya's Western province shows similar results. The average extension agent makes 57 percent of his visits to progressive farmers (who are 10 percent of the total) and 6 percent of his visits to non-innovative ones (47 percent of the total).[31] Not surprisingly, these progressive farmers tend to be relatively well-off, often owning cattle and frequently growing cash crops in what is largely a subsistence economy.[32] The follow-up of LLDP also indicates a similar tendency in that program area.

A related problem has been that the selected farmers receiving intensive assistance may not be those best suited to popularize innovations. As the

30. Johan Toborn, *The Innovation-Diffusion Process in the Gonde Area,* CADU Special Study no. 3 (Asella, Eth.: Chilalo Agricultural Development Unit, March 1971). The findings of this study have been questioned by some administrators of CADU. For instance, Bengt Negby, the former director of CADU, in his discussions with the author, has pointed out that, in CADU and MPP, model farmers have been elected by their neighbors and receive no special privileges or rewards. Only a small part of their land is used for field demonstrations. Though the farmers do not receive privileges from the program, their initial privileged position is also pointed out by another study carried out in CADU of the cooperatives, which points out the dominance of larger farmers in the programs' cooperative effort (see Chapter VI of this study for further details). Most other studies carried out by CADU's Evaluation Unit and reported in this book also bear out the low participation of tenants. As discussed in detail later in this chapter, these outcomes of the project were, of course, greatly influenced by the sociopolitical structure of the Chilalo society over which the alien management could exercise little control.

31. David K. Leonard, "Why Do Kenya's Agricultural Extension Services Favor the Rich Farmers?" Paper read at the Sixteenth Annual Meeting of the African Studies Association, Syracuse, N.Y., October–November 1973, p. 5.

32. Ibid., p.3 and passim. See Chapter X of this study for discussion of the Tetu Extension Program as part of SRDP which attempts to avoid this problem through a different training program for the extension staff. Leonard indicates a number of reasons why his investigations show that Kenya's extension service favors the more wealthy farmers. Extension workers tend to come from the uppper social strata and, therefore, naturally gravitate towards farmers from a similar background. Also, it is the more well-off farmers who are the most likely to complain to a senior officer if extension is not provided to them. In addition, richer farmers tend to be more receptive to innovation; hence, they are easier for the staff to work with.

experience in Cameroon suggests, it is quite likely that many farmer leaders in ZAPI were selected not so much for their status or authority within the traditional society but for their ability to speak French or their habit of keeping in contact with the ZAPI administration. Administrators often have preconceptions of what a progressive farmer should be and tend to select leaders based upon these preconceptions.

Such isolated model farmers or farmer leaders may frequently arouse the suspicion and apprehension of their neighbors. The innovative farmer may seem to be trying to rise above his social group and may be seen as a deviant, endangering group solidarity, or even be viewed as a traitor who has agreed to act as an accomplice of the outside world. In the ZAPIs not long ago, isolated innovators were accused of witchcraft. Belloncle and Gentil observe that for this reason the first innovators are rarely leading citizens but usually people who are already considered to be more or less marginal.

The use of a model farmer approach, however, is only one of the many reasons that may explain the concentration of extension effort on a few privileged farmers. In BDPA's Opération Arachide, although the top personnel indicate that all farmers benefit in an area in which the extension service operates, Anderson observes that in practice extension agents seem to concentrate on the farmers who are making the most progress in adopting project innovations. And when extension agents begin to introduce animal traction in their *secteurs de base* (the lowest operational level, consisting of 200–250 farmers), their efforts inevitably become more restricted (to the farmers adopting animal traction), since it is critical that these individuals succeed.

That extension workers spend much of their time with a few farmers, and that these few farmers tend to be an elite group would not be too great a problem if close relations existed between the progressive and conservative elements in the rural society. Unfortunately, personal and class rivalries may often thwart cooperation and the sharing of technical innovations. In KTDA, for instance, tea committees have provided preferential treatment to certain growers, particularly prior to 1969 when planting material often fell short of demand. The committees ensured that the more established planters received the supplies they needed, while newer, more tenuous farmers were sometimes cut short. Such interclass conflict is also a factor in Tanzania, where there has been strong resistence to *ujàmaa* in the more productive rural areas (see Chapter IX).

Neglect of Women in Agricultural Extension

Associated with the failure of many programs to reach the majority of smallholders is the tendency for agricultural extension services to focus their attention on male farmers. As noted in Chapter II, women often contribute a major proportion of the family farm labor, usually to the production of food crops and to specific tasks such as weeding. In many traditional societies it is the custom for the women to provide the major support for themselves and their children, either by supplying the family with home-grown food or by obtaining cash through the sale of their own produce.[33] Perhaps an even more important indication of the women's role in agriculture is the fact that a large percentage of rural households is headed by women.[34]

Agricultural extension programs have frequently overlooked the importance of women, both as major contributors to the farm labor supply and as significant family breadwinners. This oversight can be attributed most readily to a tendency among project planners and authorities to see African women in Western terms—i.e., essentially as domestic workers whose primary responsibility should be in the home and not in the fields.[35] Thus, the goal of extension services has frequently been not the increase in farm-level productivity of women but rather finding ways to reduce their participation in agriculture through promotion of more homebound activities. Often, such efforts have the opposite results. As pointed out in Chapter II, some farming innovations may result in increasing the burden of labor on women. Further, if emphasis is on developing male-oriented cash crops—the income from which the men often monopolize—this can divert female labor from food production with subsequent effects on the welfare of the family. Alternatively, other innovations, especially mechanization of agriculture, may eliminate female agricultural jobs and thereby also reduce female income. In all instances neglect of women's role in agriculture may act as a drag on economic growth and contribute to imbalances in the distribution of the benefits of the growth that does occur.

Too often women's extension programs have been exclusively oriented toward domestic science and home economics. Of course, improving nutritional value in food preparation, fostering hygienic practices, introducing means to conserve labor in the home, and so forth are of significant social and economic value and should not be abandoned in most cases (see Chapter VII for a discussion of the implications of social services for rural welfare and Chapter X for an analysis of some women's training programs). However, there is a need to supplement beneficial home-related programs with efforts to preserve or to improve upon women's more strictly economic functions.

The most effective course of action in this regard would generally appear to be fostering improvements in the production of food crops. At the request of local women's organizations, ZAPIs in south-central Cameroon have recently initiated a program to improve the cultivation of groundnuts. They have developed a package of recommendations (treatment of seeds, dense sowing, planting dates) that can result in groundnut yields that are six

33. Dobart and Shields report that, in many traditional African societies, there is no community of property between married couples. Men and women often live and eat separately and keep their individual earnings. See Margarita Dobart and Nwanganga Shields, "African Women: Security in Tradition, Challenge in Change," in *Africa Report,* vol. 17, no. 7 (July–August 1972), p. 18.

34. According to the ECA, 45 percent and 35 percent of the rural households in Kenya and Malawi, respectively, are headed by women. See United Nations Economic Commission for Africa, "Women and National Development in African Countries," position paper prepared by the Human Resources Development Division, Women's Programme Unit, mimeographed, February 1973.

35. For a revealing example of this perception of women's role in agriculture, see the discussion of the "Problem of Peasant Women," in *Rural Planning in Developing Countries,* ed. Raanan Weitz, Report on the Second Rehovoth Conference, Rehovoth, Israel, August 1963 (Cleveland: Western Reserve University Press, 1966), pp. 373–75.

to nine times greater than those obtained by traditional methods. Unfortunately the demonstration field approach to popularize the package has not resulted in widespread adoption—evidently either because the demonstration fields have not been distributed widely enough or because more active promotional measures are needed.[36] ZAPIs have erred, first, by postponing development of food crop technology until recently and then by failing to follow through on its extension effort. Many of the other programs reviewed under ARDS do not even show an explicit recognition of the women's role in the farming system. Consequently, they have been even more remiss in extending agricultural extension to the female half of the population.

Implications of Past Extension Experience for Organization of Future Extension

It is apparent that the attempts to encourage genuine popular participation in and support for program activities have often been ineffective. A step towards correcting this situation has been made in WADU in Ethiopia. WADU does not favor using the model farmer as a major tool for demonstrating new techniques, reasoning that, since only a few farmers may benefit from the actual demonstration process on their farms, the whole concept could be misinterpreted by non-model farmers as giving preferential treatment to a selected few. Rather, WADU has chosen a demonstrator field approach. It uses a large number of farmers, employing fields of all of them for demonstrating the profitability of various farming techniques. Usually different farmers' plots are used to demonstrate different innovations. This approach seems to have been quite successful in WADU. As pointed out earlier, there has also been a larger-than-planned increase in the number of farmers the program has reached.

However, it is unclear as to how much potential there is to use this approach successfully in other programs. As noted earlier, a similar approach has not been particularly effective in ZAPI, though this may be explained by staff shortages and insufficient scale. WADU's success seems to be largely attributable to the fact that Wolamo farms tend to be of a rather uniform size with fairly even income distribution.[37] According to WADU's management, its extension service has benefited considerably from the homogeneity of the Walamo society, which has led to a greater direct involvement of farmers in demonstrations than would have been possible in Chilalo. This involvement in turn lends credibility to the profitability of innovations, for the innovations are demonstrated within the realistic resource constraints faced on farmers' fields. Further, WADU's demonstrators are usually experienced farmers from within Wolamo province

36. ZAPIs are handicapped by their limited number of *animatrices* (female extension workers), who are able to spend only one or two days a month in program villages. This shortage of staff has adverse effects on both productive and welfare-related women's programs.

37. For a discussion of related points, see Chapter VI of this study.

who speak the local dialects and, therefore, have greater rapport with the local people.[38]

The effectiveness of involving farmers directly in the extension effort was also evidenced in the French technical assistance programs in Cameroon. On the basis of their field experience in rural French West Africa, Belloncle and Gentil devised a method of organizing a systematic group exchange of ideas and experience regarding adoption of new innovations. Through learning from each other, a process of mutual help was fostered among farmers. While this approach has not yet been applied on a large scale, it has shown a considerable potential for success when attempted by the reviewers. This chapter, therefore, ends with a summary of the approach they recommend.

Before providing any technical assistance, Belloncle and Gentil recommend sponsoring group discussions in which farmers can discuss their own particular needs and problems. These discussion sessions always ought to be focused on the implications of technical change and its probable effect on each member of the group. If properly conducted, through such discussions the farmers can come to see their individual problems as community concerns which can be dealt with most effectively through community action. The thrust of these meetings is both to instill self-reliance in the farmers and to create a more equitable relationship between them and the extension workers.

Along with group meetings, Belloncle and Gentil advocate actual demonstration of new farming methods. They stress the need for research application centers where farmers can view the results of technical schemes considered feasible for general use.[39]

These preliminary steps can spark a genuine desire for change among the participants. To transform this desire into action, it is necessary to encourage the group to select volunteers to try out different innovations. This is much like the traditional model farmer approach but with one important difference. In this case the innovators are innovators by consensus of the group, by delegation so to speak.

After an appropriate trial period, these innovators will report on their successes and failures at a self-evaluation meeting in which accomplishments of individual innovators as well as the actual specific constraints encountered by farmers in achieving the potential results can be identified. The problem then becomes one of taking steps to remove these constraints and of adopting the worthwhile innovations on a larger scale. At this stage

38. At the initial stage the Minimum Package Program experienced considerable difficulty in recruiting extension agents who could speak the local dialect. Therefore, the program had a very genuine problem of communication with farmers in some areas.

39. The crucial importance of combining discussion and demonstration is also illustrated by CADU's evaluation of its own extension program. According to Toborn, in CADU both visual and oral methods were used to promote innovations. Interestingly, visual influences were found to be more effective in advancing recently introduced innovations, while oral influences had their greatest success with well-established innovations. In addition, the more progressive farmers were more strongly impressed by extension agents and demonstration plots than were their less progressive neighbors. These non-adopters tended to rely on more familiar sources (i.e., on friends, relatives, and, only to a limited extent, on model farmers) for information on new farming techniques. Toborn, *The Innovation-Diffusion Process in the Gonde Area.*

the extension agent's expertise is required. But once again it is his relationship to the farmers which is crucial. He should act as an advisor from whom the farmers seek information which they deem important rather than as a haughty or an inexperienced stranger handing down unsolicited advice to subordinates. The review of the French technical assistance programs indicates that such self-appraisal meetings can be exceedingly successful in expediting change, in particular where there exists a spirit of rivalry between individuals within a group or between various groups.

With this approach, after a point the groups can become more or less self-perpetuating. Former innovators can then be trained to take over many of the functions of extension agents and to act as conduits for further technical information. Belloncle and Gentil argue that ideally these *vulgarisateur* peasants should draw their salary from the group itself rather than from the government. Thus, the continued grass root nature of the service and its high performance would be ensured. It is important to emphasize, however, that such a group approach can work only when there is relative equality in the socioeconomic status of the target population.

CHAPTER V

Agricultural Credit

Some Issues Related to Organization
of Agricultural Credit

In many of the countries reviewed under ARDS, little of the institutional agricultural credit has been directed towards development of smallholder subsistence farmers. Even as late as 1971, credit records of the Agricultural Finance Corporation in Kenya showed that 88 percent of the gross loans outstanding had gone to large-scale farmers, defined as those whose annual income exceeds KSh15,000. Of this, 61 percent went for the purchase of lands from white settlers and 20 percent for dairy development and cattle. Less than one percent had been distributed as working capital. Despite the increasing proportion of funds being earmarked for small farmers, in the same year over 70 percent of AFC's disbursements went to land purchases, commercial farm development, ranching, and similar large-scale uses. It is evident that AFC's loans are missing the bulk of the farmers. In the Kericho district, for example, per capita loans averaged KSh4,294—i.e., they were almost three and half times larger than the average annual farmer income in the area. A similar situation exists in Malawi, where until recently institutional agricultural credit consisted mainly of the Master Farmer Program directed towards development of the relatively larger commercial African farmers. Until the establishment of the Lilongwe Land Development Program in 1967, traditional subsistence agriculture received virtually no institutional credit.

In Ethiopia one of the main objectives in the establishment of the Agricultural and Industrial Development Bank (AIDB) was to meet the pressing needs of the agricultural sector.[1] Because of its minimum loan, collateral, and other security requirements, over 80 percent of the farming population in the country has not been eligible for credit from AIDB. Even though about 63 percent of the loans distributed during the first two years of full operation were distributed to activities in the agricultural sector, big commercial farmers and a few cooperatives were the major beneficiaries. Of about Eth$19 million distributed to the agricultural sector in 1972, three large-scale farms and 107 individual farmers accounted for nearly 79 percent of the loans. Even in Tanzania one of the major concerns of the policymakers has been to devise ways of reaching farmers who do not pro-

1. AIDB was established on August 28, 1970, by merging the former Development Bank of Ethiopia and the Ethiopian Investment Corporation.

duce traditional export crops and, therefore, have not benefited from institutional credit.

Thus, despite its magnitude in terms of the proportion of the population and the percentage of income generated, until recently the traditional subsistence sector has had to rely almost exclusively on informal sources of credit generated from within the rural areas. A strong argument is, therefore, often made for changing the composition of agricultural credit distribution through the introduction of rural development programs specially designed for small-scale subsistence farmers.

On the basis of evidence in the past small-farmer credit programs, this chapter discusses the following points:

1. The potential for mobilizing savings from the traditional rural sector and, hence, the strength of the capital constraint argument as the basis for credit programs.
2. The effect of the limited trained manpower and of the conventional approaches to the institutional credit administration on costs of credit distribution; costs of recovery; and, hence, on reaching a mass of the rural poor in a relatively short time span.
3. The factors that affect the profitability of innovations and the variance in the profitability as well as the effect of these factors on credit repayment.
4. The implications of the past experience for organization of future rural credit programs.

It is assumed that in the case of traditional high-value export crops, which require centralized procurement for further processing, delivery and recovery of institutional credit through parastatals or cooperatives is relatively easy; and the knowledge as to the organization of such credit is relatively more widespread. This chapter, therefore, deals with credit services for those crops for which the technology has usually involved high risk, the value of the crops has been relatively low, and the alternative channels for disposal of the crops have been easily available. All these factors hold in the case of most food crops and several non-food crops. They significantly increase the difficulty in organizing credit programs.

Potential for Saving in the Subsistence Sector

Few baseline surveys have been conducted in designing rural development programs prior to establishment of a credit service. Consequently, little hard information is available to program planners on the target population's saving propensities or the sources from which it obtains credit.[2] Since incomes are very low and the saving potential appears to be very small, the credit components in almost all the rural development programs reviewed

2. There is, however, considerable evidence on rural savings capacity in Africa. See, for instance, O. Amogu, "Some Notes on Savings in an African Economy," in *Social and Economic Studies,* vol. 5, no. 2 (1959), pp. 202–09; Giordano Dell'Amore, *The Mobilization of Savings in African Countries* (Milan: Cassa di Risparmio delle Provincie Lombardi, 1971); R. Galetti, K.D.S. Baldwin, and I.O. Dina, *Nigerian Cocoa Farmers: An Economic Survey of Yoruba Cocoa Farming Families* (London: Nigerian Cocoa Market Board, 1956); Polly Hill, *The Gold Coast Cocoa Farmers: A Preliminary Survey* (London: Oxford University Press, 1956); Polly Hill, *The Migrant Cocoa Farmers of Southern Ghana: A Study in Rural Capitalism* (Cambridge: Cambridge University Press, 1963); Polly Hill, *Rural Hausa: A Village and a Setting* (Cambridge: Cambridge University Press, 1972); and Polly Hill, *Studies in Rural Capitalism in West Africa* (Cambridge: Cambridge University Press, 1970); G. Hubner, "Private Savings in Uganda," in

have been based on the assumption that seasonal credit is one of the major constraints to rural development. However, von Pischke's review of smallholder credit in Kenya suggests that smallholders have a greater capacity to generate savings than is commonly assumed. For example, deposits totaling KSh15 million by 1973 (just three years after the rural banks had initiated the Cooperative Thrift Scheme) were totally unanticipated by officials in Nairobi. Also indicative of rural savings capacity is the existence of indigenous mutual savings societies. Von Pischke's survey of nineteen farmers in the Murang'a district revealed that in one such group each member would contribute KSh15 at regularly held monthly meetings, with the total amount thus accumulated then distributed to one member of the group on a rotating basis. This process would continue until everyone had received the monthly pool, whereupon the cycle would be repeated. Similar saving groups, or tontines, exist among Ewondo women in Cameroon and Chilalo women in Ethiopia.

The survey conducted by CADU's Evaluation Unit on the traditional sources of credit in two areas (Digela and Yeloma) within Chilalo Awraja, points out that agricultural investment—such as buying a new plow, hiring an extra day of labor for weeding, and so forth—has been an important reason for borrowing. Less was borrowed to fulfill consumption needs.[3]

Fifty-one percent of the farmers interviewed whose average annual family income was estimated at about Eth$300 (US$130) had some debt. Out of the 109 farmers sampled for the study, 41 percent were owner-cultivators and 59 percent tenants. Overall, 54 percent of the loans were used for improvements on the farms and 46 percent for consumption, including feast expenses, tax payments, and court case expenses. The average size of the loan was estimated to be Eth$64 for the productive loans and Eth$51 for the consumption loans. The study also indicated that only 36 percent of the total number of loans were repaid upon the agreed due dates.

The survey further showed that the major sources of credit were relatives, close friends, and other farmers. Only 6 percent of the credit was borrowed from traders and moneylenders. About 64 percent of the number of loans from relatives and friends were found to carry no interest charge, compared to only 10 percent of the number of loans from other sources; the average annual interest rate ranged from 34 percent for the loans from relatives and friends to about 110 percent for the loans from other sources. In the case of cash loans, the most common interest charged was found to be 10 percent per month.[4]

Financial Aspects of Development in East Africa, ed. Peter von Marlin (Munich: Weltforum Verlag, 1970), pp. 93–174; William O. Jones, "Economic Man in Africa," in *Food Research Institute Studies,* vol. 1, no. 1 (May 1960), pp. 126–33; Benton F. Massell, "Consistent Estimation of Expenditure Elasticities from Cross-Section Data on Households Producing Partly for Subsistence," in *Review of Economics and Statistics,* vol. 51, no. 2 (May 1969), pp. 136–42; R.A.J. Roberts, "The Role of Money in the Development of Farming in the Mumbawa and Katete Area of Zambia," Ph.D. dissertation, University of Nottingham, 1972; and Hans Seibel and Andreas Massing, *Traditional Organizations and Economic Development: Studies of Indigenous Cooperatives in Liberia* (New York: Praeger, 1974).

3. G. Bergman and H. Lindqvist, *Credit Situation in Chilalo Awraja,* CADU Minor Research Task no. 3 (Asella, Eth.: Chilalo Agricultural Development Unit, July 1969).

4. In personal communication with the author, John Cohen pointed out that loans in kind are prevalent and also carry high interest rates. According to Cohen, it is not uncommon for farmers to borrow one quintal of wheat in February and have to return three quintals during the harvest period.

Thus, although interest rates charged by moneylenders may have been prohibitive, it is by no means certain that the average effective interest rate was very high in the two Chilalo areas. In regard to the security on such loans, the survey indicates that usually some type of security was required for the loans. However, only 46 percent of the relatives and friends, compared to 95 percent of the other lenders, required security for their loans. Of the loans analyzed in the sample survey, 67 percent had some kind of written agreement, 60 percent had between one to three witnesses, 44 percent had guarantors, 9 percent of the lenders required land as a collateral, and 73 percent of the loans had a collateral of some sort. Only 27 percent of the loans were given without any kind of collateral or security.

Though the results of the Digelu-Yolema areas credit study are too limited to base conclusions for the entire CADU project area, interviews and discussions with the various CADU staff, who had been making similar observations in other parts of Chilalo, indicated that the Digelu-Yolema areas situation may, in fact, have been quite representative of Chilalo. The CADU survey indicates that the traditional rural sector may have greater potential for mobilizing savings than is generally presumed.

The survey carried out by WADU's Planning Unit is similar but covered a wider area. All areas within Wolamo Awraja, except those within the WADU project area, were included in the sample survey. The findings show a remarkable similarity with those in the Digelu and Yolema areas. For example, neighboring farmers were found to be the major lenders. Sixty-six percent of the 33,000 households surveyed borrowed from other farmers, compared to only 10 percent from traders. Twenty-eight percent of the surveyed households paid no interest at all, about 26 percent paid interest ranging from one to 50 percent per annum, and almost 40 percent of the households paid interest rates as high as 100 percent per annum. Almost all of the loans were given in cash with less than 5 percent being given in kind. This seems rather unusual; but most of the extension, credit, and marketing staff at WADU felt that it was because people in Wolamo borrowed mainly to finance feast celebrations.

A separate sample survey, conducted within the WADU project area in 1971, arrived at conclusions similar to those above.[5]

Institutional Smallholder Credit and Formal Administrative Requirements

The Case of Ethiopia

Despite this evidence in all the three Ethiopian projects, distribution of institutional agricultural credit constitutes one of the central foci of project activities. Table 5.1 shows the amount of credit distributed in these projects, while Table 5.2 shows the amounts of inputs distributed. In CADU the number of loans increased to nearly 14,000 in four years. The decline in the number of loans in the 1971/72 and the 1972/73 periods is partly related to

---

5. It is instructive to compare the interest rates charged by traditional creditors with those charged by the programs. On seasonal credit AFC charges annual interest of 7.5 to 8.0 percent. In LLDP the rate is 10 percent, while in CADU and WADU it is 12 percent.

its marketing problems discussed later in Chapter VI. The eviction of tenant borrowers also contributed to the drop in CADU's loans.[6] In WADU
over 7,000 loans were advanced in the third year, as compared to the 4,000
anticipated. In MPP areas 4,500 farms were reached in the second year.

The approach to credit administration has been generally similar in the
three programs. For example, all provide their loans in the form of farm inputs. However, there are some distinct differences. Unlike CADU and
MPP, WADU gives short-term cash loans for consumption purposes.
Wolamo farmers traditionally borrow credit from private sources for holi-
day celebrations which occur just prior to the harvest time. WADU's
justification for the cash loans is that, if it does not advance consumption
credit, the farmers' ability to repay WADU's productive credit will be
jeopardized by their need to pay off costly private loans.

There are also variations in the eligibility criteria for credit. After two
years' experience with the unrestricted participation of all classes of farmers in CADU's credit program, it became apparent that the big landlords
were the major beneficiaries of credit in the Chilalo area (see Table 5.3).
Furthermore, a combination of easy availability of credit, demonstrated
profitability of innovations, and absence of taxes on tractors and fuel contributed to the eviction of over 500 tenant families in Chilalo during 1969
and 1970. Consequently, land-owning cultivators with over 25 hectares and
tenants cultivating more than 40 hectares were excluded from CADU's
credit program in 1970. By 1972 CADU had lowered the limit to 20 hectares
for owner-cultivators and 30 hectares for tenants.[7] MPP had imposed similar restrictions since its inception. Still, landowners, who constituted less
than half the population, received the bulk of the loans (see Table 5.4).

WADU, on the other hand, had allowed all classes of farmers to participate in its credit program as long as they were full-time farmers. However,
landholdings in Wolamo have been small, averaging only 0.5 hectares, compared to 3.0 hectares in CADU. One rarely noted cultivators with over 2.0
hectares of cultivable land participating in WADU's credit program, despite
the fact that the program has been open to all categories of farmers. Thus,
although landowners received the lion's share of benefits, distribution was
actually more equitable than appears at first (see Table 5.5).

WADU's security requirements have been considerably more liberal
than in either CADU or MPP. Borrowers were asked only to present two
guarantors acceptable to the screening committee. In contrast, both CADU
and MPP required down payments, signed lease agreements between tenants and landlords, and two acceptable guarantors—one of whom had to be
the landlord if the borrower was a tenant. Apart from their use as a security
measure in absence of a land tenure reform, the one-year lease agreements
were developed by projects principally as a stopgap arrangement to avoid
eviction of tenants. According to Tecle, as a further security measure all
three projects adopted the policy of holding farmers jointly responsible for
all of the credit extended in their areas.

---

6. See Chapter II of this study and John M. Cohen, "Rural Change in Ethiopia: The Chilalo
Agricultural Development Unit," in *Economic Development and Cultural Change,* vol. 22, no. 4
(July 1974), pp. 608–14, esp. 70n.
7. Nonetheless, tenant evictions appear to have continued. Cohen estimates that 6,000 tenants may have been evicted by 1974. Ibid, 64n.

Table 5.1: Amount of Credit and Number of Loans Extended in Three Rural Development Programs, Ethiopia, 1967/68–1972/73[a]

Crop year	Chilalo Agricultural Development Unit			Wolamo Agricultural Development Unit			Minimum Package Program		
	Number of loans	Amount of loan (Eth$)	Average loan (US$)	Number of loans	Amount of loan (Eth$)	Average loan (US$)	Number of loans	Amount of loan (Eth$)	Average loan (US$)
1967/68	189	15,700	83	—b	—b	—b	—b	—b	—b
1968/69	868	158,500	182	—b	—b	—b	—b	—b	—b
1969/70	4,769	502,900	105	727	24,000	33	—c	—c	—c
1970/71	14,146	1,437,500	102	3,923	80,200	20	3,613	240,000	67
1971/72	12,624	1,063,100	84	4,791	159,300	33	4,609	370,000	80
1972/73	13,301	961,950	72	7,400	304,000	41	—d	—d	—d

a. Figures for the total amount loaned and average size loan have been rounded.
b. Program not implemented.
c. Figures were insignificant.
d. Figures were not available at the time the review was conducted.

Source: Chilalo Agricultural Development Unit figures were taken from D. Yirgou, G. Hunter, S. Bekure, and H. Ryden, *Final Report on the Appraisal of CADU and EPID* (Addis Ababa: Government of Ethiopia and the Swedish International Development Authority, May 1974), p. 11, Table 2; Wolamo Agricultural Development Unit and Minimum Package Program figures were obtained from Credit Section reports from the two projects.

Table 5.2: Seed and Fertilizer Distributed on Credit
in Three Rural Development Programs, in Quintals,
Ethiopia, 1967/68−1972/73

Crop year	Chilalo Agricultural Development Unit		Wolamo Agricultural Development Unit		Minimum Package Program	
	Fertilizer	Seed	Fertilizer	Seed	Fertilizer	Seed
1967/68	42	1,470	—[a]	—[a]	—[a]	—[a]
1968/69	2,820	4,540	—[a]	—[a]	—[a]	—[a]
1969/70	15,380	8,202	144	117	6,160	154
1970/71	41,461	13,434	1,420	367	9,280	—[b]
1971/72	35,309	2,698	—[b]	—[b]	—[b]	—[b]
1972/73	32,051	1,640	—[b]	—[b]	—[b]	—[b]

a. Program not implemented.
b. Figures were not available at the time the review was conducted.

Source: Government of Ethiopia, Chilalo Agricultural Development Unit, Marketing Division, "Preliminary Market Data for 1972/73 Annual Report," mimeographed, January 1974; and information supplied by the Credit Sections of the Wolamo Agricultural Development Unit and the Minimum Package Program.

What effect has the use of these criteria of creditworthiness had on participation of the lowest income groups? Though not definitive, interviews with some field agents and project staff have indicated that, due to the rather stringent security requirements of CADU and MPP, the poorest segments of the target population have been excluded, either because they could not afford the required down payment or because their landlords were not willing to sign the lease clause. Even in the case of WADU, where the only requirement has been that a borrower have two reputable guarantors, interviews have indicated that in some cases the poorest tenants found it difficult to find guarantors acceptable to the screening committees. Besides, under sharecropping arrangements, where all costs—including those for major improvements on the land—were borne by tenants without any compensation, tenants often did not find credit for yield-increasing inputs very rewarding. Assuming that a tenant received a favorable sharecropping arrangement, which required paying the landlord one-third of his harvest as rent plus a tithe, over a 60 percent increase in yield was necessary to make the use of improved seeds and fertilizer profitable to the tenant. By contrast, any net increase in yield was profitable to the landlord. If costs were shared proportionately, a yield increase of about 30 percent made the venture profitable to the tenant under the above assumptions.[8]

The three programs also vary in the degree of local participation in credit delivery. In CADU credit applications received preliminary approval from an extension agent and final approval from the Commerce and Industry Department. Plans had been made to employ a screening committee composed of local farmers and extension workers, but this approach had been handicapped by organizational difficulties.[9] WADU has also used a screen-

8. An evaluation team report points out that rents were often much higher, ranging up to 60 percent of the tenant's produce. The tithe or *asrat* was illegal, but many landowners continued to demand it. D. Yirgou et al., *Final Report on the Appraisal of CADU and EPID* (Addis Ababa: Government of Ethiopia and the Swedish International Development Authority, May 1974), p. 42.

9. For a discussion of some of the difficulties in building farmer committees, see Cohen, "Rural Change in Ethiopia: The Chilalo Agricultural Development Unit," pp. 607–08.

Table 5.3 Number and Percentage of Credit Takers and Distribution of Gross Benefits, by Land Tenure and Size of Holding, CADU, Ethiopia, 1968–71

Item	Tenants[a]	Landowners (holdings in hectares)						Total
		1–10	11–20	21–40	Above 40	Unknown[b]		
1968								
Credit takers								
Number	16	81	36	21	18	17		189
Percentage	8.5	42.8	19.0	11.1	9.5	8.9		100.0
Percentage of benefits	3.5	14.8	19.3	29.3	31.1	2.1		100.0
1969								
Credit takers								
Number	134	438	144	66	54	32		868
Percentage	15.4	50.5	16.6	7.6	6.2	3.7		100.0
Percentage of benefits	5.5	29.1	21.9	12.8	26.9	4.9		100.0
1970								
Credit takers								
Number	1,540	1,903	441	179	54	652		4,769
Percentage	32.3	39.9	9.3	3.8	1.1	13.7		100.0
Percentage of benefits	22.7	37.2	17.9	8.9	3.3	9.9		100.0
1971								
Credit takers								
Number	5,392	8,212	387	80	0	75		14,146
Percentage	38.1	58.1	2.7	0.6	0	0.5		100.0
Percentage of benefits	35.8	58.2	4.5	1.5	0	0		100.0

a. Approximately 90 percent of the tenant credit takers in the 1969/70 period cultivated less than 6 hectares. See Henock Kifle, *An Analysis of the CADU Credit Programme 1968/69–1970/71 and Its Impact on Income Distribution,* CADU Publication no. 66 (Assella, Ethiopia: Chilalo Agricultural Development Unit, August 1971).

b. Unknowns are farmers for whom status of land tenure or area owned was not obtained from credit applications.

Source: Johan Holmberg, "The Credit Programme of the Chilalo Agricultural Development Unit (CADU) in Ethiopia," in *Aid Small Farmer Credit,* Spring Review, vol. 8, no. 180 (February 1973), p. 55.

Table 5.4: Distribution of Inputs on Credit by Tenancy and Sizes of Farms in Nine Minimum Package Areas, Ethiopia, 1971/72

Classification	Beneficiaries		Quantity of fertilizer distributed	
	Number	Percent	Quintals	Percent
By tenancy				
Tenants	507	21.8	1,627	32.6
Landowners	1,819	78.2	3,373	67.4
Total	2,326	100.0	5,000	100.0
By area cultivated (hectares)				
0–4.9	1,325	57.0	1,573	31.5
5–9.9	600	25.8	1,604	32.0
10–14.9	233	10.0	830	16.6
Above 15	168	7.2	933	19.9
Total	2,326	100.0	5,000	100.0

Source: Compiled from Extension and Project Implementation Department credit files and Minimum Package Program loan application to the World Bank, July 1972.

Table 5.5: Distribution of Inputs on Credit by Tenancy of Farms in the Wolamo Highlands, WADU, Ethiopia, 1971/72

Classification	Beneficiaries		Quantity of fertilizer distributed	
	Number	Percent	Quintals	Percent
Tenants	199	11	128	11
Tenant-owners	112	7	75	6
Landowners	1,460	82	988	83
Total	1,771	100	1,191	100

Source: Calculated from information on the Wolamo Agricultural Development Unit Year 2 Credit Program.

ing committee, though in this case it has been composed only of farmers. The WADU committee makes the final decision as to who is eligible for credit before bulk-order dispatches are sent to the Marketing, Credit, and Cooperatives (MCC) Division. The emphasis on grass root participation has been the lowest in the Minimum Package Program. Credit applications have been processed by supervisors and their extension staff with some help from model farmers.

How effective have these programs been in fostering farmer participation in the administration of credit? CADU had difficulty even to bring committee members together, whereas WADU reports that the farmers' committees have been meeting regularly and have exerted considerable effort in trying to do a good job. Since neither CADU nor WADU has built-in incentives for committee members, it appears that the success in WADU is due to the higher level of awareness of the Wolamo people with respect to the project's functions and to the facts that the Wolamos have historically been socially cohesive and have traditionally been familiar with group actions and organizations.

As pointed out earlier in Chapter IV, the social cohesion in Wolamo seems to be closely related to the rather equitable distribution of land rights and is reflected in the broader participation of Wolamo farmers in delivery of extension. As will be discussed in Chapter VI, this may also explain the rather more encouraging start in the development of cooperatives in WADU. WADU's superior performance in repayment of credit, discussed in Section 4 of this Chapter, may also be explained by these social factors.[10] However, often the response of the Wolamo has also been attributed to respect for authority and to a lack of any past assistance by the government rather than to the social organizational factors mentioned above. Taking these various considerations into account, to what extent is the group responsibility approach in WADU replicable elsewhere? An indication of this may be obtained by comparing the three Ethiopian programs with LLDP in Malawi.

Credit in the Lilongwe Land Development Program

There was little information available to the planners of LLDP on the nature of the rural credit market in Lilongwe. In the appraisal of LLDP, it was anticipated that, although inputs may initially be distributed on credit, cash sales should acquire an increasing importance over time. However, for a variety of reasons that will be apparent in this discussion, credit rather than cash sales became the central focus for expanding the use of fertilizer and improved seeds. Table 5.6 shows, for years of operation, the sharp increase in the number of borrowers and in the total amount loaned, the gradual decline in the repayment rate in terms of the proportion of value loaned recovered, and the increasing number of defaulters. It is noteworthy that in one year the number of credit recipients in LLDP increased sharply from about 4,400 (1970/71) to almost 20,000 (1971/72).

There has been a particularly dramatic increase in the amount of credit issued for both fertilizer and groundnut seeds since the 1969/70 period (see Table 5.7). Credit has obviously been the major vehicle for the rapid promotion of purchased inputs.

Kinsey's detailed reappraisal of LLDP indicates that cash sales are lagging considerably behind projections, apparently because the credit program is serving a larger-than-anticipated number of repeat customers. For example, in the 1970/71 period it was estimated that farmers would purchase almost 3,000 metric tons of fertilizer, 1,765 of which would be paid for in cash, the remainder being purchased with credit advanced by LLDP. However, when the actual records came in, it was discovered that almost 4,000 metric tons were purchased, of which only 58 metric tons were purchased with cash.

The lack of progress on cash sales, is, however, by no means an indication of their poor potential. Farmers do, on occasion, spontaneously band

10. Some observers of the Ethiopian programs, such as Guy Hunter, have argued that, in addition to the more favorable social environment in Wolamo, the management of WADU has also made a more conscious effort to utilize the traditional social groupings than has been made in CADU. An evaluation of WADU, carried out earlier by Paulos Abraham, the former director of CADU, and reported in Chapters VI and VIII of this study, holds a much more skeptical view of WADU's management in this regard. This is despite the fact that Abraham in his personal conversations with the author emphasized that even CADU should have made greater use of traditional groupings of low-income target farmers. These conflicting assessments emphasize once again the inadequacy of systematic comparative analysis and the predominance of subjective elements in evaluation of the important institutional questions.

together and act as a group when it is advantageous to do so. For example, to take advantage of a 7 percent discount and to obtain fertilizer before program staff were posted to the locale, farmers in the southwestern Modified Input Area (MIA) grouped together to purchase on a bulk basis 505 metric tons of sulphate of ammonia fertilizer from the Chileka ADMARC market. Such group sales reportedly have been a fairly common method of obtaining fertilizer for farmers outside the program area where there is no credit program. These purchases are on a cash basis. If the southwestern MIA is considered the equivalent of two standard program units, fertilizer inputs on a cash basis here are comparable with inputs on a credit basis elsewhere in the program area. The implication is that, if credit is not available, at least some farmers are willing to pay cash for nonfarm inputs. By contrast, within the program area where credit issues received heavy emphasis, only 34 metric tons of fertilizer (less than one percent of the total issue) were sold for cash as recently as the 1972/73 period.

Table 5.6: Seasonal Credit: Amount Loaned, Number of Borrowers, and Default Rates, LLDP, Malawi, 1968/69–1973/74

Year	Total amount loaned (kwacha)	Number of borrowers	Percentage of credit recipients defaulting by August 31 of each year	Percentage of credit not repaid by August 31 of each year	Percentage of credit repaid as of April 1, 1974
1968/69	4,830	660	54	34	100
1969/70	7,040	560	7	4	100
1970/71	83,310	4,410	44	14	99
1971/72	328,660	19,800	44	21	95
1972/73	392,400	21,470	41	25	88
1973/74	495,920	25,620	— a	— a	— a
Total	1,312,160	72,520	42	22	92

a. Figures were not available at the time the review was conducted.

Source: Data supplied by the credit section of the government of Malawi, Lilongwe Land Development Program and by the program's *Quarterly Report* (n.p., January–March 1974).

Table 5.7: Total Inputs Supplied on Credit and Hectarage Covered, LLDP, Malawi, 1968/69–1972/73

Credit year	Fertilizer		Maize seed		Groundnut seed	
	Metric tons	Hectares	Metric tons	Hectares	Metric tons	Hectares
1968/69	151.3	611.3	41.3	1,672.1	12.3	101.2
1969/70	125.5	510.1	162.6	6,583.0	11.7	93.1
1970/71	814.4	3,297.2	213.6	8,647.8	102.3	830.0
1971/72	3,877.6	15,700.4	223.2	9,036.4	206.3	1,672.1
1972/73	3,820.1	15,465.6	129.7	5,251.0	227.1	1,838.1

Source: Government of Malawi, Lilongwe Land Development Program, Credit Section, *Report for the Year 1970 (n.p., n.d.);* and *Monthly Report,* various issues. Other data supplied by the program's Credit and Marketing Sections.

In a subsequent field survey in the program area, conducted as part of the follow-up of the first evaluation, fifty-nine of the one hundred farmers interviewed at random showed interest in group cash sales.

The evidence, thus, indicates that there may be far greater potential to promote either cash sales or some form of local group financing of inputs than is usually presumed in rural development programs. This form of credit mobilization may, however, require far greater flexibility in the rate of project expansion and far greater willingness to innovate and undertake the risk of not reaching ambitious targets than is usually allowed for in designing rural development programs. Since the knowledge as to the precise potential of these methods of credit mobilization is so limited, there is an uncertainty as to their results. In addition, greater time may be required for these methods to come to fruition. However, such new approaches seem to be necessary, for, as the evidence cited below illustrates, small-scale credit distribution on a mass scale, using traditional institutional approaches, seems neither administratively practical nor financially feasible.

LLDP's procedures for assessing creditworthiness are even more elaborate than those in the Ethiopian projects. The credit system has been predicated on the assumption that a credit recipient must possess a certain standard of managerial ability in order to achieve the potential benefits and high returns from packages of new farm inputs. Managerial ability is assessed by a combination of two factors:

1. A personal evaluation of the individual's ability that is made by qualified persons who are in close contact with the applicant. (Farmers are registered and placed into different credit groups according to certain personal characteristics used as indicators of trustworthiness.)
2. A cumulative rating of all growers, based on certain husbandry aspects, that is maintained by extension agents.[11]

The farmer identification list is submitted to the local village planning committee, which, with the assistance of the village headman, goes through the list and evaluates the character and reliability of each grower. This list is then forwarded to the development officer, who combines the personal evaluations with the managerial rating. The officer then forwards a list of approved applicants to the credit section, where the authorization forms are prepared.

The use of this mix of objective and subjective criteria, fairly widely applied, seems to deserve much of the credit for the high repayment rates that have been achieved in LLDP in the first few years. The system, however, imposes a very formidable work load for each extension worker (nearly 300 growers per worker). This may result in shortcuts being taken in the rating system by the arbitrary assignment of the previous year's, or any other year's, rating. The rating system has also been criticized frequently for

11. In the past this rating was expressed in terms of a percentage scale; but, as this system resulted in a very wide range of ratings and made cut-off points difficult to interpret meaningfully, it has been modified and only four ratings are now given: poor, average, good, and excellent. One of these ratings is assigned by the extension agent to each of the seven aspects of crop husbandry — ridging, planting, spacing, fertilizer use, weeding, banking (the second or third weeding), and harvesting. The evaluation of the ratings is done by the development officer in charge of the unit where the applicant lives. If the applicant resides in one of the longer established units, his rating is compared with that of the previous year in order to see if he has improved his standards of husbandry. A farmer with more than three poor ratings out of seven items is considered ineligible for credit in any event.

being applied very rigidly in the first few years of the credit operation, resulting in a spotty and selective pattern of adoption. The criticism is to some extent justified. The detailed statistical analysis of socioeconomic data carried out in the follow-up study of LLDP revealed that the credit-worthiness rating was rarely carried out as it was meant to be. Both in the 1970/71 period and the 1971/72 period, some 55 percent of the project farmers in the sample had not been rated. In some of the project's administrative units, no farmers had been rated. The analysis further indicated that farmers receiving program credit have a higher-than-average socioeconomic status, cultivate one-third more land, and have incomes that are 84 percent higher than those who do not receive program credit. Nevertheless, LLDP's concentration of credit on the relatively more wealthy farmers is lesser when compared to the government credit program which operated in the area prior to the project.

Factors Affecting Repayment of Credit

The issue of credit repayment is closely related to that of administrative procedures and raises a number of complex questions. For example, to what extent have the elaborate administrative procedures used for credit distribution assured high credit repayments? Has rapid expansion of the programs affected repayments? How feasible is it to expand credit administration on a massive scale beyond the first few thousand farmers?

In this section these questions are examined on the basis of experience in Ethiopia, Malawi, and Kenya. In addition to the interaction between administrative factors and repayment outlined above, attention is focused on the implications of overall crop profitability for repayment rates.

Repayment in CADU, WADU, and MPP

The experience of the Ethiopian projects with regard to credit repayments provides useful insights into the dynamics of social change generated by the credit programs.

Analysis of the repayment figures in the three projects shows that small-scale farmers are by no means worse defaulters than large-scale farmers. In fact, a higher percent of the defaulters were found to be the larger farmers, possibly because, being politically powerful, they feel that they can renege on their debts with impunity. The refusal of these larger farmers to settle their dues has probably led to a more far-reaching problem in the case of CADU. The due-date repayment rates have been declining gradually as the number of borrowers increased. CADU's failure to take the first defaulters to court was very likely taken as a sign of weakness by other farmers, indicating that no action would be taken against them if they failed to repay. Actually, CADU had plans to take defaulters to court, and that fact is made clear to all farmers before they are given credit. But it could not effectively litigate for a number of reasons. First, the court system has been so inefficient that prompt action, as CADU would require, was impossible under the setup that existed then.[12] Second, close cooperation by the local admin-

12. In personal communications Cohen indicated that court corruption rather than court inefficiency was the major reason that CADU had difficulty prosecuting defaulters.

istration is necessary in order to be effective in enforcing repayments; this has not been forthcoming. Third, local interest groups were taking advantage of the situation by complaining that CADU did not come to help farmers but to imprison them. Without the full support and cooperation of local institutions and the local administration, the projects had found it difficult to enforce their policies.

The Ethiopian evidence raises doubts about the general contention that, because small farmers tend to use their increased income or to divert production credit more for consumption rather than for repayment of their debts, they are a greater credit risk than large farmers. Nevertheless, CADU and MPP have required down payments. In WADU no down payment was required until recently. WADU was able to achieve repayment rates of 98 percent and 95 percent in the first two years, compared to about 90 percent, 85 percent, and 92 percent during the first three years in CADU[13] and about 90 percent in the first year in MPP.[14]

There are a number of reasons why WADU may have achieved a relatively higher repayment rate. These reasons emphasize that the profitability of investment interpreted in its broadest sense may be much more important than stringent security.

In addition to grains, farmers in the WADU project area produce cash crops like coffee, whose prices have recently remained at higher levels than those of cereals, giving the farmers a better chance of making timely repayment. In contrast, farmers in CADU and MPP have grown mainly cereals, whose prices have been declining, jeopardizing the benefit of the credit program to the borrowers and consequently reducing their potential to repay the dues. The most important reason seems to be related to the Wolamos' traditional habit of borrowing for consumption purposes, noted earlier. Since WADU decided to provide consumption credit at low interest rates, the farmers have wanted to maintain good faith with WADU by showing a willingness to repay on time. This desire was reinforced by WADU's policy, followed from the outset, of excluding all farmers from a given area from future credit programs if repayment for the area fell below 95 percent. CADU had just recently adopted such a policy. However, it is unclear as to what extent the group responsibility for repayment has been enforced rigorously in practice in CADU and further whether the Ethiopian experience with credit organization and repayment can be generalized to the rest of sub-Saharan Africa.[15] Ethiopia's unique feudalistic heritage may have facilitated interventions which would be ineffective in areas with different sociopolitical traditions.

13. Cohen has argued that CADU's final repayment rate is somewhat higher than these figures indicate, averaging around 95 percent. See Cohen, "Rural Change in Ethiopia: The Chilalo Agricultural Development Unit," 41n.

14. By contrast, AFC in Kenya has had a collection rate on both its large- and small-scale loans of only 75 percent. This is despite the fact that, according to the existing estimates, the financial rate of return to small-scale AFC borrowers is 40 percent and above. Von Pischke attributes AFC's low repayment rate primarily to poor administrative procedures in loan supervision and follow-up. Tighter discipline would increase the repayment rate dramatically. However, because the agency is a publicly supported institution, there is no pressure to make a profit in order to survive. Further, given the widespread arrears on AFC loans, there might well be political opposition to tighter loan discipline.

15. The evaluation of CADU carried out recently has urged that CADU eliminate group punishment for credit defaults, arguing that this practice unfairly penalizes small farmers. See Yirgou et al., *Final Report on the Appraisal of CADU and EPID*, p. 23.

Repayment in LLDP

Though LLDP has been quite effective in ensuring final repayment of credit, punctual repayment has been a consistent problem (see Table 5.6). Defaulters are handled in two ways: *(a)* granting of moratoria until the opening of the markets the following season to farmers who agree to certain conditions; or *(b)* taking defaulters to court. However, as in CADU, the courts' ability or willingness to enforce repayment laws has deteriorated. In certain areas defaulters appear to have read the courts' inaction as a sign of weakness, and court rulings are often held in contempt with the knowledge that no action will be taken if a defaulter fails to repay.

What explains defaults? Analysis of the data collected by LLDP's Evaluation Unit provides conflicting explanations. Default rates were found to be significantly higher for farmers growing groundnuts. Of all the borrowers in the sample, 14.7 percent defaulted, while the figure for farmers with groundnut packages alone was 18.5 percent and for those with groundnuts plus other packages, 34.6 percent. The lowest default rate, 7.0 percent, was found among those growers who had only tobacco packages. For a variety of reasons discussed earlier in Chapter III, gross returns per man day have been lower for groundnuts than for maize or tobacco, though gross returns per hectare have been higher for groundnuts than for maize. The follow-up study of LLDP indicated further that farmers receiving groundnut packages have holdings 24 percent smaller than the mean. So the high default rate of groundnut loans may have been related to the fact that groundnut farmers are poorer than average. However, the detailed statistical analysis also indicates that the farmers paying less than 100 percent of the credit were significantly better off than the average credit recipients. It is important to note, however, that the analysis also suggests that mean agricultural income is significantly greater when a member of the family is working outside the country and sending remittances to the other members remaining behind to cultivate the land. So it is difficult to establish an accurate relationship between farm income and tendency to repay credit. The lack of clarity concerning this issue underscores again the need for more appropriate data to evaluate realistically the performance of program interventions.

Both credit and defaults were distributed quite unevenly among the unit areas in Lilongwe. Again, the considerable amount of data collected in LLDP are not adequate to explain what causes the geographical variation in defaults. However, the attitude of village headmen may be playing an important role in the repayment performance and may partly account for the geographical variation. Land registration introduced under the project has been eroding their traditional power base.[16] The village headmen, therefore, often perceive the project as a threat which, in their view, weakens their position. This may be setting up groups of individuals (the village committee) that are willing to act in concert against the traditional authority. Kinsey points out that, when members of the project staff identify a village as good or bad, they have in mind the degree of cooperation obtained from

16. The chiefs have also had their traditional power altered. However, their new role as salaried institutionalized officials has enhanced their prestige.

the village headman. The attitude of the local leaders thus appears to have a substantial bearing on the effectiveness of LLDP's activities in a particular village.

The Vihiga Maize Credit (Kenya)

The experience of SRDP's Vihiga maize scheme emphasizes the importance of identifying the precise constraint to adoption before instituting a credit program. The Vihiga Maize Credit Program is far less ambitious compared to the rural development programs in Ethiopia and Malawi. Of the sample of 600 farmers selected at random to participate in the Vihiga Maize Credit Program in 1971, only 54 qualified for credit under the Program's standards of creditworthiness. Adding another 22 eligible farmers from outside resulted in 76 potential borrowers. Only 63 farmers finally utilized loans. The repayment in Vihiga was much lower than in the Ethiopian programs or in LLDP. Only 80.7 percent of the credit was repaid. In 1972 the expanded program included 383 farmers. The evaluation of SRDP carried out by IDS contends that farmers who were qualified to receive credit were not necessarily the ones who needed credit, since a considerable subjective element entered the definition of creditworthiness. The poor repayment rate may be explained by the lower-than-expected profitability of the maize enterprise.

The lower profitability seems to have resulted from the fact that credit was needed less for fertilizer, as stipulated in the program, and more for purchase of labor. Although there were rumors regarding isolated attempts to resell the material inputs made available through a credit program, the extension agents' visits to the farms appear to have been useful in ensuring the use of the inputs for the intended purpose. However, out of the twenty-two farmers who did not reapply for loans in 1972, ten indicated that an important reason was their inability to use the loan to hire labor for land preparation.

Implications of Past Credit Components
for Design of Future Programs

Whatever the specifics of individual programs, the reviews illustrate with a remarkable consistency that the credit procedures adopted in the programs are tedious, cumbersome, and highly demanding of the very limited trained manpower. Once the crop of the thoroughly screened, early credit takers is harvested and as the number of credit applications increases, the repayment rate slides and the costs of distribution and recovery rise. There is a genuine question as to whether and how the less eager adopters, who may be less able to bear the risk or may be less creditworthy, will be handled by the current approaches to credit distribution. The creditworthiness problem may be compounded if project innovations cause landlords to increase rents, as in CADU. To assure repayments through individual litigation or by goading creditors is expensive, cumbersome, time-consuming, and, judged by the experience in CADU and LLDP, by no means helpful in fostering amicable relations between the project authorities and the rural people. The long-term financial and administrative viability of such an approach to credit distribution is even more questionable if the credit is really to reach all segments of the rural population.

Some projects, such as the Salima project financed by the West German government in Malawi, consciously attempt to foster an element of private enterprise through a complex ladder rating, which rewards better managers and has a credit incentive system. However, many fear that, by neglecting to tackle the apathy of the nonparticipants, the Salima project is accentuating the differences in the economic status between participants and nonparticipants.

What explains the poor repayment of credit and how could it be alleviated? As illustrated above, a number of hypotheses have been put forward in the project reviews about the repayment rate. For example:

1. Poor extension explains low repayment. One of CADU's evaluation studies shows a high positive correlation between an independent assessment of the quality of extension supervision and the repayment rates of credit in the same area.
2. Inadequate yields from new technological packages cause low repayments, as in the case of groundnuts in Lilongwe or maize in Vihiga.
3. Low harvest prices result in low profitability and, hence, low repayment. Such is the case in CADU.
4. Repayments are inversely related to social status, as in CADU and perhaps in LLDP.
5. Overly ambitious expansion of credit facilities with inadequate followup by the government or project authority responsible for collection leads to low repayment. This appears to have occurred with AFC and to some extent in CADU and LLDP.

Most projects, however, provide little data to permit a more systematic analysis than presented above. It is critical that these various hypotheses be tested so as to be able to ameliorate deficiencies which may cause a reluctance to borrow or to repay.

On the basis of available information, it cannot even be stated how crucial the supply of credit is for adoption of innovations. On the one hand, the project reviews indicate that the existing potential for savings in the rural sector is not being exploited. On the other hand, LLDP's rate of credit expansion raises a question as to whether dramatic short-run increases in maize production in the Lilongwe district would have been possible without an emphasis on credit distribution. Few programs seem to want to take the risk to answer this question.

Nevertheless, it is apparent that traditional, individually oriented institutional credit distribution is not efficient in reaching large numbers. As in the case of delivery of extension, new group approaches may be an economic necessity in organizing credit systems. Wherever social systems will permit, group responsibility and group benefit will have to be emphasized *(a)* to reduce cost of credit distribution, *(b)* to assure repayments of credit, and *(c)* to mobilize new savings into the credit system.

This may require a far greater encouragement of spontaneous group input purchases of the type that have been occurring in Lilongwe. However, even if credit is not a constraint to adoption of innovations, as demonstrated by the cash purchases in Lilongwe, there may still be a reluctance among farmers to take up new practices due to two additional obstacles: *(a)* if the innovation does not seem sufficiently profitable in relation to its costs, or (b) if the risk of adoption seems high. Although introduction of institutional credit is frequently justified on the basis of a credit constraint, in practice credit may be more effective in alleviating these latter two obstacles to adoption. The low interest rates usually associated with institutional credit reduce the cost of adoption. And since credit is frequently provided under the same program that promotes innovations, the farmers seem to get an impression that, if the adoption fails, the credit may not have to be repaid. Such an impression, although unconscious, seems to reduce the risk of adoption.

These characteristics of institutional credit raise a question as to whether, in the intial stages of development, input subsidies may not increase relative profitability more easily than credit. During this early period when the number of adopters is low, the financial cost of subsidies is not very high. Of course, to make subsidies less demanding administratively, it is necessary that there be a far greater effort to exploit the traditional channels for input marketing. In most rural development programs reviewed, credit is given in kind; and credit programs only reinforce the need for formally administered input distribution systems.

Although input subsidies are attractive due to administrative ease, it is frequently argued that, because of political pressures, once instituted they may be difficult to remove. This problem would appear to be no more serious in the case of input subsidies than in the case of the subsidized credit provided in most programs. The other argument against input subsidies, however, is that, if subsidies are withdrawn in the later stages of development when innovations have become popular, the risk-averting, slow adopters may be bypassed by the benefit of subsidies. The late adopters may be even greater losers, since the prices of their produce may decline as a result of adoption of new innovations. There is, therefore, a question as to whether a combination of general subsidies and specific credit programs directed towards low-income groups may not be used to minimize the use of scarce administrative resources and to ensure the distribution of benefits to the lower income groups. However, such important questions as to how to use alternate means to reach the lowest income groups cannot be answered satisfactorily, since so few programs have deviated from the standard credit approach.

More attention also needs to be paid to institutionalization of rural savings through traditional organizations. Evidence discussed earlier indicates that there probably exists a considerable potential for savings in the rural sector which remains untapped. A survey carried out by LLDP's Evaluation Unit indicates that in the LLDP area people bury considerable amounts of savings under mattresses and in tin cans. The mobile savings banks being tried by the project management have not yet met with much success, apparently because the people do not trust banks which go away with their savings. Certainly some ways must and can be found to mobilize these savings and to use the local energies to carry out the mobilization.

At the same time, the sense of responsibility and participation in the rural people can be increased through their understanding of the benefits of sharing a bigger pie over time. Involving rural people in saving as well as in receiving credit will lead to more direct interest in assuring repayments. An alternative is to introduce matching credit grants in proportion to the amount of resources mobilized and effectively utilized from within the rural areas. This approach to rural credit implies that limited, formal administrative manpower would be best utilized initially for institutionalizing ways of mobilizing and distributing rural credit rather than for the rapid expansion of an institutionalized credit program. The approach suggested here is very similar to the suggestion made by Belloncle and Gentil for fostering group involvement in extension (see Chapter IV). As with extension, a group approach to credit distribution requires considerable oral exchange with the rural people. They must be able to identify for themselves their own need for credit. They should be involved in administering credit and should understand the importance of repayments to keep the pie growing.

This approach is different from using local committees to distribute externally injected credit and to bring pressure on the rural people to repay. Too often such committees are not delegated genuine responsibility at the local level. As Belloncle and Gentil have noted, planners often feel that the peasant is incapable of adopting recommended changes on his own initiative and look on adult peasants as only big children who need constant watching. The dangers of such paternalism are manifest. For example, farmers' associations set up under the Local Progress Enterprise (EPL) in Cameroon are reduced to requesting financial assistance from EPL in order to carry out projects that it has elaborated. This assistance is granted only insofar as EPL considers it justified. Associations have been forbidden by EPL to procure their own resources to finance their own investments. The inevitable result, in the opinion of Belloncle and Gentil, is a deep sense of frustration which may be transformed into aggressiveness against EPL and may lead to a belief that the enterprise is out to rob the farmers.

LLDP's experience in introducing group credit illustrates the same point. LLDP attempted to make the former village chiefs responsible for credit distribution for the village as a whole. This did not prove to be very effective. Because the chiefs were illiterate, they were poor administrators of credit. Using them led to an increase in administrative costs, as all records had to be maintained in duplicate. However, according to the former credit manager at LLDP, the lack of effectiveness of the village chiefs as credit administrators was a result of their eroding authority, caused by the land settlement program. There is probably an element of validity in both these arguments. Clearly, ways have to be devised, on the one hand, to impart basic accounting and writing skills and, on the other, to exploit the changing leadership structure in a village. Both these factors mean that it will take a lot of time and effort to build grass root institutions, a task which is neither easy nor without risks of failure.

It cannot be overemphasized, however, that at initial stages project expansion must take place at a slower pace than has been the case in the projects reviewed. Thus, considerable attention can be devoted to understanding the rural social structure and the role that it can play and gradually to delegating genuine responsibility of administration to local organizations. Such a participatory, as distinct from a paternalistic, approach to development seems critical for the long-term viability of rural development programs beyond the stage of donor involvement.

CHAPTER VI

Marketing of Agricultural Output

Inadequate marketing and transport facilities, fragmented markets, and uneconomic and unpredictable prices are generally considered to be some of the major bottlenecks to rural development. Consequently, in assessing the essential minimum components of a rural development package, marketing attracts a great deal of attention.[1] The need for and the exact nature of a marketing component are, however, very difficult to assess. Marketing involves a complex and, at times, an obscure interaction of traditional and modern institutions with broader economic policy questions, such as the determination of relative prices among crops and between sectors. Because of the fragmented nature of rural markets, the tendency in most programs is to establish elaborate formal marketing structures. Such an approach to marketing is not only demanding of the limited administrative capacity but also overlooks the potential to utilize the informal market channels already prevalent in many rural areas. There appears to be a wide scope for adopting a pluralistic approach in the development of marketing institutions so as to relieve the staffing/administrative constraint faced by many programs and to increase marketing efficiency through competition between formal and informal channels. Frequently, however, the potential benefits of a pluralistic approach are neglected; and policies are instituted which, in fact, undermine the building of viable local market systems.

This chapter draws on the evidence related to output marketing to support these arguments. There may also be considerable scope for a pluralistic approach to the marketing of agricultural inputs, once demand is created for such inputs through promotional programs and once standardization is introduced in the servicing of inputs through regulatory means related to quality control and weights and measures. Unfortunately, this avenue remains unexplored, as most projects rely almost completely on organized input channels.

Promotion of informal market channels may also generate greater growth linkages within the rural economy, since the demand for a wide range of goods and services from farm tools to radios is substantial in many project areas once incomes increase. In the initial stages of implementation, the projects have, by necessity, focused on marketing of a limited range of

---

1. For instance, this concern was strongly present in the preparation of the Minimum Package Program financed by IDA in 1973. It is reflected in the reports of the members of the preappraisal missions and in the correspondence between the World Bank's Washington office and the Regional Mission in East Africa regarding the various marketing components proposed in the Minimum Package Program.

agricultural commodities. However, frequently the traditional markets have already begun to respond to the rural demand.[2] Encouraging the growth of such informal markets through provision of infrastructure, training programs, and small-merchant loans can stimulate investment in service activities and can be a major source of employment generation.

To illustrate these points, the discussion in this chapter is focused on three questions:

1. What considerations have entered into the design of marketing components?
2. How effective have the marketing components in the past rural development programs been in meeting the objectives that prompt them?
3. What are the lessons of the past experience for designing marketing components in future rural development programs?

Factors Influencing Marketing Components

The reviews show that the substantial marketing component in package programs is usually prompted by a concern about price incentives. As the Ethiopian Minimum Package Program illustrates, production increases resulting from the introduction of new technologies may lead to a precipitous drop in harvest prices. The problem of price decline is particularly severe when production surpluses are concentrated in a small region and where markets are fragmented by lack of transport, communication, and storage facilities. The reviews of CADU and LLDP show how the marketing components in these two programs evolved from a concern for assuring farmers a guaranteed minimum price and for reducing seasonal year-to-year price fluctuations so as to provide farmers an incentive to use new inputs.

The argument for introducing a marketing component is often supported by a widespread belief that traditional trade channels are inefficient, exploitative, and generally antisocial. According to this view, the substantial regional and seasonal disparities in agricultural prices are partially explained by the exploitative nature of traditional trade.[3] Further arguments

2. In the LLDP area, for instance, a number of shops have emerged, established by residents who have returned with savings after serving in mines in neighboring countries. These shops carry a range of consumer goods, including shoes, hurricane lamps, locks, tinned food, umbrellas, and ready-made clothing.

3. To the contrary, substantial literature has amassed which confirms the potential for competitiveness and efficiency in the traditional trading channels. Much of this evidence relates to West African countries. See, for example, Q.B.O. Anthonio, "The Marketing of Staple Foodstuffs in Nigeria: A Study of Pricing Efficiency," Ph.D. dissertation, University of London, 1968; P.T. Bauer, *West African Trade: A Study of Competition, Oligopoly and Monopoly in a Changing Economy,* rev. ed. (London: Routledge and Kegan Paul, 1963); Polly Hill, "Markets in Africa," in *Journal of Modern African Studies,* vol. 1, no. 1 (December 1963), pp. 441–54; H.C. Kreisal, *Cocoa Marketing in Nigeria,* Consortium for the Study of Nigerian Rural Development Paper no. 21 (East Lansing: Michigan State University Press, May 1969). For a statement of the issues related to marketing, see Uma J. Lele, "The Role of Credit and Marketing in Agricultural Development," in *Agricultural Policy in Developing Countries,* ed. Nural Islam (London: Macmillan, 1974), pp. 413–41. Although the evidence is far more scanty, a similar potential for competitiveness has been observed in some of the East African countries. See the Kenyan case in William O. Jones, *Marketing Staple Foodstuffs in Tropical Africa* (Ithaca, N.Y.: Cornell University Press, 1972). Thoday's study makes similar observations in Ethiopia. See A.R. Thoday, *Marketing of Grains and Pulses in Ethiopia* (Stanford, Calif.: Stanford Research Institute, April 1969). On the other hand, the limitations of the alternatives frequently followed are presented forthrightly in government of Tanzania, *Report of the Presidential Special Committee of Enquiry into the Cooperative Movement and Marketing Boards* (Dar es Salaam: Government Printers Office, 1966).

in support of a marketing component relate to the ease of production credit collection. According to this view, cultivators may sell their produce to traders at low prices and, thus, will be unable to repay credit unless marketing is combined with credit.

Gross return to the farmer is dependent on the cost of inputs, the physical return to inputs, and the output price. As was documented earlier in the discussion of extension, in many projects reviewed adequate attention has not been paid to the farm-level constraints which affect the farmer's yield. Yields are often affected by lack of availability of inputs at the right time, in the right place, in the right form.[4] A considerable portion of the yield differences may still be explained by vagaries of weather. As long as yields vary substantially from year to year, a price stabilization program may lead to substantial year-to-year fluctuations in monetary incomes. The fluctuations in monetary incomes may be even more substantial in the case of small farmers, since the elasticity of marketing with respect to changes in production is likely to be greater in their case. However, in the absence of concrete empirical evidence on these questions, the extent to which incomes fluctuate with or without price stabilization programs and whether farmers respond to fluctuating incomes rather than to fluctuating prices is largely a matter of conjecture.[5] Preliminary evidence from the review of LLDP and the Ethiopian projects suggests, however, that it may well be the uncertainty about yields and the consequent risk of not maintaining a minimum level of subsistence production, combined with an unwillingness to incur unpayable debts on new inputs, which dissuade small farmers and tenants from adopting new technology (see Chapters II, III, and V). Thus, frequently the logic of the price-support program is, at best, based on shaky grounds. However, even if the efficacy of support prices is accepted, an important question is whether they are administratively feasible, given the complexity of the task, the limited administrative capability in most African countries, and the alternatives that frequently exist. To answer this question, the relative benefits and costs of the various price-support programs in the projects reviewed are examined below.

Effectiveness of Marketing Components in the Development Projects

A variety of marketing approaches has been used in the various projects reviewed. These various approaches have, however, consistently failed to show potential for a viable low-cost approach that will also provide an incentive for increased agricultural production. As will be evident from the experience reviewed below, the causes are as numerous as the various approaches tried.

---

4. In interviews the management of the German-financed Salima project in Malawi indicated that the project's effort in improving the Agricultural Development and Marketing Corporation's administrative capacity to distribute inputs has centered around ensuring that AD-MARC can estimate and distribute on time different types of fertilizers in the combinations in which they are recommended by the extension service.

5. For a discussion of the elasticity of consumption and marketing with respect to change in production, see John W. Mellor, "Agricultural Price Policy and Income Distribution," unpublished paper prepared for the World Bank, December 1974.

Formally Administered Marketing Components

One of the important factors which explains the limitations of the market interventions is that the national grain boards or their equivalents are often not interested in handling food crops. Most marketing boards have traditionally handled the export crops of commercial farmers. Commercial crops are easier to procure; their areas of production are usually endowed with relatively good marketing infrastructure of roads, storage, and processing facilities. Most marketing boards also lack the administrative capacity and the manpower required to purchase small, scattered supplies of food crops. Further, the marketing boards are frequently not interested in distributing procured food supplies much beyond the capital city.[6]

Table 6.1: Grain Purchases by the Marketing Division of CADU, Ethiopia, and Additional Benefits Received by Farmers, 1967/68–1971/72

	Wheat		Barley		Flax	
Farming season	Quantity (quintals)	Additional benefits[a] (Eth$)	Quantity (quintals)	Additional benefits[a] (Eth$)	Quantity (quintals)	Additional benefits[a] (Eth$)
1967/68	480	1,440	—[b]	—[b]	—[b]	—[b]
1968/69	2,300	6,900	—[b]	—[b]	710	2,840
1969/70	6,310	18,940	—[b]	—[b]	800	3,190
1970/71	23,980	71,940	520	1,560	6,100	24,400
1971/72[c]	93,890	281,660	12,150	36,450	3,330	13,310

a. Additional benefit is the difference between the net price paid by CADU and local market price. Figures have been rounded.
b. No purchases made.
c. During the 1971/72 season CADU also bought 1,070 quintals of peas, 900 quintals of rapeseed, and 1,900 quintals of maize.

Source: Government of Ethiopia, Chilalo Agricultural Development Unit, *Cost/Benefit Analysis of CADU for the Period 1967/68–1973/74* (Asella: CADU, 1971), pp. 4–5.

In Ethiopia CADU and WADU undertook the purchase of major crops grown in their respective program areas at specified prices. Tables 6.1 and 6.2 show the quantities of various crops handled by the marketing divisions of CADU and WADU. As can be seen from Table 6.1, CADU's marketing activities have centered mainly around wheat. However, between 1966 and 1971 the area under wheat in CADU increased from 23,700 hectares to 51,000 hectares; total output jumped from 32,000 metric tons to about 102,000 metric tons during the same period.[7] Nevertheless, in Chilalo hectarage under barley is much larger than that under wheat.[8]

6. Kinsey points out, for instance, that ADMARC has requested the Ministry of Agriculture in Malawi to encourage maize production in deficit areas in an attempt to reduce its own transportation costs.

7. G. Bergman and H. Lindqvist, *Credit Situation in Chilalo Awraja,* CADU Minor Research Task no. 3 (Asella, Eth.: Chilalo Agricultural Development Unit, July 1969); and Chilalo Agricultural Development Unit crop sampling surveys. More recent figures indicate that the area in wheat was 27,000 hectares in the 1967/68 period, 47,000 hectares in the 1971/72 period, and 150,000 hectares in the 1972/73 period. See D. Yirgou et. al., *Final Report on the Appraisal of CADU and EPID* (Addis Ababa: Government of Ethiopia and the Swedish International Development Authority, May 1974), p. 11.

8. This may be because barley has traditionally been used for home consumption while wheat is mostly marketed. CADU could easily sell wheat to big flour mills, whereas most of the other crops have to be sold in small quantities in retail markets, which CADU found to be very costly.

Table 6.2: Commodities Handled by the Marketing, Credit and Cooperatives Division of WADU, Ethiopia, 1971/72

Product	Purchases[a] Metric tons	Value per metric ton (Eth$)[b]	Total value (Eth$)	Sales Metric tons	Value per metric ton (Eth$)[b]	Total value (Eth$)	Stocks Metric tons
Coffee cherries	215.5	198.5	42,776.8	215.5	264.3	56,965.6	–[c]
Cotton	146.1	730.0	106,653.0	146.1	746.3	109,028.1	–[c]
Ginger	579.8[d]	146.0	84,650.8	–[e]	–[e]	–[e]	131.5[f]
Maize	134.8	120.0	16,176.0	100.2	255.8	25,629.8	34.6
Chilies	29.4	500.0	14,700.0	29.4	680.5	20,005.1	–[c]
Teff	252.3	190.0	47,937.0	17.6	355.5	6,256.0	234.7
Wheat	479.0	200.0	95,800.0	13.4	362.4	4,851.4	465.6
Hides and skins	9.6	832.0	7,987.2	9.6	933.8	8,964.7	–[c]
Tobacco	19.5	42.2	822.9	19.5	60.3	1,175.5	–[c]
Total	1,866.0		417,503.7	551.3		232,876.2	866.4

a. First payments.
b. Average figures, not necessarily reflective of total value column.
c. No sales handled.
d. Wet weight.
e. No stocks handled.
f. Dry weight.

Note: According to Tecle, the reliability of some of the information given in the table is questionable. Sale price of wheat, teff, and maize seems to be too high.
Source: Government of Ethiopia, Wolamo Agricultural Development Unit, *Annual Report for Year 2 Programs* (Soddo: Ministry of Agriculture, May 1972) and files of the program's Marketing, Credit, and Cooperative Division.

In the Lilongwe Land Development Program of Malawi, the marketing of inputs and agricultural output has been entrusted to the Agricultural Development and Marketing Corporation. ADMARC, by virtue of its monopoly position as a purchaser and exporter, is responsible for formulating and implementing Malawi's price policies with respect to all the major agricultural commodities. However, in practice LLDP's program management has played an important role in the purchase of maize in the program area. For example, as a way of promoting the sale of maize through program channels, LLDP has introduced a maize-shelling program. According to Kinsey, the LLDP mobile maize-shelling program has, for the moment, solved the transportation problem for many growers. The maize shellers are pulled from village to village by a team of hired oxen; and, after the maize has been shelled, a private lorry hired by LLDP comes to the village to collect it. All that remains for the farmer to do is to go to the ADMARC market to pick up his payment. ADMARC has strongly resisted the maize-shelling program and has even refused to allow LLDP to use ADMARC cashiers at the unit markets to make payments for maize purchased through the shelling program. Consequently, LLDP has had to establish mobile teams that circulate among the units, paying out for maize purchases.

Despite such efforts on the part of LLDP's program managers, it is difficult to state how important formal marketing channels have been in handling the total marketed surplus of maize in the program area. No information is available on the quantities handled by informal channels. Their role must, therefore, be surmised indirectly through estimates of production increases, domestic consumption, and so forth. As noted in Chapter III, detailed reappraisal of the program shows that estimates of maize production in the program area vary substantially, depending on which of the existing estimates of size of holding, area under maize, and yields per hectare are accepted. The estimate of marketed surplus handled by the program as a proportion of production (or of the total marketed surplus) depends on which one of these various estimates of production is accepted. Existing data, therefore, cannot resolve the question of whether to accept a substantial success in achieving an increase in the production of maize (with only a moderate success in purchasing the marketable surpluses of maize through the program's marketing channels) or, alternatively, to accept a considerable success in acquiring a major portion of the increased production through organized channels (with only a limited success on the production front).[9]

Whatever its relative importance in the total marketed surplus, the considerable initiative on the part of the program management in purchasing maize seems to be accompanied by a reluctance on the part of ADMARC to involve itself in maize purchases in the program area, at least for the time being.

9. ADMARC handles a very small portion of the marketed surplus of maize, although one of ADMARC's stated goals is to assure that the internal demand for maize in Malawi is satisfied and that there is an annual carry-over of some 7 percent of a normal season's production as a safety margin. For example, in the 1971/72 period only 7,710 metric tons of maize were sold to ADMARC in the project area, though the LLDP Evaluation Section estimated the marketable surplus to be 19,090 metric tons. According to Kinsey, the amount of maize marketed through ADMARC in any given season represents only the tip of the iceberg (about 4 percent of estimated production in the 1971/72 period) and as little as a 10 percent drop in production results in the complete curtailment of sales to ADMARC.

With respect to LLDP, ADMARC has maintained a relatively low profile in maize-marketing activities. ADMARC's management would prefer to come in on a large scale only when maize becomes a commercial crop. In the opinion of ADMARC's director, LLDP would not supply maize in commercial quantities at least until 1976. On the other hand, according to LLDP marketing staff, the price of maize cannot be reduced without a drastic drop in production and a shift by farmers away from maize growing into tobacco and groundnuts. The current national purchase price for maize in Malawi is well below the prices established for maize elsewhere in Central Africa.[10]

The price policy towards maize has been a major bone of contention between the program management and ADMARC. LLDP's experience in this regard illustrates the complexities and difficulties involved in implementing a price policy when the individual program's objectives are in conflict with those of the marketing board. For example, until the 1972/73 period the guaranteed farm-level price of maize was established by ADMARC at K2.50 per bag. Through its maize-shelling program, however, LLDP was able to pay farmers K2.70 per bag in the 1971/72 period while receiving K3.30 when the maize was delivered to ADMARC. There has been considerable dissatisfaction, both within the Ministry of Agriculture and ADMARC, over the differential price structure.

In general, ADMARC's objections appear to stem from the fact that farmers outside LLDP have become aware of the LLDP price and have been insisting upon being paid this price in other areas. ADMARC, of course, will pay only the stated price of K2.50. On occasion, the policies of ADMARC and LLDP are in diametric opposition. The best example of this occurs in a crop season when maize export prices are at relatively low levels. ADMARC, not wishing to buy and store large quantities of maize above the target surplus, would like to close the markets when it has acquired enough maize. LLDP management, on the other hand, is particularly concerned about credit repayment rates and would like to see the markets remain open so as to improve sales. Both sets of objectives are valid, but the conflict between them is very real. To fulfill its other objectives, once a marketing component is introduced in a project, the project management often ends up providing a marketing service at some guaranteed price. The problems of the project authority may, however, only begin with such an intervention.

First, there is the problem of providing a low-cost service. With intensive marketing facilities even the most efficient organized marketing schemes involve much higher costs of operations than do the traditional alternatives. According to data collected by Tecle, in CADU the unit costs (excluding overheads to the project management) of marketing wheat between Asella and Addis Ababa amounted to more than twice those of the private traders. The program's relatively higher handling costs raise serious questions as to how the Marketing, Credit, and Cooperative Division will be able to function as a viable autonomous unit in the future. Starting from the 1973/74 season, the MCC Division was expected to cover all of its marketing costs from the deductions that have to be made before making second

10. The 1971/72 pre-planting price in Zambia, for example, was K4.30 per 90-kilogram bag, compared to K2.70 per bag in Malawi.

payments to farmers. So far, salaries of the MCC Division staff and a few other costs such as depreciation of equipment have not been charged to farmers as marketing costs. LLDP's maize-shelling program suffers from similar problems of high costs of operation.

Second, there are numerous problems related to the determination of the levels of guaranteed minimum prices in the context of an overall price policy and the implementation of the minimum price. The experiences of CADU and WADU cited below show that, given the fragmented nature of the national market and the extreme unpredictability with which national grain boards often export, import, and distribute grain, even the best marketing experts can do little more than resort to their astrological abilities in predicting prices and determining the project's price policy.

The management may become a financial loser at this highly speculative game, as illustrated by the losses incurred by CADU in the 1970/71 and 1971/72 periods. For the 1972/73 season, it was decided to let farmers bear the marketing risks involved. A two-payment system with 90 percent of the prevailing local market price as the first payment was proposed. However, as local traders expressed their willingness to buy all the marketed produce at prevailing local market prices, farmers refused to sell their grains to CADU at 90 percent of the market price. This forced CADU to reverse its policy and buy farmers' grains at prevailing local prices. The decline in the number of borrowers in Chilalo in the 1972/73 period compared to the 1971/72 period has been explained by the project management as a consequence of the farmers' dissatisfaction with the wheat price, which, in its view, was exploited by the local trading-interest groups.[11]

Yet another variant of the marketing problem faced by the project authorities occurred in LLDP. It arose because ADMARC has been reluctant to pass gains from rising world maize prices on to farmers. The export price of maize in 1972 was K6.60 per bag, compared with the price of K2.50 paid by ADMARC to farmers. There has been a similar problem in the pricing policies in Mali, as indicated earlier in Chapter III. LLDP management pointed out during interviews that farmers become discontented when they realize that the prices received by them in the project markets are lower than those offered elsewhere by private traders. In the 1972 harvest season, this price differential resulted in farmers throwing stones at some of the LLDP marketing centers. Under these circumstances, the project authority may either tell the farmer that it cannot pay as high a price as offered elsewhere or suggest that the farmer sell his produce elsewhere.

WADU encounters problems similar to those faced in CADU. It handles too insignificant a proportion of the products marketed in Wolamo to be able to influence the marketing system (see Table 6.2). Since Wolamo is a net importer of grain (teff, barley, wheat, maize), WADU prefers not to buy these products. Farmers have continually been pressuring WADU to buy their grain, believing that WADU is able to offer them a higher price than

11. According to Cohen, the decline in the number of borrowers may also be explained by the fact that (a) many tenants, who were previous borrowers, have been evicted from their holdings; (b) many farmers have acquired their own seed from previous purchases and felt that they no longer needed CADU's credit to purchase CADU's seed; (c) some farmers purchased seed sold with a CADU label at the local market; and (d) in the view of the farmers, the price of CADU seed seemed high relative to the local price for wheat. See Cohen, "Rural Change in Ethiopia," pp. 595–601.

the local traders. WADU stands to lose if it buys grain, as its handling costs are much higher than those of the local traders. Nevertheless, it has decided to buy some grain in order to preserve its good relationship with the farmers. WADU has also encountered problems in implementing an ad hoc price policy, although it has allowed farmers to participate in the risk involved in unexpected price declines. WADU's policy has been to pay farmers 60 percent of the anticipated sale price of any product as a first payment and, when the product is sold, to make a second payment after deducting an amount equal to 20 percent of the first payment to cover the marketing costs. A second payment is made only if and when the realized sale price more than covers the first payment plus the marketing costs. The main obstacle to this policy seems to be WADU's inability to forecast product prices with sufficient certainty to ensure second payments. For example, WADU was unable to make second payments for ginger, wheat, teff, and maize for the 1971/72 season because large amounts of these crops were in stock as late as October 1973. Failure in making second payments generates mistrust among farmers, as indicated by interviews with some farmers, because WADU's first payments, particularly those for grains, are usually smaller than the prices offered by local merchants.

How effective is a price-support program when only small proportions of the marketable surpluses are handled by the project authorities? As they have in CADU, farmers usually develop an expectation of receiving from the project authority not only a guaranteed minimum price but also a share in the profit. Ironically, in the 1972 season farmers in the CADU area accused management of making a profit at their cost. CADU's management observed that the subsequent drop in credit applications may have been partly due to the farmers' expressed desire to boycott credit the following year, though tenant eviction was likely to have been an equally important factor in explaining the decline in the number of borrowers.

How useful is the marketing component for assuring high credit repayments? The reviews of CADU, WADU, and LLDP show that the provision of collection centers certainly aided collection of credit in the first few years when the number of credit takers was small and credit administration was relatively easy. However, those farmers who do not want to repay credit find many ingenious ways of avoiding this responsibility. In LLDP, for example, farmers are required to reveal their credit record when selling their produce at the project market. Those owing money are required to pay off their debts immediately with the cash gained from the sales. Many farmers get around this requirement by borrowing the credit records of persons whose debts are paid up. Another frequently used route is to market produce through private channels.

The performance of the marketing systems in the package programs raises doubts as to their viability in the long run. What is disturbing about the marketing systems reviewed is their inability to get at the more basic factors—e.g., if the marketing boards are not interested in purchasing the food crops produced by small farmers, what is the guarantee that they will do so after the project authority phases out?[12] Would it not be easier to im-

12. Kinsey reports that ADMARC officials are quite confident that they could cope with any amount of maize that might be marketed. However, such confidence might well be tempered by the fact that storage and transportation facilities at the Lilongwe depot already appear to be operating close to capacity. Certainly a significant increase in marketed maize over two consecutive good seasons would severely strain local facilities.

prove the traditional marketing organization that obviously already handles a substantial portion of the marketed surplus, even in such program areas as CADU, WADU, and LLDP? In any case, if the long-term viability of the project is a consideration, the question remains whether it makes sense to expand distribution of credit rapidly without developing a genuine sense of responsibility and farmer participation in the project activities and without building a more viable marketing and price policy system.

Performance of Cooperatives

As an alternative—or a complementary approach—to other marketing efforts, a number of the programs reviewed have established cooperative societies. However, an effective cooperative development requires organization, leadership, and entrepreneurial capability. Even if this is recognized, as indeed it is by many of the program managers interviewed, developing such a capability is a difficult and long-term task.

Moreover, an examination of the steps taken to introduce cooperatives causes one to wonder whether they will be successful, even in the long run. The cooperative training courses usually consist of principles of cooperation, borrowed from textbooks not dissimilar to those used in nineteenth century Europe. Courses also include training in accounting. However, they fail to cover the trading and speculative aspects of marketing food crops and the entrepreneurial skills required to deal with these problems. An evaluation of CADU's experience in cooperative promotion observed that the graduate is handicapped when he goes to the field, due to the fact that the training so acquired is not job oriented. Nor does it cover essential courses in cooperative organization and management. The lack of practical training can become a source of frustration and embarrassment to the trainees.[13] The need for trading skills is by far the most important difference between the export crop cooperatives and the cooperatives being formed for marketing food crops.

The export crop cooperatives have performed the relatively straightforward administrative function of procuring for further processing or export standard, scientifically graded crops at prices usually fixed by the marketing boards. Collinson attributes the success of the Sukuma cooperative movement for cotton in Tanzania—apart from its unique marriage with the broader political movement—to the relative simplicity of the task. For instance:

1. The cooperative movement inherited a history of government intervention in the marketing of the crop. From 1949 onwards, there were no alternative channels for selling the crop overseas. The government was the sole buyer.
2. It dealt with a crop with no domestic use. All the production was exported. The board was never forced into the position of being a buyer

13. Government of Ethiopia, Chilalo Agricultural Development Unit, "An Appraisal of CADU's Experience in Cooperative Promotion," unpublished report, July 1972. According to Cohen, to date CADU's involvement in cooperatives is rather limited; perhaps as few as 1,000 farmers belonged to such groups in 1974. However, Nekby, the first manager of CADU, has indicated in personal discussions that the CADU cooperative movement has about 10,000 members and is very active. Conflicting data of this nature highlight the need for institutionalizing systems for maintenance of regular and reliable data on numbers as well as on the degree of involvement to be able to assess more objectively the progress of institutional development.

of last resort with its inherent uncertainties, nor did it have to face illegal local and inter-farm sales; so, vis-à-vis the local producers, the
board was the sole consumer.

3. The board was formed at a period when a booming world market
   allowed it to consolidate its position with no financial problems, creating a security never threatened until perhaps the near exhaustion of its
   Price Assistance Fund in 1966.

4. The Lint and Seed Marketing Board (LSMB) took the trading role out
   of the cooperative movement in cotton. It removed the commercial
   sting which has often been the downfall of cooperatives operating in
   competition with private traders. It left the cooperative as purely a collection channel for the crop.

If the grain cooperatives are to survive, unlike the export crop cooperatives, they have to be able to compete with the private trading channels in
their ability to speculate and to operate at low costs in highly fragmented
domestic food markets.[14] In the case of ZAPI in Cameroon, trading problems are particularly difficult for inexperienced cooperatives to handle
when the latter are confronted with illiteracy, poor transport and communication facilities, and the virtual absence of financial institutions in
many rural areas. Furthermore, there is some evidence in the reviews to indicate that fraud is an extensive problem. Costs of cooperative marketing
tend to be high, even in Tanzania, which has had a relatively well-developed cooperative network.[15] Another problem is the tendency to develop a
paternalistic rather than participatory approach to cooperative development. The reviews indicate with remarkable consistency how this has adversely affected the rural people's sense of involvement in project activities
and their willingness to be involved financially and organizationally to
make project-initiated institutions viable.

For instance, Belloncle and Gentil observed that the ZAPI project in
Cameroon was seen by the farmers as a series of operations decided upon
far from them in the capital and perhaps even in France, set up by foreigners and which, undoubtedly, would last only a very short time as in the case
of the neighboring projects. Abraham, et al., who carried out an independent evaluation of WADU's Phase I, attribute the poor performance of the
WADU Group Marketing Organization (WGMO) to its emphasis on working for the farmers rather than with them. During interviews the team had
with farmers in Wolamo, both members and nonmembers believed that
WGMO was really WADU; and the idea of joint conduct of the organization's program seemed foreign and, perhaps, suspect to them.[16] The review

14. As pointed out earlier, although some of the East African countries have a less developed private trading system compared to several other countries in West Africa, there is a
considerable informal exchange of produce in rural areas.

15. For problems of cooperatives in Tanzania, see Elliot J. Berg, "Socialist Ideology and
Marketing Policy in Africa," in *Markets and Marketing in Developing Economics,* eds. R. Moyer
and S. Hollander (Homewood, Ill.: Richard D. Irwin, 1968), pp. 24–47; Stanley Dryden, *Local
Administration in Tanzania* (Nairobi: East African Publishing House, 1968); and government of
Tanzania, *Report of the Presidential Special Committee of Enquiry into Cooperative Movement and
Marketing Boards.*

16. In personal discussions Abraham, the first Ethiopian manager of CADU, indicated that
one of the lessons of CADU is the need to pay far greater attention to farmers' involvement
in the project activities from the outset so as to reduce their sense of dependence on project
activities. However, given the social and political realities in Chilalo, increased farmer involvement was difficult to institute.

of SODENKAM in Cameroon makes a similar point, as do evaluation studies conducted in CADU. However, it must be emphasized that this paternalistic attitude is by no means confined to projects financed by donors and designed and implemented by expatriates. It seems to apply equally well to the *ujàmaa* movement in Tanzania and may, in fact, explain some of the problems encountered in its implementation (see Chapter IX below).

To some extent paternalism results in subsidization of local institutions, jeopardizing the chances of developing in them a sense of financial responsibility.[17] CADU's Evaluation Unit, for example, observed that one of the ways in which Chilalo's cooperatives can become independent of CADU's benign but suffocating influence is by their involvement in financial matters. There is yet another prerequisite for success of cooperatives which must be taken into account. Evidence from the project reviews and other sources strongly indicated that, where traditional authority and power are unequally distributed, cooperatives become an instrument in the hands of the few relatively large farmers and provide little assistance to subsistence farmers.[18] There may also be a conflict between the objectives of the financial self-reliance of cooperatives and participation of the lowest income groups, since the latter may not have the ability to make financial contributions.

However, all too often it is the relatively better-off farmers who control the cooperatives and who are also subsidized through programs. The evaluation of CADU's cooperatives, cited earlier, noted that, whereas the proportion of landlords in the overall population was estimated to be about 55 percent in the project areas, landlords constituted between 60 and 95 percent of the members in the cooperative societies of Asella, Bilalo, Kechema, and Sagure. The size distribution of the landownership was not known. However, these should have been small landowners with farms of 25 hectares or less, since the large ones had been excluded from the program. The study observed that tenants who had not joined were afraid of losing their tenure, had less cash available, and had considerably less land at their disposal. Thus, though the requirements and procedures for becoming a member did not discrimate against them, tenants were very much underrepresented. It must be emphasized that it was Chilalo's social structure rather than the program's procedures that seem to be at fault in the pattern of participation. However, the question remains as to whether the relatively better-off farmers should not have been made to contribute somewhat more to the cooperative organization than they had been. Even in Tanzania, cooperatives have been embroiled in a controversy over whose interests they serve. The dominant role of the rural elite growing export crops in

17. The question of subsidization applies equally well to the *ujàmaa* movement, as will be illustrated later. To the extent that subsidization involves transfer of resources to poor regions, classes, or sectors which would not have occurred otherwise, this may be genuinely desirable. However, if such a resource transfer does not generate a long-term productive potential through augmenting technical and organizational capacity, its scope is inevitably very restricted in the long run (see Chapter IX for further discussion of this question).

18. Raymond J. Apthorpe, "Some Problems of Evaluation," in *Cooperatives and Rural Development in East Africa,* ed. C. G. Widstrand (Uppsala: Scandinavian Institute of African Studies, 1970). Also see Goran Hyden, "Government and Cooperatives," in *Development Administration: The Kenyan Experience,* eds. Goran Hyden, Robert Jackson, and John Okumu (Nairobi: Oxford University Press, 1970), pp. 296–318.

these organizations has been the basis of a conflict between the cooperative and the *ujàmaa* movements.[19]

The performance of both the formally administered marketing components and the cooperatives suggests that a simple transplant of modern marketing organizations into the traditional sector is unlikely to be viable, not only because of the shortage of skills, financial capital, and infrastructure and communication facilities, but also because of the existence of interest groups—e.g., grain boards and the commercial farmers—that stand in the way of a viable market development in the subsistence sector.[20]

Implications for the Design of Marketing Components

What lessons do the past programs offer for development of the marketing systems? First, to avoid serious marketing bottlenecks, emphasis on increased food production often needs to be gradual, geographically dispersed, and commensurate with a simultaneous development of markets rather than on highly integrated, ambitious package programs which aim at increasing marketed surpluses rapidly without devoting adequate attention at the outset to institutional development.

A second lesson of the projects reviewed is that, as soon as large rural development programs with a substantial potential food production component are identified, examination of the overall price policy and resource allocation questions should be undertaken with particular emphasis on the various marketing institutions, their performance, potential, and their relationship to the organization of the program. Price policies adopted in programs should become a part of an overall price policy rather than ad hoc measures adopted to meet successive unanticipated crises, as has been the case in the projects reviewed.

Third, the foremost shortcoming of the approach adopted in many of the programs is that it has paid little attention to making the traditional forms of marketing organization work. The existing documentation, mostly from West African countries,[21] indicates that the traditional traders (men and women) possess a highly developed trading skill and carry on an efficient marketing system. Relatively little is known about the traditional trading channels in Eastern Africa.[22]

19. As was pointed out in Chapter I, the relatively more well-to-do export crop producers who constitute the rural elite in Tanzania are, nevertheless, small farmers.

20. An extremely good illustration of the conflict between the interest of commercial and subsistence farmers was provided in an unpublished restricted comment prepared by the Kenya National Farmers' Union on the International Labour Organisation's *Employment, Incomes and Equality: A Strategy for Increasing Productive Employment in Kenya,* 1973.

21. K.R. Anschel, "Agricultural Marketing in the Former British West Africa," in *Agricultural Cooperatives and Markets in Developing Countries,* eds. K.R. Anschel, R.H. Brannon, and E.D. Smith (New York: Praeger, 1969), pp. 140–62; B.W. Hodder and N.I. Ukwu, *Markets in West Africa: Studies of Markets and Trade Among the Yoruba and Ibo* (Ibadan: Ibadan University Press, 1969); Marvin P. Miracle, "Market Structure in Commodity Trade and Capital Accumulation in West Africa," in *Agricultural Cooperatives and Markets in Developing Countries,* eds. R. Moyer and S. Hollander (New York: Praeger, 1969); Marvin P. Miracle, "Market Structure in the Tribal Economies of West Africa," in *Agricultural Cooperatives and Markets in Developing Countries,* eds. K.R. Anschel, R.H. Brannon, and E.D. Smith (New York: Praeger, 1969), pp. 120–39.

22. C.M. Good, *Rural Markets and Trade in East Africa: A Study of the Functions and Development of Exchange Institutions in Ankole, Uganda,* Research Paper no. 128 (Chicago: University of Chicago Department of Geography, 1970).

The extent to which the disappearing Asian trader is being replaced by the African trader is not known. However, existing studies show that in Ethiopia there is a well-developed network of traditional trading channels that handles substantial interregional trade and possesses its own market intelligence system.[23] Where means of communication and transportation are well developed, regional price movements are well coordinated. In Malawi LLDP project management observed that, although traditional unlicensed traders are barred in the project area, Malawian (as opposed to Asian) traders are quite active and procure a substantial portion of the marketed surplus of maize and groundnuts.

The project management further pointed out in the interviews that, had it not been for these unauthorized traders, ADMARC's attitude toward purchases in the program area would have led to a substantial drop in maize prices and discouraged farmers from growing it. In LLDP, disposal of grain through nonformal channels is facilitated by the close-knit network of feeder roads that is being developed in the program area; nearly a third of the project expenditure is allocated to the development of the infrastructure. In the Ethiopian Minimum Package Program, however, despite provisions for feeder roads, the progress in their construction has been slow. This has led to a major bottleneck, since increased surpluses in far-off and ill-connected locations do not seem to attract private traders.

The Ethiopian case illustrates the need first to remove the basic marketing constraints of poor institutional development and inadequate means of transport and communication. Only then can the more apparent constraints, such as lack of fertilizer and nonincentive prices, be effectively tackled. LLDP in Malawi, by contrast, has undertaken a very ambitious road development program, though its local institutional capability in terms of trained manpower and ability to mobilize resources necessary for road maintenance is still very limited. Both these cases indicate the need to reach a proper balance between institutional development and measurable targets, whether the latter be in terms of amount of fertilizer distributed or miles of roads constructed. Improving the means of transport and communications is critical for improving performance of traditional trade channels. The removal of these and other constraints receives relatively little emphasis in the marketing components in comparison to the attention paid to replacing traditional marketing systems.

The approach to marketing that is suggested involves attacking the constraints faced by the farmer (and/or the trader), rather than spoon-feeding the farmer through tailor-made marketing programs. This will require several simple but explicit steps to improve the farmers' knowledge of the process of price formation, of the standard weights and measures, and of the role that these factors play in causing high market margins. The studies conducted by the Evaluation Unit of CADU, the survey by Manig of the German AID Mission in Bako, and the study in marketing by the Stanford

23. Government of Ethiopia, Economic Research Division, Planning and Program Department, *Findings of a Market Structure Survey and an Analysis of Those Grains That Provide the Basic Subsistence for the People of Ethiopia* (Soddo: Ministry of Agriculture, July 1973); also see W. Manig, *Marketing of Selected Agricultural Commodities in Bako Area, Ethiopia,* Occasional Paper no. 66 (Ithaca, N.Y.: Cornell University Department of Agricultural Economics, December 1973); and Thoday, *Marketing of Grains and Pulses in Ethiopia.*

Research Institute[24] note that most price exploitation that has been observed in Ethiopian markets is covert, through false weights and measures, rather than overt. This implies that the farmer does have the potential to enjoy real bargaining power. Once the cultivators are made aware of the covert practices, the demand for correct weights and measures can be substantial. There probably could not be a better testimonial to the importance of introducing correct weights and measures than the resistance received from traders to CADU's program of making available standard weights and measures at its trade centers. Cultivators in the program area could use the facilities even if they were selling their produce to the private traders and not to the trade centers. The plan was tried on an experimental basis in four village markets and the primary market at Asella. In almost all of the areas where the program was operative, local merchants resented it vehemently; and at times they were violent. In Bekoji and Asella the municipality chiefs opposed the whole idea of the program and exhibited strong opposition to the scheme. Intervention of the *enderassie* (governor) was required to implement the program in Asella. In spite of these setbacks, during the two and a half months that the program was operative, the Planning and Evaluation section considered the experiment as a relatively successful venture and suggested that it be run in the future on an expanded basis.

Farmers also need a market intelligence program to inform them of prices prevailing in the major market centers and of the importance of these prices for the prices they should receive. A survey conducted early in 1972 in Lilongwe indicated that half of all the male growers surveyed had no idea of the current maize price and were unwilling even to hazard a guess. Among those farmers who gave a maize price, only half were within the range of the correct ADMARC price—K2.50 per bag—while a quarter knew the price offered by the program's maize shellers. Thus, of all the farmers queried, approximately three-quarters did not know the price of maize that could be obtained through the legal outlets. It is interesting to note that, of the 60 percent of male farmers stating a price that could be obtained from local traders, almost two-thirds gave a figure higher than the ADMARC price.[25] Tecle observes that, generally, the lack of adequate and reliable information at all levels of the marketing system is a primary cause of unequal bargaining power, poor producer prices, and the low level of inter-market price consonance. Manig, on the basis of his microlevel marketing survey conducted over a three-year period near Bako in Ethiopia, pointed out in personal discussions that informal exchange of price information is substantial among farmers and that farmers are generally well informed of the prices prevailing in the nearby areas. However, the extent of their knowledge about prices is closely related to their physical access to markets and to whether the crop is commercial, such as chilies, or subsistence, such as sorghum. The Bako farmers sell very little of the latter.[26]

24. Manig, *Marketing of Selected Agricultural Commodities in Bako Area, Ethiopia;* and Thoday, *Marketing of Grains and Pulses in Ethiopia.*
25. According to LLDP's management, the validity of these surveys may be questionable, since farmers are not used to thinking of prices in standard European measures. More recently in disseminating prices, LLDP has made an attempt to translate prices into units more familiar to the farmers.
26. See also Manig, *Marketing of Selected Agricultural Commodities in Bako Area, Ethiopia.*

Price information could, of course, be facilitated through improvement of feeder roads and increased farmer mobility or through extension agents. In Malawi LLDP has undertaken such a price dissemination program through extension agents and through displays of prices in marketing centers. The program has been somewhat restricted in scope, as it attempted to inform farmers only of the price paid by LLDP for purchases on behalf of ADMARC, whereas a considerable portion of the produce was sold elsewhere. The marketing service provided by programs also needs to convey to the farmer the risks involved in seasonal storage so that the cultivator will have the choice of storing for the off season if he is willing to undertake the risk.

In essence, in designing and implementing marketing components, there needs to be a shift from viewing trading as an unproductive and anti-social activity to viewing it as a productive and socially desirable endeavor which requires considerable skill and involves a great deal of risk. In developing the marketing system, it is also essential to convey to the farmers the importance of cooperation among them and to impart to them the necessary accounting and trading skills. It is possible, however, that the cultivators may decide to undertake intermediate forms of cooperation, as, for instance, organizing themselves to ensure the implementation of standard weights and measures or to build market yards or storage facilities for their common use. As another intermediate form of intervention, storage facilities may be combined with seasonal advances for grain storage by cultivators in the off season. This will allow farmers to repay their cash obligations without forcing them to sell their crops in the immediate post-harvest period, while at the same time encouraging them to share the risk of seasonal storage. Initially, at least, farmers may decide to leave the trading function to the experts. But, in any case, the important principle of sharing benefits and costs (including risks) must be conveyed to the farmers from the very initial stages in any program of market modernization.[27]

---

27. This very point was also emphasized in the report of the ILO to the government of Tanzania. See International Labour Organisation, *Report to the Government of the United Republic of Tanzania on Consumers' Cooperatives* (Geneva: ILO, 1970), p. 58.

CHAPTER VII

Social Services

The provision of social services has been of vital importance in many of the projects reviewed under ARDS. The humanitarian argument for such services is obvious. Improvement in health, water supply, diet, and education can improve the welfare of the rural population. There are also sound economic reasons for introducing social welfare services, since better health, reduced domestic chores, and higher levels of education can contribute to increases in agricultural productivity through increases in the quantity and quality of labor. Planning of social services, however, poses by far the most difficult problem of resolution between economic, social, and technical choices. This is because demand for a wide range of social services is substantial in many rural areas. However, the financial, manpower, and organizational resources for effective delivery of social services are often extremely limited. Consequently, three sets of interrelated questions are faced in planning rural development programs. First, given that resources are limited, how should additional fiscal, organizational, and manpower resources be raised from within the rural areas? Second, are such resources likely to be mobilized more easily if the services to be provided lead to a measurable impact on productivity or if they generate substantial enthusiasm for development programs among rural people? In other words, are social choices regarding allocation of resources related to social willingness to pay? Third, how can low-cost delivery of services be organized? Is greater participation in planning and/or implementation of programs more conducive to a low-cost delivery of services? This latter question of relationship between cost and participation is, of course, related to the nature of services and the degree of technical input required in planning and implementation. These various issues are dealt with in this chapter.

The existing information on social services is, however, sparse and provides little systematic evidence, either on the impact of these various social service interventions on rural welfare or on productivity. Nor does much systematic analysis exist of alternative technical and administrative choices in provision of social services or of the effect of these choices on the costs of organizing social services. What data that do exist are largely of a suggestive nature, underlining the need for more research in this critical area. Because of the paucity of hard information, the discussion in this chapter is necessarily tentative. The purpose is more to raise the important issues faced in designing rural development programs than to provide definitive prescriptions.

Because of the multiple causes of low welfare and productivity, social services are defined broadly in this chapter. They include the commonly introduced measures such as broad-based immunization against disease and provision of rural health clinics. Improved water supplies, labor-saving measures in the homes, and improvement of local diets through new varieties of food crops are no less important for rural welfare, although perhaps less evident. And, of course, educational and training programs are crucial in any effort to improve the quality of life of low-income rural populations. The implications of education and training for rural welfare are discussed separately in Chapter X.

Economic Justification for Social Services

Several project reviews have drawn attention to the generally poor health of the population and the adverse implications which ill health has for labor productivity. In the squatter settlements in Kenya, the settlers have poor resistance to diseases due to heavy energy demand of farm activities under conditions of low energy supply, inadequate medical services, and insufficient insulation against disease vectors. In ZAPI malaria and intestinal parasitic diseases and sores are predominant and are common at all ages. Among children numerous cases of bronchitis, pneumonia, and epidemic illiness are recorded. The farmers are especially susceptible to diseases because of the lack of preventative medication. It is not rare to see children and even adults die of malaria.[1]

Apart from its effect on mortality rates, the extremely debilitating effect of malaria has been well documented.[2] Chronic parasitic infection can have a similar effect on overall physical well-being and performance.[3] The reviews both of ZAPI and of the squatter settlements point out that such health problems could be reduced by simple protective measures, such as the provision of quinine to prevent malaria or the introduction of water filters to reduce the incidence of intestinal parasites.

Local food shortages, inadequate nutrition, and susceptibility to debilitating diseases form a vicious cycle in many rural areas. In Kenya, for example, WHO surveys show that throughout the year about two-fifths of the rural families consume less than 80 percent of the average protein requirements.[4] Vitamin and mineral deficiencies are also widespread throughout Africa. Insufficient dietary intake is, of course, compounded by disease and parasites, which make a higher demand for nutrients to preserve integrity.

1. In an analysis of health programs in Niger, Belloncle cited a WHO survey, according to which 93 percent of the population is affected by malaria. See Guy Belloncle, "Total Participation in Public Health Programs: Some Reflections on the Niger Experience," mimeographed (Paris: Institut de Recherches et d'Applications des Méthodes de Développement, 1973).

2. See Robin Barlow, *The Economic Effects of Malaria Eradication* (Ann Arbor: University of Michigan School of Public Health, 1968).

3. For descriptions of parasitic and other common tropical diseases, see G.W. Hunter, W.H. Frye, and J.C. Swarzwelder, *A Manual of Tropical Medicine,* 4th ed. (Philadelphia: W.B. Saunders, 1966).

4. See M. Bohadal, N.E. Gibbs, and W.K. Simmons, "Nutritional Survey and Campaign Against Malnutrition in Kenya, 1964–1968," Report to the Ministry of Health of Kenya on the WHO/FAO/UNICEF–assisted project, mimeographed, n.d.

To the extent that their health is affected by poor diets, rural people are able to devote fewer and less-productive hours to agriculture. In addition, there seems to be a relationship between malnutrition and mental deficiencies, which poses a further constraint to increased productivity.

It is obvious, therefore, that better health facilities and preventative medicine can provide only a partial solution to the rural health problem. Efforts must also be made to improve diet through increasing or altering food crop production. This is desirable, even in many cash crop schemes, where shift from food to cash crops may lower nutritional standards if increased income is not devoted to food purchases.[5] As pointed out in Chapter II, in some cases the introduction of new food crops—which replace traditional subsistence crops—may itself create imbalances in the local diet. The replacement of the more nutritious and drought-resistent cereals like millet and sorghum by maize, noted in Sukumaland in Tanzania, has also been observed in the marginal areas of Kenya by the World Bank's agricultural sector survey. In northeastern Tanzania, surveys have found that the increasing prestige of cabbage over wild spinach has limited vitamin A intake.[6] New cropping patterns may also counterbalance these developments, e.g., increased cereal/legume production can increase the availability of protein, calories, and calcium; greater fruit and vegetable production can augment intake of vitamins A and C. However, research is needed to find locally suited varieties of food crops that are both high yielding and are high in nutritional content.

Another step which could improve local diets is to foster better methods of food storage and preservation. This is important in several respects. Approximately 25 percent of the food produced in Africa is said to be lost through spoilage.[7] If these estimates are correct, better storage techniques may increase rural food intake significantly and perhaps provide a greater marketable surplus. Further, improved methods of preservation can maintain the nutritional value of stored food, prevent food poisoning and other ailments related to the consumption of spoiled food, and help eliminate the off-season hungry months. The technology involved in improved food storage and preservation need not be complicated. The use of raised cribs, protected by rat baffles, can frequently protect stored grain from rodent attack. Sun drying of fruit and vegetables is an inexpensive and widely applicable means of preserving food. Thus, there seems to be a wide scope

5. One study in Kenya found that cash crop farmers are nutritionally no better off than subsistence farmers, at least in the short run. The apparent explanation for this fact is that cash farmers preferred to spend their increased income on conspicuous consumer durables—e.g., bicycles, radios, and on education for their children. Improved diet was given a relatively low priority. It is suggested that educational programs stressing health and nutrition could help to change this situation. For details see R. Korte, "The Nutritional and Health Status of the People Living on the Mwea-Tebere Irrigation Settlement," in *Investigations into Health and Nutrition in East Africa*, eds. H. Kraut and H.D. Cremer, Afrika-Studien no. 42 (Munich: Weltforum Verlag, 1969), pp. 267–334.

6. J. Kreysler and C. Schlage, "The Nutrition Situation in the Pangani Basin," in *Investigations into Health and Nutrition in East Africa*, eds. H. Kraut and H.D. Cremer, Afrika-Studien no. 42 (Munich: Weltforum Verlag, 1969), p. 170.

7. United Nations Economic Commission on Africa, Food and Agriculture Organization of the United Nations, and the Netherlands government, *Report: 5 Workshops for Trainers in Home Economics and Other Family Oriented Fields, Eastern and Southern Africa*, mimeographed, 1973.

through home economics extension to improve the health and welfare of rural people and concurrently to increase the productivity of their labor.[8]

In addition to low labor productivity, low labor availability is also one of the chief constraints to increasing agricultural production. Poor health and lack of health facilities can have a direct effect on labor availability. For instance, residents of the Kenyan squatter settlements have to go to the Trust Land Area if they require medical attention. For the Ngwata squatters this means a trip to Makindu, a place over 25 miles away. The amount of time and scarce cash spent traveling to and from these places is considerable. Further, the number of illness periods reported by householders in the settlements is significantly greater than has been reported in the sixteen control sites. The cost of these periods of illness in the form of reduced labor availability is difficult to quantify but is higher than in other areas.

In view of the substantial effect of ill health on the allocation of time for productive activities as well as for family welfare activities such as child care, it would appear that the provision of a set of fairly simple health and welfare facilities would contribute significantly to the efficiency of time use.

However, caution must be exercised before instituting measures hastily. The provision of water supply is a case in point. It has been noted frequently that, if water supply were within easy reach of homesteads, it would significantly reduce the amount of time spent by women fetching water. However, in order to provide such facilities on an economic basis, a fairly high degree of residential concentration is frequently necessary. Particularly in unproductive areas where extensive farming is practiced, this often necessitates walking long distances to fields. The result may be little or no increase in the amount of labor time available to agriculture. The interrelations between social services and the quality and quantity of labor are, thus, extremely complex; highly variable; and, hence, need to be examined carefully. Where absence of particular social services leads to extreme adverse effect on welfare and, hence, on labor productivity, the allocation of scarce resources to such services can, of course, be justified both on productive and welfare grounds. It is where such adverse welfare and productive effects are not extreme that it becomes difficult to establish economic priorities without a substantial improvement in the knowledge of the relative effect of various services on productivity and welfare.

---

8. From the viewpoint of agricultural production, improvements in home economics can provide additional benefits. More efficient use of domestic labor can result in significant savings in time and energy, which can be transferred to other productive activities. However, far too often the identification of constraints and the interventions introduced are not very relevant to the low-income situations. For instance, an FAO study notes that in a poorly planned home a woman may have to walk more than 180 meters to prepare a pot of porridge. According to the study, rearranging the location of the stove, the food storage area, and so forth can significantly reduce the walking required in housework. The efficiency of such high-income–dominated home economics studies in the case of very small homes, frequently noted in the case of low-income rural households, seems highly questionable. However, there can be more useful, inexpensive, intermediate labor-saving technologies available for home use. For instance, in Zambia the Intermediate Technology Research Station is said to have designed a $1 manual maize huller that can reduce the time for hulling a bag of corn cobs by one-third as well as reducing wear on the hands. For a further discussion of home economics innovations and techniques, see ibid. Also see Chapter II of this study for additional points on the implications of labor-saving technology for labor allocation and productivity.

Discrepancies Between Demand for Social Services and Resource Availability

Establishment of priorities is necessitated, particularly, in view of the substantial demand for social services in many rural areas. Such demand is reflected in the eagerness with which rural people often contribute their labor to construction of schools and clinics. It would appear, therefore, that the allocation of resources to specific services may quite effectively be linked to the additional resources generated for those services. However, despite the widespread evidence of demand for services and for the potential for local resource mobilization, in practice social service programs have often been implemented primarily with central or donor resources and with little regard for utilizing grass root support. Such policies call into question the long-term viability of many social service programs, as is illustrated by the evidence from the projects reviewed.

The problems faced by LLDP management in raising recurrent resources for health services illustrate the point. Provision of health services was not included in the original design of LLDP. Further, it is the declared policy of the Malawi government that improved health remain a low priority in the immediate future. However, because of the very substantial local demand for health clinics, the project management subsequently decided to provide such facilities. Villagers contributed their labor enthusiastically for construction of clinics. However, the management has had to make ad hoc temporary arrangements through missionaries and other voluntary organizations to provide medical personnel. As of mid-1974 the project authority had not received a commitment from the government, either for the allocation of fiscal resources or for the provision of trained manpower to maintain the activities of the health centers. The LLDP example, of course, raises the question as to whether, in initially planning the health services, additional recurrent resources could not have been raised locally, given the substantial local demand and given the substantial allocation of resources to the program area, which has already had a considerable favorable effect on rural incomes.

Social Services Administration, Fiscal Responsibility, Regional Equity, and Self-Reliance

How social services are organized, of course, should have substantial implications for the extent to which resources for their provision can be generated locally. It is, therefore, useful to examine the extent to which the top down and the bottom up strategies of development provide different lessons in the organization of social services. The top down approach is an apt description of the earlier externally financed integrated programs such as LLDP, CADU, and WADU, which were in essence planned and implemented by expatriate staff (see Chapter VIII). In contrast, the bottom up approach is exemplified by the *ujàmaa* movement in Tanzania. It reflects a national political philosophy and emphasizes local participation and decentralization of the indigenous administration (see Chapter IX). Interestingly, both approaches seem to encounter substantially analogous problems in providing social services.

Difficulties related to administration, financing, and regional imbalances encountered in the top down approach are best illustrated by SODENKAM in Cameroon. In order to meet the substantial demand for health services, SODENKAM provided facilities which include six dispensaries; fourteen medical attendants; a hospital; a testing laboratory; and an advanced health center that is administered by a registered chief medical attendant, two assistant medical attendants, and three nurses. Mobile clinics are arranged weekly in those villages that have no permanent clinics. The medical supplies for the clinics are provided through SODENKAM's budget. In the 1971/72 period 110,000 consultations were provided in pioneer villages, although the total population in these areas is only 3,500. Thus, the program area has a dense health service coverage compared with neighboring areas.

However, in SODENKAM, services were organized without identification of local needs and as in LLDP without exploring possibilities of local financing. This explains the emphasis on elaborate clinical procedures rather than on simple preventive measures as well as the substantial amount of financing provided by the project authority. It also highlights the extensive regional imbalances resulting from the program. The intensity of services available to the indigenous population of the Nkondjok *arrondissement* (district), bordering on the SODENKAM settlement areas, is extremely low. The estimated 16,000 inhabitants of the area are served by nine primary school teachers, one state medical attendant, and three dispensary attendants. The comparable figures for SODENKAM are twenty-six to forty teachers and fourteen health workers for a population that is less than a quarter of that of Nkondjok. Not surprisingly, the disparity between the services provided by SODENKAM and those provided for residents of Nkondjok has generated much envy and frustration. A 1968 agricultural survey points out the danger of creating a barrier between the poorly served local population and the pioneer villages, thus providing "an ideal opportunity for what might well develop into serious friction."[9]

It could, perhaps, be argued that the SODENKAM example is somewhat extreme. Nevertheless, it does epitomize very clearly the dangers inherent in a misguidedly elaborate program which, despite it size, fails to meet the real needs of the rural people and which might, in fact, create problems which far outweigh any benefits.

The *ujàmaa* villages in Tanzania illustrate the difficulties which may be encountered in a bottom up administration. In recent years Tanzania's public expenditure devoted to the provision of social service programs has been substantially greater than that devoted to productive activities. According to the information gathered by the World Bank's rural sector survey of Tanzania, education, health, and water programs accounted for about 60 percent of the regional development budget during the 1972/73

9. P. Capot-Rey, D. Audebert, and R. Owerra, *Opération Yabassi-Bafang: Enquête Agricole* (Yaoundé, Cam.: Ministere de l'Agiculture, Direction des Statistiques, May–June 1968), p. 41.

10. The sector survey points to similar trends on a national scale—i.e., including ministerial spending. According to the information gathered, the share of directly productive investment declined from 27 percent of all development expenditures in the 1969/70 period to 13 percent in the 1973/74 period. In the three-year period ending in 1972/73, recurrent expenditures on social services increased more rapidly (11.2 percent per annum) than recurrent expenditures on economic services (7.7 percent per annum). To some extent as a result of this spending pattern, agricultural production appears to be stagnating and perhaps even declining, a question discussed later in Chapter IX of this study.

and 1974/75 periods. In the same period the share of agriculture ranged from 16 percent to 21 percent. These social service–oriented development allocations have led to a similar imbalance in regional recurrent expenditures. Health, education, and water services have absorbed 50–60 percent of the total regional recurrent expenditures during this period, while the share of agriculture has varied from 4 percent to 12 percent. In the 1973/74 period the regional budget accounted for about 22 percent of the public expenditure in Tanzania.[10]

The increased allocations to social service programs seem to have been the result of a need to elicit popular support for *ujàmaa* as well as of the government's ideological commitment to improve overall rural welfare. The recent decentralization of the rural development administration, which has assured that the needs of the poorer farmers will receive priority in the allocation of funds, has reinforced the trend towards increased social service spending. However, despite Tanzania's pronounced support for self-help, there has been little local fiscal participation in this process. Quite to the contrary, local taxing authority has been reduced; and many taxes have been eliminated as colonialist and oppressive. Consequently, funds for local development must come increasingly from the center. Because the government is able to channel resources into the country's poorer areas, it helps to avoid regional imbalances of the type exhibited by SODENKAM's social service program. However, in its emphasis on bringing about a regional balance through social services, Tanzania has basically relied on foreign assistance rather than on mobilizing additional domestic resources. Substantial assistance from bilateral donors, especially the Scandinavian countries, is being accepted without due regard to the recurrent cost implications, which are generally financed nationally. The amount of resources devoted to nonaided development programs has fallen, both in absolute amounts and relative to the total development expenditure. Given the long gestation period and high recurrent cost implications of investment in many social services, emphasis on a massive provision of social service programs seems misplaced, not only from the point of view of its impact on the domestic economy, but also in terms of Tanzania's declared policy of self-reliance.

The costs implicit in social services and the difficulties in generating additional central resources imply that, in rapidly expanding investments in the rural sector, the initial emphasis may frequently have to be restricted to those services which will increase productivity. The provision of the other services, including many social services, may be feasible only when additional local resources can be raised for this purpose. This seems necessary for the following reasons:

1. The rural sector is very large in most African countries.
2. The average income is very low, and with a few exceptions it is relatively equitably distributed in rural areas in Africa.[11]

11. Although the estimates of income distribution are the poorest for Africa, whatever evidence exists shows that, by and large, the distribution of income in Africa is more equitable. See Irma Adelman and Cynthia Taft Morris, "Who Benefits from Economic Development?" International Meeting of Directors of Development Research and Training, Belgrade, August 28–30, 1973. Also see A.M. Kamarck, "The Structure of the African Economies," in *Economic Change and Development: Tropical Africa,* ed. J. Oliver Hall (East Lansing: Michigan State University Press, 1969), pp. 59–80.

3. Consequently, there is not a significant scope for income redistribution as in many countries in Latin America. The low tax base originates in the relatively small commercial agricultural and modern industrial sectors.[12]
4. Finally, the administrative capability and the political will required to mobilize additional resources or to divert existing resources from urban to rural areas is frequently limited.

Under these circumstances the substantial allocation of central resources to social services frequently occurs at the cost of more immediately productive investments in rural areas and, therefore, may prove self-defeating in the long run.

Costs of Social Services

The provision of social services will, of course, not have to be restricted if greater attention is devoted to developing low-cost social service systems that are in line with the generally low resource base. Alternatives do exist which can lower labor costs. For example, the use of "barefoot" doctors and paramedical personnel may result in major savings in the provision of rural health clinics. The use of *harambee* or self-help labor can reduce the costs of developing local water supplies. However, programs organized with local labor to reduce recurrent costs frequently suffer from organizational constraints, thus reducing their effectiveness. The weaknesses in the Kenyan self-help program organized to provide water supply are discussed in Chapter IX. Some social services also involve considerable capital costs and technical input that can be largely inflexible and incapable of significant reduction. For instance, the construction of water facilities often involves large initial outlays for pipes, pumps, and drilling equipment. The recurrent budgetary requirements and, hence, the need for continuous resource mobilization is also limited in the case of such services.

The recurrent expenditure requirements, however, vary substantially among services, as illustrated by the Kenyan estimates for health and education on the one hand and for roads, waterways, and agriculture on the other (Table 7.1). Compared to the Kenyan estimates, Tanzanian data show even larger recurrent shares in the case of health and educational services (Table 7.2). Consequently, although the scope for direct local mobilization of resources varies between types of services, the high recurrent expenditures involved in some services may also create insupportable financial burdens. This is particularly true where large capital outlays have been made to provide physical facilities, such as school buildings or health clinics. It is these complex relationships between the capital and recurrent

12. D. Ghai, "Towards Tax Reform in East Africa," in *Readings on Economic Development and Administration in Tanzania,* ed. H.E. Smith, Institute of Public Administration, University College, Dar es Salaam (London and Nairobi: Oxford University Press, 1966), pp. 195–208; G.K. Helleiner, "The Fiscal Role of the Marketing Boards in Nigerian Economic Development, 1947–1961," in *Economic Journal,* vol. 74, no. 295 (September 1964), pp. 582–605; A. Ogunsheye, "Marketing Boards and Domestic Stabilization in Nigeria," in *Review of Economics and Statistics,* vol. 48, no. 1 (February 1966), pp. 69–78; USAID, Statistics and Reports Division, "Central Government Finances: Kenya," in *AID Economic Data Book for Africa,* revision no. 286 (Washington, D.C.: U.S. Government Printing Office, October 1972); and I. Wallerstein, "The Range of Choice: Constraints on the Policies of Governments of Contemporary African Independent States," in *The State of the Nations: Constraints on Development in Independent Africa,* ed. M.F. Lofchie (Berkeley: University of California Press, 1971), pp. 19–36.

costs of various social services and the associated technical input which determine the scope for provision of inexpensive welfare benefits to the rural people and for mobilizing resources directly for specific services.

Table 7.1: Estimated Development/Recurrent Expenditure Ratios for Public Services,[a] Kenya, 1966-70

Roads	5:1
Waterways	5:1
Agriculture	2:1
Education	1:3
Health	1:3

a. Development expenditures are primarily capital investment.

Source: Government of Kenya, *Development Plan for the Period 1965/66-1969/70* (Nairobi: Government Printers Office, 1966), p. 40.

Table 7.2 Estimated Capital/Recurrent Expenditure Ratios for Education and Health,[a] Tanzania, 1973-80

Year	Education	Health
1973	1:10	1:5
1974	1:8	1:5
1975	1:7	1:6
1976	1:8	1:6
1977	1:8	1:6
1978	1:7	1:6
1979	1:7	1:5
1980	1:7	1:5

a. Based on proposed capital and recurrent expenditures.

Source: Government of Tanzania, *Annual Manpower Report to the President* (Dar es Salaam: Ministry of Economic Affairs and Development Planning, 1971) and working figures of the Ministry of Health.

Implication for Resource Mobilization and Increasing Participation

Social services provide considerable potential for involving, as opposed to merely reaching, rural people. The project reviews suggest that there may be a close relation between the degree of politicization and the willingness and ability of the rural people to articulate their demands for social services. How can policy measures mobilize the maximum potential of local administrative talent and financial resources? At least in some cases, local participation and resource mobilization provide a means of overcoming the problems of the high recurrent costs of many social services. It could be argued, however, that a self-help type of approach might contribute to widening regional disparities, since the more productive areas may be able to generate more resources for social services. If this is the case, encouraging a self-help approach might require some fairly direct policy interventions, particularly in the initial stages, to correct regional disparities, in particular through the allocation resources to generate a productive potential. Experience in Kenya, however, suggests that mobilization of local resources is not necessarily related to income and, indeed, the poorer areas may frequently be more successful in initiating self-help activities.

There have been a large number of spontaneously initiated *harambee* projects in the squatter settlements in Kenya. These schemes have blossomed in Ngwata and the Ngoliba areas where the need for schools and health clinics is urgently felt. In Ngwata in 1973 local self-help projects were attempting to raise KSh180,000 from the area's residents in order to fund both a secondary school and a medical center. Similarly, in the Ngoliba settlements primary schools have been built with volunteer labor.[13] Mbithi and Barnes attribute these remarkable instances of local initiative to the isolation of the area from government services and infrastructure, thus forcing the people to unite in their struggle for maintaining a minimum decent standard of living. While it may not be possible to undertake self-help health or education programs on as massive a scale as the above in less disadvantaged communities, it may, nevertheless, be feasible to attempt to mobilize local resources through fund-raising drives or through the charging of small fees for the service.[14]

In addition to demonstrating the potential for resource mobilization, the Kenyan self-help projects emphasize an additional important point— namely, the need to arrive at the optimum degree of government intervention. Experience in the Tetu district in Kenya—an area with a long history of local initiative—provides much insight into this question. In an evaluation of SRDP, Almy and Mbithi contend that the number of self-help schemes has actually declined subsequent to the introduction of SRDP in 1970. Before 1968 seventy-seven such projects had been started and sixty-five others were added in the next two years. In 1970, however, the number of new projects registered dropped off dramatically to only twenty-two.[15]

Almy and Mbithi attribute this to the rather heavy-handed attempts of SRDP at integrating into the on-going self-help projects. They note: "Self-help in Tetu has been overtaxed by the large number of Harambee projects pushed by aspiring politicians in the last few years ... Poor farmers can only contribute a limited amount to development, but the politicians do not recognize this local problem in their struggle for national recognition. Field workers report that there are in fact a number of new self-help groups forming in these areas, but they are avoiding registration so that their project is not expanded by politicians or administrators beyond what they can afford."[16]

Like SRDP, ZAPI has occasionally pushed peasant organizations to do too much too soon. Although the evidence suggests that such clumsy intervention as that in SRDP or ZAPI is likely to prove self-defeating, projects must also avoid the paternalism evinced by LLDP, SODENKAM, and

13. At one school built in 1970, money from local inhabitants was used even to pay teachers' salaries.

14. As indicated earlier in Chapter V of this study, tontines, or savings clubs, were observed in many of the project areas.

15. S.W. Almy and P. Mbithi, "Local Involvement in the SRDP," in *An Overall Evaluation of the Special Rural Development Programme, 1972,* Institute for Development Studies Occasional Paper no. 8 (Nairobi: University of Nairobi, 1973), Section G, p. 13.

16. Ibid., Section G, pp. 14–15.

ujàmaa. The approach recommended here is to allow the people to delineate for themselves their critical needs and to identify the remedial steps that
the people are willing to take. The programs could then provide the relevant
technical, pedagogical, and other forms of assistance, making it possible to
alleviate pressing social or welfare problems without overburdening the
local resource base.

Implementing this approach will mean taking steps similar to those suggested by Belloncle and Gentil for mobilizing popular participation in extension, as outlined in Chapter IV. Belloncle indicates that there has been
considerable success in Niger in organizing public health programs along
such lines. Health officials begin these programs by sponsoring group meetings at which villagers discuss their medical problems. During the discussions the formally trained medical personnel are made cognizant of the
villagers' explanations of and cures for the most common diseases, for it
seems much easier for the staff to explain Western techniques, once they
have a knowledge of traditional medicine. If the villagers have shown an interest in improving their health, they are asked to choose a volunteer for
training at the nearest dispensary and to collect money to purchase a village
medical kit. The prospective medic is given a brief course in which hygiene,
preventative medicine, and first aid are stressed. The more highly trained
medical personnel working in the area make follow-up visits to check on
the village health worker and to replenish his supplies. The villagers are
asked to repay their medic by helping him with his farm work and by bringing him gifts in kind.

Of the hundred such health workers trained in Marandi province in
Niger in 1971, eighty were actively engaged in their villages. During the first
six months of the year, they received visits from 83,600 patients, or about
half as many patients as were received by the eighteen dispensaries in the
province. Of course, these medics are not able to treat all diseases; but they
can deal with a wide range of common ailments and do have the knowledge
to recognize problems which need professional care.[17]

Similar steps could be taken to organize other social services. Village
women could be organized to identify their key needs in the field of home
economics. One of them could be given brief training and returned to the
village to advise her neighbors. Similarly, farmers could be brought together
to discuss their water supply needs and alternative solutions. Though new
wells may be necessary, it may be possible to delegate one farmer to carry
out the job of distributing the water on a community-wide basis with the
use of a cooperatively owned ox cart. In practice there are a myriad of potential solutions to social service needs. In most cases the appropriate
choice of interventions must depend largely on what the rural people are
willing to do for themselves.[18]

17. See Belloncle, "Total Participation in Public Health Programmes: Some Reflections on
the Niger Experience." One problem encountered with this approach has been resistance on
the part of traditional witch doctors or healers. The problem does not appear insurmountable,
however, since conceivably these traditional practitioners could be brought into such programs. Belloncle also notes success in a similar program for training village midwives.
18. See the related discussion on the education of rural people in Chapter X of this study.

CHAPTER VIII

Forms of Rural Development Administration 1: Autonomous Projects

Issues Related to Project Authorities

Although both Ethiopia and Malawi have low levels of income, they also have a few regions with obviously high development potential. These appeared to offer a good opportunity to make a substantial impact on the levels of living of the low-income rural populations in selected regions. However, even by contemporary African standards, the two countries were endowed with relatively little physical or institutional infrastructure or trained manpower.[1] Therefore, to make a noticeable impact in a short period and to deal with the complementarities in production and to some extent in consumption, substantial simultaneous investment was deemed necessary in a number of activities, including agricultural extension, credit, marketing, roads, soil conservation, training, cooperative development, and water supply.[2] Because the rural administrations in Ethiopia and Malawi have had very limited capacity to absorb and utilize finances at the district and divisional levels (or their equivalents), both countries were ill-equipped to take on large-scale development functions. For example, in Ethiopia the local-level administration had been primarily a tax collection and a law enforcement agency and lacked developmental capacity almost completely.[3] With perhaps a few exceptions, the past Ethiopian leadership had been apathetic towards, if not at odds with, the concept of mass participation in rural development. In these two countries the inadequacy of the existing institutions to administer complex multisectoral programs and the absence of well-articulated national commitments to bring about substantial political and administrative improvements led expatriate planners to

1. See Colin Baker, "The Administrative Service of Malawi—A Case Study in Africanisation," in *Journal of Modern African Studies,* vol. 10, no. 4 (1972), pp. 543–60. Also see chapter on "Education" in American University Foreign Area Studies, *Area Handbook for Ethiopia* (Washington, D.C.: U.S. Government Printing Office, 1971), pp. 185–206.

2. Improved water supply was expected to improve health, increase availability of labor for productive activities by reducing time allocated to fetching water, and to motivate people to participate in the programs. See Chapters II and VII of this study for further discussion of these points.

3. For a discussion of local government in Ethiopia, see John M. Cohen and Peter H. Koehn, "Local Government in Ethiopia: Prospects for Reform in the 1970s," paper presented to the Seventeenth Annual Conference of the African Studies Association, Chicago, October–November 1974.

view the establishment of autonomous project authorities as a logical way of making a noticeable impact and, thus, of exercising a demonstration effect on policymakers, administrators, and, of course, on the rural people.

The relatively little initial emphasis placed on improvement of the indigenous administrative systems in the resulting rural development programs, such as CADU, WADU, and LLDP, is partly a reflection of the lack of indigenous participation in planning and implementation of these programs. Furthermore, Africanization of administration had not been as important an issue in these countries as it has been in Kenya or Tanzania. The Malawian government's strategy did not preclude extensive use of expatriate manpower to maintain administrative efficiency.[4] In Ethiopia, which did not have a colonial history comparable to that of many other African countries, there also was relatively little concern about the use of a substantial number of expatriates in managerial positions at the time the programs were conceived. Establishment of project authorities involving substantial concentration of expatriate staff was, thus, more feasible in Ethiopia and Malawi than it would have been in Kenya or Tanzania.[5]

The project authorities in these rural development programs have carried out functions of several departments (or ministries) and local institutions involving a wide range of activities related to agriculture, transportation, health, community development, credit, and marketing. It must be noted that the new project authorities are, thus, different from the earlier export crop authorities in at least two important respects: (a) they actually or potentially substitute a range of activities that are already the responsibility of the normal governmental structure, and (b) they look to the fulfillment of a broad range of sociopolitical objectives. For these reasons the new project authorities sooner or later face the pressure to integrate with the existing administrative structure.

The first step towards integration is, of course, Africanization of the top-level management of the project authorities. The second step is to pass on the responsibility for the various functions carried out by the project authorities to the appropriate departments of the central government, local governmental institutions, and commercial organizations without significantly jeopardizing the administrative efficiency achieved by the project authorities.

To assess the progress of integrated programs in Africanization and integration, it is necessary to note the characteristics which distinguish project authorities from the normal governmental structure. The managers of the

---

4. The controversial statement of Dr. H. Banda, President of Malawi, regarding Africanization in Malawi quoted below is obviously a contrast with the emphasis on Africanization in Tanzania and Kenya. "I do not want to dismiss any European just because he has a white skin . . . Our African civil servants . . .must be patient, they must be trained, they must become efficient before they can expect me to promote them into the jobs now occupied by the Europeans. I would rather be shot dead . . . than Africanize just to please anyone who wants Africanization." As quoted in Baker, "The Administrative Services of Malawi—A Case Study in Africanisation," p. 557.

5. It must be noted, however, that, despite Kenya's emphasis on Africanization in recent years, as much as 41 percent of the aid to Kenya consisted of technical assistance. In comparison with many other countries, Kenya has been one of the largest recipients of financial and technical assistance on a per capita basis. The effectiveness of such assistance in accelerating the process of Africanization has, however, been questioned. See H. W. Singer and A. C. Doss, "Technical Assistance in Kenya: Some Thoughts on Flows and Programming," in *Eastern Africa Economic Review*, vol. 1, no. 1 (June 1969), pp. 17–27.

projects have the clear responsibility and the necessary authority to coordinate activities and to supervise performance of a number of different departments. Compared to indigenous administrations, the project authorities, of course, benefit from a clearer orientation towards achieving visible and measurable results within a specified time frame and enjoy considerably greater independence. This situation is the result of the greater coincidence in formation and implementation of work programs and a shorter chain of command in autonomous projects. Further, project authorities usually have greater financial resources and considerably more technical and managerial expertise with the potential for providing the indigenous staff with more training, additional administrative incentives, higher salaries, more fringe benefits, and greater job satisfaction.

However, there is an additional characteristic of the integrated programs central to their design and performance. Because there are no easy objective criteria by which to judge such accomplishments as the training of manpower or the development of administrative abilities, investment in these integrated programs tends to be judged primarily by the criterion of an acceptable internal rate of return, calculated on the basis of quantifiable production targets. These targets are derived from standard input–output coefficients for physical inputs, such as fertilizer and seed, and do not explicitly take into account some of the crucial complementarities in realizing production objectives—namely, the supply of trained manpower to administer an input delivery, system, the effectiveness of administrative procedures, or the existence of other physical infrastructure such as roads to facilitate the movement of inputs. Thus, the larger the proportion of expenditure in a given project on these latter types of components, the greater appears to be the need for ambitious production targets to carry the burden of these indirectly productive activities, so that the project can be acceptable in terms of its internal rate of return. This may necessitate setting ambitious production targets in the short run, introducing a contradiction in the project design from the very outset,[6] for such targets may distract the attention of the project authorities from acquiring and training competent indigenous staff, from evolving administrative procedures that will last long past the stage of donor financing, and from developing effective working relations with the normal administrative structure. The greater administrative flexibility and financial resources of the autonomous project authorities and the higher salaries and administrative incentives that they may offer to the local staff may also become a source of annoyance and envy to the indigenous administration. An elitist project administration may develop that is not capable of establishing rapport with the normal administrative structure. These tensions will persist unless the performance and the incentives in the normal governmental administration are improved or unless the autonomous projects lose their special characteristics in the course of integration. Alternatively, or to some extent, concurrently, the tendency of the

6. In LLDP over a third of the expenditure of $1.2 million during the first four years of Phase I was allocated to development of physical infrastructure (capital costs) and $925,000 to staff salaries, manpower training, and so forth. To justify this expenditure along with the expenditure on production inputs, 23,000 farmers had to be reached through inputs (and credit) during the first five years to bring about the necessary targeted increase in agricultural production. It is noteworthy that the number of credit recipients in LLDP increased from 4,000 to 19,000 in one year to keep up with the targets. See Chapter V of this study.

governmental administration may be to avoid making the modification in regulations necessary to improve the administrative environment for the indigenous staff in the project authorities, thus affecting the availability of indigenous trained manpower to project authorities.

In any case, unless there is far-reaching reform of the indigenous rural administration, it seems unlikely that in the long run the objectives of rural development can continue to be realized simply through the establishment of autonomous project authorities. Thus, even if project authorities are to be established as a way of alleviating the constraint of absorptive capacity and of creating a noticeable impact in the short run, there is an important advantage in facing the problem of its integration with the existing government structure at the outset in that it facilitates the necessary adjustments in project design, thus increasing the long-run effectiveness of the project. On the basis of the experience related to project authorities, this chapter points out the need for adjustments in respect to three factors: *(a)* the availability of trained manpower and the steps needed to increase their supply, *(b)* the degree of coordination between various government departments and the effort needed to increase it in the foreseeable future, and *(c)* the overall administrative and institutional performance and the steps necessary to improve it. Without these adjustments and, equally important, without the necessary national commitment to tackle these problems, rural development programs are unlikely to be effective in the long run.

Africanization of Management in Autonomous Projects

Although the importance of indigenous management is recognized and early Africanization is proposed in most donor-aided rural development programs, in practice turning a project over to African management is beset with many difficulties. For example, in the case of LLDP, IDA proposed that a qualified Malawian be appointed to the post of deputy program manager and that other qualified Malawians, who lacked practical experience, spend at least one year as understudies to more experienced officers. The major division chiefs and other senior positions were to have understudies, and a number of supernumerary training posts were to be created for some forty professional and technical positions in the program that were currently filled by expatriates.[7] Because of difficulties in hiring qualified Malawian staff, none of these proposals had been put into effect by October 1973 — i.e., six years after the program had been under way. Only one candidate had proved qualified for a top-level management position; he subsequently transferred to the nearby German-funded Salima project.

WADU in Ethiopia experienced similar difficulties in hiring both expatriate and Ethiopian staff to occupy high-level positions and had particular difficulty in retaining Ethiopian staff. Of the nine expatriate staff posts, only four were filled at the commencement of the project; and, four years

---

7. The Phase I appraisal of LLDP envisaged eighty expatriate positions, though only thirty of these have been filled at any one time. The explanation for the limited use of expatriates appears partly to have been the result of a conscious decision by the project management to use indigenous personnel whenever possible. Also, the project has been unable to find enough foreign manpower to staff the expatriate positions.

after establishment of WADU, none of the expatriate staff posts had been taken over by Ethiopians. Two expatriate staff positions were altogether vacant. By the end of 1972, twelve graduate-level Ethiopian staff (including the deputy project director) had left WADU.

Salaries, Administrative Incentives, and Africanization

Staffing problems appear to be compounded by the terms, conditions, and administrative salary scales that are defined by the public service commissions and applied to nationals. At the current salary levels, there does not appear to be the incentive to take on jobs of considerable responsibility involving the disadvantages of living in remote rural areas. Frequently, the moral commitment of the type noted among some Tanzanians is also lacking among most staff serving in development projects.

The reluctance on the part of the governments to change the rules and regulations applicable to the indigenous staff in project authorities seems to arise from the far-reaching implications of such changes in salary structures for rural administrative staff generally. The close relation of regular government pay and promotion regulations with lack of progress on Africanization of staff is evident in LLDP in Malawi. The project authority must pay salaries according to the government scales. Promotions must be tied to a rigid scale of time served in any given position rather than being based on ability or experience in a given project. Unless he has the requisite number of years at the next lower level, Malawi government statutes also forbid the payment of full salary to an individual who holds a post in an acting capacity. It is not possible to pay two men simultaneously for the same position, however briefly; hence, there can be no overlap between old staff and new and no opportunity for outgoing staff to introduce new staff to either the program or the post they will fill. Statutory regulations also forbid the paying of salaries to staff in training, making it difficult to upgrade staff within LLDP. The project encounters additional problems in staffing due to the complex relations of the project's administrative structure with the normal government administration and the lack of security that this creates for the government staff who might otherwise join the program.

In order to permit flexibility and limit long-term government liability, a dualistic staff structure was created especially for LLDP. This structure consists of two types of posts: established posts, which were permanent and which would continue beyond the life of the program, and nonestablished posts, which were anticipated to last only for the active life of the program. Any officer serving on an established basis cannot resign his post and re-enter government service at a later date, whatever the circumstances of his resignation. As a result, all nonestablished posts are blocked to serving established officers. To compound the problem, the program has experienced difficulty in keeping nonestablished staff once they have been trained, since many are anxious to enter established posts elsewhere in government so as to obtain job security.

WADU's management explains the high turnover of its indigenous staff in terms of similar factors. In WADU the remoteness of the project area is combined with the ability of many of the degree-level staff to find attractive positions elsewhere. Frequently, such positions have prospects for further training and long-term careers. Interviews with Ethiopian staff indicate that

WADU's staffing problems may also have arisen from working conditions that seem unacceptable to the indigenous staff. According to them, WADU had unfair recruitment procedures (different fringe benefits promised for the same-level staff) and an unbalanced salary structure (different beginning salaries offered for staff with similar qualifications). In the view of the persons interviewed, the project also suffered from the incompetence of some of the senior staff (both Ethiopians and expatriates), a lack of disciplined working conditions, and from the deliberate exclusion of some staff when making certain important decisions.[8]

Whether prompted by legitimate or perceived grievances, the dissatisfaction of WADU's staff illustrates the vicious circle created by initial staffing problems; poor working conditions; and inadequate training given to the available indigenous staff and, hence, inadequate incentive for them to remain in project authorities. Because of staffing difficulties, project authorities are generally left with relatively few, if any, African employees in management positions and with a considerable concentration of expatriate manpower at the project headquarters. As pointed out earlier, at the time the review of LLDP was carried out, the project had only one inexperienced Malawian in a managerial position, compared to over thirty expatriates. The minority position of indigenous staff is also not very conducive to a profitable interaction between the expatriate management and the few relatively less trained and less experienced African counterparts. Some of the Ethiopian staff in WADU pointed out that this was also one of the problems in WADU.

Quite understandably, management practices of the project authorities gravitate towards the style of the expatriate expert, to which Africans often find difficulty adjusting. For instance, both LLDP and WADU, like many other agricultural projects in East Africa, suffer from a shortage of well-trained African accountants. This is one of the many reasons why these projects have poor cost records. Such shortcomings could be rectified by instituting a simple cost-accounting system which could be followed by indigenous staff with a reasonable amount of practical training. CADU is one of the few projects reviewed which has managed to introduce such a simple cost-accounting system and teach African staff to implement it.

How does the pace of the projects affect the building of viable managerial systems staffed by African nationals? The projects are frequently geared to meeting ambitious targets. As pointed out in Chapter III, many of these are by necessity based on the poor initial information at the disposal of the preparation teams. Management procedures for the fulfillment of many of the targets are also poorly specified. As is to be expected, many unanticipated problems arise at the stage of implementation. The managerial task in many of the autonomous programs is frequently comparable in complexity to that of a small corporation, involving use of funds from various sources, international procurement of items, and the establishment of effective working relationships with many government structures and with donors. Ad hoc managerial procedures to tackle these various problems evolve based on the individual manager's ability to adapt to the system within the

---

8. The staff made similar complaints to Paulos Abraham, the first Ethiopian director of CADU, and others during their independent evaluation of WADU undertaken for preparation of WADU's Phase II application to IDA. (Based on discussions with Paulos Abraham.)

very severe time constraint under which he operates. Such procedures frequently disappear with the departure of expatriate managers, since the managers often cannot develop a systematic who-will-do-what-when-and-how management organization which can be imparted to African counterparts.

Not all projects, however, have been beset with manpower problems of the magnitude experienced in LLDP and WADU. CADU had a greater task of Africanization with an initial input of forty expatriates, compared to eight in WADU. However, in the first four years, CADU made significant progress in developing Ethiopian management. The number of expatriate staff had declined to twenty-four by 1972 and to eight by 1974.

CADU's progress can be attributed in part to its successful removal of some of the same constraints which LLDP has been unable to tackle. In establishing CADU, provisions were made to employ staff on contract basis with a three-months' notice of termination. This system proved to be effective and had been retained in the Extension and Project Implementation Department (EPID) in the Ministry of Agriculture for all package projects. This worked favorably for CADU in comparison with the procedure employed by the Central Personnel Agency (CPA), which hired all regular government employees. CADU's project director acknowledged that contract employment contributed significantly to the effectiveness of its work program, as it allowed promotions and salary increments to be based on performance rather than on tenure, unlike in other government agencies. CADU also seemed to have gradually gathered highly motivated Ethiopian staff who have had amiable working relations with their expatriate counterparts. The staff attributed this to the meaningful jobs that CADU provided and to the quality of leadership at all levels of the project. In addition, CADU has provided in-service training for many of its staff and sent others abroad for further studies.

Among other programs, which seem to have succeeded in attracting, training, and retaining talented indigenous employees, are the older parastatal organizations such as the Kenya Tea Development Authority and the recently formulated Tanzanian Tobacco Authority, which retains much of the staff trained by the British American Tobacco Company and the Tanganyika Agricultural Corporation. Although the parastatals may have trained their own qualified indigenous staff, the diversion of the best African manpower to parastatals may, however, itself inhibit improvement of the existing government departments. The Kenyan Ministry of Agriculture has experienced repeated staffing difficulties as a result of the drain of skilled employees to KTDA. This drain is likely to continue, since the Ministry has made commitments to provide KTDA with its manpower needs through the 1977/78 period.[9]

Some Contradictions in Africanization of Management

Trained manpower is a scarce factor and, therefore, commands high return in the form of attractive salaries in private or parastatal jobs, city life, fringe benefits, and foreign training. At the same time, the terms and condi-

9. See government of Kenya, *Kenya Tea Development Authority Third Tea Project* (Nairobi: Government Printing Office, 1972), p. 15. KTDA estimates that it will require thirty-nine additional agricultural assistants for its Fourth Plan. This would amount to 11 percent of the graduates of the Embu Institute of Agriculture between 1973 and 1978.

tions dictated by the manpower shortage in recruiting and retaining staff for rural development programs poses the danger of further widening the existing differentials in salaries and leading to increased disparities between the salaried classes and the rural people. Once integrated programs are established, they, therefore, face a difficult dilemma in dealing with the conflicts arising from the realities of the labor market. Both Tecle and Abraham in their independent evaluations of WADU point out that WADU's inadequate salary and fringe benefits have affected its progress towards Ethiopianization. However, Abraham also attributes WADU's inability to establish satisfactory rapport with the Awraja administration largely to the high salaries of the WADU staff and the envy that they invite from the local administration.[10]

When the reviews were carried out, it was too early to judge whether LLDP would encounter difficulties similar to those encountered by WADU (if differences in incentives received by its staff and the staff of the regional agricultural office were maintained) or whether it would lose its best staff (if incentives between the project and the non-project staff were equalized). However, the effect of different working conditions on performance and attitude of LLDP's field staff are already apparent and hint at the problems likely to be encountered in integration with the existing administration.

LLDP has tried to ensure that fieldworkers do not allow their formal training to deteriorate and, moreover, that they learn to translate and apply effectively this training in actual circumstances. There is little doubt that LLDP field staff enjoy working conditions superior to those of the regional staff; this superiority appears to extend as much to the ability, enthusiasm and effectiveness of the senior staff as to the material benefits—good housing, transportation, and so forth—available in the program. Junior staff voiced their strong support for an administration that gets things done and tries to minimize red tape.[11]

Politics, Management, and Africanization

Apart from questions of salary structures and staff incentives, the integration of autonomous projects with normal administration also raises questions of the effect of likely political influences on the long-run performance of rural development programs. To a considerable extent the project authorities are free, once the program planning is completed, from social and political pressures concerning such matters as which areas will receive priority in road construction or in soil conservation measures or which areas will receive credit. However, for the same reason, the job of the expatriate project manager is often made more difficult, compared to his indigenous counterpart, by the fact that the many sociopolitical constraints faced by local administrators are not always easily communicated to an

---

10. Conflicts between WADU and the local government have also been a result of political factors. Local landlords and merchants, who often found WADU's initiatives at odds with their own interests, tended to pressure local officials into opposing the program. See the later discussion in this chapter.

11. For a further discussion of staff incentives in LLDP and other projects, see Chapter IV of this study.

alien project authority. As the manager of LLDP in Malawi indicated, much of the perspective he had acquired on the marketing organization (ADMARC) and the interest group orientation of its management were based on the lessons he had learned from the problems faced by the project vis-à-vis ADMARC and not through an open discussion of issues between the two parties (see Chapter V for further details on the relationship between LLDP and ADMARC).

Even if an alien in a project authority is somewhat more cushioned from administrative pressures than his indigenous counterpart, problems are likely to arise in the post-integration period. Expatriates may underrate the difficulties of establishing linkages between project authorities and the existing government administration and may, therefore, make inadequate efforts to establish effective links. Ethiopians have contended that WADU would probably have established better rapport with the administration of Wolamo Awraja if the top management had been Ethiopian. But, did the problems encountered by WADU's management with the local administration arise because the project management was alien or because the objectives of WADU were at odds with the interests of the local landowners and merchants? They appear to have resulted from a combination of the two. Although Wolamo has had a less staunch feudal structure compared to Chilalo, WADU's settlement activities still led to a considerable protest from the landowners in the region.

The review of the autonomous groundnut operation in Mali comments on some of the additional problems that are likely to arise from political and administrative pressure. The integration of the groundnut operation under the Ministry of Production presents challenges (especially for the future as French expatriates are phased out) in defining the relationship between the operation and the Malian administrative structure. Prior to the establishment of the operation, indigenous agricultural staff were frequently subject to direct interference from officials in the local administration. For example, a circle commandant (roughly the equivalent of a district officer) could request the vehicle of an agricultural officer for a week's trip. The latter had no choice but to comply and, thus, was unable to carry out his own duties in supervision and training of extension agents at the local level.

Holmquist (in his case study of the cattle dip program initiated by the district administration in Kisii district in Kenya) also points out how the inadequate ability of various levels of government to resist counter pressures (administrative and political) lead to very considerable changes in the outcome during the course of implementation, which were not anticipated when the program got under way.[12]

CADU provides by far the most striking illustration of the conflicts arising from sociopolitical pressures exerted by the local power structure and the extent to which they can be resisted by indigenous and alien staff. CADU was one of the first comprehensive rural development programs undertaken by SIDA. CADU involved far more careful planning compared to

12. See Frank W. Holmquist, "Implementing Rural Development Projects," in *Development Administration: The Kenyan Experience,* eds. Goran Hyden, Robert Jackson, and John Okumu (Nairobi: Oxford University Press, 1970), pp. 201–29.

SIDA's earlier efforts in North Africa.[13] The Comilla project in East Pakistan (now Bangladesh) had a considerable influence on CADU's strategy. CADU is often described as the Comilla of Africa. However, in a recent visit to Ethiopia, Akhter Hameed Khan, the founder and former Director of Comilla, pointed out an important difference between the Comilla Project and CADU: while CADU was implemented through a parallel administrative structure, Comilla aimed, among other things, at transforming the Thana police station, the only local governmental institution of any consequence, from a law enforcement agency to a development agency responsible for all the major development activities.[14] According to Khan, the level of institutional development in East Pakistan in the 1950s, when Comilla was conceived, was probably not much superior to that in Ethiopia.[15]

To a considerable extent the noninvolvement of Chilalo's local government in CADU is explained by the opposition of the past landlord-dominated power structure to mass-oriented rural development.[16] Given the little or no direct involvement of nationals, the Swedes, as outsiders, experienced considerable difficulty in establishing close links with the local administration and with the mass of rural people. It is also true, however, that greater national leadership in a rural development program that aimed at tilting the scale in favor of the small farmer would have been unlikely under the political structure that then existed in Ethiopia. Nor should the difficult task of developing local institutions and the time required for it, particularly in a relatively unsympathetic environment, be underrated. The confrontations with landowners encountered by CADU in introducing land leases and credit ceilings or with merchants in introducing standard weights and measures illustrate the strong conflicts of interest that arose concerning the means of rural development. There is a real question as to whether CADU would have had as many accomplishments on its balance sheet, including a considerable increase in agricultural production and a substantial initiative in getting a nationwide development effort under way, if the project had taken on the additional uphill battle of developing local institutions in an alien and unwelcome environment. Thus, the fact remains that,

13. Bengt Nekby, *CADU: An Ethiopian Experiment in Developing Peasant Farming* (Stockholm: Prisma Publishers, 1971).

14. Based on a series of personal discussions with Dr. Khan during Development from Below Workshop organized by the Overseas Liaison Committee of the American Council on Education and Association for the Advancement of Agricultural Sciences in Africa, Addis Ababa, October 12–20, 1973.

15. There are, however, also the interrelated questions frequently raised as to whether the Comilla experiment had been successful in providing transferable lessons for developing the overall developmental administration in the former East Pakistan and as to the extent to which Comilla's success is explained by Dr. Khan's charismatic personality. See Arthur R. Raper et al., *Rural Development in Action: The Comprehensive Experiment at Comilla, East Pakistan* (Ithaca, N.Y.: Cornell University Press, 1970). Also see the review of the above book by Harvey M. Choldin, in *Economic Development and Cultural Change,* vol. 20, no. 3 (April 1972), pp. 594–601.

16. Cohen argues, however, that the previous central government's attitude towards rural development has also been a major constraint on CADU's success. He points out that, while the central authorities supported the basic goal of rural development, they had been opposed to the local political changes that this implied. Consequently, in Cohen's view, they did not offer the national commitment necessary to ensure the realization of CADU's objectives and, in fact, may have lent their prestige to tactics that were incompatible with CADU's ultimate success. See Cohen, "Rural Change in Ethiopia: The Chilalo Agricultural Development Unit," in *Economic Development and Cultural Change,* vol. 22, no. 4 (July 1974), pp. 608–10.

despite CADU's achievements on other scores and despite its considerable effort at the time the review was conducted, it had not yet had a significant success in augmenting the indigenous administrative capacity in Chilalo or in developing viable grass root institutions.[17]

Compared to that of the Swedes, the Ethiopian management of CADU was, of course, more open to sociopolitical pressures, particularly those generated by local vested interests. To some extent the departure of CADU's first Ethiopian manager is explained by the demoralization that resistance to such local pressure prompted.

But then how useful are the short-run achievements when in the long run the projects will be run by nationals who are more subject to domestic sociopolitical considerations? To what extent does national commitment affect the realization of the participatory and productive objectives of the projects subsequent to national takeover? To what extent can the two objectives be reconciled without substantial emphasis on development of an effective, indigenous administration? A comparison of the Tanzanian and Kenyan parastatals with the Ethiopian experience is instructive in this regard.

In 1963 the Urambo Tobacco Scheme in Tanzania was taken over by the Tanganyika Agricultural Corporation from the Village Settlement Commission (VSC). TAC was directly responsible to the Prime Minister's office.[18] The tobacco scheme in Tumbi, however, remained with BAT, a commercial organization geared to meet export demand. The yield differences between Urambo and Tumbi and the absolute decline in tobacco yields in Urambo subsequent to 1964 (see Chapter IV) seem to be explained at least partially by the adverse effect of the takeover on Urambo's management. Though much of the staff of VSC was retained in the transfer, many of the decisions regarding project implementation were no longer made in Urambo but in Dar es Salaam. Less stringent criteria were used in the selection of tobacco farmers in Urambo, compared to Urambo's earlier criteria or compared to those of BAT. In contrast, BAT continued to use only trained and experienced farmers and weeded out those who did not perform well. Even after the Tabora Tobacco Growers Cooperative Society was registered in 1964, BAT remained largely in charge of management of the Tumbi scheme, while the company gradually trained the cooperative staff. Complete responsibility for the Tumbi scheme went to the cooperative staff only in 1969. In the BAT scheme there has also been stricter discipline enforced in repayment of credit than has been possible in the Urambo cooperative.

17. Nekby, the first director of CADU, has argued that more significant changes had begun to occur in the recent period. For instance, the appointment in 1974 of Ato Tesfa Bushen, then the Minister of State for Agriculture, as Governor-General of Arussi province, along with advancements in cooperative organization were beginning to lead to an integration of CADU with the administration that existed in Chilalo at the time. In Nekby's view this indicated that autonomous, foreign-inspired projects can lead to viable rural development. Hunter in his assessment of CADU has argued, however, that the program's policy was not to develop local institutions but to bypass them altogether. In his view the program's paternalism towards indigenous organizations has been its major shortcoming. This difference in perception is another example which points to the need for specification of more assessable criteria by which to judge institutional achievements, since they are so crucial for the realization of rural development objectives.

18. In 1965 VSC was dissolved and replaced by the Village Settlement Division (VSD) of the Ministry of Lands, Settlements and Water Development.

Observers of KTDA in Kenya attribute KTDA's administrative effectiveness and productive efficiency to similar strict discipline and little political interference in management. By the 1971/72 period KTDA had reached 66,500 smallholders. Since KTDA caters to small farmers—their average tea plot is about 0.4 hectares—it would appear to have been highly effective in realizing the objective of broad participation in growth. However, the very discipline imposed on farmers—for example KTDA's emphasis on not providing credit for tea seedlings (so as to include only the motivated farmers and to foster mobilization of local savings)—seems to have excluded some of the poorest farmers from growing tea. Often they have neither the credit nor the financial ability to divert the best part of their small plot to tea cultivation or to bear the gestation lag in returns from tea.

When the resource constraints are different between farmers, obviously there are some conflicts in growth and participation, particularly when the trained manpower available for devising alternative strategies is limited. An effective solution to these conflicts requires monitoring performance of programs from the point of view of participation and developing appropriate strategies over time so as to broaden the distribution of benefits. Instead of following such a systematic, sequential approach to participation, the tendency of an indigenous administration may often be either to neglect participation altogether, as has been the case in Ethiopia until recently, or to adopt a strategy participatory in style rather than in substance. The decline in tobacco production in Tabora, Tanzania, subsequent to IDA financing in 1970 illustrates the latter case. The decline was prompted by the commencement of a policy to move smallholder tobacco farmers into *ujàmaa* villages and to collectivize tobacco cultivation. The government faced considerable resistance to villagization and collectivization from tobacco farmers, adversely affecting tobacco production as well as the distribution of benefits. As a result, the administrators had begun to show flexibility in the extent of collectivization and the rate at which it will be introduced.[19]

Direction and Coordination in the Transfer of Functions to the Regular Administration

Transfer of the functions of the autonomous project authorities to the regular administration raises questions, not only of the possible conflicts between sociopolitical and economic objectives, but also about the logistics of the effective transfer of functions to ensure a high level of administrative performance. These questions are of particular importance because, unlike project authorities administered by expatriates which turn towards the center of power in the capital city, it is the improvement of the lower levels of government administration and other institutions that is critical for the long-run performance of the programs.

To the extent that project authorities undertake functions which the existing administration is ill-suited or ill-prepared to carry out, transfer may involve at least a temporary, adverse effect on the performance of the project. If adequate attention is not given to bridging the gap between the project authority and the existing governmental structure at an early stage, the project's performance may be significantly affected in the long run.

19. See Chapter IX of this study.

Integration involves administrative choices and improvements at several levels. First, there are the considerations related to overall direction and coordination, an important feature of the project authority. Second, there are questions related to the transfer of individual components carried out by the project. Some components—such as roads, soil conservation, boreholes, community development, health clinics, housing, and training—involve transfer of responsibility to the regional or local government administration. Others (as, for instance, input and output marketing as well as credit distribution) involve transfer of responsibility of a commercial nature. Third, there are questions related to local participation and integration of the local committee structure created by the project with the existing local government administration.

LLDP in Malawi is at such a transitional stage where the gaps between its accomplishments and the existing rural administrative capability in the region are substantial. In Lilongwe difficult problems of overall direction and coordination arise because the administrative units of the regular government structure—namely, regional and district administrations and agricultural divisions—do not correspond to the units and sectors of the project.[20] Though this has perhaps given the project a measure of freedom from entrenched bureaucratic groups, it has also raised such elementary questions as *(a)* which levels of administrative units in the Ministry of Agriculture should be strengthened to perform which specific functions of policy and field administration coordination, and *(b)* the more difficult questions of how to implement these changes in administrative responsibility. Traditionally, the region and the district have been the administrative units coordinating a number of technical and social service departments. Therefore, the headquarters of the district administration are also usually located in the same town as the headquarters of the district councils. The district, therefore, has several advantages in coordinating interdepartmental functions. In contrast, divisions, which are larger administrative units than the districts, have traditionally been the center of agricultural activities. Since agriculture constitutes the backbone of LLDP, divisions are the more appropriate coordinating point to reinforce staffing for improved planning and implementation of the agricultural activities. However, coordination of the project activities involves the resolution of policies as well as the administration of field staff. Under the present administrative setup, the policy formulation could best be done at the regional level.

In transferring individual components, many other problems arise. For example, coordination between the Ministries of Agriculture and Public Works is necessary during road construction. The maintenance of roads, on the other hand, has to be transferred to the appropriate body (i.e., the upkeep of major thoroughfares must be made the responsibility of the Ministry of Public Works, while district and local roads should be transferred to the district and village councils). These transfers require strengthening the appropriate units with manpower and financial resources so that they may perform their functions satisfactorily. Health clinics, of course, involve coordination between district and village councils, the health ministry, and—if they involve any self-help—the Ministry of Community Develop-

20. In LLDP the unit is the basic administrative unit and is smaller than the agricultural divisions. It is viewed as a potential growth center consisting of forty to fifty villages.

ment. The same applies to women's extension which involves health, nutrition, child care, and so forth. Which of these various ministries or departments should be assigned to pay staff salaries, supervise field administration, or perform the central coordinating function are less important issues which need to be resolved.

The transfer of commercial services is equally important. In Malawi the Agricultural Development and Marketing Corporation is responsible for input delivery and output marketing. However, as discussed in Chapter VI, the performance of ADMARC seems to have been less than satisfactory. The extent to which ADMARC will take over the major responsibility of ensuring the continued expansion of LLDP's delivery systems remains to be seen.

Administration of credit after LLDP phases out is even more difficult. This is not only for the various reasons discussed earlier in Chapter V but also because, at present, there is no logical administrative organization that can take over the credit function. A more diversified and low-cost approach to provision of inputs and credit (i.e., an approach which develops local commercial institutions and involves group sales, commercial credit, private trading channels, and personal savings) still remains largely unexplored. Organization of medium-term credit for purchase of capital goods will also need attention as investment demand increases.

The role of the various committees created under the project authority and of their relationship with the more traditional district councils raises a different set of questions. The village-level committees are meant to be participatory bodies. Their purpose is to provide a forum for communicating new ideas, for identifying the needs and aspirations of the rural people, and for fostering self-help efforts. But, as pointed out in Chapter V, these committees have at times been used for recovery of loans which promotes dissension between local groups. Guy Hunter, in his assessment of LLDP's administrative structure, therefore recommended that as far as possible local committees should not be used to serve objectives other than those for which they were formulated.[21] The status of the higher level consultative committees vis-à-vis the district councils in planning, implementation, and maintenance of activities is also unclear at this stage. This is partly because LLDP's administrative units do not correspond with the regular local government institutions. For example, there is no governmental equivalent to the project's unit centers which would constitute the growth nuclei. However, even more important, the role of the local leadership and its relation to the political party or other authority that may be assigned to the various project and non-project committees for mobilization and allocation of resources remains to be specified.

Concluding Statement

The problems faced by parallel administrative structures are many and are admittedly complex. They include the hiring and training of national staff; establishing rapport with the indigenous institutions to improve effectiveness of administration; and, finally, the task of integration with the

---

21. Based on discussions with Hunter.

regular governmental administration without jeopardizing the performance of the project. As has been pointed out in this chapter, without the resolution of many of these problems, the gap between the initial promise of the integrated programs and their long-term performance can be substantial, despite the considerable initial capital and trained manpower input that they involve. Realizing the full potential of donor-aided programs must mean not only short-term production increases but also the development of effective rural administration and the concurrent training of indigenous manpower. To this end, far greater national involvement in planning and implementation of rural development programs is necessary than was possible in the autonomous projects reviewed under ARDS. However, if participation of nationals is to be meaningful in the long run and if programs are to benefit from knowledge of local needs and local constraints, it is also essential that rural people and local-level officials, who possess such knowledge, play a major role in planning and implementing rural development programs. The improvement of administrative capacity and technical competence at the regional and lower levels is necessary to ensure that sociopolitical considerations do not become the exclusive criteria for the allocation of development resources. In the following chapter the alternative of self-generated, internal improvement of existing administrations is discussed.

CHAPTER IX

Forms of Rural Development Administration 2: Nationally Planned Programs

Objectives of national administrations tend to be broader than those of project authorities. In addition to increasing production and incomes, national administrations may use rural development programs as a vehicle to broaden political participation, reinforce political patronage, or realize ideological objectives. These multiple and, at times, conflicting objectives have often rendered overall rural development strategy inconsistent and sometimes even self-defeating. Government planners, therefore, have the difficult job of reconciling the needs for growth as well as for broadening participation and of finding a coherent rural development strategy which is politically feasible and economically sound and can be implemented administratively.

Such planning is by no means easy to realize. Priorities have to be set with regard to an appropriate production mix (i.e., between cropping combinations, livestock activities, and small industrial enterprises) and with regard to an appropriate activity mix (i.e., a balance between productive and social services). The production mix must take into account the technical constraints outlined in Chapters II and III which vary widely from area to area. The activity mix must also be highly area specific and must depend upon the existing availability of productive facilities and upon the need and support for social services. Yet while the sheer complexity and diversity of local socioeconomic systems necessitate individually tailored development programs, this same complexity and diversity require considerable coordination between the many departments and agencies usually responsible for rural development. National planning, thus, has to reconcile two apparently conflicting but basically interdependent goals: *(a)* the need for decentralization to take into account local potential and constraints and to channel the knowledge and energies of millions of rural people into the development process; and *(b)* the need for central control to foster national integration, regional specialization, and outside stimulus.

In the past, national administrations have rarely been able to strike a proper balance between these twin goals. Centralized control of the rural development planning process has tended to predominate, often leading to what Chambers has called "planning without implementation."[1] The tendency has been to draw up broad sectoral plans that are little more than shopping lists and may bear little relation to local resource endowments. Because of this planning vacuum, there has frequently been "implementation without planning,"[2] i.e., self-help groups or activist administrators channeling resources into local programs that are at times in conflict with national objectives.

What explains such uncoordinated planning? To some extent the centrist tendency has been necessitated by the shortage of administrative capacity in many African countries. The limited trained manpower has led to a concentration of expertise at the center, inevitably weakening the capacity at the local level. Central control of the administration has often also been a result of the narrow political base of many of the governments and the corresponding lack of national identity among large segments of the population. Frequently, these tendencies towards centralized administration have, of course, been reinforced by inadequate appreciation of the need for area-based planning.

This chapter analyzes the performance of the planning and implementation of the Special Rural Development Program (SRDP) in Kenya and of the *ujàmaa* movement in Tanzania. It discusses the efforts being made in these two countries to improve planning and implementing capacity, the nature of the problems encountered in increased national participation in planning and implementation, and the possible ways in which some of these problems could be dealt with in future rural development programs. The purpose of the discussion is to raise three questions:

1. To what extent have the existing administrative structures been able to carry out the development task effectively?
2. To the extent that there are deficiencies, how can these administrative structures be made more innovative and effective in initiating and administering the growing number of rural development programs?
3. How can rural development programs help improve administrative capacity?

The Special Rural Development Program in Kenya

Until recently, the administration of rural development programs in Kenya has been highly centralized. This has resulted in several problems in the design and implementation of various specific projects. First, the hierarchical structure of the various ministries involved in rural development has resulted in most decisions having been made in Nairobi and

1. Robert Chambers, "Planning for Rural Areas in East Africa: Experience and Prescriptions," in *Rural Administration in Kenya,* ed. David K. Leonard (Nairobi: East African Literature Bureau, 1973), pp. 15–18.
2. Ibid., pp. 18–19. For an interesting example of implementation without planning, see the discussion of the Kisii cattle dip program in Frank W. Holmquist, "Implementing Rural Development Projects," in *Development Administration: The Kenyan Experience,* eds. Goran Hyden, Robert Jackson, and John Okumu (Nairobi: Oxford University Press, 1970), pp. 201–32.

passed down to the field staff. As a result, much of the rural development planning has been based on inadequate knowledge of local constraints. Second, different programs have been the responsibility of different agencies. Given the generally inadequate interministerial coordination, many services have been duplicated while others have been completely omitted.[3] Third, while there has been general agreement that the government should pursue the course of African socialism, i.e., the "participation of all people in the task of nation building as well as in the enjoyment of the fruits of progress,"[4] the specific means for achieving these goals have often been poorly articulated.

Because no simple, clear-cut solutions existed to the problems outlined above, a conference was held in Kericho in 1966 on the interrelated issues of education, employment, and rural development. As an outgrowth of the proposals made at the much-debated Kericho conference, the government initiated the Special Rural Development Program to increase interministerial cooperation and to bring about more realistic divisional planning. As originally conceived in 1967, SRDP was to involve a number of comprehensive pilot programs which would pull together all aspects of rural development within a coordinated strategy. These programs were to be specific, concrete, and based upon detailed baseline surveys of the divisions involved. The decision-making locus was to be shifted away from the center. The special nature of SRDP lay in its capacity for testing the effect on rural development of various additional efforts over and above extant programs and policies.[5] Since all of SRDP's programs were also to be undertaken with a view to their replicability elsewhere in Kenya, they were to be handled through the existing government machinery and with only minimal additional resources. While donors would be invited to participate, it was intended that they would form a consortium from which the program would allocate funds for the various divisional projects.

As SRDP developed, it departed from its initial objectives. However, its accomplishments and shortcomings provide useful insights into the process of program planning and implementation and into the role of communication and coordination *(a)* between various ministries, *(b)* between the civil servants and researchers involved in planning, *(c)* between the central and the local-level bureaucracy, *(d)* between the bureaucracy and the rural people, and *(e)* between national administrators and donors.

3. Hyden notes the proliferation of specialized civil service ministries in Kenya (there were twenty in 1969) and the consequent problem of interministerial coordination. The proliferation of ministries is partly a result of a need to patronize large numbers of supporters in a politically heterogeneous society. See Goran Hyden, "Basic Civil Service Characteristics," in *Development Administration: The Kenyan Experience,* eds. Goran Hyden, Robert Jackson, and John Okumu (Nairobi: Oxford University Press, 1970), pp. 3–25.

4. Government of Kenya, *African Socialism and Its Application to Planning in Kenya,* Sessional Paper no. 10 (Nairobi: Government Printers Office, 1965).

5. According to a statement approved by the National Rural Development Committee on January 23, 1970, the purpose of SRDP was "*(a)* to increase rural income and employment opportunities and *(b)* to establish procedures and techniques for acceleration and self-generating rural development programs which can be repeated in other similar areas and, in particular, to improve the developmental capacity of Kenyan government officials in the field." It is this latter purpose which has made SRDP unique. As the IDS study of SRDP concludes, it is "a truly remarkable and innovative program because it seeks to build the functions of Research and Development into the government machinery for rural development." Institute for Development Studies, *An Overall Evaluation of the Special Rural Development Programme, 1972,* Occasional Paper no. 8 (Nairobi: University of Nairobi, 1973), p. xii.

Administrative Structure of SRDP

Overall responsibility for the program was held by the Ministry of Finance and Economic Planning (MFEP). In order to coordinate the program at the top, the National Rural Development Committee (NRDC) was organized in 1969. This committee was made up of the secretaries of MFEP, the Ministry of Agriculture, the Treasury, and the other ministries involved in rural development. Interdepartmental cooperation was to be facilitated by the establishment of a system of linkmen in the various ministries. When problems of coordination between ministries arose, the appropriate linkman—usually a senior officer in his ministry—was to be contacted and a decision worked out. The coordination of activities within the specific project area was the responsibility of the area coordinator, who was also an administrative officer in the provincial administration. In addition, the area coordinator was to serve as a communication link between the divisional, district, and provincial administrations. In order to provide input from local people, the District Development Committees (DDC) and the Provincial Development Committees (PDC) were brought into the decision-making process.

NRDC laid down very specific procedures for the preparation of SRDP programs. First, a provincial planning officer (PPO) was to conduct a survey of the proposed project area to discover local constraints and potentials. Based on this data, the PPO, in consultation with the district heads of technical departments, was to draw up a general project strategy. These plans were then to be forwarded to NRDC, where they would be evaluated with assistance from the concerned ministries. Approved plans would be returned to the PPO for clearance with DDC and PDC. After clearance had been received, detailed plans were to be drawn up and forwarded to NRDC. The committee in turn would secure the necessary approval from the departmental headquarters. Only when this process was successfully completed would implementation begin—the sequencing and phasing of which were largely the responsiblity of the area coordinator.

Coordination Between Ministries

The objective in establishing NRDC was largely to bring sufficient prestige and attention to SRDP so as to facilitate the interministerial cooperation vital to the program's success. Such cooperation was not easy to achieve. While MFEP was generally supportive of SRDP, both the Treasury and the Ministry of Agriculture were ambivalent towards the program. NRDC lacked adequate staff and authority to resolve these tensions quickly. Thus, despite substantial prodding, NRDC found it difficult to convince the Treasury either of the novelty of SRDP's content or of the validity of its purpose.[6] Consequently, the Treasury blocked the release of funds for the program in June 1970, despite the fact that the program had been discussed for three years at the national level and had been announced publicly. It became readily apparent that further delays in implementation might jeopardize the entire effort. The urge to press on led NRDC to abandon its earlier position of seeking external assistance towards a central consortium in favor of allowing donors to fund specific geographic units. The

6. See J. R. Nellis, "The Administration of Rural Development in Kenya," in *East Africa Journal*, vol. 9, no. 3 (March 1972), pp. 10–17.

Norwegian Agency for International Development (NORAD) had been interested in backing SRDP in the Mbere district and received the green light from NRDC. FAO, SIDA, USAID, and other agencies were permitted to fund SRDP in other districts.

While it enabled the program to get under way, this form of funding compromised SRDP's original goals of experimentation and replicability. Some of the donors demanded replanning of the individual projects as a precondition of their support.[7] In addition, the donors offered technical as well as financial assistance, which raised more questions about the programs' replicability.

It was only in January 1971, after the Treasury had been amalgamated with the Ministry of Economic Planning, that the government finally released funds for SRDP. By this time, however, the external agencies were heavily involved in specific projects.

Other problems have occurred with the linkman system in the various ministries, largely because ministry staff has tended to be skeptical of SRDP. Many of the linkmen have had only nominal functions and have often lacked experience and the authority within their respective ministries necessary to acquire resource commitments to the program. Nevertheless, progress has been made in smoothing interministerial coordination. A personalized network has developed among the various linkmen, NRDC, and the area coordinators. This has helped circumvent the bureaucratic hierarchy and overcome delays. In addition, SRDP has developed a reporting system to close the gap between project planning and implementation.

Coordination Between Civil Servants and Researchers

In order to prepare SRDP plans, extensive baseline surveys were carried out in the target districts by researchers of IDS in Nairobi.[8] SRDP surveys were useful for understanding the characteristics of the regions studied and for pointing out that major economic breakthroughs of a technological miracle variety could not be expected and that the problems in rural development could be solved only by slow, steady, incremental change on a broad front.[9]

The planning, however, suffered from considerable delays. While members of IDS were insistent about the minimum data needs for planning, administrators in Nairobi became impatient that nothing useful was resulting from the surveys. The division of responsibility between the civil servants and researchers in the formation of strategy, as distinct from the conduct of baseline surveys, remained unclearly specified. As a result, the bureaucrats

7. For example, subsequent to its involvement, USAID replanned the program in the Vihiga district. According to IDS's evaluation, under American prodding the program was focused on the promotion of a single product—hybrid maize. Though an original objective of the program had been to involve all classes of farmers, the American-designed maize credit package was made available only to those farmers cultivating between 0.81 and 1.62 hectares of maize. Moreover, this particular crop is unlikely to be suitable for poorer and less skilled farmers. The IDS evaluation of the Vihiga program concluded that it had "lost most of its experimental content..." and had become a straightforward development project. See *An Overall Evaluation of the Special Rural Development Programme, 1972,* Section F, p. 16.

8. J. Heyer, D. Ireri, and J. Moris, *Rural Development in Kenya* (Nairobi: East African Publishing House, 1971). Although the surveys were conducted in fourteen districts which were initially selected, only six districts had programs under way in 1971.

9. Ibid.

felt that there was no emphasis on setting priorities, while the researchers, being cognizant of variability, emphasized principles of planning rather than specifying the content of individual plans.

SRDP's planning experience, nevertheless, emphasizes the need for: *(a)* a clear specification of objectives of the surveys; *(b)* the identification of critical data needs; *(c)* to the extent possible, the standardization of survey techniques; *(d)* a realistic assessment, in light of stated objectives, of the time required for conducting baseline surveys; and *(e)* a clear specification of responsibility for information gathering as distinct from that for setting priorities.

Coordination Between Central and Local Bureaucracy

SRDP illustrates the need for an adequately long-term horizon in bringing about the meaningful participation of district and local administrators in planning.

Planning of SRDP suffered from lack of such a long-term perspective and adequate forward planning. Steps necessary to correct the inadequacy of the planning capacity at the local administrative level were not taken. In addition, the precise procedures for the actual planning responsibility between the provincial planning officers (PPO) and the district and local officers and the criteria for setting priorities were ill defined. Thus, although PPOs were expected to serve as catalysts, provoking and drawing together the ideas put forward by the district officers, in absence of guidelines the districts provided only long shopping lists.[10] The idea of training district officers for producing better plans and the delays that might result because of time taken to train them seemed intolerable to the central authorities in Nairobi. Finally, plans for Vihiga and Kwale were produced only after prodding of local officials by a squad of central ministerial staff. As pointed out earlier, these plans were changed substantially in the course of implementation as donors stepped in. Among the plans the Tetu extension training program, involving heavy participation of IDS staff in planning, has shown a great deal of imagination and potential for replicability. The program is discussed in Chapter X.

The temporary staff provided by the donors, unlike some of the IDS staff, was often unable to provide such on-the-job instruction in planning as distinct from simply carrying out planning and implementation. Creating local planning and implementing capacity, therefore, takes much longer than if more experienced staff were available under technical assistance.

Coordination Between the Bureaucracy and Rural People

Local people in some SRDP areas have been neither consulted during program planning nor informed in advance of program implementation.[11] The District Development Committee had been intended to serve a major role in providing local input during the planning of various SRDP projects. However, as the IDS staff noted, DDC has generally been relegated to a subordinate position in planning, merely approving project design

10. Guy Hunter has pointed out to the author that the PPOs were generally inexperienced and lacked influence within the Ministry of Agriculture.
11. See Chapter X of this study for further details on local involvement in SRDP.

rather than actively participating in the design process itself.[12] In addition, they observed that DDCs frequently do not involve the local community but serve more as a forum for government officials and local politicians.[13]

In the Migori district some steps have been taken towards correcting this situation through the development of a local project advisory committee. Established mainly at the initiative of the local area coordinator, this committee includes the district officer, extension staff, as well as elected farmers. It has been developing most of the SRDP proposals for the project area.[14]

Local participation in project implementation has largely involved a few self-help schemes, such as the construction of roads, cattle dips, and water projects. However, even in these cases many bottlenecks have been encountered. For example, in the Mbere district the SRDP's Cotton Block Scheme called for the construction of an 88-kilometer water pipe. The plan originally assumed that the digging of the pipe trenches could be done by *harambee* labor. However, because the pipe installation was a long-range project without immediate benefits, it was feared that any initial popular support for the pipe would soon wane. In addition, the pipe leads from a relatively well-watered area to a drier one, so enthusiasm was greater at the far end. Consequently, the project was started with contract labor. The work went quickly, and 6.5 kilometers were dug within three weeks. Because of its high cost, however, contract labor was abandoned shortly thereafter; and efforts were made to use the self-help labor originally planned. Subsequent performance on the trench was poor—only 560 meters were dug over the next two months. Whatever the initial *harambee* support for the project might have been, an attempt to get people to work without pay on a job which they had previously been paid for was bound to run into difficulty. Clearly, if the local people had been consulted more carefully during the planning stage, these problems in sequencing could have been dealt with more effectively.[15]

Coordination Between National Administrations and Donors

With respect to the role of the expatriates and the donors in SRDP, it has been frequently observed that, had there been a greater Kenyan content to SRDP from the outset with experienced Kenyans of high rank and prestige stimulating the effort, much of the delay in planning could have been avoided.[16] For although the expatriates were technically qualified, they simply did not have the authority or the position to elicit the action re-

12. *An Overall Evaluation of the Special Rural Development Programme, 1972*, p. 39.

13. Ibid., p. 50

14. Ibid., p. 39. Oyugi, however, is highly critical of the Migori SRDP. He quotes one SRDP staff member as telling local people at a *baraza* (meeting) that, "There is a plan being drawn up for this area. As soon as it is out, we will let you know what you are expected to do." The make-up of the local advisory committee is determined by the district commissioner and the DDC. According to Oyugi, this committee does not meet regularly, and what meetings do take place tend to be poorly attended. See W. O. Oyugi, "Participation in Planning at the Local Level," in *Rural Administration in Kenya,* ed. David K. Leonard (Nairobi: East African Literature Bureau, 1973), pp. 59–66.

15. See ibid., Section C, pp. 41–43.

16. See J. R. Nellis, "The Administration of Rural Development in Kenya." The IDS group has made a recommendation that a Kenyan be appointed to the post of the deputy secretary rank. See *An Overall Evaluation of the Special Rural Development Programme, 1972.*

quired by the Kenyan bureaucracy. This was particularly apparent during the funding stage when excessive delays occurred due to different expectations of the Treasury and the districts about the nature of specification of the plans and, in fact, about the very objectives of SRDP.

The fate of the Master Farmers Scheme in Migori district is a prime example of a communication breakdown between donor agencies and national administrations. This scheme was largely the brainchild of the FAO/SIDA team leader assigned to Migori, though it was worked out in close conjunction with local agricultural assistants. The team leader remained in contact with the responsible officers at the Ministry of Agriculture as well. According to IDS's evaluation, the team leader's plans received preliminary approval. However, three months after he had submitted his final proposals, the Ministry rejected the scheme. This not only embittered the team leader but also necessitated replanning and delays in the implementation of a development program for the project area.[17] One of the individuals in the Ministry responsible for rejection of the plan has argued, however, that there were bona fide administrative reasons for the decision. Whatever the precise reasons behind the Ministry of Agriculture's action, the problems encountered by the FAO/SIDA team leader are indicative of the lack of intra-ministerial communications frequently noted in LDCs.

The Future of Decentralized Planning in Kenya

As much of the preceding discussion indicates, SRDP has been handicapped by its somewhat ambivalent nature. On the one hand, it was expected to serve a pilot function of finding transferable solutions for planning and implementing rural development projects. On the other hand, it has been expected to be successful in the traditional sense of increasing visible benefits. In the short run these two objectives not always been compatible.

The Kenyan government is proceeding with plans to expand the district planning capacity. Currently, planning primarily involves the disaggregation of the centrally devised national budget. Each district has an individual plan identifying the area's projects and expenditures. Planning at the district level is, thus, confined to the identification of new needs and of unforeseen gaps in the plans. It does not extend to setting an overall district strategy. A district development fund is presently in operation to take care of some of these contingencies, but its use is restricted to projects which do not require recurrent funding. The extent to which SRDP has provided lessons and guidelines for this effort is an open question. However, given the problems which SRDP has encountered, it would be unrealistic to expect that the nationwide administrative decentralization of planning and implementation of rural development will have a noticeable impact in the immediate future. Indeed, the disappointment of many observers of SRDP stems not so much from the deficiencies of the program itself as it does from the fact that similar shortcomings are not being tackled in the district planning exercise.

The various administrative reforms being undertaken in Kenya may aptly be described as deconcentration of administration in which the center

17. Ibid., Section D, pp. 6–8.

of administrative authority is being shifted from Nairobi to the representatives of the technical ministries in the provinces or districts. For instance, in 1969 the Ministry of Agriculture was reorganized to grant wider discretion to field officers. However, according to the observers of the decentralization effort, such delegation of authority to lower-level administrators has not resulted in changes in basic policy or value orientation.[18] Nor have these reforms meant a transfer of decision-making power from the civil service to elected officials. Under Kenya's 1970–74 National Plan, the most active development organ at the provincial level is the Provincial Development Committee, which consists of the heads of the provincial technical departments. There is no political representation at this level. Popular input to the planning process takes place primarily at the level of the District Development Committee. Even at this lower level the ability of the masses to influence development plans appears to be limited. Indeed, in 1970 responsibility for many social services was transferred from the county councils to the respective technical ministries. Thus, the allocation of resources is increasingly being influenced by technical and national priority considerations rather than by local needs or constraints.[19] As the preceding experience of SRDP indicates, the neglect of local input has had an unfavorable effect on the performance of the rural development effort.

A question, therefore, arises as to whether the future attempts to improve administrative performance should not place less emphasis on structural changes within the rural development administration, such as those discussed in this chapter, and more on improving the procedures followed in program planning and implementation.[20] Proper procedures have to include consultation with rural residents, careful identification of local needs and constraints, intelligent application of appropriate technical and institutional criteria, and a feedback mechanism to assess progress and to remove obstacles in the way of its realization. The successful institution of such procedures is, however, frequently blocked by bureaucratic inertia and political pressures that result in following or abandoning certain programs, irrespective of their intrinsic merit. The Tanzanian experience is, therefore, reviewed below to examine the extent to which the far more politically oriented strategy adopted in Tanzania is able to overcome the sorts of limitations encountered in the Kenyan effort.

18. David K. Leonard, "Communications and Deconcentration," in *Development Administration: The Kenyan Experience,* eds. Goran Hyden, Robert Jackson, and John Okumu (Nairobi: Oxford University Press, 1970), pp. 91–111.

19. Thomas Mulusa, "Central Government and Local Authorities," in *Development Administration: The Kenyan Experience,* eds. Goran Hyden, Robert Jackson, and John Okumu (Nairobi: Oxford University Press, 1970), pp. 233–51. Also see Nicholas Nyangira, "Relative Modernization and Public Resource Allocation in Kenya," paper presented to the East African Universities Social Science Council, Eighth Annual Conference, Nairobi, December 19–23, 1972. For a conflict of interest between the local desires to control expenditure and pattern of education in rural areas and the central tendency to take over traditionally local programs, see L. G. Cowan, *The Cost of Learning: The Politics of Primary Education in Kenya* (New York: Teachers College, Columbia University Press, 1970). Cowan also discusses alternate ways of financing and administering primary education in a decentralized manner. Also see Goran Hyden, "Local Government Reform in Kenya," in *East Africa Journal,* vol. 7, no. 4 (April 1970), pp. 19–24.

20. Robert Chambers, "Planning for Rural Areas in East Africa: Experience and Prescriptions," pp. 31–35. See Chapter X of this study for a discussion of attempts to improve administrative procedures through improved training of management and field staff.

Decentralization and the Ujàmaa Movement in Tanzania

The Genesis of Ujàmaa

Ujàmaa vijijini, or rural socialism, is Tanzania's unique approach to rural development. As much an ideology as a program, the concept of *ujàmaa* was worked out over a number of years in the writings of Julius Nyerere and crystallized in the now-famous Arusha Declaration of 1967.[21] Central to the *ujàmaa weltanschauung* are *(a)* the belief that the traditional African extended family represents an indigenous form of socialism, *(b)* an associated view which sees free enterprise and private property as foreign institutions that are without deep roots in Tanzania, and *(c)* a faith that Tanzania can be developed along socialist lines within the framework of its unique social and cultural heritage. The explicit vision of *ujàmaa* is, thus, of a nation of communal farm units based on equality, cooperation, and non-exploitation.

Prior to the Arusha Declaration, the central policymakers were unclear as to the specific means for realizing the objectives of *ujàmaa.* Indeed, many of the earlier initiatives of the government in the rural sector seemed to be in conflict with this goal. The Village Settlement Scheme—a high-cost program for establishing cooperative farms on virgin land—suffered from too little farmer participation and too much bureaucratic control.[22] The so-called improvement approach to development, which implied a continuation of conventional extension methods, was perceived as leading to the creation of a rural bourgeoisie. In short, rural development appeared to be neither benefiting the peasant masses nor restructuring their society.

With the Arusha Declaration a transitional stage was reached. The Tanganyika African National Union (TANU)—the nation's sole political party—and the government reaffirmed their commitment to *ujàmaa* and began to delineate the specific steps to create an egalitarian and socialist society. The linchpin in the new strategy was the creation of *ujàmaa* villages. As Nyerere described these communities: "A group of families will live together in a village, and will work together on a common farm for their common benefit. Their houses will be the ones they build for themselves out of their own resources; their farm will be owned jointly, and its produce will be their joint property. The activities of the village, and the type of production they undertake, as well as the distribution of crops and other goods they produce, will all be determined by the village members themselves. . . . In other words, we shall have an up-to-date and larger version of the traditional African family. . . ."[23]

---

21. See, for example, Julius K. Nyerere, *Freedom and Socialism* (Dar es Salaam: Oxford University Press, 1968); *Freedom and Unity* (Dar es Salaam: Oxford University Press, 1966); and *Socialism and Rural Development* (Dar es Salaam: Government Printers Office, 1967).

22. For a discussion of one such settlement at Kaluku, see Clyde R. Ingle, "From Colonialism to Ujamaa: Case Studies in Tanzania's Search for Independence," paper delivered at the Conference on the Political Implications of Change at the Local Level in Africa, University of Toronto, January 28–30, 1971. In 1969 the government announced that no new villages would be initiated under this scheme and that the settlements already established would be reorganized along *ujàmaa* lines.

23. Nyerere, *Socialism and Rural Development,* p. 15.

The formation of the villages was to be based on persuasion and step-by-step transformation. Where families were scattered, peasants would be encouraged to move into a central *ujàmaa* village.[24] In areas marked by preexisting village settlements, villagers were to be encouraged to alter their community along *ujàmaa* lines. Total communalism was not an immediate goal; initially most *ujàmaa* villages would contain both private and communal plots, with the former to be gradually phased out as the *wajàmaa* became better equipped to handle cooperative agricultural production.[25]

Decentralization of the Rural Development Administration

By 1971 it became apparent to the national leadership that the goals of *ujàmaa* were not being achieved as rapidly as hoped. Part of the reason was that the existing administrative procedures and structure were inadequate to handle the implementation of *ujàmaa* villages. First, there was too little horizontal integration—i.e., programs for villages were prepared, priorities worked out, budgets allocated, and personnel deployed by the sectoral ministries in Dar es Salaam. Field staff were responsible to their parent agencies and rarely acted as members of a unified development team.[26] Second, the vertical set-up was weighted in favor of the central bureaucracies with too little lower echelon input. Decisions took an inordinately long time to reach the field personnel and often overlooked local resource endowments and environmental factors. Consequently, farmer initiative and cooperation were often strangled.[27] Third and perhaps most important, in TANU's view the party had insufficient control over decisions within the existing administrative structure. Though the party had representation on the committees at all levels and was responsible for overall policy, it did not have veto power over specific plans and was not linked directly to the crucial technical ministries. Frequently, TANU–sponsored initiatives were either sidetracked or watered down by bureaucratic elements that were lukewarm, if not hostile, towards the *ujàmaa* village program.

It thus seemed that some administrative reform was needed if *ujàmaa* were to be more than a set of high-sounding ideals. In 1972 the government responded to these concerns by decentralizing the administration of its rural development program. The result of this action was *(a)* to reduce the authority of the sectoral ministries, *(b)* to grant TANU wider power to implement its policies, and *(c)* to give the Prime Minister's office an important role in coordinating the overall *ujàmaa* strategy.

24. Villagization—i.e., the moving of scattered farmers into a central location—may allow economies of scale in the provision of services such as extension, marketing, credit, input supplies, and health and transportation facilities. However, where land potential is poor, congregation of population may also mean walking to distant areas for cultivating land or for fetching water, thus increasing the labor requirements for other household activities. See footnote 33 of this chapter for further discussion of this question.

25. See government of Tanzania, *Second Five Year Plan, July 1969–June 1974*, vol. 1, General Analysis (Dar es Salaam: Government Printers Office, 1969), for a detailed discussion of the *ujàmaa* village program.

26. For example, in an *ujàmaa* village, agricultural extension would be the responsibility of the Ministry of Agriculture; a clinic, that of the Ministry of Health; and so forth.

27. See Lionel Cliffe and John S. Saul, "The District Development Front," in *Socialism in Tanzania*, vol. I, eds. Cliffe and Saul (Nairobi: East African Publishing House, 1972), pp. 302–28.

More specifically, under decentralization the regional and area commissioners (who are also chairmen of the corresponding party organ) are granted wide responsibility for planning and implementing activities in *ujàmaa* villages. In administrative terms the regional administrations have, in fact, become the equivalent of a ministry, since they have assumed direct control over ministerial expenditures and staff operations that take place at the regional level. The role of the central ministries is reduced to one of developing broad policies and providing specific technical advice. They no longer have a direct role in *ujàmaa* village activities.[28] TANU retains membership in various development committees. In addition, all plans have to be submitted to the appropriate party body for preliminary approval. For instance, district plans go to the TANU District Executive Committee before being passed on to the Regional Development Committee. The Prime Minister's office, in turn, becomes the major coordinating body, as all regional plans are supposed to be funneled through it for consolidation with national rural development objectives.

Under these reforms, in principle development plans are to be initiated at the very bottom of the administrative structure (the *ujàmaa* villages), passed through the district and regional organs, and brought up to the central political authority for approval. Policy guidelines and plan approval flow in the opposite direction. These reforms have resulted in some degree of administrative devolution—i.e., the transfer of decision-making power concerning development from the sectoral ministries to the regional commissioners and, indirectly, to the party. However, despite the relative autonomy of the regional administrations, ultimate authority remains vested in the high-level party and government offices.

Paradoxically, the devolution of power has meant somewhat less-direct farmer participation in the planning process. One of the problems under the old system had been the potential for elected farmer representatives to support policies directed towards commercial farming and individual entrepreneurship. One component of the reform was to reduce officially the number of locally elected farmers sitting on the various development committees. Though an apparent setback for democratic control of the planning process, this step is counterbalanced somewhat by the greater role of TANU, which, at least in principle, represents the interest of the majority of peasants. Nevertheless, as the review of *ujàmaa* carried out under ARDS noted, there are only limited formal procedures for local people to influence TANU officials, leaving little more than good will to assure that these officials will, in fact, protect peasant interests.[29]

Concurrent with the decentralization of the rural development administration, steps have been taken to centralize taxing power. According to the World Bank's rural sector survey carried out in Tanzania, the authority of

28. This does not apply to programs (such as training institutes, research centers, road systems, and so forth) cutting across regional boundaries. Also, some sectoral ministries have not been decentralized—e.g., defense, foreign affairs, and information.

29. The peasants' main source of access to the party is through their elected TANU cell leaders. In principle, these leaders are supposed to articulate the views of their constituency to higher-level officials. In practice, however, they are often reluctant to report views that are critical of the party or that run counter to party policy. See Clyde R. Ingle, "The Ten-House Cell System in Tanzania: A Consideration of an Emerging Village Institution," in *Journal of Developing Areas,* vol. 6, no. 2 (January 1972), pp. 211–25.

the district-level committees to raise revenues was revoked in 1969; and now all expenditures come from funds provided by the central government. This step seems to have been motivated by the national government's commitment to social equality and frontal development. Given the substantial regional disparities in income and access to social services, it was feared that local financing of development activities would favor the more endowed areas and cause uneven growth. Central fiscal authority offers a potential counterweight to these imbalances. Further, the subsequent creation of separate regional budgets helps to insure that local and regional expenditures will be in line with national policy objectives.

The growth of *ujàmaa* villages since the Arusha Declaration has been impressive. According to the figures obtained from the Rural Development Division of the Prime Minister's office, between 1970 and 1972 the number of registered villages increased from 1,196 to 5,556, while membership as a percentage of rural population increased from 4.3 percent to 15.3 percent. The implementation of the *ujàmaa* village program accelerated considerably in the middle of 1974. Between 2 to 4 million people are estimated to have been settled during the last half of the calendar year 1974. However, as of 1971, 90 percent of the settled villages were classified as Stage I villages, i.e., without "significant communal productive activity."[30] Even more significant in terms of the government's avowed policy of nationwide *ujàmaazation,* the villages are concentrated in the poorest areas of the country. Robinson and Abraham report that in 1973 nearly 70 percent of the population residing in *ujàmaa* villages was located in five regions, which together contributed less than 25 percent of the 1967 GDP. By contrast, economically more developed areas of Tanzania (e.g., Kilimanjaro, Bukoba, East Lake, and Rungwe) had not made much progress in forming *ujàmaa* villages.

Voluntarism and Constraints in Tanzanian Rural Development

What is the relationship between the *ujàmaa* policy and the reforms which have taken place in the administration of rural development? As indicated above, the implementation of *ujàmaa* villages is a means to an end. The ultimate goal is the transformation of society; *ujàmaa vijijini* is to accomplish this by raising the consciousness of the rural society and by shifting the balance of political power in favor of the poorest classes. Administrative decentralization, by granting TANU greater control over the allocation of human and financial resources, provides the economic muscle to achieve these social and political aims. In this sense, the move towards decentralization complements the *ujàmaa* policy. However, the decentralization, which has allocated greater power to the regional authorities and the party, may also subvert some of the basic tenets of *ujàmaa,* such as its emphasis on self-reliance of the rural people. There seems to be an inherent contradition in the *ujàmaa* philosophy of peasant voluntarism and spontaneity on the one hand and the official policy of central control and direction on the other. The discussion in the remainder of this chapter, therefore, examines whether the recent administrative reform resolves or accentuates these various tensions.

30. See government of Tanzania, *The Economic Survey, 1970–71* (Dar es Salaam: Government Printers Office, 1971), pp. 54–55.

The Tanzanian policy to decentralize administration provides an interesting contrast with the Kenyan experience. First, compared to Kenya, the Tanzanian effort is based on a far greater national commitment to the goal of decentralization. This is reflected in the greater regional autonomy which has been granted in Tanzania. In this regard the provision of the Regional Development Fund (RDF) to finance plans at the district level is of particular interest. Although, at present, RDF is a small portion of the national budget, it is expected to increase in size and to help overcome the type of delays in the allocation of resources experienced in Kenya. Second, compared to SRDP, *ujàmaa* has had a greater indigenous content from the outset. Therefore, high-priority programs are more likely to be in line with the government's goals.

However, as suggested in the previous discussion, the decentralization of the rural administration in Tanzania also raises questions as to: *(a)* the authenticity of the grass root participation in program planning and implementation; *(b)* the efficiency of the new administrative structure; and *(c)* the effectiveness with which the restructured administration allocates resources and services from the point of view of long-term, nationwide development, as distinct from short-term achievements. These various factors are discussed below.

Decentralization and the "Class Conflict"

The sources of resistance. The *ujàmaa* movement is based on the explicit assumption that rural development means more than economic progress. TANU's February 1971 policy statement, "Mwongozo,"[31] advocates sacrificing rapid economic growth and concentrating instead on social and political gains—i.e., improving the living standards of the poorest segments of the population and organizing rural life on a collective basis.

Obviously, TANU's policies and, in particular, the *ujàmaa* movement are intended to be of greatest benefit to the impoverished social groups, such as the landless or underemployed peasants. Conversely, at least in the short run, the relatively more prosperous small-scale commercial farmers stand to lose the most from the redistribution of resources. The costs of the *ujàmaa* policy are, therefore, being borne by the more developed areas of the rural sector. This has created considerable political opposition to *ujàmaa,* particularly among the smallholder commercial peasants.

The antipathy of this class seems to stem from three major sources:

1. Small-scale commercial farmers are likely to lose their share of government assistance in services such as credit, technical advice, and crop inputs. Given the limited governmental resources and given TANU's determination to provide services on a frontal basis, there will simply not be enough funds to satisfy the needs of both the subsistence and commercial farmers. This problem has been, of course, aggravated by the low priority received by production-increasing programs in the allocation of resources (see Chapter VII). A shift, however, toward emphasis on productivity may have begun.

31. Tanganyika African National Union, *TANU Guidelines, 1971* (Dar es Salaam: Government Printers Office, 1971).

2. At least initially, collectivized farming seems to lead to a decline in agricultural productivity and, hence, to a fall in living standards. There is little hard evidence to support this argument, though the recent shortages of food in many cities and towns suggest that the organization of *ujàmaa* villages has had an adverse effect on overall rural productivity.[32] Further, sources within the government report that in the Ismani area, where coercion was used to collectivize maize growing, maize production fell by 70 percent in two years. Such a decline may be caused more by initial opposition to collectivization than by any inherent inefficiency in the collective farming system.[33] Nevertheless, popular resistance to *ujàmaa* could lead to prolonged civil strife with adverse social and, in particular, economic consequences. The Ismani case cited above ended violently in December 1971 when the regional commissioner responsible for the drive was murdered by an embittered well-to-do farmer.

3. Land-owning peasants seem to be determined to hold onto their land holdings.[34] This is aptly illustrated by the experience of the IDA–financed tobacco project, initiated in 1970. The project was to enlist 15,000 small farmers in tobacco production. Development was to take place along *ujàmaa* lines, which was initially interpreted to mean private farms and common processing and grading facilities. The number of farmers participating in the program grew moderately during the first year of activity. However, in 1971 government pressure led to calls for the immediate collectivization of all tobacco production within the scheme. Recruitment became a serious problem, and over the next six months there was a 25 percent decline in the number of growers participating in the project. Tobacco yields also declined significantly. This trend was reversed only after President Nyerere visited the area and proclaimed that the farmers could retain their individual holdings. In the three months following Nyerere's visit, 844 new farmers joined the project.

32. Imports of grain in Tanzania increased from 15,000 metric tons in 1973 to 463,000 metric tons in 1974. Imports of an additional 430,000 metric tons are estimated to be needed in 1975. Although initially drought was thought to be the major reason, later analysis indicates that the main cause was an acceleration of the forces which have caused demand to outgrow supply over the last seven years.

33. Where settlers are moved into entirely new *ujàmaa* villages, there is usually a temporary drop in production, even if collective farming is not introduced, as the villagers have to abandon their established plots and begin by clearing new land. Such a drop has frequently been accentuated by poor timing of the movement, which has hindered completion of the old crop cycle in the existing settlements and the beginning of a new one in the newly settled villages. In these situations the government has had to supply food to carry the farmers through to their first harvest, increasing the need for central supplies, although such distribution has also not been very reliable.

34. In many areas in Tanzania, as, for example, in Sukumaland, peasant farmers have rights to land use rather than to formal land ownership. Under this system of tenure, the land is held communally and distributed according to native law or custom by village authorities. Typically this results in de facto private ownership, since there tend to be no limits on how a farmer may use the land to which he has rights. Farm income is consumed privately, and frequently the land itself can be transferred to a farmer's sons or rented to his neighbors. As Kenneth Shepiro observed in his field investigations, if for no other reason, farmers in Sukumaland have frequently resisted leaving their traditional land holdings because of the practice of burying ancestors on one's own holding. Such resistance has, of course, been reinforced by the fear of cotton farmers that their incomes may decline as a result of the move to *ujàmaa* villages. The two other major forms of land tenure in Tanzania are leasehold and

Given the antipathy of small commercial farmers to *ujàmaa,* it is not surprising that the villages have grown most rapidly in areas where commercial agriculture is least developed. However, in general, a go-slow policy has been adopted toward enforcing collectivization, although the rate of villagization has been accelerated.[35] It has been reported that in December 1973 the goal of collectivizing the country's agriculture was changed in favor of individual plots arranged in a block pattern. Despite abandonment of the policy of collectivization at the official level, resistance to villagization remained significant in 1974, partly because the fact that collectivization had been abandoned was frequently not known in the villages and partly because the short-term, adverse effect on production continued to be experienced as a result of the various constraints encountered in implementing villagization rapidly.

The commercial farmers appeared to be supported in their opposition to *ujàmaa* by the technical ministries. This support may be rooted in two factors: *(a)* As Lionel Cliffe has pointed out, the bureaucratic bourgeoisie often have a similar class background to commercial farmers and tend to identify with their interest. According to Cliffe, resistance from this source can be expected to grow, since the children of commercial farmers have had greater access to education and are filling the ranks of the civil service at an ever-increasing rate.[36] *(b)* Personnel in the technical ministries often possess a bias in favor of efforts to increase economic productivity over programs geared towards improving social welfare. Opposition from this quarter may dissipate, however, for there appears to be a growing number of young educated technocrats dedicated to the ideals of improving the lot of the peasantry.

Generating grass root support. Though difficult to document, the evidence suggests that, to be successful in the long-run, *ujàmaa* villages must offer clear-cut material advantages over traditional modes of social organization—not only to the most impoverished members of the rural proletariat, but also to the relatively more prosperous peasants. The attraction of the material incentives is illustrated by a survey in Bukoba, a cash growing area, in which 90 percent of the *wajàmaa* cited economic motives for joining vil-

rights of occupancy. For further details see government of Tanzania, Bureau of Resource Assessment and Land Use Planning, "Preliminary Report of the Sukumaland Interdisciplinary Research Project," BRALUP Report no. 40 (June 1970), pp. 43–59.

35. Despite the fact that the creation of new village settlements disrupts short-run production, villagization per se does not have to result in a long-term production decline. The fact that it has frequently been associated with stagnating or declining production seems to result from several factors: *(a)* villagization has often been hastily implemented, leading to the location of villages in areas with poor land potential; *(b)* in some cases, increased time is spent by farmers traveling to their fields; *(c)* a decline in farm-level management practices is caused by the farmers' lack of proximity to their fields and by the poor quality of agricultural services in new villages; and *(d)* inadequate incentives exist where collectivized production has been stressed. None of these problems seems insurmountable and probably could be corrected through more careful study of potential village sites, improved technology, and greater production incentives and services. However, given Tanzania's limited financial and manpower resources, whether the investment to achieve villagization can be justified on a massive scale in the short run remains questionable, although interest in its realization is understandable as a political goal.

36. Lionel Cliffe, "The Policy of Ujamaa Vijijini and the Class Struggle in Tanzania," in *Rural Africana,* no. 13 (Winter 1971), pp. 5–27.

lages.[37] In seven of the eight *ujàmaa* villages visited by ARDS researchers, villagers had reaped clear benefits in the form of government inputs and/or increased access to agricultural services. As noted in earlier chapters, promising tractor services, schools, health facilities, and other services has been resorted to in order to entice local people to form *ujàmaa* villages. Given Tanzania's limited resources, its policy of national self-reliance, and commitment to frontal development, such inducements can be offered indefinitely only if substantial increases in production are realized to carry their cost.

Despite the vital need for production increases, the government appears to be gauging the success of its program primarily on the rate of villagization. This is reflected in the paucity of data on the economic achievements of the *ujàmaa* policy in contrast with the data available on numbers of villages and people settled. Robinson and Abraham have argued that there is a real danger that the government and party officials will mistake the form of the program (the creation of socialist villages) for its content (improving the lives of the peasant majority). Too much emphasis already seems to have been placed on the program's rapid expansion and not enough on substantive economic achievement. In the absence of such achievement, continued resistance can be expected from commercially oriented peasants; and growing dissatisfaction may develop, even among the poorest classes.

In response to these realities, there appears to be a growing effort in the recent months to increase resources allocated to production activities. However, concomitant with the shift in emphasis in the allocation of resources is a tendency among high officials to accept the possibility of using force, both to create *ujàmaa* villages and to ensure correct behavior on the part of the *wajàmaa*.[38] Aside from the obvious conflict of force with the principles of *ujàmaa,* Tanzania also lacks administrative capability to enforce cooperation in rural activities on a national scale. Thus, both from an ideological as well as a practical standpoint, increasing the positive incentives to join *ujàmaa* villages would seem to be the only avenue for effecting successful nationwide *ujàmaazation* in the foreseeable future. The key test of the administrative decentralization exercise is whether it can facilitate

37. David J. Vail, "Technology for Socialist Development in Rural Tanzania," mimeographed, n.d., background paper for the Seventeenth Annual Meeting of the African Studies Association, Chicago, November 1974. The fact emphasized elsewhere in this study that the so-called prosperous farmers in much of sub-Saharan Africa are often affluent only in degree rather than in kind should be borne in mind throughout this discussion. The Tanzanian philosophy is directed more against reinforcing this class distinction over time rather than towards abolishing an existing exploitative class. This is probably an important distinction between the liberation movement in Tanzania and that in many other countries, including mainland China and Cuba. It is the lack of an obvious exploitative class in the rural sector as a social enemy that may be making the Tanzanian struggle somewhat more difficult. However, it also makes positive economic incentives far more essential to the success of the effort.

38. Intimidation and imprisonment have sometimes been used to force individuals into *ujàmaa* villages and to compel their participation in village activities. For an overall discussion of the various incentives used in the *ujàmaa* village program, see Dean E. McHenry, "Policy Implementation in Rural Africa: The Case of Ujamaa Villages in Tanzania," paper read at the Sixteenth Annual Meeting of the African Studies Association, Syracuse, N.Y., October–November 1973. Also see Cliffe, "The Policy of Ujamaa Vijijini and the Class Struggle in Tanzania" and Clyde R. Ingle, "Compulsion and Rural Development in Tanzania," in *Canadian Journal of African Studies,* vol. 4, no. 1 (Winter 1970).

such positive incentives through the planning and implementation of programs and through innovations which will benefit the mass of farmers. The mere fact that coercion has been discussed among some quarters as a means for rural development seems to indicate at least a partial setback of the decentralization effort to deliver goods in this important regard.

The Effect of Decentralization on Planning and Implementation

Because decentralization is new, far too little is known about the actual decision-making processes in the bottom up committee structure and the factors influencing allocative or implementing decisions except in a general way and on the lines discussed above. Whether the network of committees ranging from the village to the regional level, through which plans must be forwarded, is too elaborate and time consuming to ensure prompt decision making remains to be seen, although the spirit of participation of the structure must also receive important consideration. There is also a question as to whether transfer of the most competent staff from Dar es Salaam to the regional offices will necessarily ensure their effective use in local planning, given that there is little direct-line authority or communication in the technical ministries. It is mainly through the district and regional heads of administration that line communication and direction seem to take place under the present system. Although the regions are endowed with the best technical staff, as yet the new organization has not facilitated the use of its expertise in planning programs at lower levels. The limited amount of trained indigenous manpower creates further difficulties with such area-based planning.

Moreover, as pointed out in Chapter II, there is some evidence to indicate that the decentralized administration may be committing errors similar to those made under the preexisting system as, for instance, with regard to "the persistence of the mystique which equates modernization with electrification and motorization." [39] Though appropriate intermediate innovations and implements do exist, it remains to be seen whether this avenue will be exploited fully and introduced on a significant scale by the decentralized administration.

The Effects of Decentralization on the Allocation of Resources and the Distribution of Benefits

The decentralization and the consequent increase in the power of the party may explain the imbalanced allocation of resources to social services. The loss of power at the technical ministries has further enforced the asymmetry in the allocation of resources between social and productive programs (see Chapter VII for further discussion of this issue).

Tanzania's frontal approach to planning has meant opting in favor of spreading the few manpower resources thinly to avoid regional imbalances.

39. Vail, "Technology for Socialist Development in Rural Tanzania." Vail estimates that just providing the *ujàmaa* villages existing in 1972 with tractors would require an initial investment of $25 to $30 million, or roughly one-third of the entire development budget of the Ministry of Agriculture under the Second Five Year Plan.

A mid-term evaluation of Tanzania's Second Plan noted that, because of the extremely limited manpower available for planning and implementation of programs in the agricultural sector, the actual expenditure has been even lower than the planned expenditure. Due to inadequate planning and implementing capacity at the lowest levels, much of the expenditure in the agricultural sector has been incurred on the relatively larger irrigation projects and main roads rather than on small irrigation schemes, storages, and feeder roads.[40] Rapid expansion of *ujàmaa* village settlements has taken place, often without assessment of technical potential and, hence, of carrying capacity prior to movement of people.[41] It must be realized that, in the case of some villages, the population was scattered precisely because of the low level of carrying capacity of the land.

As noted earlier, despite the commitment to the frontal approach to development planning, there has been a countervailing tendency towards concentrating public resources in select *ujàmaa* villages located in low-income areas. Vail notes that, where villages have been most successful in establishing a cooperative production base, it is usually due to privileged access to infrastructure, capital inputs, cash crop technologies, and so forth.[42] The temptation to indulge in showpiece projects often also seems irresistible. It is still too early to judge if the decentralized administration will be able to overcome the tendency towards concentrated allocation of resources.

Under decentralization there has been little, if any, improvement in quality of the extension service and related training. Regional specialization in crop production, which has been one of the major objectives of Tanzania's development plans, has not been realized due to poor knowledge of crop potential and technological possibilities. Consequently, regional production plans do no more than provide a shopping list of all the crops that can be grown in the region.[43] Because there have been no clearly defined targets for production of crops, assessment of performance of the delivery system and, in particular, of extension has received little attention. The result has been a much slower rate of growth of agricultural production than had been anticipated in the Second Plan.

The Future of the Ujàmaa Village Program

Tanzania's strong commitment to broad-based rural development appears to be well warranted, given the overwhelming number of rural resi-

40. A similar phenomenon is noted in the Kenya plans. See Colin Leys, "Kenya's Second Development Plan: Political and Administrative Aspects," in *East Africa Journal*, vol. 7, no. 3 (March 1970), pp. 6–12.

41. In a number of cases, farmers were persuaded or forced to move into *ujàmaa* villages in new areas with little or no previous knowledge on the part of the government and party officials of soil characteristics, amount and pattern of rainfall, suitability of the crops farmers were to grow, or disease situation of the area (including the possible incidence of tsetse, malaria, and so forth). In some cases farmers were made to move into new areas with no provision for food during the build-up period. Because of the lack of data and of operation-oriented studies, the government is not in a position to advise on the range of productive activities that would be appropriate to the various village areas.

42. Vail, "Technology for Socialist Development in Rural Tanzania."

43. I. Livingstone, "Some Requirements for Agricultural Planning in Tanzania," and "Production, Prices and Marketing Policy for Staple Foodstuffs in Tanzania," in *Agricultural Policy Issues in East Africa*, ed. V. F. Amann (Kampala: Makerere University, May 1973), pp. 15–38 and 208–42.

dents and the generally low levels of incomes and services available to them. *Ujàmaa vijijini* is an innovative and potentially effective means of realizing broadly participatory economic growth and of improving the welfare of the rural masses. The decentralization of the rural development administration offers the hope that the *ujàmaa* movement can become more viable through the building of a planning and implementation capacity that will be able to take account of diverse local constraints and potentials. Whether the *ujàmaa* program will be successful in the long run, however, depends largely on how effectively the government and the party can generate realistic area-based planning and ensure genuine grass root support.

A positive feature may, however, be the evaluations carried out by the Tanzanian government, many of which reflect concern with shortcomings identical to those discussed in this study. Tanzania's tendency towards self-criticism suggests that the strategic difficulties with *ujàmaa* may eventually be ironed out internally, provided the political roadblocks do not prove insurmountable.

External assistance can play a useful role in augmenting Tanzania's planning and implementing capacity. With this approach the emphasis in donor assistance can be on improving the long-run effectiveness of the resources provided externally and on mobilizing additional domestic resources, rather than on utilizing external resources for creating a noticeable but temporary impact or for substituting assistance in place of a domestic effort. This approach is also in the spirit of self-reliance that the Tanzanians intend to follow.

Future efforts in Tanzania need to augment the supply of technical manpower (such as plant breeders, agronomists, hydrologists, and civil engineers) who can identify technical constraints and provide technical solutions.[44] Further, there is a need to improve the performance of planners and administrators so that administrative functions are clearly specified, deadlines to fulfill these functions are set, and procedures for improving coordination between various ministries and for decision making within individual agencies are devised. The more basic political issues will, of course, have to be resolved by the domestic policymakers.

---

44. The general lack of knowledge of technical factors is frequently a major constraint to planning. For instance, little is known about potential for water development as well as of the interactions between water supply and improved health or productivity. See government of Tanzania, "Water Development—Tanzania, A Critical Review of Research," BRALUP Paper no. 12 (Dar es Salaam: University College, April 1970); and government of Tanzania, "Rural Water Supply in East Africa," in *Proceedings of the Workshop on Rural Water Supply,* ed. Dennis Warner, BRALUP/Economic Land Use Paper no. 11 (Dar es Salaam: University College, May 1970). These two publications also emphasize the considerable shortage of trained manpower required for planning, implementing, and evaluation of water supply.

CHAPTER X

Training for Rural Development

In previous chapters it has been argued that, for rural development to be viable in the long run, far greater attention to local involvement and to development of rural institutions is necessary than has been provided in the programs analyzed. Local involvement and institutional development are not likely to be very effective unless training is provided at three levels:

1. In its broadest sense, to sensitize rural people and, thus, to increase the receptivity and ability of rural people to respond to development programs as well as to encourage local initiative.
2. For the field staff, to improve technical and administrative performance.
3. For higher-level administrative staff, to improve the quality of policy formulation, degree of coordination, and overall effectiveness of implementation.

Training Programs and the Rural Population

Stimulating Local Initiative

Local participation may mean involvement in planning, including assessment of local needs. Even if local people do not participate in planning, at the very minimum they should be informed of the plans designed for their areas if they are expected to consent and to cooperate with program implementation. Participation in planning and implementation of programs can develop the self-reliance necessary among rural people for accelerated development.

But the most ambitious efforts to foster popular involvement can be thwarted by subtle forms of paternalism. Even where development of local participation is an important objective of rural development and where political education in mass participation is a key element of the development strategy, as in Tanzania, programs have not developed genuine participation and responsibility among the rural people.

In SRDP of Kenya, participation of the rural people in the planning and even in the implementation of programs has been very limited. Since SRDP evolved into essentially an agricultural program, its projects have been planned by technical government departments; only in the self-help schemes, such as construction of cattle dips, and a few community development activities, such as women's extension, have rural people participated at the stages of implementation. Even in these schemes local participation does not appear to have been very effective.

Concerning SRDP's program in the Kapenguria district, Barnes observes: "Community participation is seriously lacking. At times the people of a given area are not even informed of project implementation in their area.... At other times, after plans are made, the community is informed through formal meetings (at which a few questions are permitted) where the officers justify their plans, but modification is not considered."[1]

Perhaps the most striking instance of this lack of communication with Kapenguria residents involved the SRDP's road building project in the area. As Almy and Mbithi report: "To the people of Sook [location within the division] a road meant more police coming to arrest their cattle-raiding activities, but SRDP *barazas* [meetings] to discover their needs and offer to help with them were scheduled for after completion of the road. When tractors appeared unannounced and began to cut down their trees, the Sook objected vigorously; police were sent to guard the tractors and the antipathy to the road (and possibly SRDP) was consolidated."[2]

SRDP's initiatives in the Kwale district attempted to avoid these basic problems. Public opinion in this district was particularly skeptical of government programs, so great pains were taken to prevent the local residents from over-anticipating the program's ultimate benefits. SRDP concentrated its attention on popular projects with highly visible and immediate results. This cautious, step-by-step approach came to be labeled the Sequential Implementation Program (SIP). Apparently, SIP has worked quite well. In the Kikoneni water project, which was introduced by this method, public support was even greater than anticipated. Original plans had called for the project's trenches to be dug by hired labor. As the project got under way, however, it became possible to rely entirely on self-help labor for the trenching operations. Those who have analyzed the Sequential Implementation Program have been most enthusiastic and have advised SRDP to use a similar approach in districts other than Kwale.[3]

On the whole, the programs designed by national governments have not provided much training to people in genuine local participation. It is not surprising, therefore, that foreign-financed and -managed projects have provided even fewer opportunities for utilizing local support. In an unpublished paper on the social implications of LLDP in Malawi, Phieps points out the difficulty an outsider has in identifying local attitudes. Ordinary survey techniques are not well suited for discerning popular opinion in rural Africa. Phieps cites the case of one farmer who was characterized by researchers as "modern or progressive-minded" on the basis of his answers to survey questions. This same farmer's behavior, on the other hand, raised

1. C. Barnes, "Kapanguria SRDP: An Evaluation," in *An Overall Evaluation of the Special Rural Development Programme, 1972*, Institute for Development Studies Occasional Paper no. 8 (Nairobi: University of Nairobi, 1973), Section A, p. 20.

2. S.W. Almy and P. Mbithi, "Local Involvement in the SRDP," in *An Overall Evaluation of the Special Rural Development Programme, 1972*, Section G, p. 26.

3. Ibid., pp. 35–36. For related experiences in the Vihiga district, see Section G, pp. 19–20. For details on similar events, see Holmquist's excellent case study of the cattle dip program in the Kisii district, which also illustrates the very substantial local initiative that can generate new rural development programs. See Frank W. Holmquist, "Implementing Rural Development Projects," in *Development Administration: The Kenyan Experience*, eds. Goran Hyden, Robert Jackson, and John Okumu (Nairobi: Oxford University Press, 1970).

doubts as to how genuinely modern he really was. Only later it was discovered (from an African assistant) that the man, in fact, had not responded frankly to the survey questions. Rather, he had given the answers he thought the researchers wanted to hear. Phieps concludes that "this desire to please the white man has invalidated many an enquiry in Africa."[4]

Although Phieps's observations are valid in many an expatriate-managed program, there are also contrary examples. Despite the program's paternalism in certain respects (as, for instance, in organizing its marketing component) and its initial adverse effect on development of self-reliant local organization, CADU appears to have been a major factor in the identification and assertion of socioeconomic rights by the rural poor in Chilalo. The marches by Chilalo's small farmers— members of a feudalistic and authoritarian rural society— to demand feeder roads from the Awraja governor and higher prices from CADU have been indicative of their increasing participation in what had been a major social experiment under the sociopolitical structure that then existed in Ethiopia.

Programs for Development of Local Skills

Functional literacy. Illiteracy has been one of the major constraints in introducing a wide range of programs to rural people in the projects reviewed. Illiteracy of the village headmen in LLDP, who were made responsible for administering credit, created problems for the maintenance of proper records. This contributed to the failure of the earlier group credit approach. Belloncle and Gentil indicate that, both in ZAPI and SODENKAM in Cameroon, illiteracy is a constraint in broadening participation in rural development programs and poses a serious risk that the educated will exploit the illiterate. The only way to prevent malfeasance at the marketing level is to give the pioneers the training they need in order to be able to check the weighing of produce and understand the year-end statements. Similarly, the deception of cultivators by village traders in Chilalo, Ethiopia, is in no small part due to the peasants' inability to count. Although illiteracy is a major constraint, the projects reviewed do not include adult literacy programs of any significance.[5]

Adult training can be effective if imaginative teaching techniques are used. In Niger, over a period of six years, Belloncle has been able to help develop viable cooperatives. In his view, "Pedagogy must be active, concrete, imaginative, and repetitious, in the form of the theatre."[6] In practice this meant that village meetings were often turned into a dress rehearsal in which the farmers acted out a scene in the marketplace or an encounter with a credit agent. Even in teaching the farmers about so simple a device as an ordinary scale, words were often insufficient. Farmers were encouraged to use a scale under as realistic conditions as possible. Therefore, when market day arrived, they were able to understand the proceedings at the weigh-

4. B.A. Phieps, "Evaluating Development Schemes: Problems and Implications, A Malawi Case Study," mimeographed (Dar es Salaam: East African Universities Social Science Council, Annual Conference, December 1970), p. 14.

5. In CADU the lack of a literacy component was explained by the fact that Unesco was running such a program in the project area.

6. As indicated by Belloncle in personal discussions.

ing area.[7] This graphic and practice-oriented teaching technique needs replication on a far wider scale.

Nonagricultural vocational skills. Several efforts are under way to provide vocational training to adults. In Mali CFDT, for example, has undertaken a training program for local blacksmiths to enable them to repair multicultivators, plows, and other implements. The program was begun when CFDT was unable to obtain enough spare parts from Service du Crédit Agricole et d'Equipement Rural (SCAER) for the implements in Fana. Twenty-three blacksmiths were taught how to repair implements and to make spare parts such as bolts, plowshares, and flanges. After the training program CFDT furnished interest-free loans for the new equipment and assigned the villages from which each blacksmith could draw his business. Further, the project also fixed the selling price of certain parts and supervised the quality of the spare parts made by the blacksmiths. When the review was conducted, twenty-one blacksmiths had bought improved equipment; ten had an anvil; and four had welding equipment with which they could begin to repair the increasing number of bicycles and motor bikes in the program area. The program seems to have had a significant effect on work time and on the income of the blacksmiths.[8]

In Ethiopia CADU expected to promote training in small-scale manufacturing of goods in the rural sector during its third phase. With this in view, CADU recently completed a consumption survey to identify potential goods and services which would have a particularly buoyant demand as a result of increased incomes.[9]

In contrast to these relatively modest and phased efforts is the USAID-supported program for promoting small industries in northern Nigeria. Started in 1962, the Industrial Development Center (IDC) at Zaria was intended to provide technical know-how and managerial expertise to small businessmen. The scope of the program was wide ranging, from blacksmithing and auto repairing to leather working and carpentry. IDC has been running week-long workshops. Unfortunately, up to 1970 these workshops did not provide training in how to operate the new equipment which the businessmen had acquired under the program. Lately IDC had shifted to more specific training, but the problems remained. There was apparently a great need for immediate, on-the-spot technical assistance at the local level, which had not been forthcoming from the project. The center had been conducting one-week management seminars, which had also proved disappointing. Small-scale entrepreneurs have often found it difficult to leave their businesses for this length of time. The long journeys frequently required to attend the seminars have also been a constraining factor. Those who did manage to get to the seminars often found the

7. See G. Belloncle and D. Gentil, "Pédagogie de l'Implantation du Mouvement Coopératif au Niger," in *Archives Internationales de Sociologie de la Coopération,* no. 23 (January–June 1967), pp. 47–73.

8. One blacksmith estimated that his income had doubled as a result of the program. Through better methods and equipment, the time he required to make certain spare parts decreased from 1.5–2.0 working days to one morning.

9. CADU's strategy of phased planning of rural industrial development seems highly sensible. If properly conducted, its consumption survey should provide a number of useful insights as to the types of goods and services which may be facilitated in the subsequent periods of development.

material offered either too general or not particularly relevant. This is because the technical skills required in cement block manufacturing, for example, are very different from those needed in a bakery. The review of IDC has linked these shortcomings to the limited number of competent personnel available to the program, noting that the shortage of staff prevents any direct technical or managerial counseling to the small enterprises.

There seems to be an additional important explanation for the limited success of the USAID small-industry project. Given the practical difficulty of improving the management and efficiency of many small and scattered rural enterprises, it is only where rural enterprises enjoy a buoyant demand for their services that increase in their profitability can occur. In most cases this implies that rural industrial development must be concomitant with, if not preceded by, a dynamic agricultural sector and a growing rural economy. Frequently, rural industries have been promoted from within a broad but simplistic view of rural development which fails to recognize adequately the important linkages of small-scale industrialization with effective consumption and investment demand in the rural sector.[10]

The USAID program is instructive in an additional important regard. It points out that, whether offered through vocational schooling or through training programs, most of these training efforts directed to development of technical skills suffer from severe shortages of trained manpower. There exists considerable scope for the use of international voluntary services to compensate for the shortage of middle-level trained manpower in donor-assisted programs. Although bilateral agencies have, by and large, made greater use of volunteers compared to the projects financed by the World Bank, this important potential still remains relatively unexploited.

General training for rural needs. Although efforts have been made to promote manufacturing skills in the rural sector, the main thrust of rural training has been on activities related to agricultural and social services. Compared to the earlier export crop projects, the more recent integrated programs have substantially broadened the scope of training in development of local skills.

For instance, WADU's program in Ethiopia trains lower echelon field agents. These demonstrators, who have ninth- to eleventh-grade education, are given field training on extension practices. More recently, WADU has started offering a month-long course in principles at its training center. LLDP in Malawi provides training in a very wide range of activities, including general agriculture, nutrition, and committee procedures. In the 1971/72 period forty-eight residential and nonresidential courses involving 920 persons were held for the project's staff, some at Colby College located in the project area. LLDP also carries out an internal training function through a procedure of understudies and supervision of field staff. According to Kinsey, during the first two program phases, LLDP will have spent 3.5 percent of the program expenditure, or $542,000, on training.

10. For a discussion of the linkages between rural industries and consumption demand, see John W. Mellor and Uma J. Lele, "Growth Linkages of the New Foodgrain Technologies," in *Indian Journal of Agricultural Economics,* vol. 28, no. 1 (January–March 1971). For an analysis of the linkages between industrialization and investment in the rural sector, see Bruce Johnston and Peter Kilby, *Agriculture and Structural Transformation* (New York: Oxford University Press, 1975).

CADU has also had an elaborate training component. Its farmer training program involves training model farmers, as well as holding field days and using demonstration plots to show the results of new techniques. Although most of CADU's high- and middle-level Ethiopian staff are trained in various Ethiopian institutions, CADU trains its own lower level field staff and some of those needed by the Minimum Package Program. CADU has also trained Ethiopian managerial staff. The French West African programs, i.e., ZAPI, SODENKAM, BDPA, and CFDT, also have similar training programs.

Women's training programs. LLDP in Malawi has an active women's training program. It includes training in home economics, nutrition, needlecraft, child care, and a wide range of domestic skills. LLDP staff report that the gap between acquisition and application of knowledge is smaller in the case of women's courses as compared with men's courses. Because of the focus of their courses, women are able to put into practice what they learn immediately. Unfortunately, not all women's training is very relevant. One home economics agent, giving a demonstration to a group of African women on child care, was observed washing a baby doll in an imported plastic bathtub filled with warm water. Neither water nor a plastic bathtub seemed easily available to the women in the audience. With the help of the doll, the agent also demonstrated the use of an imported disposable diaper. The relevance of this entire demonstration is obviously questionable. The program is handicapped by a serious shortage of qualified female staff: courses have to be run on a rotational rather than a daily schedule. This situation is unlikely to improve in the near future, as LLDP's instructor training programs at Colby College and the Tuchilla Farm Institute have been producing only twenty new instructors a year. A similar situation exists in LLDP's community development work. The staff in this field are employed by the district council, not by the program, and reflect the generally poor investment in women's trainers. Kinsey notes that their training is inadequate and their salaries low; hence, there is a very high rate of turnover.

CADU has also employed a Women's Extension Unit, which had twelve agents in 1971. Their activities centered largely on welfare, such as hygiene, nutrition, meal preparation, and gardening. Expansion of this program had been halted, pending evaluation of its effectiveness.

Despite such efforts, by and large the training of women has been insufficient in almost all the programs reviewed. It is not only the social welfare training programs oriented towards the more traditional role of women that are judged generally inadequate. All too frequently, women's training programs also seem to miss the important point that the traditional role of an African woman has often been quite different than in the West. As noted in Chapter II, women have constituted an important portion of the productive rural labor force; yet their participation in agricultural training programs has been very limited.[11]

---

11. For example, as discussed in Chapter IV of this study, women in ZAPI would like to receive training in increasing the production of groundnuts, since groundnut production is primarily their responsibility. So far they have received little effective response from the program. Out of the fifty-five farmers selected for a farmer training program in one of the branch associations in ZAPI, a study shows that only one trainee was a woman; and she was a nurse!

The experience of LLDP is typical. Kinsey points out that, although women constitute 30 percent of farm managers in the Lilongwe area, their participation in LLDP's farmers' training courses is very low.[12] This is despite the fact that Chewa women generally interact freely with men in all major rural activities and play an important role in decision making. In this matriarchal society, land, among other things, is inherited through female members of the family. An earlier World Bank study points out that women were responsible for subverting the earlier land allocation program.[13]

In spite of its limited success in the formal training of women, LLDP has shown a very considerable sensitivity to the societal position of women and has made an effort to include women on village planning committees.[14] Because of the important role women often play in traditional African societies, it may be possible to increase the impact of many programs through the greater involvement of women, both in the planning and implementation of interventions. For example, there would appear to be wide scope to foster savings by tapping the female tontines that were observed in many of the program areas.[15] Similarly, the promotion of food crops, which are often grown by women, could probably be made more effectual through training programs directed explicitly towards women.

Farmer training programs. As part of their extension strategy, most programs offer training in improved agricultural practices on a regular basis to groups of farmers through residential and nonresidential courses. The objective is to impart technical knowledge suited to particular farming conditions faced by farmer leaders on their own farms so that, through the example of increased production set by them, other farmers may emulate the improved practices. To the extent that the leaders are representative and able to gain the confidence of other cultivators, the farmers' training program can be effective in spreading innovations rapidly. Yet, selection of representative farmer leaders seems to be a consistent problem in the projects reviewed. As noted in Chapter IV, farmer leaders tend to be young men with far more education and income than is representative of the rural population. The deficiencies of the typical model farmers approach are often compounded by the training program. First, it is the extension staff rather than the village planning committees which recruit students for these courses. Consequently, the majority of participants comes from progressive villages. Second, the formal classroom environment, complete with printed handouts (which the participants often cannot read) is alien to those who take part. Courses so conceived and conducted can have little effect on the level of agricultural knowledge in the general population.

12. This has largely been due to difficulties in recruiting women for courses and in hiring female trainers. The project management has felt that women need female trainers for a course in agricultural methods. Recently, however, it has been recognized that male trainers may be equally effective in reaching women farmers.

13. John C. de Wilde, *Experiences with Agricultural Development in Tropical Africa,* vol. 1 (Baltimore: Johns Hopkins Press, 1967), p. 140.

14. Village leadership is passed through the matriarchal family in Chewa villages. One village remained without a leader for six months because women did not agree on election of a leader who did not happen to be a maternal uncle.

15. For instance, women in the Ewondo society in Cameroon have traditionally practiced a lottery system of saving by which all members of the group contribute a fixed amount to the fund, which is used in turn by individual members of the group. See Chapter V of this study for a discussion of similar lotteries among peasants elsewhere in Africa.

SRDP's extension training program in the Tetu district of Kenya avoided this problem. The purpose of this program was to aim at more widespread adoption of innovations to assure greater equity. Initially, the program concentrated on improving the training imparted to the extension service, since the extension service was considered to be a principal educational agent. The training program was carried out with the assistance of IDS in Nairobi.[16] Information was gathered on 354 farmers who were randomly selected and the data used to list the adoption of various practices and procedures in various locations. The farmers were ranked according to the degree of progressiveness and divided into four categories. The findings of the study were discussed in considerable detail with the provincial, district, and divisional officers to form a relevant curriculum for extension personnel. The objective was to train extension workers "*how* to teach *what content* to *whom* with *what effect.*"[17] The next step was to organize farmers into homogeneous groups based upon progressiveness and place them in the appropriate course level. After they had mastered the particular level of techniques, the farmers were given the next course until they had graduated to the most progressive level.

Perhaps the most promising feature of the Tetu training program has been the way local officials have been able to modify course content and design in response to field conditions. Under their initiative it was decided to concentrate on only one crop — hybrid maize. Similarly, the decision to use an intensive three-day format was made at the field level. As an evaluation of SRDP points out, "the Tetu experience suggests that continuous modification *can* make a positive contribution. . . ."[18]

Brief but specific training courses like those in Tetu seem to have considerable potential for widespread replication. Belloncle and Gentil recommend in their review of ZAPI in Cameroon that training should be given in short sessions, scheduled for the periods of least activity, and should focus on the evaluation of the work just ended and the preparation of the following work phase.

Kinsey also speculates that in Malawi the nonresidential one-day courses offered at the unit centers in LLDP are more effective than the residential courses. More farmers are able to attend the one-day courses. Since short courses emphasize only a few simple points at a time, the participants appear to find it easier to remember what they are taught. Finally, because they are local, these courses can disseminate very specific information.[19]

16. For a detailed discussion of the Tetu extension project, see J. Ascroft, N. Roling, J. Kariuki, and F. Chege, "The Tetu Extension Project: A First Report on a Field Experiment," paper presented at the East African Universities Social Science Council, Eighth Annual Conference, Nairobi, December 1972. For an analysis of the effectiveness of communication of the extension system in Kenya, also see David K. Leonard, "Some Hypotheses Concerning the Organization of Communication in Agricultural Extension," Institute for Development Studies Staff Paper no. 72 (Nairobi: University of Nairobi, 1970).

17. C. Barnes, J. Heyer, and S.W. Almy, "The Tetu SRDP: The Extension Pilot Project and 4K Club Project," in *An Overall Evaluation of the Special Rural Development Programme, 1972*, Section E, p. 6.

18. Ibid., Section E, p. 17.

19. Moris does not agree with the judgment of the value of short, nonformal training, at least for youth. In Moris's opinion certain kinds of learning, such as an understanding of technical and scientific concepts, can be conveyed only through extended formal instruction. As he notes: "Our recent analysis of peasant farming indicates that farmers do have a real need for the kinds of learning that would normally be emphasized in school agriculture [courses],

Training of Field Staff

Much of the preceding discussion has emphasized three points. Training of rural people, whether they be men, women, or children, can be effective only under the following conditions: *(a)* the trainers are technically competent; *(b)* they possess an ability to translate their knowledge in the context of the specific constraints and potentials which face their target populations (and, therefore, by implication, possess knowledge of the environment in which the target population lives); and *(c)* they are able to communicate their knowledge effectively to the rural people. Training programs must also involve continuous and critical evaluation to ascertain if they are effective in fulfilling the objectives of the programs and, if not, what modifications should be made. This is a tall order. Unfortunately, most training offered to the field staff is deficient in these respects.

A critical evaluation of the performance of SODENKAM's field staff in Cameroon indicates a low level of both technical competence and teaching ability. The reviewers observed that three or four well-trained supervisors would probably be worth twenty of the present staff who are frequently unable to diagnose the maladies of the plantations and to prescribe effective remedies to them. The review of BDPA arrived at a similar conclusion about BDPA's extension staff in Mali. In ZAPI the paucity of technical knowledge on the part of the field staff is often compounded by their ignorance of the rural social structure and by their poor ability to communicate effectively with the rural people. The staff that was in direct contact with the people lacked sociological and pedagogical training.

According to Belloncle and Gentil, merely mastering a local dialect does not ensure effective communication. A great many technical terms often have no direct African equivalents. For staff members, who themselves frequently have problems with Western terminology, the temptation is to pepper their instruction and explanations with unfamiliar jargon. Of course, this communication problem works in both directions. Farmers have their own peculiar phrases and metaphors, which are often equally incomprehensible to the field staff.[20]

Designing training programs that emphasize high technical competence as well as effective means of communication is by no means simple. Since

---

and it is the lack of this underlying conceptual foundation which limits their subsequent effectiveness...." Jon Moris, "Agriculture in the Schools: The East African Experience," mimeographed, n.d., its earlier draft was presented as a paper at the Annual Symposium of the East Africa Academy, Dar es Salaam, 1972, p. 34. Far too little systematic evidence exists to arrive at firm conclusions as to the desirability of one approach over the other. It is true, however, that low levels of formal schooling do reduce the effectiveness of short-term training. In this sense the two approaches would seem to be complementary rather than in conflict with each other.

20. Belloncle and Gentil observed that, even when speaking Ewondo to local farmers, the indigenous staff in ZAPI would use terms such as *association fonctionelle, association dynamique, structuration,* and *production potentielle.* How well the staff themselves understood French is questionable. At one meeting an association head explained that he had a great deal of trouble "corrupting" the planters to reimburse their loans.

The proverbs and images used by the farmers are also interesting. Soo and Mollet have reported several examples. Concerning staff behavior, farmers were heard to say: "You don't call a dog with a stick in your hand." And the following was an explanation of why ZAPI should reimburse old debts contracted at the stabilization bank: "If you want to have someone's wife, first give back the dowry to the first husband." See G. Soo and A. Mollet, *Esquisse d'une Problématique pour les EPL de Mengueme, N'goulemakong, et Zoetele* (Yaoundé, Cam.: Direction des ZAPI du Centre Sud, 1970).   (Footnote continues on next page.)

farmers often know a great deal more about the various technical innovations than do extension workers,[21] the ideal in-training program to strive for, of course, is one which relies largely on the rural people and improves their technical competence. This will require a strong adaptive research effort and its close tie with extension and training. An additional worthwhile step may be to make provision for visits by senior African trainers to other relatively more successful projects in countries with similar technical or social constraints rather than relying heavily on Western teaching methods and content. For instance, in organizing training for extension workers, which has so far been rather ineffective in Tanzania, a visit to the Tetu extension program in Kenya or to ZAPI in Cameroon may, indeed, be a great deal more useful than a visit to Sweden or England.

Training of Managers

The training of Africans for managerial positions is a concern in almost all the programs reviewed. The specific training required seems to vary widely, depending on whether the program is administratively autonomous or whether it is being conducted through an established administrative structure. These two types of programs place very different demands upon administrators and pose very different training problems.

Autonomous Programs

Autonomous programs have usually had expatriate management from the outset. If these programs are to remain viable, Africans must be trained to take over positions initially held by foreigners.

Five general factors appear to influence effectiveness of training programs in autonomous projects:

Close expatriate-national interaction. A close interaction between expatriates and nationals seems very important. Without some effort in this regard, any plan to replace foreign managers with Africans is hamstrung from the beginning. Tensions between indigenous and expatriate staff can be a major threat to effective training. In some cases, problems may arise even without a genuine discrimination by the expatriates against the local staff as a result of the perception of the local staff that they are not being treated equally. However, in cases such as this, perceptions are as important as reality.

Many projects have been successful in overcoming these problems. CADU, BDPA, and ZAPI are among those in which local managers developed excellent rapport with expatriate staff; the social interaction outside working hours between expatriate and local staff noted in these programs

---

Nekby observes that lack of knowledge of local dialects was initially a major obstacle in establishing a dialogue with rural people in Chilalo. He emphasizes the role played by Ethiopian staff in overcoming this difficulty. Bengt Nekby, *CADU: An Ethiopian Experiment in Developing Peasant Farming* (Stockholm: Prisma Publishers, 1971).

21. The German volunteers dealing with women's extension in SODENKAM illustrate the problems faced by foreigners in working in an alien environment. Belloncle and Gentil report that they had a great deal of difficulty understanding a society so different from their own and in ridding themselves of their race-centered reactions. For instance, one of them said, "What can you do with these women who do not even love their own children?"

was far less evident in other programs. The Swedish experience in CADU is particularly interesting in this regard. Ethiopians were recruited for a wide variety of jobs. This recruitment was not done on a counterpart basis, in which one Ethiopian would be specifically groomed for a particular job. Rather, large numbers of them were placed in various administrative positions. Those who did well were advanced rapidly, often becoming the superiors of the Swedes. This approach to training seems to have been based on the perceptive view that a Swedish subordinate is more likely to make suggestions to his Ethiopian boss than would a local subordinate to an expatriate boss.[22] Such feedback from lower administrative levels is essential in learning management skills, and the Ethiopians interviewed considered this to be an important feature of CADU's training.

Administrative flexibility. A second factor which appears to influence effectiveness of training programs in autonomous projects is the need for administrative flexibility. The approach taken in CADU can occur only where requirements for advancement are determined on the basis of performance, so that even a competent junior staff member can be promoted rapidly if he performs well. LLDP faced difficulties in hiring and promoting junior local staff because of the rules and regulations established by the Public Service Commission. With rigid administrative rules, capable and energetic Africans are often locked into low-level jobs, even if they are capable of handling higher positions. Only when the programs are able to respond quickly to provide deserving Africans with genuine managerial experience before the expatriates leave will the quality of management be maintained.

Adequate training budget. A third point is that programs must have an adequate training budget if they are to hire a large enough number of local people to fill managerial positions. This budget must be in addition to normal operating funds, so that the program can recruit many more people than it actually needs. The selection process will achieve maximum results only if there is a large initial pool of manpower to choose from. Such a special budget has been useful in acquiring and training management personnel in ZAPI. The lack of such a budget appears to have been one of the explanations of LLDP's inability to hire Malawian staff.[23] To tackle this problem, it may be useful to provide a large number of training posts within the project at middle or high levels in addition to normal staffing. Such a policy would enable the project to be manned at all times with full staff with the simultaneous promotion of trainees into the mainstream of project management.

22. The CADU experience is, in many respects, unique, however, for Swedish expatriates are in an unusual position vis-à-vis their Ethiopian co-workers. As CADU's observers explained in personal discussions, while the Swedes had not been colonizers, the Ethiopians had, in essence, not been colonized. Neither suffered from the complexes from the past. For both, English was a foreign language. Furthermore, CADU was one of the first rural development projects undertaken by the Swedes; so they could admit mistakes more easily, since not everything had been tried before.

23. Of course, merely providing funds for training of expatriate replacements will not in itself ensure an adequate supply of talent or manpower at the middle or high administrative levels. Rates of pay and promotion policies must be such that trainees are attracted by adequate future pay and career prospects. This goal may be difficult to realize, given the competing requirements in the normal civil service, government policies, and the urgent staff needs of the project itself. See the discussion of staff incentives in Chapter VIII of this study.

Expert assistance. The fourth point concerns the need for short-term consultations with experts to solve specific organizational and technical problems and, hence, the need for a budget for this purpose. Any number of unusual difficulties requiring special advice may arise during project operation, as in organizing branch associations in ZAPI or in getting livestock development under way in LLDP. It is important that local managers learn to deal with these particular problems and, more generally, that they become accustomed to the occasional use of outside expertise. This seems to have been an important feature of ZAPI's training program.

Research and evaluation. A final requirement for management training is a constant emphasis on research and evaluation. Expatriate personnel must not pass on to African managers a rigid formula dictating proper program maintenance. Managerial excellence requires an open-minded, pragmatic attitude and a willingness to modify policy in light of experience. Belloncle and Gentil note that in ZAPI such a spirit of continuing evaluation and self-criticism was generally passed on to the Cameroonian personnel in charge.

Administrative Structures

Management training requirements in existing administrative structures appear to be quite different from those in autonomous administrations. First, the problems of take-over and native–expatriate relations do not exist in the same form in regular administration, even if there are expatriate technical advisers. Second, in the regular administration, managers are usually working within a much longer chain of command. Third, such managers tend to have a more limited set of resources at their disposal. Fourth, regular administrators generally have broader concerns and wider areas of responsibility than do autonomous project managers. Last, if training is to be effective in regular administrative structures, a very different emphasis in training is required. Autonomous programs stress managing a given set of resources effectively within a specific format. Regular administrations have to place a premium on innovation and ability to improve performance within existing administrative constraints posed by inadequate specification of decision-making responsibility and lesser congruence between rule making and rule implementation, and so forth.

The primary emphasis in training for indigenous administrations must be on improving the efficiency of the existing structure rather than on maintaining the efficiency of a new structure. This may mean introducing apparently trivial technical changes, such as a new filing system. It may also mean fostering major procedural changes within the bureaucracy itself.

One interesting attempt at internal improvement has been the Programming and Implementation Management System (PIM) of SRDP in Kenya. The Kenyan project had been suffering from a lack of internal coordination and confusion as to project goals. PIM was designed to combat these problems through streamlining and clarifying administrative procedures. For example, prior to PIM, project goals were often unrealistically high since they were set by high government officials not particularly familiar with local constraints. This often had negative results in the field as lower officials struggled vainly to reach their quotas and deadlines. To correct this situation, PIM established procedures to provide input and feedback from the lower administrative levels. An annual programming exercise was instituted in which all concerned parties worked in unison to draw up priorities and lay down program goals. Targets were quantified and reasonable deadlines established. Responsibility for given tasks was clearly delineated so as to avoid confusion about who-was-to-do-what-when. The annual meeting was followed up by monthly sessions in which managers reported their progress in implementing project goals. On the basis of these periodic meetings, short project reports were drawn up in which achievements, delays, and possible remedial action were discussed. An evaluation of this new system notes that while "PIM is by no means a panacea. . . . The evidence so far suggests that it is one way of improving the performance of government staff and programs in rural areas."[24]

Experiments like PIM certainly warrant more attention, for upgrading existing administrations is crucial to the future development of rural Africa. The training of African staff within autonomous projects is of relatively less importance in the long run because, for most of these autonomous projects to continue, they must eventually be integrated with regular administrative structures. Even the best managed autonomous projects may flounder if merged with a poorly run governmental ministry. Integration itself is no solution to the management problems of the existing structure, for the efforts required for administrative improvement in the two types of administrations may be quite different, although the skills required may be similar.

This is not to suggest that indigenous managers trained in integrated programs will not make a useful contribution in the future rural development of their countries. There is considerable evidence that the Ethiopian staff trained in CADU is playing an important role in planning and implementing development programs in Ethiopia. Nevertheless, to a considerable extent, this has been made possible by the larger contribution of Swedish technical assistance in transforming the Ethiopian Ministry of Agriculture into a development-oriented administration.

24. Deryke Belshaw and Robert Chambers, "PIM: A Practical Management System for Implementing Rural Development Programs and Projects," Institute for Development Studies (Nairobi: University of Nairobi, 1972), p. 18. See also H. Chabala, D. Kiiru, S. Mukuna, and D. Leonard, "An Evaluation of the Programming and Implementing Management (PIM) System," Institute for Development Studies Working Paper no. 89 (Nairobi: University of Nairobi, March 1973).

CHAPTER XI

Summary and Conclusions

Some Major Issues Related to Designing Rural Development Programs

The performance of the rural development programs reviewed can now be summarized with a view towards drawing lessons for the design and implementation of future programs. In doing so, it is important to emphasize at the outset that knowledge of rural development is still at a rudimentary stage. Interactions among policies, institutions, trained manpower, physical resources, and technology are complex and immensely diverse. No single program package is universally applicable. Nor is there a systematic framework that can realistically be applied to establish priorities or to identify complementarities on a mass scale, given the extreme paucity of information and, in particular, of the trained manpower and institutional capability for planning rural development in Africa.

There is only a catalog of insights based on the analyses of the constraints and potentials encountered in designing and implementing the programs reviewed, of the mechanisms that have evolved to deal with them, and of the effectiveness of these mechanisms in improving the performance of the projects. In presenting a view of rural development derived from these insights, it is assumed that in the future the objective of rural development will be not only to reach a mass of the low-income rural population but also to make the process of their development viable in the long run. The discussion therefore focuses on the following questions, which are closely interrelated:

1. Were the reviewed programs directed towards low-income populations?
2. To what extent have the programs been effective or shown a potential to be effective in improving living standards of the mass of the low-income rural population?
3. What constraints have been experienced in realizing this objective?
4. How have these constraints been ameliorated in the programs reviewed?
5. What are the implications of the performance of the past programs for the choice of target groups, types of targets, policies, and institutions if the objectives of rural development are to be realized?

It is apparent from the description of the programs in Chapter I that, with the exception of the spontaneous squatter settlements in Kenya, all the programs selected for analysis were at least partially directed toward improving living standards of the low-income rural populations. Although the Agricultural Finance Corporation and the livestock schemes in Kenya have aimed at the development of both the existing commercial and the traditional subsistence sectors, a certain portion of their resources has been allocated specifically to the development of the low-income subsistence sector. Even the earlier export crop schemes, such as KTDA in Kenya and BAT in Tanzania, involved development of low-income smallholders. Although these programs represent a considerable step towards realizing the objectives of rural development, on the whole they have been less than fully effective in making the process of development of the low-income sector self-sustaining.

Their limited effectiveness cannot be attributed to the inadequate or inappropriate specification of target groups but rather to a combination of factors. First, the objectives of rural development have changed considerably over time. Many of the projects reviewed were designed with what now appear to be limited objectives, as, for example, increasing export crop production among smallholders. The projects were also based on more limited knowledge than is now available of broad sector and policy questions and of their possible impact on the performance of the individual programs. Frequently, despite the fact that the likely impact of domestic policies and institutions was anticipated, for a variety of reasons analyzed in this study, national policies could not be changed to improve project performance. The programs were often based on inadequate knowledge of technological possibilities and of their suitability to small-farm conditions. Experience with regard to the appropriate forms of administrative institutions and their transferability was limited when many of these programs were planned.

They also suffered from poor knowledge of the sociocultural and institutional environment in which they were to be implemented. Consequently, the programs were rarely designed with a view to anticipate the effect of sociopolitical factors on the response to interventions or with an intention to introduce modifications in plans in the course of implementation to achieve maximum effectiveness. Finally and most importantly, the programs often experienced extreme scarcity of trained local manpower.

These various factors largely explain the limitations of the past programs and have important implications for future sectoral policies and for the planning and implementation of future rural development programs. The past experience suggests that, first, if the objective of participation of the lowest income group is to be ensured, examination of the particular country's existing sectoral policies and plans as well as of the indigenous institutions available for rural development has to be oriented explicitly toward assessing the extent to which these effectively reach the lowest income groups in the rural areas. Such examination will allow explicit recognition of the existing government policies which are inconsistent with the goals of rural development. For example, if the land tenure situation precludes participation of the lowest income groups in rural development programs, land reform may be essential for realizing the potential of a particular program. If the marketing boards have a vested interest in certain pricing policies which affect the distribution of benefits to the lowest income groups, perhaps a change in price policies is necessary for improving benefits of a specific rural development program. But these questions have to be resolved by national governments. Because they were not resolved prior to implementation, many of the programs reviewed have had only a limited impact on low-income groups. It must also be recognized, however, that in some cases the necessary changes in national policies are not easy to bring about. In such cases the choice for planners, whether they be nationals or from donor agencies, is between opting for only a limited impact on the rural population versus not undertaking programs at all, in either case with the hope that policies will change eventually.

Second, the past programs indicate that substantially greater planning effort is necessary than was possible in most of the programs reviewed if effectiveness is to be maximized. To this end a number of pertinent questions must be resolved. For example, are technologies actually profitable at the farm level? Do existing marketing systems serve low-income farmers effectively? Given the social ties that often exist between peasants and traders and given the extreme scarcity of trained manpower available to implement market interventions, will a new marketing system—which may seem desirable in principle—actually benefit the lowest income groups? Or will it merely aggravate the tensions between the cultivators and the merchants with adverse effects on the cultivators, as has been the case in ZAPI in Cameroon and CADU in Ethiopia? In sum, what really are the critical constraints to development in a specific situation? How feasible is it to remove these constraints, given the existing manpower and institutional development? What steps are necessary to develop the necessary capability? And what is the time horizon implicit in the results to be expected from the program?

To answer such questions, planning of rural development programs will, of course, require considerably greater trained manpower and effort. Given the extreme scarcity of trained manpower to plan and implement rural development programs, one of the following alternatives usually has to be accepted:

1. To use the existing scarce trained manpower to acquire all the necessary information to perfect the design of only a few rural development programs in the hope of maximizing their effectiveness. This approach frequently results in a substantial time lag between planning and implementation.

2. To adopt an approach of learning by doing—i.e., undertaking pilot programs with an explicit recognition that, if they are based on limited knowledge, performance may fall short of expectations but that, nevertheless, such programs may allow eventual replication of their successful features on a broader scale. To some extent this is what SRDP, LLDP, CADU, and WADU have been attempting. However, in these programs monitoring of performance and flexibility in program implementation has received substantially lesser attention than is neccessary if the programs are to be modified during implementation to improve their effectiveness and to enable their replicability. Although the importance of such flexibility is recognized in principle, analysis of the past programs indicates that in practice numerous obstacles emerge which frustrate the programs' ability to adapt to changing circumstances. Particularly because pilot programs tend to be too resource intensive to be replicable on a wide scale, overt empha-

sis on innovativeness, monitoring, and modification seems essential in such programs to ensure that transferable lessons are derived.

3. To attempt to reconcile the desirable features of the first two approaches—namely, planning based on systematic acquisition of local knowledge and flexibility in the course of implementation. This alternative is the one recommended here. However, this approach differs from the first two in two important ways: (a) it can allow broader geographical coverage than is implicit in the first two approaches; and (b) it places substantially greater emphasis on involvement of local people and officials in planning and implementation, thus using their knowledge in place of much (but by no means all) of the formal data gathering and research.

The approach recommended in this study involves beginning programs with only the few simplest interventions to remove the most critical constraints, and allows the programs to evolve in scope through time-phasing of activities. Program evolution ought to be based on the specific knowledge acquired; the constraints identified; and the indigenous human, institutional, and financial capability developed during the course of earlier stages of program implementation. The various implications of this approach for design of future programs are best illustrated by summarizing the effect of the various factors listed earlier on the performance of the past programs.

Effect of National Policies on Past Programs

Land Policies

The Ethiopian and the Kenyan experience have indicated that, where acute inequity in the distribution of land rights exists, the full potential of the programs in improving benefits to the lowest income groups is not realized by simply targeting programs towards low-income groups and devising temporary tenurial arrangements, as has been done in the Ethiopian programs. In such circumstances a more permanent change in the distribution of land rights should be an integral part of the rural development strategy.

In Ethiopia exclusion of large farmers from the programs' services both in CADU and in the Minimum Package Program has had several positive effects on the lowest income groups.[1] This policy slowed the widespread eviction of tenants that commenced with the introduction of new technologies in the CADU area. It also facilitated the distribution of credit to small farmers and, thus, tilted the programs' benefits in favor of the low-income rural population. However, these steps did not ensure full participation in program activities by the lowest income groups, in particular the tenants. In 1973 only 5 percent of the credit recipients in the MPP areas were tenants. Yet, a land tenure survey conducted by the Ethiopian government

---

1. See Chapters II, V, and VIII of this study for discussion of Ethiopia's land tenure system, its relationship to the local power structure, and their impact on the design and performance of the various programs.

in 1969 noted that tenants constitute between one-third to two-thirds of the population in the various target areas.[2] The low participation of the tenants resulted from insecurity of tenure and high and uncontrolled rents. For the tenants an innovation had to increase net yields by at least 30 percent if it were to be profitable. For the landowners, on the other hand, any net increase in yield was profitable (see Chapter V for further details). Most tenants also encountered considerable difficulty in obtaining the yearly lease that was necessary to qualify for the program's credit.[3]

Have the incentive problems been dealt with more effectively through collectivization of cultivation? The Tanzanian experience is of interest, particularly because of its commitment to mass participation. It indicates, however, that, if collectivization is to have a noticeable impact on the productivity and incomes of subsistence farmers and is to receive broad popular support, the critical organizational questions encountered in managing collective farms (who will do what, when, how, and at what wage rate) need much greater attention than they seem to have. Also, if continued uncertainty of land rights is not to have a disincentive effect on production, the decisions as to whether to introduce collectivization across the board and whether collectivization is possible only through persuasion cannot be postponed indefinitely.

In the absence of the resolution of these policy questions, the agricultural services provided to the collective farms and the managerial standards on the farms have frequently been inadequate. The incentive for the cultivator to allocate his scarce labor to collective cultivation seems to have been low; and, consequently, the yields on collective plots are noted to have been generally lower than those on private plots. In addition, there is some evidence that uncertainty with regard to villagization and collectivization is affecting yields on private plots (see Chapter IX). The resistance has been substantial, particularly in the predominantly export crop-growing regions, such as Tabora and Sukumaland, where the potential losses to commercial farmers from joining *ujàmaa* villages are considerably greater than in the case of subsistence farmers. In summary, despite the substantial donor assistance available for development of the low-income agricultural population in Tanzania, effectiveness of the agricultural programs has been limited by haphazard policies and by the neglect of critical organizational questions. The lack of effectiveness of these efforts recently led to the policy decision of not pursuing collectivization, although the rate of villagization has been accelerated.

2. The proportion of tenant participation was 40 percent in CADU. However, this is because CADU's Swedish management introduced a policy of denying credit to landowners who would not sign temporary leases for their tenants (see footnote 3 below). MPP has not had such "muscle" to bring to bear. Still, the tenancy problem created much tension in CADU, showing effectively the limits of rural development when there is little national will to change policies, as was the case at the time.

3. In the absence of a land reform, the programs introduced temporary lease clauses to prevent eviction of tenants by landowners, at least during the period when tenants received credit from the program. However, the efficacy of the leases became a much debated issue. For instance, according to a recent evaluation, these leases did not prove to be useful and in some cases may even have been counterproductive. See Yirgou et al., *Final Report on the Appraisal of CADU and EPID* (Addis Ababa: Government of Ethiopia and the Swedish International Development Authority, May 1974), p. 43. In personal discussions Cohen has indicated that, when CADU had its lawyer attempt to enforce several leases, the project was charged with disrupting the community.

Technology

Where considerable effort has been made to adapt technology to suit small-farm conditions, as in KTDA in Kenya or CADU in Ethiopia, the response of small farmers to innovations has been truly dramatic (see Chapters II and III). Even without such effort, where transplanted technologies have been responsive to local agronomic and climatic conditions, the adoption of innovations has been rapid and has often surpassed projections, as in WADU. However, in many other programs—such as the *ujàmaa* villages in Tanzania, ZAPI and SODENKAM in Cameroon, and SRDP and the small-farmer credit programs in Kenya—inadequate adaptive research appears to have been a major constraint to increasing productivity and incomes of low-income farmers (see Chapter III).

The research gap has been particularly severe in the case of food crops. This is one of the reasons why in many earlier export crop schemes there existed considerable reluctance to introduce services for food crops.[4] In these schemes promotion of the relatively more profitable export crops has led to rapid substitution of hectarage from food to export crops. Such substitution has considerably increased cash incomes of the farmers who have taken to export crops (see Chapter III). However, it has also reduced the overall off-seasonal food supplies available for local consumption in the predominantly export crop areas as, for instance, in Sukumaland in Tanzania or in the groundnut operation in Mali. These shortages have not been corrected by marketing systems, which are of a fragmented nature (see Chapter III and Chapter VI for details). Excessive specialization in export crop production in early stages of development, thus, appears to have adversely affected rural welfare, particularly of the low-income farmers who are deficit in food but too poor to purchase food at high off-seasonal prices (see Chapter III).

The neglect of technology for food crops not only affects rural welfare; it also arrests rural growth. The need to grow the minimum supply of low-productivity food crops for domestic consumption has frequently restricted the supply of scarce labor for production of high-value export crops (see Chapter II).

The experience of the export crop schemes indicates that, even if export crop development is highly justified, in most cases mixed cash and food crop development may be essential if the objective is not only to increase cash incomes of participants but also to improve general welfare in the program areas (see Chapter III). Although this approach has been adopted in many recent programs, including many reviewed under ARDS, all too often its effectiveness seems to have been limited by the inadequate adaptive agricultural research. Such research needs to be oriented to develop technological packages that are profitable, not only on research stations and demonstration plots, but on the small farmer's field as well. The importance of such adaptive research and the present technological gap cannot be overstated.

If effective national research systems are to be developed along with national commitment to their continuation, substantial resources may have to be allocated specifically for this purpose.

4. See Chapter III of this study for other reasons for this reluctance.

Pricing and Marketing Policies

Pricing and marketing policies, particularly towards food crops, have had a substantial adverse effect on the performance of rural development programs. They have often led to considerable income disparities among food and non-food crop producers, even within program areas. In Lilongwe the gross return from a hectare of tobacco is three times that from maize, despite the fact that new technologies exist for maize. Where no new technologies exist for food crops, as in the squatter settlements in Kenya, the incomes of food crop producers are even lower (see Chapter III).

Low food crop prices have discouraged expansion of food crop production for the market. Often, even when grain has to be imported to meet national food deficits as in Mali and Ethiopia, program managers have encountered considerable difficulty in convincing indigenous policymakers to establish prices high enough to provide an incentive for increasing domestic food production. When the programs have attempted to generate substantial marketed surpluses in the absence of coherent national price policies, their individual pricing and marketing efforts have become successive reactions to a series of unanticipated crises, arising from inconsistencies between program and national objectives. Such ad hoc price policies have not only contributed to a decline in the rate of adoption of new technologies in the program areas, as, for instance, in the case of wheat in Chilalo in 1972, but have also required substantial subsidization of marketing operations in programs, as has occurred in WADU, CADU, LLDP, and ZAPI (see Chapters V and VI). But even more important, these price policies have resulted in diversion of scarce administrative talent from the problems of long-term development to the solution of the short-term crises that are caused by the problem of disposal of marketable surpluses.

The pricing and marketing problems seem to have been frequently aggravated by the excessive dependence of the programs on unwilling marketing boards or inadequate farmers' organizations to handle the increased marketable surpluses. In many program areas, as, for instance, ZAPI, LLDP, CADU, and WADU, much of the marketed surplus is already handled by private trading channels. However, due to the common view of the private trading systems as being exploitative and antisocial, their development has received relatively little attention. The surpluses generated have tended to outstrip the capacity of the organized marketing channels.

Despite the considerable efforts devoted to correcting marketing problems, much of the marketed surplus procured in integrated program areas has found its way to the capital city or has been exported. Due to the poor market development in the rural areas, there has not been much increase in food availability in the non-program rural areas, except that which has frequently trickled through the traditional marketing channels (see Chapter VI).

But then, why cannot the surpluses sold in the cities or exported abroad provide resources for development of other regions? To answer this question, it is not enough merely to estimate the magnitude of the surplus; it is also necessary to examine who is likely to have control of the resources generated by these surpluses. In Malawi ADMARC has earned substantial profits from the high market margins in the export of the increased maize surpluses in LLDP.[5] So far these profits have helped reduce the past deficits of ADMARC, which are said to have arisen from handling the marketing operations of traditional export crop producers at low margins. These profits also seem to have led to substantial investments in large-scale commercial enterprises. The maize surpluses in Lilongwe, thus, appear to have resulted in a substantial redistribution of income from small-scale maize producers to traditional commercial farmers. However, this phenomenon is by no means confined to Malawi. In Tanzania it is not rare to find that the resources generated by smallholders are lost to a few members or officials of the inefficient cooperative societies.

The experience of the past programs indicates that, if the objective of rural development programs is not only to generate substantial marketed surpluses but also to ensure minimum availability of food and income to low-income populations in rural areas, three steps are necessary in rural development programs: *(a)* broad geographical coverage of services in bringing about production increases; *(b)* a commensurate, simultaneous improvement of the marketing systems, including traditional trade channels where these already play an important role; and *(c)* development of the rural infrastructure, in particular of roads and storage facilities.

Manpower Policies and Participation

Trained manpower poses a particularly severe constraint to the expansion of rural services in African countries. Substantial investment in manpower training of field-level and administrative staff is, therefore, necessary if rural development programs are to reach a mass of the low-income rural population.

In the programs reviewed several interrelated factors have affected supply of trained manpower and, thus, limited the expansion of services to the target populations. The countries started with a low base of trained manpower. Malawi, for example, is said to have had ten college graduates when it became independent in 1964. Because of the considerable demand generated by a combination of increased development expenditure and Africanization of the existing positions, there has been a severe shortage of trained manpower in the early years of development. Investment in training of manpower does not seem to have been commensurate with the substantial investment in rural development programs. Therefore, employment of the trained indigenous manpower by the programs has frequently meant depriving other regions and departments of their existing manpower with adverse effect on their development (see Chapter VIII). However, in other cases where the programs have been bound by the domestic public service commission rules regarding salaries, promotions, and benefits, both the programs and the normal administrative structures have lost manpower to private enterprises and parastatals (see Chapter VIII). Although establishment of project authorities has temporarily bypassed several inefficien-

---

5. ADMARC earned as high as K6.6 per bag for the maize it exported in 1972, whereas the maize producers received only K2.5. Kinsey reports that in 1974 such policies resulted in ADMARC earning a profit of K27 million, a substantial portion of which was siphoned off to the investments of prominent politicians. These factors have been a major source of contention between the program management and ADMARC. See Chapter VI of this study for further details.

cies of the existing administrative structure, it has not resolved the difficult basic problem of wage disparities and administrative incentive systems that continue to deter manpower from serving the rural sector. This problem is by no means easy to tackle. Frequently, it is argued that higher salaries are necessary to attract trained manpower to the rural sector. However, attempting to maintain parity with rising urban salaries rather than controlling the latter further increases the disparities between the educated and the uneducated. The constraints posed by these structural problems, however, seem to receive little attention in policymaking. Often, ad hoc measures are adopted in programs, making the manpower problem more complex over time (see Chapter VIII).

The administrative and technical quality of the available staff has also been poor, restricting the scope for expansion of services. Quality of the indigenous manpower can, of course, be increased relatively quickly, provided there are effective programs for their training. Performance of the programs on this score has varied considerably. CADU, KTDA, BAT, and ZAPI have played a very effective role in training administrative staff. However, most other programs reviewed have been deficient in this respect.

In Ethiopia even the substantial training of field staff being carried out by programs such as CADU and by the additional nationally run training centers has not been adequate relative to the manpower needs. The supply of trained extension staff remains one of the major constraints to expansion of even the very modest level of services that the Minimum Package Program aims to provide. Low levels of technical competence among the field staff and poor incentive systems remain an equally severe constraint to improved performance in Kenya and Tanzania, although in comparison with Ethiopia the latter two countries have been better endowed in terms of numbers of extension workers.[6] (See Chapter IV.)

This raises a question as to whether programs directed at low-income target populations can, indeed, carry out training on the scale and of the quality which are essential for providing a guaranteed minimum level of services to all the low-income rural populations in the foreseeable future. Substantial investment seems to be necessary in training programs to release this major constraint. To improve the content of training and to make it more practical, training programs can, of course, be linked to specific rural development programs.

Obviously, the need for formally trained manpower is largely determined by how delivery of agricultural services is organized. Many programs follow conventional forms of credit administration based on complex criteria of creditworthiness of the applicant, which involve processing of a number of complicated forms. These administrative procedures are highly demanding of scarce trained manpower, a constraint which limits the number of small farmers that can be reached through credit (see Chapter V). Similarly, the use of personal visits in the introduction of innovations, an approach followed in many programs, restricts the number of farmers that can be reached through extension services (see Chapter IV). All too often

---

6. It has been frequently observed that development of an effective network of field staff may be easier in Ethiopia, where the slate is clean, than in Kenya and Tanzania, where administrative reform poses a major constraint.

the administrative systems used in the delivery of services and the man-power they require seem to be a far greater constraint to the expansion of coverage than are finances.

The manpower constraint also creates a conflict between realizing growth and achieving distribution, since reaching fewer, more responsive farmers within the target populations is the easier way to realize growth in the short run. This tendency to concentrate on progressive or innovative farmers was frequently noted in the programs reviewed (see Chapters IV and V).

To alleviate this problem, some of the programs, including KTDA, ZAPI, CADU, and WADU, have introduced a modest element of responsibility to the program participants in the provision of extension services, in the deliv-ery of credit, and in the marketing of inputs and outputs. The experience of these programs indicates that, if properly developed, there may be substan-tial potential for local participation in the delivery of services. However, this potential has so far not been exploited sufficiently, primarily because the knowledge as to how to organize such services is limited.

Whether the planners of the programs are expatriates or indigenous ad-ministrators, their understanding of the rural people and of local leadership traditions often seems poor. There also seems to have been little tendency to innovate in organizing services and little willingness to delegate respon-sibility to the rural people. Reviewers of the programs emphasize that the paternalism of program administrators is one of the severe constraints to development of strong, viable local organizations. This attitude tends to lead to excessive protection and subsidization of local organizations at the outset, resulting in inefficiencies and a lack of willingness on the part of the rural people to share responsibility along with benefits.

Credit Policies

In the programs reviewed target populations have been eligible for short-term institutional credit at an annual interest rate of 7 to 12 percent, pro-vided they meet the criteria of creditworthiness. Although these criteria vary substantially between programs, they are generally cumbersome. In some cases the requirement of a down payment—which the poorest farm-ers often cannot afford—excludes many farmers from credit services. Despite this fact the credit policies in the programs reviewed have, by and large, not been discriminatory towards the low-income groups; nor has the amount of credit distributed in these particular programs been restricted by the supply of credit. Rather, in most cases the availability of manpower to administer credit and the profitability of the innovations affecting the de-mand for credit seem to have been the critical limiting factors in reaching small farmers (see Chapter V). Often during implementation in the quest for measuring success of the programs by the number of farmers reached through credit, these constraints appear to be overlooked and emphasis placed on credit expansion. When innovations are profitable, however, the repayment rate of even the lowest income farmers can be as high as, if not higher than, that of the large farmers, as illustrated by the rural develop-ment programs in Ethiopia.

Since priorities must be established in the use of scarce administrative manpower, in the initial stages in many of the programs reviewed the devel-opment and extension of technology and the improvement of the marketing systems seem to have been far more critical before credit could become the central focus of the programs. When profitable innovations and markets for output exist, even small farmers are frequently noted to purchase inputs with cash or to organize themselves spontaneously to take advantage of group sales, as illustrated by the Modified Input Areas in Lilongwe. Where feasible, it, therefore, seems desirable to encourage such spontaneous group or cash sales of inputs. This approach has the advantage of minimizing complex credit administrations, of mobilizing rural savings, and of developing viable farmer organizations. Alternative approaches to credit administration, such as an input subsidy, also need to be explored more systematically. The programs reviewed have, however, rarely departed from the credit focus.

Interregional Allocation of Resources and Participation

There are several special features of the African countries which seem to require particular attention if mass participation of the lowest income groups is to be realized in the foreseeable future. A majority of the rural population in Africa earns low incomes. Although relative income disparities are substantial, with a few obvious exceptions, incomes of even the prosperous rural classes are generally low.[7] The low-income population is not concentrated in a few regions, as is the case in some Latin American countries, but encompasses the entire rural sector. The widespread incidence of low productivity and incomes means that in Africa potential target groups are large relative to finances and, in particular, to the trained manpower and institutional capability available for planning and implementing rural development programs. Therefore, if masses are to be reached and if their development is to be viable in the long run, the primary emphasis in rural development programs has to be on establishing a few clear priorities, such as increasing productivity; generating additional resources; and, equally important, augmenting indigenous institutional capability to undertake the more complex tasks of development over time.

Intensive development of certain high-value export crops or of high-potential regions is, therefore, often justified, not only because of its direct impact on the selected target populations, but also because of its potential to generate substantial additional resources for development elsewhere.

However, as has been pointed out earlier, emphasis on intensity of services in an early stage of development may also divert scarce manpower and financial resources away from other regions or activities. Further, even if it generates additional resources, the form in which the resources are generated or the institutions that control the resources may not in practice always ensure the mobilization and allocation of these resources to other low-

7. Although a tea farmer in Kenya may earn an annual cash income of $40 compared to $7 earned by a subsistence farmer, he can hardly be placed in the class of the Latin American *latifundio* (estate). The relatively equitable income distribution in Africa is underlined by a comparison of the proportion of the national income going to the lowest income groups in Africa and Latin America. For example, in Kenya and Tanzania the poorest 20 percent of the population earns, respectively, 7.0 and 9.5 percent of the national income, while in Brazil and Colombia the poorest 20 percent earns 3.5 and 2.2 percent of the income. (See Irma Adelman and Cynthia Taft Morris, "Who Benefits from Economic Development," International Meeting of Directors of Development Research and Training, Belgrade, August 28–30, 1973, Appendix.) The problem in Africa is, therefore, frequently one of fostering participation of the poor rather than attempting exclusion of the rich.

income regions. This is one of the many dilemmas faced in rural development. It would seem, however, that in many cases the objective of mass
participation of low-income groups may be better served by a more equitable allocation of resources at the outset to ensure a minimum level of services and institutional development for removal of the most critical constraints before a few regions benefit from substantially greater allocation.
There are, of course, exceptions when unusually profitable opportunities
may justify intensive development.

In several programs the argument against initial intensity can be made
particularly strong in the case of investments in social services. Social services are heavily in demand in most program areas and can be frequently
justified on the basis of need. Consequently, in both top down integrated
programs (such as LLDP and SODENKAM) and in bottom up programs
(such as *ujàmaa*), many social services are provided, often without instituting mechanisms for generating additional fiscal resources in the program
areas, without examining economic ways of providing the services, without
training additional manpower, and without developing the necessary institutions to ensure their long-term viability. These oversights may occur
despite the fact that the intensive provision of productive services has led
to considerable increases in income in some of the program areas, such as
LLDP or SODENKAM (see Chapter VII).

Particularly, because many social services such as health facilities involve
substantial recurrent budgetary resources, ensuring their continuity without
additional resource mobilization means either continued reliance on
foreign assistance or diversion of resources from productive investments
elsewhere. This diversion of resources may frequently affect long-term
growth as well as distribution, as is feared may be the case in Tanzania. The
knowledge of the effect of social services on increasing productive capacity
as distinct from improving welfare must, of course, be highly region
specific. Such knowledge is generally very poor. Where social services cannot be justified on the basis of extreme need on either productive or welfare
grounds, the question of their initial efficacy focuses on the interrelated
considerations of long-term feasibility and regional equity: e.g., why should
people in Lilongwe benefit from substantial productive services, intensive
land-use planning, roads, soil conservation measures, water supply, and
health clinics, while several other regions in Malawi do not receive even the
minimum level of agricultural services?

Through their visibility and the demonstration effect, integrated programs have undoubtedly helped to focus attention on problems of rural development, as is evident from the role of CADU in energizing the Ethiopian Ministry of Agriculture and in getting a massive rural development
effort under way. However, where the peasantry is politically conscious, as
in Kenya, a few regional programs can also generate substantial political
tensions. This explains partly the rather lukewarm attitude of the Kenyan
government towards regional programs, so labeled, since SRDP got under
way.

Institutional Development in Past Programs

Constraints are also imposed by inadequate development of administrative, commercial, and elective institutions which have had a profound

effect on the scope for development of the subsistence sector. Institutional development takes time, even if the commitment to its realization exists and the necessary decisions for its development are made. Frequently, however, the time required for institutional development and the changes in the distribution of political and administrative power that such development implies deter policymakers from taking the necessary steps, despite the attention that institutional reform may receive in policy pronouncements. For reasons of ideology or preconceptions, in choosing between different types of institutions, far too much emphasis is also placed on the form rather than on the substance of institutions, discouraging competition between different types of institutions and reducing their overall effectiveness. This is despite the fact that, frequently, substantial scope exists for institutional pluralism.

Besides, for political, administrative, psychological, and other conventional economic reasons, success is easier to measure when it is in the form of an immediate increase in the amount of fertilizer distributed, the number of health clinics established, or the number of *ujàmaa* villages settled than when programs aim at bringing about participation more slowly and indirectly, as, for instance, by simultaneously increasing the administrative capacity of ADMARC to ensure that the fertilizer will be distributed in the program areas after the program phases out; or by developing viable local organizations in ZAPI that can plan and implement health clinics; or by improving the technical and administrative competence of the local leaders to organize and implement *ujàmaa* villages.

This is why it is important to examine the performance of SRDP in Kenya and the decentralization of rural development administration in Tanzania. For unlike the integrated programs, these two efforts have been undertaken ostensibly with the objective of improving institutional capability and self-reliance.

Decentralization of Administration

For several reasons SRDP has had a rather limited success. The form in which it evolved did not have adequate commitment of high-level Kenyans to bring prestige to the concept and to push the program through the many difficult domestic administrative obstacles, including obtaining funding from the influential but conservative Treasury. Frequently, such tasks cannot be carried out by expatriate technical advisors, even with the greatest of will and commitment to a program's concept (see Chapter IX).

As is so often the case, for short-term political reasons far too many quick results also seem to have been expected of SRDP, even though local administrators responsible for planning were inexperienced and lacked technical ability. In practice SRDP has, therefore, suffered from an ambivalence: on the one hand, it has attempted to serve a pilot function and, thus, to be innovative in bringing about administrative improvements; on the other, it has been under pressure to show immediate visible results. There has also been considerable reluctance among the administrators in Nairobi to delegate authority to the provinces and districts and inadequate willingness in the individual ministries to coordinate their activities.

SRDP has, nevertheless, made a modest beginning in improving area-based planning and implementing capacity and in institutionalizing an administrative system to improve interdepartmental coordination (see Chapter X). The disappointment with the program results is not so much due to the limitations of SRDP as much as the fact that, in planning the overall district decentralization exercise in Kenya, many of the same mistakes seem to be repeated.

Development Administration and the Role of Elective Bodies

The Tanzanian effort has benefited from an immense national commitment to the idea of decentralized and participatory administration. This is already reflected in the greater delegation of authority to the regional administrations and the more explicit role given to the political party in rural development planning. The Tanzanian experience is too new to be able to assess its performance. Nevertheless, its potential for accomplishments and its possible limitations are beginning to be apparent.

The Tanzanian emphasis on regional equity in the allocation of resources is worthy of emulation in other African countries. However, the increased role of the elective bodies in planning seems to have led to the allocation of far too high a proportion of the development expenditure to provision of social services without a commensurate effort at resource mobilization. Paradoxically, welfare expenditures on such a scale appear to have been possible, mainly because the emphasis on self-reliance has attracted donors to Tanzania, leading to a considerable increase over the short run in the availability of resources (see Chapter VII).

In the long run, increased competence of the regional administrators can exercise an important influence in bringing about a more rational allocation of resources and a more effective use of the resources allocated. This is why considerably greater attention needs to be devoted in donor-assisted programs to improving the indigenous planning and implementing capacity. In the programs reviewed, including those in Kenya and Tanzania, donors have taken an excessively short-term view of aid. They have tended to design their own programs and to implement them mainly so as to avoid risk of failure. This attitude has, of course, been reinforced by the frequent lack of national will to make policy decisions that touch upon the existing distribution of political and administrative power. The role of technical assistance in improving the indigenous planning and implementing capacity has, therefore, been far short of its potential.

The Role of Semi-autonomous Administrative Structures

As the time approaches for transferring administrative responsibility for some of the autonomous integrated rural development programs from the project authorities to the indigenous administrations, the gap between the capability of the two administrative systems has become a subject of particular concern to persons involved in designing rural development programs.

Paradoxically, the institutional gap seems to have arisen because the integrated programs have set themselves to accomplish far too many visible results in too short a time period and, therefore, have been able to allocate only a limited time and effort to development of institutional capability. The gap exists at three levels. First, the indigenous regional administrations do not have the capability to carry out the policy and coordinating functions

at the regional headquarters. These are now being carried out by autonomous administrations. This capability is critical for administering complex integrated programs, since they involve activities of a number of
departments and local governmental agencies as, for instance, agriculture,
transportation, and health. Second, the institutions to handle the commercial aspects of the programs, such as agricultural credit and input and output
marketing, either do not exist (since the programs have handled these functions) or do not yet have the administrative capability to manage the activities on a scale on which the programs have carried them out. Third, the
local organizations and local administrative units being developed by programs do not correspond to the existing local governmental institutions,
raising difficult questions related to maintenance and expansion of the
various local services.

LLDP is now faced with these complex problems. Although CADU and
ZAPI have been more effective than LLDP in training indigenous administrators, their progress in establishing liaison with the regional administrations, in developing commercial institutions, and in fostering vigorous local
organizations seems to have been limited.

The experience of the integrated programs indicates that, if there is not to
be a considerable sag in the program activities after expatriate managers
have departed and project authorities have dissolved, programs may have
to undertake only those activities on such a scale which, in the foreseeable
future, can realistically be taken over and managed by indigenous manpower and institutions, even with ambitious assumptions about manpower
training and institutional development.

Implications of the Findings of ARDS
for Designing Rural Development Programs

The experience of the past points again to several special features of the
African countries which seem to call for greater attention in designing
future programs if the new objectives of rural development are to be
realized (see Chapter I).

Because the bulk of the rural population in Africa is poor and because
this poverty is spread over the entire rural sector, target groups in Africa are
large relative to the financial resources and, in particular, to the trained
manpower and the institutional capability frequently available for development. Therefore, if the emphasis in rural development is to be on mass participation and on the viability of the process of rural development, it would
seem necessary that rural development programs be viewed as part of a
continuous, dynamic process rather than as an extensive versus an intensive or a maximum versus a minimum effort. The emphasis on mass participation also means that a sequential approach may be necessary in planning
and implementing a rural development strategy, involving establishment of
clear priorities and time-phasing of activities.

Given the low productivity of the subsistence rural sector, for a variety of
reasons discussed earlier, in many cases an initial emphasis on broad-based
increases in productivity through a certain minimum level of services and
institutional development may well be a more effective way of ensuring
viability of mass participation than the substantial initial concentration of
resources in a few regions.

Some constraints to improvement of productivity, such as lack of a profitable technology, ineffective extension, and inadequate fertilizer, may be common to all of subsistence agriculture, whereas others, such as ill health caused by malaria (in the squatter settlements in Kenya) or the inadequate incentive system and organization (in the *ujàmaa* villages in Tanzania) may be location specific. A single package is, therefore, not universally applicable. The establishment of priorities needs a combination of a few critical, general interventions applicable to several regions along with emphasis on development of capability of the regional administrations to identify and ameliorate additional constraints specific to the individual regions.

However, in all cases, including the case of priorities that may be established at the national level, the effectiveness of implementation depends on the efficiency and the coordinating ability of the regional administrations and of the general institutional development at the regional and local level. This is why a regional focus in development is necessary from the outset, even when a broad coverage of services may be aimed at. This is especially the case if more complex programs involving a number of sectors are to be planned and implemented by regional administrations over time.

The first step may well be to improve regional administrative capability for effective planning and implementing of programs directed towards only a few productive activities, including food crops. Attention to food crop production seems critical, since a majority of the low-income population derives its livelihood from this activity. The results of the mixed crop approach are already noticeable in the more recent integrated rural development programs. However, they have been confined to a few regions.

The sequential approach implies efforts to improve indigenous institutional and technical capability in several regions. If per capita agricultural production is to increase, the first phase of sequential development may involve an objective of achieving an overall annual growth rate of 4 to 5 percent. The time required to achieve such an annual growth rate may, of course, vary between regions, depending on their potential and on the effectiveness with which the necessary steps are implemented. However, the first phase of development may be planned for from four to seven years. In a few cases in which an effective technical and institutional capability to coordinate and deliver the necessary services already exists, the first phase of development may be skipped.

Increased intensity in agricultural services of the type undertaken in integrated programs (including improvement of the overall farming systems through rotational improvement, integration of crop and livestock production, soil conservation, and land registration) may constitute the second stage of development. Realistically, the overall growth rate of production may not exceed 4 to 5 percent per year even during the second phase. However, consolidation of the growth rate through a more diversified agricultural productivity may require an intensive effort.

In this case the bridge between the first and the second stages of development will often be land-use planning.[8] The intensive effort needs considerable technical and administrative input, both at the planning and implementing stages.

8. The timing of land-use planning, of course, depends on the preemption of other choices. For example, if an area is being settled rapidly through migration, as in Tanzania, some degree of land-use planning may be essential, regardless of the stage of program activities.

To plan a strategy for intensive agricultural development, data are needed on factors such as agroclimatic zones (including soil conditions, rainfall patterns, present yields, existing farming systems, erosion, and fertility problems); density of settlement; sociocultural factors; and opportunities for expansion of cultivated area and grazing land, required investments in road and water development, soil conservation, and the optimal farming systems (i.e., crops, management practices, rotations, and so forth).

The data gathering and planning of this second phase may be combined with the implementation of the first phase. Phased planning has several advantages which were not derived in many of the programs reviewed. It may allow greater first-hand knowledge of the specific technical, administrative, and sociocultural constraints. It may also permit greater efficiency in the acquisition of such knowledge through greater indigenous participation in planning. Both these factors are important for improving effectiveness of the strategy. The phased approach may also facilitate training of indigenous manpower geared specifically to planning and implementing regional programs. Equally important, it may allow a relatively balanced national coverage of services in the foreseeable future.

For a variety of reasons discussed earlier, planning and implementation of services, such as community centers, drinking water supply, health clinics, women's extension programs, and so forth, require considerations substantially different from those in agricultural planning. It seems necessary to allow greater scope for social choice and for local participation in the organization and delivery of these services. This is also true about promotion of small-scale manufacturing and servicing, the success of which frequently depends upon its linkages with the development of the agricultural sector (see Chapters II and IX). In many cases such planning may have to wait until the second phase—i.e., until incomes and effective demand for such services increase, local skills and administrative capability for planning and coordinating such programs are developed, mechanisms for increasing savings and raising fiscal resources are instituted, and local institutional capability to implement programs is fostered through an explicit emphasis on the necessary preplanning in the first phase.

Given the substantial shortage of trained manpower and administrative capacity, in each phase only those components which are not likely to be undertaken without planned public intervention may be provided. These, of course, vary substantially between regions, depending on what does and does not exist in the form of institutional development. Therefore, no single blueprint for planning is possible. However, in the first phase, provision of technology, extension, inputs, manpower training, and a feeder road network may be the most frequently needed components. A facilitative role may be provided in fostering other activities. For instance, encouraging cash or group purchases of inputs may be desirable where the savings potential in the traditional society is demonstrated to be significant. Once intensity of cultivation increases and manpower and institutions are developed, credit may become the major thrust of the programs.

Marketing services may also fall in the category of a facilitative development at an early stage. The initial emphasis may be on providing intermediate forms of interventions and on improving the bargaining position of the farmer, as, for instance, through construction of public facilities for seasonal storage, improvement of roads and market information systems, and standardization of weights and measures. Introduction of high-cost administrative marketing monopolies or hurried development of farmers' marketing organizations should perhaps be avoided in the early stages. Such organizations are likely to develop more spontaneously once the preconditions for their development are established.

Given the extreme constraint of trained manpower, even with the establishment of priorities in provision of services, mass participation rarely seems feasible in the short run through delivery systems oriented towards individual farmers. Therefore, some delegation of responsibility to the rural people is necessary. Many recent programs have already made a beginning in this direction. They have shown a considerable potential for success, provided local involvement is promoted gradually and is accompanied by a genuine delegation of responsibility to the rural people.

Considerable emphasis on the training of field and administrative staff is needed so that the intensity of services and the number of services may be increased gradually over time. Manpower training is critical to achieve production targets as well as to broaden participation.

Finally, and of importance, the past programs indicate that, if the process of rural development is to be viable, there is need not only for expanding administrative coverage but also for improving the performance of the indigenous administrative systems. Technical assistance may be needed not mainly to manage projects but to assist in developing local, regional, and national capability to plan and implement rural development programs. To realize this objective, it seems necessary that nationals be actively involved from the early stages of project formulation and implementation. It also seems desirable that expatriates not be highly concentrated in project authorities in which effective interaction with local staff and indigenous administrative institutions is frequently inhibited, hampering the development of the latter.

Wherever possible, technical assistance needs to be provided to develop administrative systems which incorporate clear definitions of objectives and targets, ways of implementing and evaluating these targets, and incentive systems which will encourage improved administrative performance as measured by the realization of these targets.

Use of the sequential approach tends to facilitate the incorporation of several desirable features found in the programs reviewed. First, it helps to focus attention on the frequent need for broad-based development of the subsistence sector. Second, it helps to highlight the crucial role of indigenous manpower and institutional capability, not only in terms of the effectiveness with which interventions are implemented, but also in planning rural development programs to take account of variability. By revealing the need for emphasis on manpower and institutional development in early stages of program implementation, it tends to assure the smoother and more effective expansion of the scope of programs over time. Finally, in using the sequential approach, it is assumed that an increase in productivity of the subsistence sector frequently constitutes a major, but only the first, step in improvement of the welfare of subsistence rural populations.

Glossary

Acronyms and Non-English Terms Used in the Text

ADMARC	Agriculture Development and Marketing Corporation (Malawi)
AFC	Agricultural Finance Corporation (Kenya)
AIDB	Agricultural and Industrial Development Bank (Ethiopia)
ALDEV	African Land Development Board
animatrices	female extension workers (Cameroon)
ARDS	African Rural Development Study
arrondissement	district (Cameroon)
asrat	tithe (Ethiopia)
baraza	meeting (Kenya)
BAT	British American Tobacco Company
BDPA	Bureau pour le Développement de Production Agricole (Mali)
bwana shamba	agricultural field agent (Tanzania)
CADU	Chilalo Agricultural Development Unit (Ethiopia)
CDC	Commonwealth Development Corporation (United Kingdom)
CFDT	Compagnie Française pour le Développement des Fibres et Textiles (Mali)
CINAM	Compagnie d'Etudes Industrielles et d'Aménagement du Territoire (Company for Industrial Studies and Territorial Development, France)
CPA	Central Personnel Agency (Ethiopia)
CREA	Rural Marketing and Supply Cooperative (Cameroon)
CTS	Cooperative Thrift Scheme (Kenya)
CUT	Cooperative Union of Tanganyika, Ltd. (Tanzania)

dah	vegetable fiber used in ropes and sacks (Kenya)
DDC	District Development Committee (Kenya)
DDPC	District Development and Planning Committee (Tanzania)
ECA	United Nations Economic Commission for Africa
enderassie	governor (Ethiopia)
EPID	Extension and Project Implementation Department (Ethiopia)
EPL	Entreprise de Progrès Local (Local Progress Enterprise, Cameroon)
ERB	Economic Research Bureau (Tanzania)
FAC	Fonds d'Aide et de Coopération (France)
FAO	Food and Agriculture Organization of the United Nations
GMR	Guaranteed Minimum Return Program (Kenya)
harambee	self-help labor (Kenya)
IDA	International Development Association
IDC	Industrial Development Center (Nigeria)
IDS	Institute for Development Studies (Kenya)
IRAM	Institut de Recherches et d'Applications des Méthodes de Développement (France)
IRAT	Institut de Recherches pour l'Agronomie Tropicale (France)
KfW	Kreditanstalt für Wiederaufbau (West Germany)
KLDP	Kenya Livestock Development Project
KTDA	Kenya Tea Development Authority
latifundio	Latin American estate
LDCs	less developed countries
LLDP	Lilongwe Land Development Program (Malawi)
LSMB	Lint and Seed Marketing Board (Tanzania)
MCC Division	Marketing, Credit, and Cooperative Division (WADU, Ethiopia)
MFEP	Ministry of Finance and Economic Planning (Kenya)
MIA	Modified Input Area (LLDP, Malawi)
moniteur	team head (Cameroon)
MPP	Minimum Package Program (Ethiopia)
NORAD	Norwegian Agency for International Development
NRDC	National Rural Development Committee (Kenya)
OPAM	Office des Produits Agricoles du Mali

PDC	Provincial Development Committee (Kenya)
PIM	Programming and Implementation Management System (SRDP, Kenya)
PPO	provincial planning officer (Kenya)
PSC	Public Service Commission (Malawi)
RDC	Regional Development Committee (Tanzania)
RDF	Regional Development Fund (Tanzania)
RMEA	Resident Mission in East Africa (Kenya)
SCAER	Service du Crédit Agricole et d'Equipement Rural (Mali)
SCDA	Special Crops Development Authority (Kenya)
SCET–Coopération	Société Centrale pour les Etudes du Territoire-Coopération (France)
secteurs de base	lowest operational level (Mali)
SEDES	Société d'Etudes du Développement Economique et Social (France)
shambas	field or plot (Tanzania)
SIC	Small Industry Credit Schemes (Nigeria)
SIDA	Swedish International Development Authority
SIP	Sequential Implementation Program (SRDP, Kenya)
SODENKAM	Société de Développement du Nkam (Nkam Development Corporation, Cameroon)
SRDP	Special Rural Development Program (Kenya)
TAC	Tanganyika Agricultural Corporation (Tanzania)
TANU	Tanganyika African National Union (Tanzania)
TTA	Tanzania Tobacco Authority
TTB	Tanzania Tobacco Board
TTGC	Tabora Tobacco Growers Cooperative (Tanzania)
ujàmaa	familyhood (Tanzania)
ujàmaa vijijini	rural socialism (Tanzania)
UNIDO	United Nations Industrial Development Organization
USAID	United States Agency for International Development
VSC	Village Settlement Commission (Tanzania)
VSD	Village Settlement Division (Tanzania)
vulgarisateur	extension worker (Cameroon)
WADU	Wolamo Agricultural Development Unit (Ethiopia)
wajàmaa	*ujàmaa* villagers (Tanzania)
wazungu	Europeans (Kenya)

wazungu dawa	fertilizers (Kenya)
weltanschauung	philosophical world view
WGMO	WADU Group Marketing Organization (Ethiopia)
WHO	World Health Organization
ZAPI	Zones d'Action Prioritaires Intégrées (Integrated Priority Action Zones, Cameroon)

National Currencies and Exchange Rates, 1972

Country	*National currency*	*Ratio of national currency to US$1.00*
Cameroon	CFA franc (CFA Fr)	256.25
Ethiopia	Ethiopian dollar (Eth$)	2.3
Kenya	Kenyan shilling (KSh)	7.143
Malawi	kwacha (K)	0.8547
Mali	Malian franc (MFr)	470.85
Nigeria	Nigerian pound (£N)[a]	0.6579
Tanzania	Tanzanian shilling (TSh)	7.143

a. On January 1, 1973, Nigeria converted to the naira (1 naira = 2 £N).

Source: United Nations Monthly Bulletin of Statistics, vol. 29, no. 1 (January 1975), Table 66.

Equivalents of Weights and Measures

metric ton	1,000,000 grams	1.1 tons
quintal	100,000 grams	220.46 pounds
kilogram	1,000 grams	2.2046 pounds
kilometer	1,000 meters	0.62 mile
centimeter	0.01 meter	0.39 inch
millimeter	0.001 meter	0.04 inch
hectare	10,000 square meters	2.47 acres

Project Reviews

Cameroon

Zones d'Action Prioritaires Intégrées (ZAPIs); Société de Développement du Nkam (SODENKAM)

The Integrated Priority Action Zones (ZAPIs) in the South Central province and the East province and the SODENKAM Land Settlement Scheme in the Littoral province are experiments in integrated development which seek to bring together all crucial factors involved in achieving rural development. Each program is headed by a single financially independent non-governmental development company which acts as the primary promoter of development in the particular geographical area. The establishment of a development company permits the adoption of a commercial management style, financial autonomy, and the opportunity to coordinate under one authority the functions in development which are usually dispersed among numerous departments.

The idea behind the creation of ZAPIs grew out of the drafting of Cameroon's Second Five-Year Plan, which was concerned with regionalization. The Company for Industrial Studies and Territorial Development (CINAM), a private French firm specializing in planning, presented the proposal to the government of Cameroon in 1966. Between 1967 and 1971 the ZAPI program was implemented in seven areas—Mengueme, Zoetele, N'goulemakong, and Ngoumou in the South Central province and Nguelemendouka, Doume, and Abong-Mbang in the East province. These regions were chosen because of their high development potential—the people were receptive to new ideas, there was sufficient access to main roads, and the population density was such as to permit economies of scale in the provision of services.

The development company in each ZAPI, the Local Progress Enterprise (EPL), covers a region populated by 2,500–4,000 farmers. EPL plans and implements development projects across a wide range of activities through its two divisions—the Development Division and the Business Management Division. Although EPLs were financed completely by governmental sub-

---

Note: Boundaries and locations of project areas shown in the maps on the following pages are based on the best information available but are not necessarily precise. The political boundaries shown do not imply endorsement or acceptance by the World Bank and its affiliates.

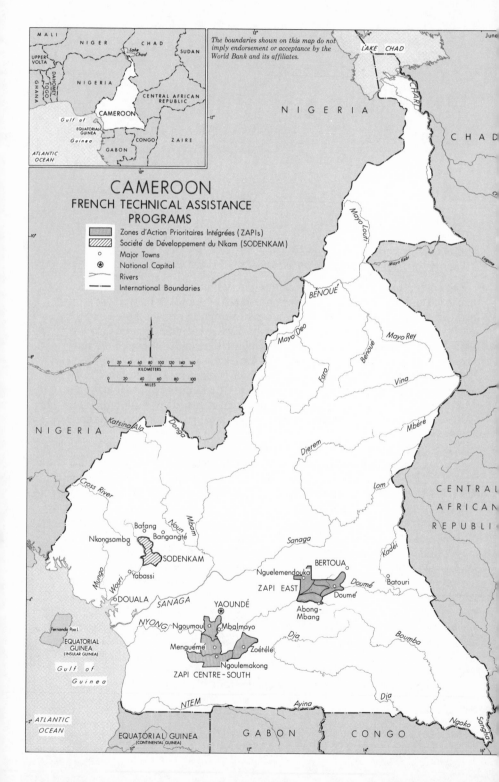

CAMEROON
FRENCH TECHNICAL ASSISTANCE
PROGRAMS

sidy at their onset, this subsidy was to be phased out over a five-year period as EPL attained financial viability. Profits from marketing operations were expected to cover the expenses of EPL and provide a growing surplus for reinvestment.

Each EPL has three to five branch officers presided over by a manager who has responsibilities in credit and marketing. He also controls four to five advisors who are charged with promoting the adoption of new agricultural techniques. There is one advisor for every 150 farmers. At the provincial level, the Regional Mission of Zones creates new zones, trains EPL managers, and coordinates inter-EPL activity.

Farmer organizations have been created to promote participation, and it is hoped that the farmers will gradually assume control of EPLs. At the village level, associations made up of thirty to fifty farmers are responsible for marketing operations and the granting and repayment of credit. The associations have no financial resources at their disposal and must request funds from EPL for development activities.

A farmer subcommittee at the branch level, made up of one representative from each farmer association, serves as a liaison between the association and EPL. An EPL committee of ten to fifteen groups elected from the subcommittee members participates in activities at the EPL level.

Results of the programs carried out in the South Central ZAPIs have been mixed. Although no figures are available, the production of cocoa, the region's major cash crop, seems to be increasing steadily. By 1972 anti-capsid bug treatment and treatment against brown rot had reached 83 percent and 44 percent, respectively, of the area planted to cocoa. Eight hundred and sixty thousand new cocoa seedlings were distributed in 1972. Projects involving banana production and peanut production have also exhibited some success. Little progress has been achieved, on the other hand, in fermentation and drying of cocoa beans and in introducing a crop rotation system.

The marketing of cocoa and foodstuffs has been unsuccessful, and the four ZAPIs showed a loss of Fr7.6 million in the 1971/72 period for marketing operations. Lack of training and motivation at the local level and embezzlement seem to be major problems. Marketing at the village level is self-operating in name only, as EPLs have tight control over the operations.

During the 1971/72 period Fr92.97 million were loaned out in the South Central ZAPIs. Bad loans account for approximately 10 percent of this number and seem to be spreading in many areas, as enforcement is lax. The system vacillates between individual and collective responsibility for repayment.

In general, EPLs seem reluctant to entrust the farmer organizations with any real responsibility. Training of personnel and farmers does not have high priority. The cost of the ZAPI program in the South Central province between November 1966 and June 1972 was about Fr218 million.

The programs carried out in ZAPIs of the East province have been more successful. Statistics on output for the Nguelemendouka ZAPI, the only one for which data are available, show an increase in coffee output per planter from 70 to 150 kilograms and for cocoa from 159 to 266 kilograms over the period 1967/68 to 1971/72. The regeneration of coffee trees, the treatment of cocoa trees against brown rot, and the distribution of fertilizer have received priority.

Marketing operations, most of which involve coffee, have been successful and are self-operated by village associations. The profits, however, are managed by EPL. Total loans granted by EPLs were valued at Fr11.7 million in 1972, and credit problems are similar to those in the South Central ZAPIs.

Supplementary programs are more developed than in the South Central ZAPIs and include women's aid programs, training programs aimed at young adults, health campaigns, and housing improvements.

EPLs in both regions have been relieved of the goal of self-sufficiency. They are now run as commercial enterprises with the goal of maximum turnover with minimum profit and as promotion enterprises receiving subsidies from the government to foster development. In the future decentralization will permit the transfer of planning and decision making from EPLs to the branches.

The SODENKAM project, located in the Littoral region in western Cameroon, was begun in 1966 as an experimental, integrated, low-cost settlement scheme extendable to larger areas. The completion of the Yabassi-Bafang highway in the early 1960s opened up much of this sparsely populated region of 120,000 hectares to development; and the SCET–Coopération, which did the preliminary planning for the project in 1964, chose the area as a good place for a settlement program. Settlers began arriving in 1966; by June 1972 there were 1,180 settlers present, as compared to the 2,230 which had been projected for 1971.

In 1970 administration of the program was transferred from SCET–Coopération to the newly established Company for the Development of the Yabassi-Bafang Region, which was charged with achieving the integrated development of the pioneer villages. An administrative director (responsible for business, finance, and marketing) and a technical director (responsible for installing the settlers and follow-up on the technical level) were appointed by the board of directors. It was hoped that the settlers themselves would eventually take control of the company.

By 1971, 1,040 hectares of land were under coffee and cocoa cultivation; and in 1973, the first year of production, 100 metric tons of coffee were marketed. The Rural Marketing and Supply Cooperative (CREA) was established to market produce and to supply materials and consumer goods; but it has performed poorly.

SODENKAM's Technical Support Center has distributed 400,000 coffee seedlings, 300,000 cocoa seedlings, and 70,000 fruit seedlings. No applied research has been conducted in the area, however; and the extension workers are young and poorly trained.

SODENKAM's supplementary programs include the building of ten schools serving 1,800 pupils in 1972, six health dispensaries, a cultural center, and a training center.

The program's major problems include its relations with the indigenous population, its poor recruitment performance, and the lack of technical support for the settlers. Marketing problems may emerge as more and more cash crops are produced.

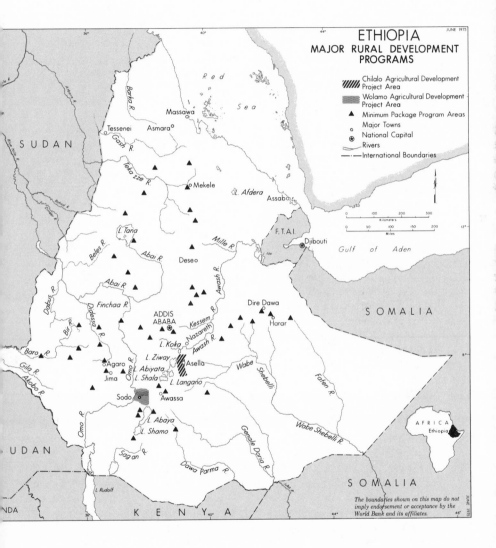

ETHIOPIA
JUNE 1975
MAJOR RURAL DEVELOPMENT
PROGRAMS

▨ Chilalo Agricultural Development
    Project Area
▨ Wolamo Agricultural Development
    Project Area
▲ Minimum Package Program Areas
○ Major Towns
⊛ National Capital
— Rivers
— ∙ — International Boundaries

The boundaries shown on this map do not
imply endorsement or acceptance by the
World Bank and its affiliates.

Ethiopia

Chilalo Agricultural Development Unit (CADU);
Wolamo Agricultural Development Unit (WADU);
Minimum Package Program (MPP)

In order to initiate and accelerate economic growth and development, Ethiopia initially adopted an integrated rural development strategy in which scarce resources were concentrated within clearly defined geographical areas in the form of package projects. The Extension and Project Implementation Department (EPID) was established within the Ministry of Agriculture in 1971 to administer the one extensive nationwide project, the Minimum Package Program, as well as the two existing intensive projects. EPID is, of course, expected to coordinate all the activities related to agricultural development in Ethiopia.

CADU was established in 1967 and is located in the center of Chilalo Awraja in the Arussi province on the eastern side of the Rift Valley. The project covers 10,000 square kilometers and 400,000 inhabitants. CADU's goals are to achieve economic and social development; to enhance local participation in development; to improve employment opportunities; to ensure that attention is given to low-income farmers; and to stress research, training, and transferability. Phase I (1967/68–1970/71) program costs were Eth$13.8 million. Costs of Phase II (1970/71–1974/75) are estimated at Eth$30.5 million. The Swedish International Development Authority (SIDA) covers the expense of its own staff plus 67 percent of the remaining project costs; the balance is covered by the Ethiopian government. In the 1972/73 period CADU's extension workers reached about 15,000 barley, wheat, and dairy farmers; at least 34,000 farmers were expected to be reached in 1975. From 1966 to 1971, largely due to improved marketing, credit, and the use of improved seeds and fertilizer, the area under wheat production expanded from 23,700 to 51,000 hectares; average wheat yields increased from approximately 10 quintals per hectare to 21 quintals per hectare. The net revenue per hectare from the use of improved seeds and fertilizer has been estimated at Eth$126. The economic rate of return on investment for CADU is estimated at 18–19 percent over a ten- to thirteen-year period.

CADU's research efforts have resulted in the development of high-yielding wheat and other seed varieties, labor-intensive farm implements, and high-milking crossbred cattle. Extension methods involve the use of model farmers and demonstration plots. The marketing strategy consists of a purchase and storage program for the seasonal stabilization of grain prices and to assure the farmer an incentive price. Other activities include water resource surveys, rural health programs, soil conservation, women's extension, and feeder road construction. The Ethiopianization of the program staff has progressed smoothly.

WADU was established in 1970 and is located in Wolamo Awraja in Sidamo province on the northeastern edge of the Rift Valley. The project area covers the highland areas of Sodo and Bolosso with a population of 236,000 and the largely uninhabited lowland areas of the Abela and Bele with a population of approximately 3,500. The goals of WADU have been

(a) to raise the per family cash income of 6,000 small-scale highland farmers from Eth$200 to Eth$325 per year; (b) to establish or reorganize 1,750 settler families (10,000 persons) in the lowlands with a target annual income per family of Eth$435; (c) to promote a shift from subsistence to cash crop agriculture; (d) to increase the government's tax revenue; and (e) to demonstrate the value of development projects in Ethiopia. WADU's 1969–74 costs are estimated at Eth$11.7 million, of which 69.4 percent were to be financed by an IDA credit, 4.8 percent by the United Kingdom, 2.5 percent by the World Food Program, and the remaining 23 percent by the Ethiopian government. The economic rate of return on investment is expected to be 11–13 percent (10 percent in the highlands and 17 percent in the settlements) over a twenty-year period. Due to impoved seed and fertilizer use, maize yields have increased from 10 quintals per hectare in 1969 to 22 qunitals per hectare in 1972. The net revenue per hectare resulting from the use of these inputs is estimated at Eth$60 in the highlands and Eth$200 in the settlement areas. By late 1972 the project had reorganized 460 old settlers and accommodated 207 new settlers in the lowlands. In the same year, WADU's extension service reached over 7,000 farmers.

Despite shortages of staff and research facilities, WADU's research team has made some progress in improved maize varieties and livestock breeding. The program uses the demonstrator field extension approach. Usually only one innovation is demonstrated on any one farmer's land. Credit is given in kind and in cash. The program's marketing component is organized along cooperative lines and involves both cash and subsistence crops. WADU's aerial survey and soil conservation activities had proved successful. However, at the time when the review was conducted in 1973, there had not been much progress in road construction, staff training, water improvement, home economic instruction, land consolidation, destocking, and in the betterment of rural health—activities initially proposed by WADU.

Though CADU and WADU are essential parts of the development process in Ethiopia, they are costly in terms of finance and trained manpower. Therefore, MPP was established in 1970 to provide the *minimum* services required by peasant farmers throughout the nation. MPP employs the methods and innovations developed and tested in the comprehensive projects; its goals are similar to those of CADU. The total cost of the program (1970–76) is expected to be Eth$70 million. Technical assistance from IDA and FAO as well as Ethiopian government funds covered the costs of MPP's first three years (Eth$16 million). The 1973–75 costs (Eth$54 million) are to be covered by an IDA credit (81 percent), SIDA technical assistance (9 percent), the Ethiopian government (7 percent), and farmers' down payments (3 percent). The economic rate of return on investment is estimated at 16–17 percent over a twenty-five–year period. Due to the use of improved seeds and fertilizer, teff yield in the program area has increased from 7 quintals per hectare to 15 quintals per hectare. A total of 3,600 farmers in the 1970/71 period and 4,600 in the 1971/72 period participated in the credit program. Over 100,000 farmers were expected to participate by the year 1975/76.

The basic unit of MPP is the minimum package area, each containing approximately 10,000 farmers and located in close proximity to a 75 kilometer stretch of all-weather road. MPP is designed to involve the entire population of Ethiopia, though it initially has been restricted to the Addis Ababa region due to the lack of all-weather roads elsewhere in the country. Each MPP area is divided into extension areas, each of which has its own marketing center and a one-hectare trial demonstration plot.

MPP is constrained by shortages in trained manpower and financial resources. The participation of the affected population in decision making is encouraged in the program. Each MPP area will gradually become more comprehensive as more development components are added to the minimum package. MPP's extension effort involves model farmers and demonstration plots. The program gives credit only in kind, particularly in the form of fertilizer and improved seed. Other activities include livestock improvement, soil conservation, road building, home economics, and cooperative programs.

Kenya

Kenya Livestock Development Project (KLDP)

The Kenya Livestock Development Project is a comprehensive approach to the first step of long-term range development in Kenya. It embraces five different types of livestock production systems, all of which are managed as combined operations for breeding, raising, and fattening beef cattle. The objectives of KLDP are (a) to make life in rural areas attractive, given the absence of greater urban-industrial employment; and (b) to promote the necessary capital formation to further future employment potential and alleviate rural population pressure.

The project supports group, company, and individual ranches with the aim of improving the traditional production sector. Existing commercial ranches have been assisted to improve their productivity. Grazing blocks were proposed to develop marginal pastoral land. IDA and SIDA have provided KSh81 million to KLDP for the period 1970–74. The program's credit operations provided loans for long-term development and short-term working capital. The scheme also finances the facilities and services of a number of government agencies involved in range development. In addition, KLDP is sponsoring land tenure reform to define the rights and duties of specified individuals or groups with respect to specified sections of land.

The commercial ranches backed by KLDP are located on the Laikipia Plateau and in the Rift Valley from south of Lake Naivasha to Baringo district north of Nakuru as well as in Machakos district. Most of the thirty ranches which received loans were underdeveloped and suffered from lack of capital. They are owned by both Europeans and Africans. Loans were administered through AFC at 7.5 percent interest. Loans worth KSh6.4 million have been finalized for feedlot operations; another KSh8.4 million are to be allocated for ranch development, steer purchase, and operation capital. Commercial ranches absorb 54 percent of KLDP's total loan resources and offer an economic rate of return on investment of 23–25 percent. The commercial ranches have low employment potential; their combined capacity to provide additional employment is limited to 300–400 men per year. However, the tax revenues generated from these ranches are expected to help the government provide rural services to other needy areas.

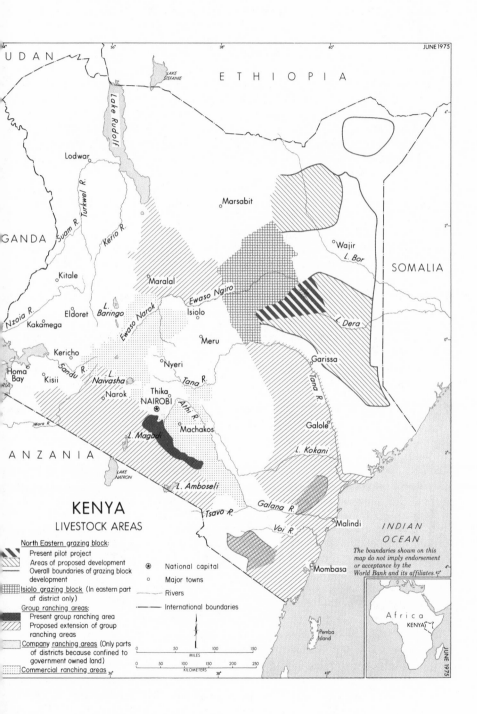

JUNE 1975

UDAN

ETHIOPIA

LAKE STEFANIE

Lake Rudolf

Lodwar

Marsabit

GANDA

°Wajir

L. Bor

SOMALIA

Suam R. Turkwel R.

Kerio R.

Kitale

Maralal

Ewaso Ngiro

Eldoret L. Baringo

Isiolo

L. Dera

Nzoia R. Kakamega

Ewaso Narok

Meru

Garissa

Kericho

Nyeri

Tana R.

Homa Bay Kisii L. Naivasha

Sandu R.

Narok

Thika
NAIROBI

Athi R.

Tana R.

Galole

Mara R.

L. Magadi

Machakos

L. Kokani

ANZANIA

LAKE NATRON

L. Amboseli

Galana R.

L. Kokani

Tsavo R.

Voi R.

Malindi

INDIAN
OCEAN

KENYA
LIVESTOCK AREAS

North Eastern grazing block:
Present pilot project
Areas of proposed development
Overall boundaries of grazing block development

Isiolo grazing block (In eastern part of district only)

Group ranching areas:
Present group ranching area
Proposed extension of group ranching areas

Company ranching areas (Only parts of districts because confined to government owned land)

Commercial ranching areas

⊛ National capital
○ Major towns
— Rivers
—·—· International boundaries

The boundaries shown on this map do not imply endorsement or acceptance by the World Bank and its affiliates.

Mombasa

Pemba Island

Africa

KENYA

JUNE 1975

0   50   100   150
MILES

0   50   100   150   200   250
KILOMETERS

The company ranches financed by KLDP are located in the unoccupied coastal areas of Taita, Tana, and Kilifi districts. The ranches are owned by the state and leased for twenty years. Seven company ranches were granted leases for tracts of 2,000 to 45,000 hectares. The emphasis in these ranches is on steer fattening, ranch development, and the production and marketing of immature steers. Some health, veterinary, water, road, extension, and school services are available to these ranchers. Approved loans totaled about KSh2.7 million (i.e., 33 percent of KLDP's loan funds) and are expected to earn an economic rate of return of 10–20 percent. The employment potential of these ranches is limited to approximately 250–420 men per year. The Galana Ranch, another company endeavor financed by KLDP, is a special effort to bring 300,000 hectares of empty, low-potential land into production.

Forty-two individual ranches were established in pastoral areas originally designated as Masai trust land, eleven of them in Loitokilok (320–800 hectares each) and thirty-one of them in Kaputiei (764–939 hectares each). The average loans for these ranches were KSh90,000 and KSh130,000 in the two locations. Water development and steer purchasing were the main loan items. These individual ranches account for 9 percent of KLDP's loan funds and offer an expected rate of return of 6 percent. They present a low capacity to generate employment but may have already had a significant impact on capital formation.

Group ranching in pastoral areas is a new concept and embraces 37,500 square kilometers of the Masai-occupied Kaputiei section of the Kajiado district. There are twenty-five of these ranches, averaging 18,000 hectares in size and supporting a total of over 1,500 ranchers. They account for 4 percent of the total loan funds but are expected to offer a 13 percent rate of return. The direct employment effect of group ranches is negligible; pastoralists are already underemployed, and little additional labor will be required in the establishment of these ranches.

Grazing block development is designed to replace seminomadism by permanent ranching without regulating the movement of livestock, except for block rotation purposes. This is to be accomplished through range water investments, stationary cattle husbandry, increased commercial off-take, and controlled grazing. Range water surveys and investments began in 1970 in three grazing blocks (700,000 hectares) in the Gashi-Kalalut area in Garissa and Wajir districts. These blocks are expected to cost $1.5 million, which will be financed by USAID and administered by the Kenyan government. On every block there are 150 to 300 cattle owners, each holding 114–228 head of cattle. Investments are direct grants-in-aid to the people; all services are free. The rate of return to investment is 5 percent, and the employment potential is low relative to the high capital investments.

Agricultural Finance Corporation (AFC) and other Farm Credit Schemes

Kenya's agricultural credit system includes an array of financial institutions and schemes. There are programs to support the transfer of agricultural land from European to African ownership. There are older structures oriented toward large-scale agriculture—i.e., suppliers of agricultural inputs and equipment, commercial banks, a public sector farm mortgage lending

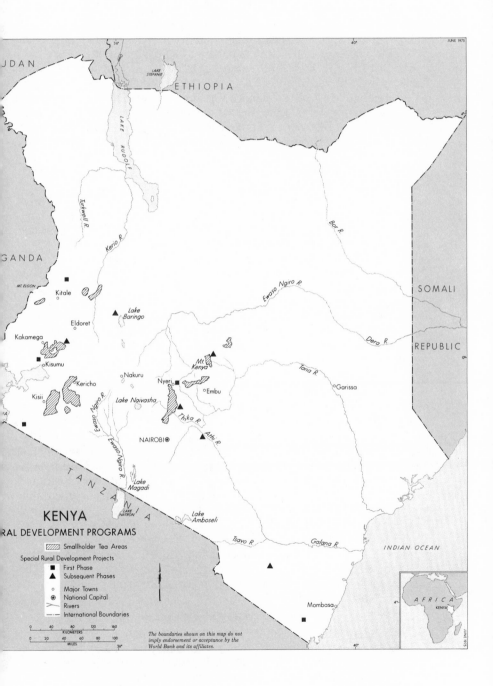

KENYA
RAL DEVELOPMENT PROGRAMS

Smallholder Tea Areas

Special Rural Development Projects
- First Phase
- Subsequent Phases
- Major Towns
- National Capital
- Rivers
- International Boundaries

The boundaries shown on this map do not
imply endorsement or acceptance by the
World Bank and its affiliates.

program, and production and storage finance arrangements for large producers of wheat and maize. There are also newer institutions and programs serving smallholders. These include cooperative structures, crop marketing authorities, and pilot projects. Estimates of agricultural credit use in Kenya indicate that, in 1972, 100,000 small-scale farmers borrowed KSh371 million and 7,000 large-scale farmers borrowed KSh558 million.

The British Land Transfer Program began in 1961 to transfer 2.82 million hectares of European-owned land in the scheduled areas to African proprietorship. Most of the finance was supplied by the United Kingdom. The main components were the Settlement Scheme, the British Land Transfer Assisted Owners Scheme, and the Stamp Purchase Plan (which provided for the Agricultural Development Corporation farms and the Harambee Settlement Scheme). Many of these funds were channeled through the Agricultural Finance Corporation (AFC), which was established in 1963 as the primary specialized agricultural credit institution in Kenya and the only lender aimed at both the small- and large-scale farmers.

In addition to its land purchase and development loans, AFC's large-scale loan activities include loans for ranching, funded by IDA and Sweden, as well as the allocation of West German development loans. The KSh81 million IDA/SIDA-financed Kenya Livestock Development Project (KLDP) began in 1970 and attempted to involve traditional pastoral societies in commercial beef production. The West German Kreditanstalt für Wiederaufbau (KfW) Large-Scale Loan Project began in 1969 and provided DM2.5 million for the establishment of state-owned animal breeding farms and for the rationalization of large-scale African farms in the Trans-Nzoia district.

AFC is also involved in three small-scale loan programs. The World Bank's Smallholder Credit Project began in 1967 and was designed to provide credit for on-farm development to smallholders as well as loans to machinery contractors for the purchase of tractors. IDA provided $3.6 million and the Kenyan government $1.4 million. The project was intended to reach 8,100 borrowers with net annual cash incomes of KSh1,300 within four years. By December 1972 it had approved over 10,000 smallholder loans worth an average of KSh3,350 and had disbursed 50 tractor loans worth a total of KSh1.1 million. In 1973 a second phase was instituted, focusing on livestock and poultry development, crop production, and tractors. IDA provided about 60 percent of the project's total cost of $9.2 million. The KfW Smallholder Credit Project began in 1969 in Kisii and Kericho districts to provide credit to 3,600 farmers. The project was expanded in 1972. KfW has contributed funds totaling about $1.4 million. AFC began the internally funded Small-Scale Loan Project in 1965. This project was intended to finance land registration, fruit production, and neglected small farmers.

Addditional components of Kenya's credit system include:
1. The Guaranteed Minimum Return (GMR) Program, which furnishes seasonal production credit for growers with more than 6.1 hectares in wheat and hybrid maize and which provides crop insurance, guaranteeing compensation in the event of a crop failure;
2. Agricultural development loans for crop finance and intermediate development finance, provided by the Kenya Commercial Bank,

Barclay's Bank International, Standard Bank, and the Cooperative Bank of Kenya;

3. The Cooperative Production Credit Scheme, a credit program geared towards cooperative marketing of agricultural produce and strengthening of cooperatives in Kenya;

4. The Kenya Tea Development Authority, which provides fertilizer on credit, and the Pyrethrum Marketing Board, which furnishes planting materials on credit;

5. The Kenya Farmers Association, a national cooperative organization which sells a myriad of articles and inputs to farmers on credit as well as buys wheat and maize (this group is also involved in GMR and AFC);

6. FAO pilot schemes for fertilizer distribution, financed by grants from the fertilizer industry in Western Europe and Japan, and AFC's pilot smallholder credit schemes, which have been restricted to the Vihiga and Tetu districts.

Recently, Kenya's credit programs have emphasized improving the distribution and the amount of credit available to smallholders. Analysis of a nonrandom sample of thirteen smallholder borrowers of AFC/IDA credits and six smallholder non-borrowers, all in Murang'a district, tends to indicate that the individual farmer's commitment to farming, his education, and his experience are the most vital factors in the determination of internal rates of return on agricultural enterprises.

Kenya Tea Development Authority (KTDA)

Kenya's smallholder tea project was established with the objective of increasing smallholder tea production on both sides of the Rift Valley, in Kiambu, Murang'a, Nyeri, Kirinyaga, Embu, Meru, Kericho, Kisii, Nandi, and Kakamega. Originally administered by the Special Crops Development Authority in 1960, the project became the sole responsibility of the Kenya Tea Development Authority in 1964. KTDA's gross expenses from 1960 to 1971 of KSh111.3 million have been covered by internal revenue from planting material sales, taxes from growers, and loans from the Kenyan government, the West German government, IDA, and the Commonwealth Development Corporation (CDC). Massive input of capital and skilled supervisory manpower have been essential ingredients. During the first two plans, from 1960–1971, tea hectarage of smallholders increased from 1,482 to 24,912; the number of smallholders increased from 9,062 to 66,500; production of green leaf increased from 4,618 quintals to 311,562 quintals; and the return to farmers (including taxes to be paid to KTDA) increased from KSh471,580 to KSh35.3 million. The project yielded a total gross return of more than KSh140 million in increased income for the tea-growing areas. The increased tea output has been a valuable source of foreign exchange; the export value of tea has increased from KSh88.2 million or 12.5 percent of total exports in 1960 to KSh254.1 million or 17.7 percent of total exports in 1970. Growth of rural infrastructure attributable to the tea project has had beneficial secondary effects for the local Kenyans, such as increased social mobility, commercialization, and dairy cattle ownership.

The third plan (1968–1973) called for an increase of 14,170 hectares of tea, 26,000 growers, and fifteen new factories. The goal of this plan was to limit the number of new growers in order to increase the intensity of the tea areas, reach optimum average tea plot size of 0.40 hectares per farmer, and decrease operational costs. A fourth plan began (1973–1978) with the goal of including 18,219 more hectares of tea, 24,000 more growers, and twenty-two new factories. KTDA also planned to offer credit to all new growers and to take over factory management during this plan.

In order to maintain a high-quality product and yield, KTDA maintains tight control and supervision over all production and operations. Until recently it has been the only legal source of planting material and the only legal buyer. The KTDA Board, comprised of both growers and lenders, makes all major policy and financial decisions. Local tea committees, composed of growers' representatives, advise KTDA and provide vital feedback and information links between farmers and KTDA. KTDA maintains a field grading system, grower recognition days, a fertilizer credit campaign, and legal orders of prosecution in order to enforce KTDA policy. By increasing tea-planting density and improving tea access roads, KTDA has not only reduced its own major costs of leaf inspection and collection but also reduced the marketing constraint faced by growers. KTDA's extension involves intensive field training. In the 1970/71 period, on the average, each grower received six visits from the local extension office. KTDA has also emphasized technological research; its efforts, along with those of the Minsitry of Agriculture and the Tea Research Institute at Kericho, are aimed at increasing smallholders' returns and decreasing operational costs of KTDA. The vegetative propagation package has reduced the constraints faced in expansion of planting. Subsequently, the annual planting program increased from 1,946 hectares in 1966 to 3,073 in 1971.

The Kenyan government has contributed to the establishment of KTDA through a loan of KSh400,000 for the first plan and numerous short-term loans thereafter. It has also borne the responsibility of improving the vital tea road network by increasing and upgrading 3,100 kilometers of roads by 1974 at a total cost of KSh166 million.

By 1970 smallholders produced 21 percent of total Kenya tea output and held almost half of the total hectarage. Average hectarage per family has increased from 0.15 hectares to 0.38 hectares since 1960. In the 1970/71 period in the low-yielding areas, the per hectare average net return to the grower without hired labor was KSh1,830. It was KSh5,400 in high-yielding areas. With hired labor the average net return was KSh940 in low-yielding areas and KSh4,000 in high-yielding areas.

Special Rural Development Program (SRDP)

The Special Rural Development Program was formulated in the late 1960s as a major government initiative to carry out integrated rural development and to incorporate the nation's productivity and welfare goals into government policies and programs. The Kericho Conference, which took place in 1966, involved participation of the Ministry of Planning and Development and included members of the University of Nairobi Planning Committee, the Institute for Development Studies, and the Overseas Development Administration. This conference provided most of the ideas and preliminary planning on which SRDP was based. Delays in the actual planning and implementation of SRDP were largely a result of problems involving interministerial and government-donor relationship.

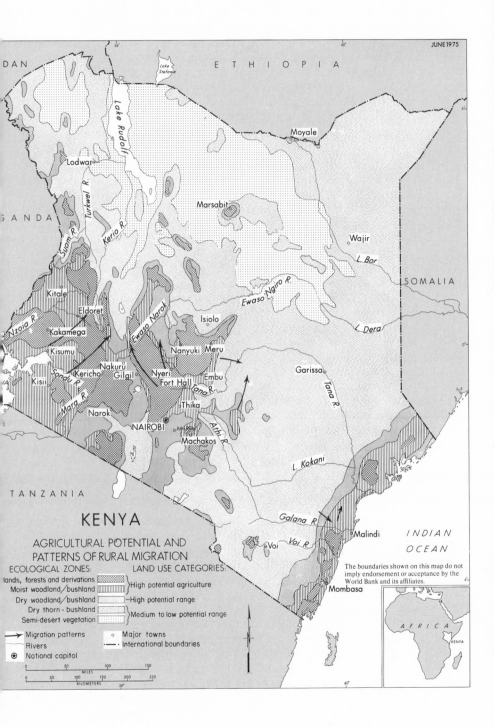

JUNE 1975

SUDAN

ETHIOPIA

Lake Stefanie

Lodwar

Lake Rudolf

Moyale

Marsabit

Wajir

L. Bor

SOMALIA

UGANDA

Swam R.

Turkwel R.

Kerio R.

Kitale

Eldoret

Nzoia R.

Kakamega

Kisumu

Sondu R.

Kericho

Kisii

Mara R.

Narok

Ewaso Narok

Isiolo

Nanyuki Meru

Nakuru Gilgil

Nyeri Fort Hall

Thika

Tana R.

Embu

Ewaso Ngiro R.

L. Dera

Garissa

Tana R.

Athi R.

NAIROBI

Machakos

L. Kokani

TANZANIA

KENYA

AGRICULTURAL POTENTIAL AND PATTERNS OF RURAL MIGRATION

Galana R.

Voi R.

Voi

Malindi

INDIAN OCEAN

Mombasa

ECOLOGICAL ZONES: LAND USE CATEGORIES:

lands, forests and derivations
Moist woodland/bushland ‖‖‖ — High potential agriculture
Dry woodland/bushland — High potential range
Dry thorn-bushland
Semi-desert vegetation — Medium to low potential range

→ Migration patterns   o Major towns
— Rivers   — International boundaries
⊛ National capitol

The boundaries shown on this map do not imply endorsement or acceptance by the World Bank and its affiliates.

AFRICA

KENYA

MILES
0   50   100   150
0 50 100 150 200 250
KILOMETERS

The Program, which began in 1971, focused on the initiation of numerous projects within six program areas which covered approximately 8 percent of Kenya's population. These programs were carried out at the divisional level and were chosen to cover an ecological and socioeconomic cross section of the nation to design and test various approaches to development. SRDP received large external inputs in planning and technical assistance as well as in financial aid. The areas chosen, the chief projects within the areas, and the principal sponsors of the programs were:

1. Migori—The Master Farmers Project, an extension service program for progressive farmers, and the Migori Road Project to build feeder roads utilizing labor-intensive techniques, financed by the Food and Agriculture Organization and the Swedish International Development Agency.
2. Mbere—The Cotton Block Project, emphasizing agronomic research, financed by the government of Norway.
3. Tetu—The Extension Pilot Project, designed to concentrate on increasing hybrid maize production, and the Special 4-K Project to concentrate on youth and to interest them in the production and preparation of high-protein foods. Financed by the Kenyan government.
4. Vihiga—The Maize Credit Package to encourage the wider adaptation of hybrid maize through the provision of credit and intensive extension supervision, financed by the United States Agency for International Development.
5. Kapenguria—The Livestock Marketing Project to increase cattle trading and foster the creation of organized ranches, financed by the government of the Netherlands.
6. Kwale—The Sequential Implementation Procedure, a broad variety of schemes financed by the government of Great Britain.

Not all of these projects were fully implemented.

As an outgrowth of the SRDP experiment, since 1972 the government has been involved in the extension of decentralized integrated planning to all districts in Kenya. The post of district development officer was created to facilitate local planning, and the basic planning unit was expanded from the division to the district.

The primary objectives of SRDP were to increase rural incomes, employment, and welfare. The focus of the strategy was to identify critical gaps and bottlenecks in development, emphasizing the testing of new ideas and projects. The major principles of SRDP included experimentaion, the use of government machinery for carrying out the programs; an emphasis on transferability of programs, and a systematic evaluation of the progress made.

A major emphasis in both planning and implementation was on organizational (interministerial) coordination and interdisciplinary (multifaceted "package" projects) coordination. The National Rural Development Committee, made up of the President and all permanent secretaries of ministries involved in rural development, was set up to consider and approve projects, coordinate donor assistance, and draw the attention of operating ministries to specific bottlenecks and constraints.

According to an evaluation carried out two years after its inception, the major achievements of SRDP were mainly in the field of narrowing the planning/implementation gap through the establishment of innovative and flexible procedures within the government organization. A major problem which the program encountered was the conflict between the desire for establishing viable programs which would be replicable throughout the country and the pressure to create individually successful programs which, for many reasons (especially including high costs and manpower constraints), were not transferable.

Spontaneous Land Settlement

Squatter settlements in Kenya have occurred as a result of the spontaneous movement of potential farmers and unemployed persons to occupy land for which they have no title for the purpose of establishing residence and cultivation. Between 1947 and 1969 the squatter population in rural Kenya grew from approximately 200,000 people to 300,000 people and is currently growing at an annual rate of about 5 percent. The major areas of inflow include the Coast and Rift Valley provinces, while the sources of migrants are primarily the Central, Western, and Eastern provinces. Intraregional migration is also substantial in many areas.

The squatter settlements are by no means a new phenomenon in Kenya, having resulted both from colonial policies and traditional customs and rules. The squatter problem first became critical as a result of the 1912–1925 colonial labor laws which encouraged Africans, already displaced or experiencing population pressure due to European settlement and land alienation, to settle on European land as labor tenants. When land alienation ended in 1960, there was a very low population density in the high-potential White Highlands area and a high population density in the low- and medium-potential "native reserves."

Kenyan squatters can be broadly categorized into four groups:

1. Traditional squatters who continue to live on large-scale farms;
2. Settlers who migrate due to famine, drought, or land pressure;
3. Traditional squatters within the 10-mile wide coastal strip under the Muslim land tenure system; and
4. Illegal residents within settlement schemes.

The squatter settlements studied were chosen to be representative of squatter problems in Kenya. The Ngoliba B and D schemes in central Kenya are government squatter settlement schemes. Most of the farmers were squatters on the land when it was owned by white farmers.

The Muka Mukuu Cooperative, a large cooperative farm in central Kenya, has squatters who are newcomers as well as those who were labor tenants of the former white owners.

The Kibwezi-Mtito-Chuyulu Hills zone, located near Tsavo National Park in southeastern Kenya, has absorbed both legal and illegal settlers from all the major tribes in Kenya.

Several aspects of Kenyan society are currently exacerbating the squatter problem. First, increasing population density in relation to the carrying capacity of the land in many areas is pushing people off the land. Second, Kenya's high annual population growth rate of 3.3 percent is accentuating this trend. Third, alternative non-farm employment is scarce—urban employment is increasing at an annual rate of only 2.5 percent while migration to urban areas ranges between 8 and 15 percent. And fourth, the current land tenure system allows the existence of extensively cultivated large-scale farms and intensively exploited, technically underdeveloped traditional farming areas.

The level of living of a squatter household is generally lower than that of a typical rural household. What little governmental activity there is in squatter areas is rarely designed to accelerate development. Squatter farming is characterized by low levels of investment due to insecurity of tenure, low levels of technology, poor yields per hectare, and poor conservation techniques.

Government programs focusing on the squatter problem have emphasized settlement schemes, even though it has been noted that, with existing technologies, there is insufficient land in Kenya to provide for all or even most of the children of the present generation of farmers.

The first program carried out by the colonial government was a settlement scheme at Gide in 1937. The African Land Development Board (ALDEV), which operated from 1946 until independence in 1961, emphasized reconditioning and reclamation of land in African areas, as land for resettlement was unavailable. Approximately 14,000 families were resettled during this period. In 1955 a land registration drive was begun, aimed at increasing the productive use of land. However, it resulted in negating the traditional ways of absorbing the landless and thus worsened the squatter problem.

In 1962 the Kenyan government began the "Million Acre Scheme," in which large European estates were purchased by the government and parcels were distributed to African farmers. By 1970, 430,190 hectares had been apportioned to about 34,000 families. The number of landless squatters who were resettled in this program is not known.

In 1965 a special commission was established to supervise the registration and resettling of squatters. By late 1969 the commission had registered about 46,000 squatters; by 1972, 15,000 of these had been settled on about 67,200 hectares of land.

Malawi

Lilongwe Land Development Program (LLDP)

LLDP is located in the Lilongwe district, Malawi, and is administered through a project authority under the Ministry of Agriculture and Natural Resources. The program was approved for funding by IDA in 1967; its total costs were originally estimated at K17.7 million over a period of thirteen years. LLDP is a focal point in Malawi's large-scale project approach to rural transformation. Aimed at increasing local agricultural production, the program's components include marketing, credit, extension, land reorganization, and the improvement of the rural infrastructure. It is expected that production increases will be of sufficient magnitude to affect the national economy.

The project presently covers an area of 465,600 hectares and a population of approximately 550,000. The soils are well suited for maize, groundnuts, and tobacco. The people are accustomed to cash cropping and seem receptive to land registration and improved farming. Benefits accruing to LLDP

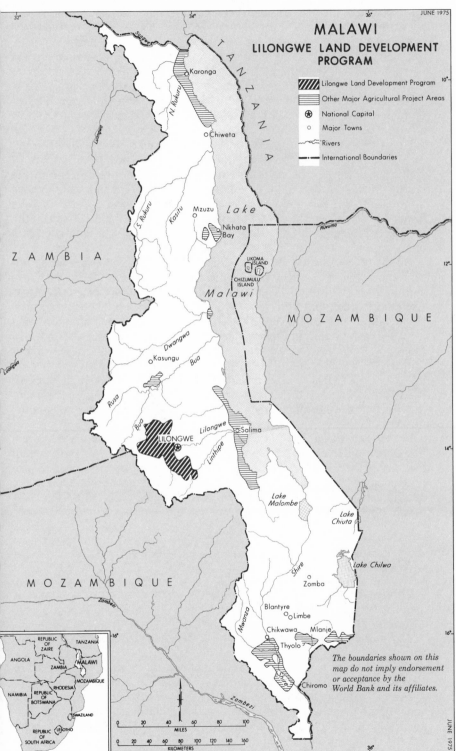

JUNE 1975

MALAWI
LILONGWE LAND DEVELOPMENT PROGRAM

▨	Lilongwe Land Development Program
▤	Other Major Agricultural Project Areas
⊛	National Capital
○	Major Towns
	Rivers
	International Boundaries

The boundaries shown on this map do not imply endorsement or acceptance by the World Bank and its affiliates.

are expected to include *(a)* an average increase in net annual income of K29 per farm family, *(b)* an exportable surplus worth K4.4 million, *(c)* increased government revenues and taxes, *(d)* the establishment of a commercially oriented and stable pattern of agriculture, and *(e)* the formation of a corps of experienced development officers. Maize yield per hectare is expected to increase from 11.2 to 22.7 quintals by 1980. Groundnut yield is projected to increase from 6.4 to 8.1 quintals per hectare in the same time span. The internal rate of return from LLDP was anticipated to be about 13 percent over a twenty-year period.

Up to 1972 the results of the program have been ambiguous. For example, compared to regions outside the project area, the rate of growth of yields per hectare of maize in the project area had not been significantly greater. Yields per hectare of groundnuts in the program area seem to have declined for the first four years of implementation and seemed to have begun to rise only in the 1973/74 period. Both the income increase and the portion attributable to LLDP's activities could also not be estimated precisely within existing data.

On the other hand, between 1969/70 and 1971/72 there has been a significant expansion in the hectarage of maize (from 13,360 to 41,296 hectares) and groundnuts (from 3,479 to 11,818 hectares). The net export earnings from these two crops in this latter year totaled K568,000. The value of marketed output per capita has increased at 10 percent per annum. Total recorded cash receipts in the program area increased from K71,000 to K1.75 million. LLDP has constructed 1,373 kilometers of roads, fifteen major bridges, and 340 boreholes. Twenty-five thousand farmers received training in 1972, while 23,000 growers received K390,000 in seasonal credit loans. In the 1970/71 period, 160 medium-term loans were made for ox carts, hammermills, and other equipment. The program also trained a substantial number of extension workers.

Phase II of LLDP (1972–1975) included increased emphasis on animal husbandry and livestock development. As part of this strategy, the program has started the 65,182-hectare Dzalanyama ranch, which is planned to produce about 3,400 cattle per annum by 1974. Annual beef production in the program area is expected to increase from 366 metric tons (1970/71) to 1,924 metric tons by 1983.

Mali

*Compagnie Française pour le Développement
des Fibres et Textiles (CFDT);
Bureau pour le Développement
de Production Agricole (BDPA)* — *Opération Arachide*

CFDT, similar to a French government consulting firm, was created in 1949 with the goal of increasing cotton production in French Africa. CFDT has been operating in Mali since 1951. The European Development Fund supplied aid for price support input subsidies and trucks from 1965 to 1971; and Fonds de Aide et de Coopération (FAC) gave aid for expatriate personnel and storages from 1969 to 1972. In the 1971/72 period the CFDT cotton

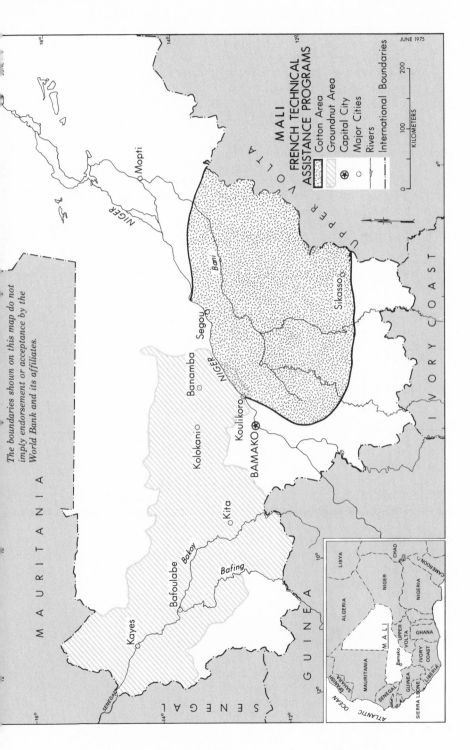

The boundaries shown on this map do not imply endorsement or acceptance by the World Bank and its affiliates.

MALI
FRENCH TECHNICAL
ASSISTANCE PROGRAMS

Cotton Area
Groundnut Area
Capital City
Major Cities
Rivers
International Boundaries

JUNE 1975

KILOMETERS
0   100   200

zone in Mali covered more than one million people, including 72,000 farmers and over 2,400 villages. Essentially all cotton in Mali is produced within the CFDT operation. Total cotton production has increased from 6,000 metric tons in 1961 to 68,000 metric tons in 1972, and average yield has increased from 139 kilograms per hectare to 874 kilograms per hectare. Cotton accounted for one-third of Mali's exports in 1968 and has made a significant contribution to Mali's foreign exchange reserves and government revenues.

CFDT's four main activities include ginning, garage maintenance for vehicle repair, an operation to increase production of *dah* (a vegetable fiber used in rope and sacks), and extension to increase cotton production. These activities are accompanied by a program to improve food production. CFDT's cotton production extension operations have been characterized by a slow shift from an authoritarian approach in the 1950s and 1960s to an advisory method in 1972. CFDT provides both training in new techniques and interest-free credit for new inputs supplied by the government. The resultant increase in productivity, combined with increased producer prices, have enabled many farmers to purchase new farm implements, carts, and livestock to increase their hectarage and yield.

After Mali's independence in 1960, CFDT in Mali shifted its emphasis from serving French economic interests to more national concerns. The company's office in Mali has some independence from the headquarters in Paris and is responsible for finance and administration of the program. The director of the office is Malian, but his subordinate administrators are primarily French. There has been substantial effort to Africanize the top administrative staff.

CFDT's Opèration Fana was a three-year experiment which took place in the Fana region between 1967 and 1970. It was designed to intensify extension efforts in order to increase cotton production, food production, and the use of new implements. It involved field demarcation in order to facilitate use of livestock and harvesting, a rural education project to teach literacy and new techniques, a livestock program, and blacksmith training in equipment repairs.

BDPA's Opèration Arachide was established in 1967 to improve groundnut production and marketing. The operation, an independent organization with financial autonomy from Mali, was funded by FAC with technical assistance provided by BDPA. The operation's area in groundnut production increased from 46,000 hectares in 1967 to 92,000 hectares in 1972; the population covered by the program increased from 270,000 to 730,000; the production increased from 18,000 to 75,000 metric tons; and the marketed production increased from 10,500 to 44,000 metric tons. Yield per hectare in the 1971/72 period was 810 kilograms, compared with 474 kilograms outside the operation.

The first stage of Opèration Arachide involved the establishment of a market network in the groundnut region, followed by extension, training, and a functional literacy program to increase yields through the adoption of more productive cultivation methods and modern techniques. The second step, which the majority of the farmers were entering in 1973, involved the introduction of a livestock program and animal-drawn implements. The World Bank is assisting in a project designed to increase the production of millet and sorghum through the functional literacy program, blacksmith training, health services, well digging, and road improvement. The World Bank's efforts are intended to facilitate the operation's evolution from a purely cash crop production scheme to an integrated rural development program.

BDPA's extension approach has been one of collaboration and voluntary participation. BDPA had proposed to train Malians to take over the program administration from expatriates by 1973.

The CFDT cotton operation and the BDPA groundnut operation began with extension services, supply of inputs and credit, and marketing facilities for crops. The administrative organizations and marketing systems are similar in both operations. Both have succeeded in expanding cash crop production and raising productivity, in increasing farmer and government revenues, and in decreasing the migration of youths from rural areas. To some extent, each has depended upon increases in producer prices in addition to the adoption of new techniques to enable farmers to finance new agricultural implements. Each has succeeded in becoming more self-supporting financially. The two projects differ primarily in the style of their extension services and in their relative success in training Malians to replace expatriate administrators.

Nigeria

Industrial Development Centers (IDC) and Small Industry Credit Schemes (SIC)

Over the period 1958–1971, Nigerian industrial output increased at an average rate of 15.3 percent per year; and the rate of growth of small-scale industrial output was 11.4 percent per year. Although small-scale industries have not been considered in detail nor any planned targets or goals set forth, the Nigerian government has in recent years begun to create institutions to serve the small-scale sector. The intentions have been to achieve maximum utilization of resources, increase employment, stimulate local entrepreneurship, and effectively disperse industries so as to foster rural development and balanced regional growth. The Federal Ministry of Industry defines a small-scale industry as any enterprise having fixed assets of £N30,000 or less and a paid labor force of less than fifty people.

The Industrial Development Centers and the Small Industry Credit Schemes are the government institutions having the most influence on the small-scale industrial sector. These organizations operate within the Small-Scale Industries Division.

The first two IDCs were established in 1962 at Zaria and in 1963 at Owerri to serve the northern region and eastern region, respectively. USAID provided assistance for both centers. A third center to serve the western region was planned for but had not yet been constructed. UNIDO was expected to provide the technical expertise for this center. Because of the Civil War, IDC at Owerri was closed in 1967. It is currently being reactivated.

IDC at Zaria functions autonomously, although it is nominally under the jurisdiction of the Federal Ministry of Industry. The major concern of IDC

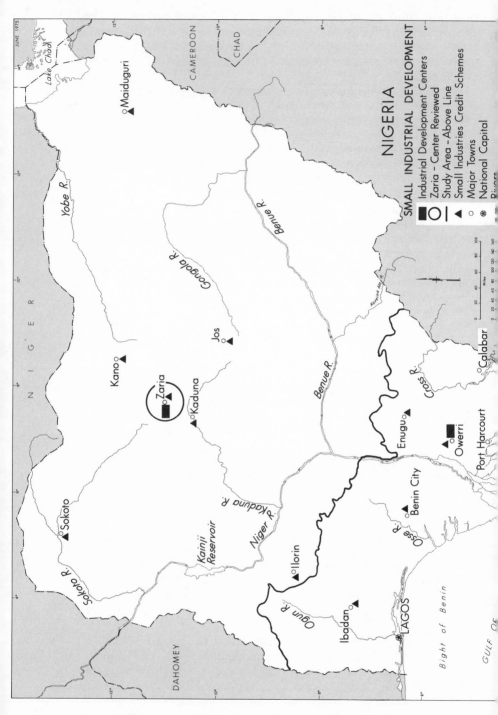

NIGERIA

SMALL INDUSTRIAL DEVELOPMENT

Industrial Development Centers
Zaria – Center Reviewed
Study Area – Above Line
Small Industries Credit Schemes
Major Towns
National Capital

has been to prepare feasibility studies for loan applications which have been received and screened by SIC. The center also attempts to provide guidance on investment opportunities; training in technical and managerial fields; workshop facilities for service, repair, and research; and assistance in the implementation of projects.

The USAID technical assistance program was phased out in 1972, and almost all functions are now carried out by Nigerian civil servants. Training programs and courses, which are rendered free of charge, have reached over 2,800 Nigerians since the program's inception. IDC studies about 150 projects per year, about one-quarter of those for which assistance is requested. Approximately 80 percent of those projects studied are approved.

SIC was formed in 1966 with the principal task of financing new firms and helping in the expansion of existing small enterprises. Although empowered to make independent policy decisions, SIC is responsible to the State Ministries of Trade and Industry. Loans are limited to a maximum of £N10,000 and are issued in kind. Loan terms depend on the loan size and the projected profits.

Over the 1969–1972 period 194 enterprises received IDC technical assistance and loans worth £N900,000. Sixty-four percent of these enterprises were located in rural areas. The major industries to which loans have been granted include printing operations, cement block industries, bakeries, vehicle repair shops, and cattle and poultry farms. Since 1966 the average loan size has tripled to over £N3,000. The owner's contribution in the initial investment is about 30 to 40 percent of the total.

There was much variation in the performance of the projects undertaken. Among the most successful included carpentry projects, cement block factories, printing operations, apparel manufacturing, metal-working projects, and furniture production. The provision of an assured market through government orders has been a principal determinant of the success of most of these projects.

The most important problem in both the IDC and the SIC schemes is the shortage of competent personnel. In addition, IDC is characterized by poor management, scant workshop facilities, and an inability to provide timely assistance when needed. SIC loans have a high default rate.

The Federal Ministry of Industry has recommended a considerable expansion of staff and upgrading of personnel. The personnel recurrent budget for the two schemes was corrected to increase from £N42,130 in 1973 to £N108,577 in 1974. IDC was to be reorganized to emphasize industrial counseling.

Tanzania

Smallholder Tobacco Schemes in Urambo and Tumbi

Between 1964 and 1971 tobacco production in Tanzania increased from 20,866 quintals to over 118,842 quintals, about 80 percent of which is flue cured. A great deal of this recent increase in production has taken place in the Tabora region in western Tanzania. The two schemes in this area, the Tumbi and Urambo Settlement Schemes, accounted for over one-third of the country's entire production in 1970. Both schemes have similar climatic and sociological conditions, but their administrative structures and procedures of operation are very different.

The Urambo project was begun in 1951 by the Tanganyika Agricultural Corporation. Management has changed hands several times since then—to the Village Settlement Commission in 1963, to the Village Settlement Division in 1965, and to the Ministry of Agriculture in 1969. Due to the management problems encountered by the organization, since 1971 the Urambo Farmers Cooperative Society, founded in 1963 to provide transport, baling services, and credit to farmers, was managed directly by staff of the Ministry of Agriculture.

Tobacco production at Urambo increased rapidly between 1960 and 1965 from 749 quintals to over 14,825 quintals but remained at this level during the next five years. The increase in the number of farmers from 100 in 1960 to 2,408 in 1970 was the primary cause of the production increases. Yields per hectare increased from 4.56 quintals to 8.85 quintals between 1960 and 1965 but then dropped to 5.33 quintals by 1970. There was also a fall in the quality of tobacco produced during the 1960s which was partially responsible for the decline in price from TSh687.84 per quintal in 1960 to TSh485.01 per quintal in 1970. Average tobacco hectarage per farmer was 1.2 hectares, requiring the use of hired labor in most cases.

The extension service at Urambo was characterized by very loose control of field officers and a high degree of job security. The farmer/field officer ratio increased drastically after 1965, from 323 to 802 farmers per field officer.

The Tumbi operations began in 1954 with the purchase of land primarily for tobacco research by BAT. In 1964 the Tabora Tobacco Growers Cooperative (TTGC) was organized to supply credit, transport, and baling services to farmers. Following a five-year training agreement with BAT, TTGC took complete control of the Tumbi operations in 1969.

BAT began to promote tobacco production among smallholders at Tumbi after independence in 1961 because of the emigration of many of the European large-scale growers, the opening of a cigarette factory in Dar es Salaam, and the imposition of restrictions on tobacco imports. Tobacco production increased from 354 quintals at Tumbi in 1960 to 7,056 quintals in 1965 to 22,669 quintals in 1970. As was true for Urambo, the increase was primarily a result of the increase in the number of farmers, from 379 in 1960 to 4,600 in 1970. Yields per hectare increased from 3.44 quintals in 1960 to 5.83 quintals in 1965 to 7.00 quintals in 1970. The quality of Tumbi's produce improved during the 1960s, and average gross return per hectare was over twice that of Urambo in 1970. Average tobacco hectarage was 0.69 hectares per farmer in 1970.

Field officers at Tumbi were under close supervision, and the farmer/field officer ratio increased less rapidly than at Urambo. Unlike Urambo, applications for credit and by new farmers entering the scheme were carefully screened.

Average cash income of tobacco growers in the schemes range from TSh1,080–TSh2,930, while incomes of local subsistence farmers are about TSh175–TSh350. Substantial benefits have occurred to the region and the nation as well. Tax revenue on tobacco is collected by both national and regional governments. A number of industries related to tobacco production, such as cigarettes and wooden crate factories, have sprung up. In 1966 Tanzania began to produce tobacco for export, and in 1970 tobacco accounted for 2 percent of the country's export earnings.

An IDA credit was granted in 1970 to cover 60 percent of the total cost of a project designed to increase production of tobacco by 90,720 quintals by 1978. The program will cost $14.7 million and will reach 15,000 to 30,000 farmers in 150 *ujàmaa* vilages. Baling, processing, and grading facilities are to be organized collectively; but each farmer is to own his own tobacco farm.

As of late 1971 only 65 hectares of tobacco had been planted, compared to the original target of 729 hectares. The primary explanation of this shortfall seems to be the local Regional Development Committee's policy of complete collectivization of production, which from September to December 1971 resulted in a decline of 25 percent in the number of farmers participating in the project. In addition, collectivization of production resulted in higher costs in supplying water and a greater need for management skills. In March 1972 President Julius K. Nyerere announced that farmers would be able to retain individual ownership of the tobacco crop, and a large influx of farmers was reported during the following months.

Sukumaland Cotton Development

Cotton production in Sukumaland, an area in northwestern Tanzania with a population of 2.5 million, increased over tenfold between 1950 and 1970 from a level of 40,000 bales to 405,000 bales. This expansion in production was not the result of a highly organized program but rather the result of the response of Wasukuma farmers to increasing returns from cotton production, which was fostered by governmental intervention in key areas.

The improvement in the profitability of cotton production was largely a result of two factors. First, reflecting world market conditions, cotton prices increased substantially over the period 1950 to 1962 from $55.12 per quintal to $123.46 per quintal. In addition, between 1948 and 1967, through the introduction of improved seed varieties, yields per hectare increased over 40 percent from 3.36 quintals of seed cotton to 4.72 quintals.

The expansion in production was facilitated by both the flexibility of the traditional system of agriculture to absorb changes and the initiatives undertaken by the government to promote production. At the local level, the number of farms producing cotton in Sukumaland increased from 203,000 in 1948 to 315,000 in 1967. While average farm size remained constant at 3.12 hectares, the average per farm hectarage allocated to cotton increased fivefold from 0.27 hectares in 1948 to 1.36 hectares in 1967. This increase was brought about through the substitution of cotton and relatively intensive food intercrops for extensively grown grains. The migration of farmers to open lands south, east, and west of traditional farming areas has also alleviated population pressure on land as well as providing an easy source of increases in production. Although farms are worked mainly by family labor, the use of hired labor is increasing.

Government initiatives and policies have had differing effects on production. Tsetse fly clearance and the provision of domestic water points have encouraged migration to open areas. The establishment of a cotton research

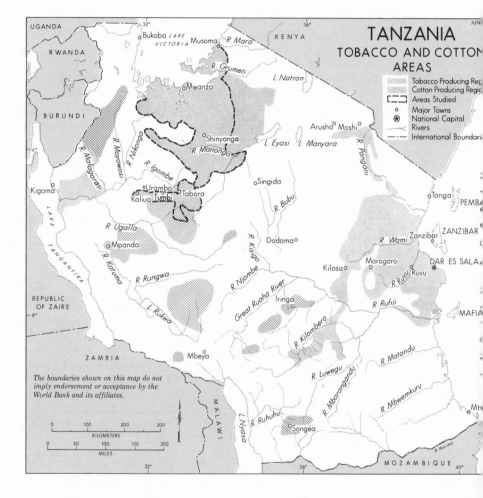

The boundaries shown on this map do not imply endorsement or acceptance by the World Bank and its affiliates.

center and the Lint and Seed Marketing Board have each played an important role in the expansion of production.

However, the government's efforts to improve yields through better husbandry and the provision of credit, extension service, and modern inputs have not had significant results. Efforts to introduce new systems of production in the middle 1960s through villagization and the introduction of block farms were recognized to be failures.

The cooperative movement, which was started in the 1930s, developed rapidly after 1952 and included over 590 primary societies by 1970. The cooperatives have had a monopoly over cotton buying since 1961 and also own most of the ginning and milling facilities. Small farmer loans financed through the cooperatives were estimated to have reached over 100,000 farmers during the 1969 crop year. Beginning in 1966, IDA Credit TA-80 provided both funds and technical assistance to permit expansion of the credit program.

The benefits of increased cotton production are many. Cash incomes from cotton have risen from TSh40 per farm in 1950 to TSh700 in the late 1960s. The proliferation of industries related to cotton production, such as transport, ginning, seed crushing, and textile production, has been accompanied by the growth of small-scale industries encompassing a wide variety of activities.

At the national level, cotton was Tanzania's leading single source of foreign exchange in 1966, accounting for 20 percent of all export earnings. The use of locally grown cotton in new textile mills has provided substitutes for imports. In addition, government revenues have grown as a result of the increased income generated by cotton production.

Ujàmaa *Village Program*

Ujàmaa, which means familyhood in Swahili and connotes the mutual obligations and expectations found in the institutions of the extended family, is Tanzania's unique socialist development strategy. Although *ujàmaa* is often associated with the creation of communal villages, it actually refers to the total integrated strategy of enabling farmers to participate in and eventually be responsible for planning and decision making in production, marketing, distribution, and for defining the quality of their social and political lives. Social equality, self-reliance, emphasis on rural development, and closing of income gaps are also important aspects of *ujàmaa.*

In the first half of the 1960s, *ujàmaa* remained a set of ideas and ideals without an operational program. Both the improvement strategy, emphasizing continuation of the conventional extension approach to individual farmers, and the transformation strategy, characterized by the creation of highly capitalized, isolated village settlements, were seen by the government as failing to bring about the social and economic changes implied by the philosophy of *ujàmaa.*

President Julius K. Nyerere's Arusha Declaration in 1967 announced a change in rural development strategy focusing on the creation of communally organized, self-help villages throughout the country. Between 1967 and 1973 the number of *ujàmaa* villages increased from 48 to 5,631, including over two million people—more than 15 percent of Tanzania's rural population. Implementation of the *Ujàmaa* Village Program was accelerated considerably in the middle of 1974. Since then and until the end of 1974, an additional 2 to 4 million people are estimated to have been relocated into new *ujàmaa* villages. Villagization has progressed most rapidly in Tanzania's least developed, most sparsely populated areas. In 1973 four of Tanzania's eighteen regions—Mtwara, Mbeye, Iringa, and Lindi—accounted for over 55 percent of the total number of villages. Average village size increased from 272 persons in 1970 to 360 persons in 1973.

Although there has been a wide variety in organization, management, and functioning of these villages, reflecting governmental flexibility and differing regional conditions, certain principles and trends may be noted. The villages are usually formed by encouraging traditional villages to "go *ujàmaa*," or by moving people from within a 5- to 10-kilometer range into a central area, creating a new village. The government then provides the credit and services necessary until the village can become economically viable. *Ujàmaa* villages have generally farmed some of their land communally and were supposed to have been progressing towards full communal ownership and production. However, the degree of communal cultivation varied significantly between villages when the review was carried out. The policy of communal cultivation has since then been abandoned due to the considerable resistance of the rural people to the policy. Villagization is, however, proceeding rapidly; and by the end of 1975 the entire rural population is expected to move into villages. Self-help projects are emphasized in *ujàmaa* villages. Elected leaders form committees which are expected to make decisions on social, political, and economic matters. In addition to providing economies in the provision of government services, *ujàmaa* villages are viewed as being important nation-building units, as defense units, and as units of political mobilization. Unfortunately, as yet there are almost no concrete data relating to achievements of the *ujàmaa* policy, although the existing evidence indicates that the achievements of the productive nature have been extremely limited..

The promotion of *ujàmaa* villages is primarily the responsibility of Tanganyika African National Union, Tanzania's sole political party, and the regional and area commissioners. A major decentralization program in 1972 transferred the planning and implementation of programs in *ujàmaa* villages from the national ministries to the regional and district administrators. *Ujàmaa* village development committees are expected to provide a direct link between the village and the district government.

*Postscript to the
Third Printing:
A Revisit to African
Rural Development*

A number of significant developments at the international and national levels have occurred in the field of rural development since *The Design of Rural Development* was published in 1975. This brief revisit is different from the previous work in two respects. First, rather than being an update of the particular projects reviewed earlier, it is a broad-brush examination of some of the important policy and operational issues that I see emerging from the recent experience in rural development. Second, rather than being based on systematic analysis of evidence of the type carried out earlier, it is based on a changed personal perspective. My new perspective arises from having transferred to an operational assignment from having been an outside researcher. Since this transfer, I have been involved in the preparation, appraisal, supervision, and evaluation of individual projects, in the analysis of sectoral policy issues, in the formulation of the Bank's lending strategy in some East African countries, and in discussions on policy and operational matters with government policymakers and staff of various bilateral and multilateral donor agencies. In a sense this whole chapter is thus a personal note. With the limitations of time and space in which it has been prepared, it deals with only those national issues which have a commonality among groups of countries and those international issues which are generalizable among donor agencies. Given my greater familiarity with World Bank assistance, however, many of the observations necessarily draw on that experience.

The purpose of this review is threefold: (a) to reassess and as necessary to strengthen, supplement, qualify, and broaden the understanding of the major development issues identified earlier through project analysis; (b) to judge progress in the resolution of those old and the other new issues; and (c) in a most general way to provide my own views about some of the implications of this reassessment for policies and action needed at the international and national levels.

To serve this purpose, it will be desirable first to review the objectives of rural development and the major features of project design that I had outlined in this book and that bear on the later discussion. Progress toward the

NOTE: I am grateful to James Adams, Wilfred Candler, Stephen Eccles, James Hendry, John Mellor, and Gene Tidrick for detailed comments on the earlier draft of this manuscript.

implementation of these earlier findings is then surveyed. The changed international and national situation referred to above is reviewed. Finally, the new and the old issues that appear to me to be important in this changed context are discussed and their implications are examined.

Rural Development Objectives and Principal Findings of the Previous Analysis

In the earlier project analysis, rural development was defined "as improving living standards of the mass of the low-income population residing in rural areas and making the process of their development self-sustaining." This simple definition was seen to have three important features with substantial implications for how rural development programs are designed and implemented:

> "1. Improving the living standards... involves mobilization and allocation of resources [among sectors] so as to reach a desirable balance over time between the welfare and productive services...
>
> "2. Mass participation requires that resources be allocated to low income regions and classes and that the productive and social services actually reach them.
>
> "3. Making the process self-sustaining requires development of the appropriate skills and implementing capacity... at the local, regional, and national levels to ensure the effective use of existing resources and to foster mobilization of additional financial and human resources for continued development of the subsistence rural sector."

Self-sustenance was thus seen to mean "involving, as distinct from simply reaching, the subsistence populations through development programs."

Rural development was also seen to be basically a national phenomenon in which achievement of aims requires interaction of three types of factors:

1. Appropriate national policies for technology development, land rights, commodity pricing and marketing systems, wages and interest rate structures, manpower allocation, and so forth.

2. The degree of centralization-decentralization of the governmental structure.

3. The extent of institutional pluralism: that is, the distribution of development responsibility among the normal government structure; semi-autonomous government agencies; private, commercial, and traditional institutions and elective bodies (all preceding from p. 20).

Viewed in this broad context, the earlier project analysis led to the conclusion that the limited effectiveness of the projects in realizing rural development objectives cannot be attributed to their inadequate or inappropriate specification of target groups but rather to a combination of factors: narrowly defined project objectives, short time horizons, ambitious project targets, inadequate understanding of the broad sector and policy issues and of their impact on realizations of project objectives, lack of (profitable) technical packages, poor knowledge of the sociocultural environment and its impact on project interventions, extreme scarcity of trained manpower, and inadequate planning and implementing capacity of national institutions (p. 176).

The past experience suggested that "if the objective of participation of the lowest income groups is to be ensured, examination of the particular country's existing sectoral policies and plans, as well as of the indigenous institutions available for rural development, has to be oriented explicitly toward assessing the extent to which these effectively reach the lowest income groups in rural areas."

For example, with regard to the technology policy, the analysis led to the conclusion that excessive specialization in export crop production in early stages of development had adversely affected both rural welfare among low income farmers and productivity of export crop production. The research gap had been particularly severe in the case of food crops grown by most low income farmers (p. 180).

It was observed that if effective national research systems are to be developed and if national commitment to their continuation is to be ensured, substantial resources may have to be allocated specifically for this purpose. Only then will foodcrop development among subsistence farmers be effectively achieved.

As to pricing and marketing policies, the study similarly observed that low foodcrop prices and the inability of the marketing boards to purchase foodcrops had discouraged expansion of food crop production.

It therefore recommended (a) a mixed food and export crop approach, (b) broad geographic coverage of services, (c) improvement in the pricing and marketing systems, and (d) development of roads and storage facilities.

With regard to manpower policies, the earlier analysis pointed to the conclusion that investment in training of manpower had not been commensurate with the substantial investment in rural development programs. Employment of the trained indigenous manpower had therefore led to depriving other regions and departments of their existing manpower with adverse effect on their development elsewhere (p. 182). Establishment of project authorities had temporarily bypassed several inefficiencies of the existing administrative structure but had not resolved the difficult basic problem of wage disparities and administrative incentive systems—a problem that is, however, by no means easy to solve. Manpower constraint had created a conflict between realizing growth and achieving distribution. It had also led to excessive protection and subsidization of local organizations at the outset, resulting in inefficiencies and a lack of willingness on the part of the rural people to share responsibility along with benefits (p. 184). The analysis concluded that such examination of sector issues will allow explicit recognition of the existing government policies that are inconsistent with the goals of rural development (p. 176). These policy questions, however, would ultimately have to be resolved by national governments, in some cases the necessary changes in national policies may not come about easily. In such cases the choice for planners, whether they be nationals or from donor agencies, is between opting for only a limited impact and not undertaking programs at all, in either case in the hope that policies will change eventually (p. 177).

As to issues related to project design, the earlier analysis led to the observation that, unlike the situation in parts of Latin America and Asia, the bulk of the rural population in Africa is poor, and this poverty is frequently spread over the entire rural sector. Target groups in Africa are thus large relative to the financial resources and, in particular, to the trained man-power and institutional capability frequently available for development. Therefore, if the emphasis in rural development is to be on mass participation and on viability of the process of rural development, rural development programs have to be seen as a continuous, dynamic process rather than as extensive versus intensive or maximum versus a minimum effort. The emphasis on mass participation also means that a sequential approach would be necessary in planning and implementing, involving establishment of clear priorities and time phasing of activities (p. 189). The study also led to the conclusion that in many cases an initial emphasis on broad-based increases in productivity through a certain minimum level of services and institutional development may well be a more effective way of ensuring mass participation than the substantial initial concentration of resources in a few regions. A single package, however, is not likely to be universally applicable. Some constraints to improvement of productivity, such as a lack of a profitable technology, ineffective extension, and inadequate inputs, may well be common to all of subsistence agriculture, whereas others, such as ill health or an inadequate incentive system and organization, may well be location specific. Therefore, a combination is needed of a few critical general interventions applicable to several regions along with development of capability of the regional administrations to identify and ameliorate constraints specific to individual regions (p. 189).

The earlier project analysis thus pointed out the desirability of phased planning, in which intensive projects would be undertaken gradually in the later stages. The analysis indicated that phased planning had many advantages that were not derived in the projects that had been reviewed. First, systematic data gathering is essential for effective project planning and implementation and can be combined with the implementation of the more modest early phases. During this time firsthand knowledge of the specific technical, administrative, and sociocultural constraints may be acquired. Second, phasing permits greater indigenous participation in planning, thus ensuring greater reliability in the knowledge acquired than is possible for outsiders. Third, phasing facilitates training of manpower that is crucial for fostering long-term national planning and implementing capacity.

The project approach and donor assistance for it was considered essential in the African context, since the domestic planning and implementing capacity in most African countries is at present greatly limited. A broader policy context and the perspective of long-term development was, however, considered essential for the project approach to be effective.

Review of Recent World Bank Assistance to East African Rural Development[1]

How does the World Bank's recent lending to rural development projects compare with these findings?

---

1. The Eastern Africa Region is defined in the World Bank to include eighteen countries south of the Sahara, from Sudan and Ethiopia in the north to Botswana, Swaziland, and Lesotho in the south. Zaïre is also included in the Eastern Africa Region.

The Bank's Changing Role

A comparison of this type is of particular interest because the Bank has been an important source of ideas on development strategies and on lessons of experience. Especially in African agriculture, there has been a tradition in the World Bank of learning from systematic analysis of its own and other project experiences. John deWilde's analysis of agricultural projects and subsequently my own of rural development projects have been followed by a number of systematic albeit limited in-house studies of Bank experiences both with rural development projects in Sub-Saharan Africa generally and with individual project components specifically (that is, monitoring and evaluation and training).[2]

This effort is to a large extent a result of the limited planning and implementing capacity of the African countries. There is the consequent recognition of the greater role that an external agency has to play in both these respects, compared even with countries having similar per capita income levels, such as those in South Asia. The extent to which outside personnel have had to play a major part in project preparation and implementation in Africa is illustrated by the fact that, of the ninety-five continuing projects in the World Bank's Eastern Africa Region with training components for which the preparation agencies were identified, in only three were these prepared exclusively by the borrowing countries. In all others the major responsibility for preparation lay with outsiders. These proportions would come close to being the reverse in South Asia.

The Bank's influence, which has been derived from its role in financing African rural development, is much more difficult to discern, even though it has been an important source of finance especially since Robert McNamara's presidential address to the Bank's Board of Governors in 1973.[3] Comparisons over time with South Asia and among sectors are telling of overall trends, relative importance of various sectors and of their present absorptive capacity, and of the Bank's role both in the present and the future rural development strategies.

The Bank's share in net foreign assistance is much smaller in the Eastern Africa Region (close to a quarter in its bigger borrowing countries) compared with its share in South Asia (close to a half).[4] The share of World Bank assistance going to agriculture and rural development—although the most important—has also increased less steeply (from 27 percent in 1970–74 to 29 percent in 1978) than in South Asia (from 23 percent in 1970–74 to 55 percent in 1978).[5] This difference reflects the limited absorptive capacity of African agriculture due both to the preponderance of rainfed agriculture (compared with South Asia's potential for irrigation) and to its present limited institutional capacity (on which more is said later).

2. John C. deWilde, *Experiences with Agricultural Development in Tropical Africa* (Baltimore: Johns Hopkins Press, 1967), 2 vols.

3. Robert S. McNamara, *Address to the Board of Governors,* Nairobi, Kenya, September 24, 1973. World Bank lending for agriculture and rural development rose from an annual average of $70.4 million in the 1970–74 period to $165.1 million in 1978 in Eastern Africa. (*World Bank Annual Report, 1978,* p. 38).

4. Calculated as proportion of net inflow of public and publicly guaranteed loans on an annual basis. Based on World Bank data.

5. Based on tables in *World Bank Annual Report, 1978,* pp. 38 and 56.

At the project level the World Bank nevertheless plays a far more significant role in the financing of rural development in the Eastern Africa Region than in South Asia. This is partly because external assistance on the whole plays a far more important role in domestic investment in African countries than in South Asia, even with the similar per capita income levels of the two regions. In 1976 the share of inflow of public and publicly guaranteed loans in annual domestic investment was three to six times as great in Tanzania, Ethiopia, Malawi, and Kenya as in India.[6] Similarly, at the project level the Bank is considerably more involved in a leadership role with other donors in East Africa, although at the aggregate level the Bank plays a far more active role as chairman of the aid consortia in South Asia. For instance, compared with the $165.1 million lent by the Bank for agriculture and rural development in East Africa in 1978, over half as much, $93.7 million, was cofinanced by bilateral and multilateral donors in the Eastern Africa Region, in comparison with the $899 million lent to South Asia, in which only $2.7 million were cofinanced.[7] The recent World Bank's experience in rural development reviewed here is thus more generalizable to other donors in Africa than it would be in Asia.

The Bank's assistance to two other related sectors is worth reviewing in view of the various issues raised later. The average annual lending to transport in the Eastern Africa Region rose from $85.1 million in 1970–74 to only $99.0 million in 1978, implying a significant decline, both in real terms as well as in the share of total lending, from 31 percent to 18 percent.[8] It went down considerably more in South Asia in real terms ($73.5 million in 1970–74 to 22.0 million in 1978) and as a share of lending (from 14 percent to 1.3 percent).

The lending to education, which was $18.9 million in 1970–74, went up to $57.7 million in 1978 in East Africa. As a percentage of Bank and IDA lending, however, it went down from 15 percent to 10 percent. Bank financing for education has never been significant in South Asia, mainly because of the less perceived need for outside assistance there.

Evolution of Projects

Concern in the World Bank with the overall planning of agricultural development, as well as with individual elements essential for successful implementation of those kinds of strategies identified in my earlier project analysis, has increased considerably since 1974 and is reflected in the types of projects financed in the Eastern Africa Region in the last four years. There are, of course, a series of projects involving traditional export crops, such as in tea, coffee, sugar, pyrethrum, or tobacco production. But a major part of Bank assistance includes national agricultural development projects to provide a broad coverage of services to improve productivity of all

---

6. Based on World Bank data.

7. Based on World Bank data. This high level of cofinancing is partly the result of higher per capita aid levels referred to earlier in East Africa than South Asia and partly of the more limited planning and implementing capacity.

8. *World Bank Annual Report, 1978,* p. 38. In both regions these figures understate the investment in transport, because the figures above refer to major trunk roads, whereas much of the feeder-road construction and maintenance is included in agriculture and rural development.

or a major part of the low-income traditional farming populations producing mainly foodcrops. The Integrated Agricultural Development Program
in Kenya (1976), the National Maize Program in Tanzania (1975), the National Rural Development Program in Malawi (1978), and the Basic Agricultural Services Program in Lesotho (1977) are illustrations of the new
projects financed at the national level. Each of these projects aims at improving the planning and implementing capacity at the national level: that
is, of the ministries of agriculture in these countries. To a limited degree
they each attempt to strengthen the abilities of the provincial-regional, district, and local governmental administrations to provide agricultural field
services such as adaptive trials and extension. They also involve support
for the related existing institutions that handle input distribution, output
marketing, and agricultural credit.

These new projects are in contrast with projects analyzed earlier in this
study, such as the Wollamo Agricultural Development Unit in Ethiopia or
the Lilongwe Land Development Program in Malawi, which were basically
enclave projects implemented relatively autonomously. Their field services (such as agricultural extension, credit, input distribution, and output
purchases and management) frequently lay outside the purview of the existing institutions and the normal governmental structure. They involved
large numbers of expatriates in line managerial positions, most of whom
were from countries that had colonized Africa. The projects tended to emphasize realization of limited, visible short-term results and were not
reproducable on a national scale in the foreseeable future. It was this
realization that led to the concept of national programs addressed to institutional development and broad coverage.

To strengthen particular national support services that were identified in
the African study as being the principal constraints in relatively large
countries, the Bank has already financed or undertaken to finance development of the national agricultural research systems (Sudan, 1977, and
Tanzania, 1980) with a view to improving technical packages. Several additional activities already being financed or proposed for Bank financing in
Tanzania illustrate the concern with sectoral support services of the policy
planning type also referred to above as a constraint to realizing rural development objectives at the project level. For example, in Tanzania support is
being provided to the Market Development Bureau, which is a price policy
advisory body, and to project planning and monitoring teams in the ministry of agriculture and the prime minister's office. To deal with the marketing constraints identified in the previous analysis, support is being considered for the principal commercial parastatal activities in food marketing
and processing.

World Bank financing to agriculture is nowhere else in Africa as comprehensive as in Tanzania. Similar institutional support has been provided
elsewhere, however: for instance, in Kenya to the Agricultural Sector and
Project Planning Unit in the Ministry of Agriculture, to the Central
Statistical Bureau for data collection and analysis, and to the Agricultural
Finance Corporation, the principal agricultural credit institution. An agricultural extension and training project has also been financed in Somalia.

Both within and outside the Bank, the new-style projects directed toward
direct alleviation of poverty have received the greatest attention, in comparison with the other Bank activities in the agricultural and rural sector

referred to above. According to the Bank's rural development sector policy paper:

1. [The new-style projects] are designed to benefit large numbers of the rural poor, while ensuring an economic rate of return, that is, at least equal to the opportunity cost of capital.
2. They are comprehensive in their approach to small-scale agriculture and provide for a balance between directly productive and other components (where inclusion of the latter is appropriate.)
3. They have a low enough cost per beneficiary, so that they could be extended to other areas, given the availability of additional resources.[9]

Three such projects have already been financed in Tanzania: Kigoma (1974), Tabora (1975), and Mwanza/Shinyanga (1978). Other integrated regional projects are under consideration for Bank financing there and elsewhere in Africa.

To the extent that they have attempted to reach large numbers of the rural poor, the aim of the new-style projects is consistent with the approach espoused earlier in this book. Despite the findings of this study and other experience the first new-style projects in the Eastern Africa Region have, however, been complex: that is, they involve many more activities in the productive and social service sectors at the outset than was considered feasible in the African Rural Development Study at early stages in view of the limited planning and implementing capacity and trained staff, which had been identified as constraints. Their targets of achievement have also been more ambitious than the existing capacity would permit. The more intensive new-style projects are also difficult to replicate nationally. In view of this experience, the future new-style projects are likely to be modest in their aims, more along the lines recommended in this study. More is said later in this chapter about the appropriate balance between the projects geared to relieving sectoral constraints and those addressed to direct alleviation of poverty.

Many of the recent Bank-financed projects show an explicit recognition of the longer time horizon needed to achieve results; therefore, they follow a phased approach. Although this approach was followed in some projects previously (as in the Lilongwe, Shire, and Karonga projects in Malawi), it is now much more widespread. Two or three phases of a long-term program, each consisting of four or five years, may now be financed by the Bank, although justification for financing of each additional phase has to be self-contained.

The extent of technical assistance being provided is not expected to decline as yet, especially in view of the increased resources being committed to the rural sector and the severe shortage of trained national manpower in most African countries. But on the whole the sensitivity of donors to the African aspirations of self-management has increased. Larger numbers of senior managerial positions in Bank-financed projects are being held by nationals. Expatriates are being recruited, largely for technical rather than managerial jobs.

---

9. *Rural Development,* Sector Policy Paper (Washington, D.C.: World Bank, February 1975), pp. 60–61.

The projects designed and financed by the Bank since 1974 reflect greater concern for manpower training than previously. Half of the projects financed in the Bank's Eastern Africa Region before 1974 had training components, compared with 75 percent in the projects approved since 1977. In the case of the agricultural and rural development projects, these percentages were 55 percent before 1974 and 93 percent since 1977. The cost of training as percentage of total project cost went up from 3.5 percent to 4.4 percent in the projects approved since 1977.

The recently designed projects also incorporate greater awareness of the importance of monitoring and evaluation in the planning and implementation of projects. According to the World Bank statistics in 1977, 81 percent of the agricultural and rural development projects financed by the Bank's Eastern Africa Region incorporated some monitoring and evaluation, compared with less than 50 percent in 1974.

Incremental local cost financing has been financed by the Bank for some time. This issue now, however, generally receives greater attention than before. More is said on local cost financing later.

Perhaps the three most significant differences in the Bank's approach to agriculture and rural development projects in the recent years relate to (a) recognition of the range of factors that affect project performance, (b) the limited knowledge on which the projects are designed, and (c) the flexibility in dealing with the consequent unforeseen circumstances. There is a wider recognition of the inability of an external donor to take fully into account the broader environment in financing project activities. To deal with this problem—apart from supporting technology development, policy advisory bodies, marketing agencies, manpower training, and monitoring and evaluation mentioned above—there is a considerably more flexible attitude toward project implementation. Although project appraisal documents are considered to be a useful guide with which to compare progress, they are no more considered the "bible" for implementation they once were. Many more projects are likely to be modified during the course of implementation than previously to reflect better the greater knowledge of the broader environment acquired during implementation. Such modifications are also generally seen to be constructive: that is, to increase project effectiveness rather than to accommodate to project failures.

Sometimes the knowledge of likely responses to project interventions is known to be limited, as when technical packages need to be developed or when new modes of organization need to be tried out. In such situations the use of small pilot projects is being considered. This approach has, however, not yet been used extensively, partly because of the general reticence about experiments, especially among the Bank's borrowing countries, and partly because of the difficulties recognized in replication of a successful experiment on a large scale. If projects were to be modest in their aims in initial stages and if there were to be the flexibility in their implementation, along the lines suggested in this book, fewer pilot projects might be necessary than otherwise.

Most of the new directions outlined above are consistent with the findings of the African Rural Development Study and of the more recent in-house project evaluations referred to earlier. The progress reported above is indeed substantial. And to the extent that national planning and implementing capacities have to be developed on the basis of experience, the recent projects provide a wealth of insight from which to make further improvements. But three types of gaps are highlighted by the recent experience. First is the gap between the resources required for African rural development in the form of knowledge, finances, physical inputs, and institutional development and those resources which are at present available. The knowledge about the resource requirements may itself evolve over time. Thus, the need identified in my earlier analysis for additional input into training, physical infrastructure, and institutional development is reinforced by the more recent experience, with one major difference: the recent experience points to far greater need for investment in formal education than was identified in this book.

The World Bank's sectoral allocations presented earlier already show a cognizance of these particular African requirements: a greater share of its resources is allocated to education and transport and a relatively smaller share to projects oriented to direct alleviation of poverty than in South Asia. The recent experience, however, shows that this balance needs to be tilted further in favor of the former two in the short and medium run. This argument is documented later in this paper.

Second is the gap between the state of knowledge and resources available at any particular time and those which are brought to bear both nationally and internationally in designing and implementing rural development programs. These gaps were illustrated in the earlier analysis and are documented once again throughout the remaining part of this chapter. Third is the gap between expectations (based on the knowledge and the resources deployed) and achievements. This gap results both from the facts that existing knowledge and resources are not fully reflected in the project design and expectations and that the resources and the knowledge required are considerably greater than are presently available.

Although it would be possible to bridge some of these gaps through evolution of policies and practice of the type discussed earlier, either considerable time or radical rethinking and policy changes may be required to tackle others. This suggests that rural development will be a slower, more difficult, and more long-drawn-out process for many African countries than is generally reflected in the national expectations and forms of rural development assistance. This fact itself needs to influence the nature of policies and priorities in the field of rural development, as will be argued below.

Expectations and Achievements

"The [World Bank's] objective ... is to help raise standards of living in developing countries by channeling financial resources from developed countries to the developing world."[10] Disbursement lags may therefore postpone realization of development objectives in the short run, although if the activities to which they are directed are carefully selected, these activities will in the long run improve the development performance.

The *Annual Report* for 1978 states that IDA disbursements in fiscal 1978 dropped by 18 percent over the previous year and that these disburse-

10. *World Bank Annual Report, 1978,* p. 1.

ments were below expectations. A review by the Bank of the causes of slow growth indicates that implementation in many Bank-assisted projects has been adversely affected as borrowing governments have tried to adjust to inflation, to balance-of-payments difficulties, and to rising budgetary deficits. As a result, counterpart funds needed for the full financing of Bank- and IDA-assisted projects are in short supply, affecting project implementation. The review also shows that disbursements in certain major sectors, particularly agriculture, will for several years be somewhat lower than could be expected on the basis of past disbursement experience. New-style projects are not only technically complex; they also involve new agencies and institutions carrying out new activities to benefit groups of people previously considered outside the reach of most government programs.[11]

The experience of the Eastern Africa Region has been generally consistent with that reported for the Bank as a whole, with one difference: the Region's disbursements were slower than the Bank average in agriculture and faster in transport, power, and education. More is said later on the issue of sectoral composition of lending in the Eastern Africa Region.

Comparison of expectations and achievement is difficult to make with regard to project impact. There is little hard evidence on the 'impact' variables. There are also methodological problems: for example, the control group outside the project areas may be benefiting from the project-related interventions, affecting "with-project" and "without-project" comparisons. Project output may frequently be marketed outside official channels. There is also a problem of establishing reliable trend lines under highly variable weather conditions and the limited period covered by the data.

But for the four-fifths of the twenty-one rural development projects in the East Africa Region for which some data are available, evidence indicates that nearly 90 percent of the projects are having a slower impact on output than had been anticipated in appraisals. These results are consistent with the analysis done under the recent Operations Evaluation Department review of smallholder projects in Sub-Saharan Africa. The reasons advanced in both reviews are similar to those advanced in deWilde's and my earlier project analysis: (a) difficulties of developing technical packages under highly variable rainfed conditions, (b) problems of mobilizing farmers under conditions of poor communications, and (c) serious staffing and institutional constraints. The resemblance between these results and those evaluated earlier indicate partly the magnitude of the problem of raising agricultural productivity in Africa and partly the fact that the findings of earlier research were not fully reflected in the design of these projects.

The training and the monitoring and evaluation components of rural development projects provide similar illustrations of the gap between expectations and achievements.

Some 70 percent of the training components in the East Africa Region's agriculture and rural development projects have experienced substantial delays in implementation or have reduced their outputs. In the case of

---

11. *Ibid., 1978*, p. 9.

many types of technical and high-level training, especially for overseas visits and courses, the in-house analysis indicates that aggregate funds available from various donors are frequently far greater than there are nationals available with the necessary qualifications to make use of the resources provided. Similarly, a myriad of local training institutions established by the various donors remain underused because of a lack of qualified expatriate or locally trained manpower to carry out training, the inadequacy of relevant teaching materials, a lack of recurrent budgetary resources to pay the salaries of trainers, and a shortage of people with the necessary educational background who can be trained. The problem is, of course, often exacerbated by inadequate coordination among activities financed by various donors. Different donors often establish separate training institutions for their own particular purpose. Yet there remains a tremendous dearth of trained manpower in most African countries, in positions ranging from relatively simple bookkeeping and accounting to complex financial management and storage technology. This situation indicates the limited capacity of many African countries to exercise control over the broader problem of institutional development and coordination needed to carry out training effectively.

What applies to training components also holds true in the case of the monitoring and evaluation components. A great deal of the data collected under some of the rural development projects have remained unanalyzed. In most cases, however, even data collection has not been possible. Again, analysis of this problem has indicated that this is due partly to lack of qualified local or expatriate manpower to carry out data collection and analysis, and partly to the inadequate recognition among planners and implementers at both the national and the international level about the importance of factual information on a routine basis in improving the quality of planning. Among local administrative and political officials the problem may sometimes go beyond the stage of indifference to resistance to the gathering facts related to planning and implementation of programs.

Experience with regard to disbursements, output increases, and the training and the monitoring and evaluation components can be generalized more broadly. Project achievements have usually been short of expectations. This holds regardless of whether achievements are judged by the targets established for given period in projects for inputs (such as number of local and expatriate staff to be recruited for project implementation by certain dates, number of agricultural trials to be carried out effectively, amounts of fertilizer and other inputs to be distributed, vehicles to be purchased, or buildings and roads to be constructed and maintained) or by the end results (such as the extent of increase in yields expected, the number of staff to be trained, or administrative or financial accounting procedures to be instituted).[12]

To the extent that the gap between expectation and achievement is the result of overoptimism (and thus does not fully reflect the existing knowledge about the various constraints analyzed in this book), it does not

---

12. Many of these same projects nevertheless realized rates of return close to those which had been expected earlier. This is because the less than expected increases in output were more than compensated for by the unexpected increases in the output prices.

reflect a failure in achievement. A certain amount of setting high standards in projects is desirable to encourage maximum effort so as to achieve better results than could be achieved otherwise. But setting too high standards can also lead to a greater sense of failure (at least implicitly attributed to the countries, since they are responsible for implementation) than the knowledge of their present capacity would warrant. High expectations thus have the danger of being counterproductive.

The Unfinished Business: New Issues and Old

The recent experience once again raises some of the old issues of inadequacy of the policy and strategy framework, government priorities to realizing rural development objectives, trained national manpower, financial and institutional constraints in a new context. It also raises new issues about the divergence between the national and international priorities attached to achieving objectives of rural development. It is argued here that because of both these old issues and the new issues, the role that external agencies can play in immediate alleviation of poverty is much more limited in the short run than is usually recognized internationally. Although such emphasis must continue so as to keep the problem in focus, a greater emphasis on development of national institutions, manpower, and physical infrastructure is required to alleviate old constraints and simultaneously to reduce the divergence between national and international objectives.

It is interesting that much of the outside criticism of Bank projects is geared toward the Bank's inability to change income distribution through its projects because of the choice of project beneficiaries and the means adopted to reach them. Most of it does not show adequate understanding either of the extent of evolution of Bank policies and practices over time or of the nature of the development problem or of the various types of gaps referred to above. This refers especially to the gap between expectations, as set out in appraisal projections, and achievements, the gap between the national and the international priority attached to alleviation of poverty, and the role that outsiders can and should properly play in the realization of that objective. These issues are discussed below.

Achieving National Unity

The issues of national unity—and thus the priority that is attached by African countries to development—did not receive as much attention in my earlier analysis as seems necessary in retrospect. Many African countries have not yet fully established their territorial integrity or achieved domestic political stability. In recent years Sudan, Somalia, Ethiopia, Uganda, Kenya, Tanzania, Rwanda, Burundi, Zaïre, Equatorial Guinea, Nigeria, and Ghana—to name a few—have all undergone either intense internal conflicts or border clashes with neighboring countries. Their national priorities and their limited resources in food surpluses, trained manpower, means of transport, recurrent resources, and infrastructure have for sustained periods of time been diverted from economic development to achieving national integration and identity. This has frequently also meant diversion of domestic and international resources, both directly and indirectly, from high-priority rural development projects to conflict resolution, leading to adverse effect on the implementation of projects under way and for the planning of future projects. In many countries not only has much scarce trained national manpower been lost in the course of these internal conflicts, but it has been reduced further by substantial emigration of the educated or by the lack of willingness or acceptability of those remaining for recruitment outside their own regions. The Eritrians in Ethiopia and the Ebos and the Yorubas in Northern Nigeria exemplify this phenomenon, which requires high-cost imported technical assistance for jobs that nationals could do.

The area of relative priorities between defense and development is not one in which international development agencies can exercise any useful direct influence, although they can raise national consciousness and provide differential levels of assistance to countries depending on their commitment to development. What assistance is provided in this respect is largely after the fact, however, and is confined mostly to restoring the material and financial resources rather than to reconstructing the countries' sociopolitical or institutional fabric. This latter is inevitably the responsibility of the nationals and is likely to be a long-term process.

The Development Objectives

The changing international role. Concern and debate about the equity issue in the international donor community is considerably more extensive now than in 1975 when the book was published. This concern is partly the result of the world food crisis of 1973–74. It has since expanded, however, to incorporate a much broader set of considerations such as alleviation of poverty, assurance of basic needs, environmental protection, women's rights, and even human rights. Phrases such as the "lowest 40 percent," "integrated rural development," "target groups," urban bias," and "basic human needs," which have become commonplace in the international development parlance, were not in circulation in the early 1970s. A myriad of policy papers, research publications, popular articles, conference proceedings, and operational guidelines have been prepared on these various topics.

The principal difference since the book's publication is the close scrutiny of, and the persistant attacks on, the activities of the international financial institutions, and especially the World Bank. These arise especially from the liberals in the traditional donor countries. The criticisms are no more the occasional protestations by the socially conscious college campus groups. Rather, they originate in the duly constituted bodies that authorize funds for aid. The increased consciousness of the equity issue and the perceived impotency of the donors to deal with it is one reason for these attacks. There is also apprehension that the poor in developed countries have to assist the rich in developing countries. It is a logical corollary of the realization that the trickle-down approach has not been working as expected and that the majority of the poor in developing countries have been bypassed in the developmental process.

The World Bank's justification for shifting lending to agriculture and rural development, and within that sector to the poorest 40 percent of the income earners in developing countries, is based partly on the recognition of the limitations of the trickle-down approach. Further, there is a premise that even if the unit cost of reaching small farmers is frequently greater than that of reaching large farmers, the higher productivity of the resources allocated to small-farmer development would in most cases more than compensate for the higher cost of reaching them. Emphasizing smallholder development would thus not adversely affect the overall rate of economic growth.

The Bank's precise justification for emphasizing lending to agriculture and rural development has, however, evolved considerably over time. Mr. McNamara's Nairobi speech of 1973 referred to developing countries and the World Bank "adopting a socially oriented measure of economic performance . . . [which] would give credit for some redistribution of the benefits of growth toward the lower income groups."[13] Subsequent publications emphasized the empirical and the theoretical basis for the theme of redistribution with growth.[14] The later policy statements have, however, tended to stress eradication of absolute rather than relative poverty. The rural development policy paper states, for instance, that "where economic dualism prevails, a rural development program may be an effective way of both redistributing income and expanding output by increasing the share of the budget allocated for services to low-income groups. Elsewhere, economic circumstances may dictate that the primary emphasis be on increasing short-run output to generate increased income."[15] The Bank's emphasis on raising productivity of small farmers rather than redistributing incomes has also meant directing investments toward "those who have access to some productive assets such as land, even if only as tenants,"[16] and not necessarily to the poorest of the poor. Much of the outside criticism of the Bank projects is, however, geared to the Bank's inability to improve incomes of the very poor and the landless through its projects.

Although there may have been ambivalence about the Bank's emphasis on redistribution, there never has been any in the role of national governments relative to outside agencies in reorienting development policy. McNamara's speech stressed "that unless national governments redirect their policies toward better income distribution, there is very little that international agencies such as the World Bank can do to accomplish this objective."[17]

Where national capacity to prepare projects for external assistance and to formulate an appropriate set of policies and the overall strategy is limited, outsiders certainly end up playing a major role. This was argued to be the case in the Eastern Africa Region. But for the reasons outlined later, this role is usually greater at the project level than at the overall policy and strategy level. Besides, even if outsiders do play an important role, without national commitment to the realization of rural development objectives,

13. McNamara, *Address* (Nairobi), p. 12.

14. See, for example, Hollis Chenery and others, *Redistribution with Growth,* (London: Oxford University Press, 1974), and Lyn Squire and Herman G. van der Tak, *Economic Analysis of Projects* (Baltimore: Johns Hopkins University Press, 1975).

15. World Bank, *Rural Development,* p. 18.

16. World Bank, *World Development Report, 1978,* (New York: Oxford University Press, 1978), p. 26.

17. McNamara, *Address* (Nairobi), p. 11.

the external influence cannot have a significant meaning at either level even in the short run—and especially in the long run.

International assistance can and does, however, play an important role in the long run by increasing national consciousness about certain issues, by improving the rationale for policies and making the effect of various policy options on different income groups more explicit, and by strengthening gradually over time those national forces which can bring about changes in the desirable direction. This is done through education and training, as well as by increasing the effectiveness of the government's capacity for policy planning and implementation. The role that international development agencies can play in changing the basic asset or political power distribution in recipient countries is generally extremely limited, a matter that should not surprise those who respect rights of sovereign nations.

It is frequently the naivete of the critics that causes a failure on their part to distinguish between the types of outside influence and the areas in which it should and can be exercised realistically. Thus, directing Bank projects to benefit lower-income groups is far easier than directing governments to reorganize their socioeconomic and political structures so radically in a short period of four or five years to ensure that cooperatives will effectively include the poor or that effective rates of subsidies do not go to the rich.

From this point of view, to what extent have national governments in Africa reoriented their development policies?

The changing national role. Awareness within individual African countries about the development of their traditional agricultural sectors is generally greater now than when the study was first undertaken. Although the concern was precipitated by the severe drought and the consequent food crisis of the 1973–74 season, food self-sufficiency has remained an important national objective in most countries in the subsequent period of good-to-excellent harvests. This has led to increased recognition among national policymakers of the importance of agricultural research systems, chemical fertilizers, improved seeds, credit programs, and incentive marketing and pricing policies in realizing this objective. Prices of foodcrops in many African countries are considerably more favorable now than when the study was undertaken.

National participation in agricultural sector planning, policymaking, and project preparation has also increased considerably as newly trained African graduates have begun to emerge from the domestic and foreign training institutions. As a result, informed and committed nationals in important policy and operational positions are more likely to be found now in comparison with the early 1970s, when most such positions were occupied by expatriates.

In some countries there have been varying degrees of effort to restructure administrative institutions to achieve development objectives. Two such efforts in decentralization—in Kenya and Tanzania, which were discussed in the previous analysis of projects—have evolved further. More is said on these later. There is generally also greater emphasis in national planning on universal primary education and on supply of rural social services, including drinking water, health facilities, and education in nutrition.

Despite these various changes, in most African countries policymakers think of development basically in terms of industrialization, urbanization, and the use of modern technology. To the extent that modernization of the agricultural sector is seen to assist in the fulfillment of the industrialization objective, it is through quick generation of food surpluses for the urban centers and export surpluses for capital formation.

Food and export crop surpluses in Africa typically are produced by a combination of smallholder agriculture and large private or state farms. Too often policymakers see the best way to produce agricultural surpluses quickly to support urban development as being through capitalized large farms rather than smallholder peasant production—and in giving those large farms priority in the use of the extremely scarce recurrent budgetary resources and manpower. Yet in contrast to the perception at the national policymaking level, experience indicates that large tractorized farms, especially in the public sector, are economically inefficient in comparison with peasant production. They are demanding of scarce capital, have poorer employment potential, and to ensure efficiency of the resources employed they require much experienced, technically qualified managerial staff and an appropriate incentive system, requisites that are frequently lacking. It is also not certain that they generate food surpluses more quickly than peasant producers if the latter are provided appropriate services and incentives. Mobilization of surpluses for urban consumption is, however, quicker and cheaper with large farms than through development of a marketing system geared to millions of small peasant producers, especially in view of the infrastructural problems discussed below. In all likelihood it is the political imperative to ensure urban food sufficiency that causes the emphasis on large-scale production.

The discussion is not meant to imply that large-scale production should not be undertaken under any situation. There are examples of successful export crop production schemes such as the oil palm production in Ivory Coast, in which large estates have been the nucleus around which smallholder production has developed. They have ensured a supply of raw materials to utilize the costly processing investments in early stages of development, demonstrated the use of modern management practices to peasant farmers, and allowed the necessary time to develop effective services to the smallholder sector to ensure their successful participation over time. Most of these circumstances do not obtain, however, in the case of foodcrop production.

Even in cases in which smallholder production is seen as an important generator of surpluses, the policy and institutional requisites of its development—in the form of appropriate technology, economic incentives, profitable technical packages, an effective delivery system, assured marketing channels, and availability of consumption and investment opportunities—are not always fully recognized. Modernization of agriculture is viewed more as changing the organization of traditional agriculture; that is, as cooperative, collective, or block cultivation instead of individual farming, as moving to single cropping from traditional intercropping, as using tractors instead of ox ploughs, and as constructing modern silos for the surpluses produced instead of regional godowns. Commenting on such a common Tanzanian view of modernization, President Julius Nyerere candidly observed, "The present widespread addiction to cement and tin roofs is a kind of mental paralysis. A bati roof is nothing compared to one of tiles. But those afflicted with this mental attitude will not agree. Cement is basically earth; but it is called 'European soil.' Therefore, people refuse to build a house of burnt bricks and tiles; they insist on waiting for a tin roof and 'European soil.' If we want to progress more rapidly in the future we must overcome at least some of these mental blocks!"[18] Again, experience indicates that modern silos take a long time to construct, are two to three times as expensive per unit of storage area if constructed so as to yield benefits in reduction in storage losses, require grain-purchasing policies that are highly discriminating in the condition of grain, and necessitate bulk drying, handling, and transport facilities. Effective silo management also demands a highly disciplined and trained managerial staff. Few of these conditions exist in most African countries.

Differences in national and international perceptions seem to result from a variety of factors. Although much general research exists on some of these problems, as in the area of appropriate technology, there is little if any cross-fertilization of ideas among (largely foreign) researchers and domestic African policymakers. The dissemination of the findings of such research is almost entirely confined to the research and the international development community. There is also relatively little specific documentation on problems of particular African countries and situations. Consequently, there is a tendency to conclude that what did not work in a given situation may not necessarily be ineffective in a different situation. International agencies such as the World Bank have for instance, spent relatively few resources on relevant research and on the extension of its research results, in much the same way that agricultural research and the extension of its results have suffered nationally.

Research in Africa has suffered as the acceptability of independent outside researchers from the former metropolitan countries has declined. A growing number of educated nationals, even from universities, are moving into administrative and policymaking positions, but many are residing outside their countries because of the pull and the push factors mentioned earlier.

As has happened in many Asian and Latin American countries, the fascination with a simple transplanting of Western technology would undoubtedly wear off with greater development experience, growth of a larger educated class, and its increased participation over time at the political and administrative level.[19] In the meantime it remains a major limiting factor in the adoption of an appropriate development strategy.

In countries in which individual smallholder farming is recognized as holding development potential and is supported appropriately through government policy and services, as in Kenya and Ivory Coast, growth in small-farm productivity and income has been much more significant. Nevertheless, these countries have experienced considerable inequality in the

---

18. Julius Nyerere, *The Arusha Declaration: Ten Years After* (Dar-es-Salaam, 1977), p. 31.

19. After all, the first major resistance to the wholesale adoption of Western technology came from Gandhi in India and the economic justification for incorporating the concept of appropriate technology in development plans came from his fellow countrymen as early as the 1950s. Both Gandhi and his compatriot economists were highly educated and most, including Gandhi, were Western trained.

distribution of benefits among small farmers in various regions and tribes. Given the concern about income distribution and participation, this phenomenon is generally not favorably viewed in the international community.

Planning and Implementing Capacity of the Bureaucracy

Administration. On the one hand, the shift in the focus of international lending agencies from autonomous project entities to improving effectiveness of the normal governmental agencies to deal with traditional agriculture has increased the demands on the latter's performance. On the other hand, the creation of national identity has also required reorganization of the entire sociopolitical, agricultural, and administrative structure to achieve national identity and development objectives. Policy decisions made in Tanzania in the last decade concerning villagization, decentralization, abolition of the cooperative movement, and appointment of village managers are examples of attempts to reorganize institutions for development.

Decentralization of administration has undoubtedly created in Tanzania an administrative structure that in the long run has considerable potential to be responsive to local needs and constraints. In the short run it has, however, exacerbated the problem of realistic planning and effective implementation. Demands by regions for complex, integrated regional projects have increased in the hope that donor-aided projects would ensure the legitimacy of their claim on scarce national resources. Consequently, the need in planning for strong central coordination and for policy and technical guidance from technical and coordinating ministries has also increased to reconcile conflicting demands. But decentralization has made it difficult to staff either central ministries or regional administrations with the needed manpower, as it has spread the existing manpower too thinly. Frequently, this shortage of manpower and institutional capability has been compounded by other institutional changes such as the abolition of cooperative societies and the transfer of the existing field staff to positions of village managers, which have placed immense burden on the existing limited administrative capacity.

Although institutional changes have not been so frequent, a shortage of trained manpower exists in varying degrees of severity in all African countries. One consequence is that there is a relative vacuum at the policy, planning, and budgetary level in parent ministries. Important policy decisions related to pricing of inputs and crops, interest rates, and allocation of trained manpower and budgetary resources among regions and sectors are frequently based on a combination of welfare considerations, political imperatives, and advice of short-term visiting experts from donor agencies; all tend to be of an ad hoc nature rather than being based on well-analyzed, well-considered policy options and long-term development objectives.

This means that even if decisions that follow are correct and even if there is support among nationals who matter for those recommended by outsiders, there are substantial lags in policy formulation and implementation, which helps to explain delays in project implementation. Without commitment on the national level, the decisions do not, in effect, get implemented. Visiting experts frequently take a highly fragmented view in recommending policy changes, because they do not have to deal with the consequences of those decisions nor work within the system to implement them. The delays also mean that the administrative system is not geared to adjusting decisions quickly to changing circumstances. This may result in prices of certain commodities continuing to be too high when there have been successive good harvests, partly in response to previous price increases, or in budgetary expenditures continuing to be generous based on an expansionary policy arising out of the improved foreign-exchange earnings of a few years ago. For example, production of traditional export crops declined in some East African countries during 1976–78 because of delays in relative domestic price adjustments—to the extent of affecting the nations' export earnings significantly. The budgetary expansion resulting from the coffee price increases of that period has not, however, been retracted despite subsequent declines in those prices.

Pressure for policy decisions and resource allocation of the type noted in many African countries is not less prevalent elsewhere in the developing or the developed world. Longer institutional development means, however, that agencies with more clearly defined and recognized responsibilities carry out policy and planning analysis. Greater education, technical training, and administrative experience of the civil service and the advisory staff helps to reduce political influence on policies and allocation of resources to a greater extent than is now realistically possible in most African countries. Budgeting and allocative procedures for using the limited resources are also more explicitly established and communicated on a routine basis to various levels of governmental administration involved in planning and implementation. The development of infrastructure and communications facilitates exchange of ideas and movement of government officials and information on a scale that is not yet possible in many African countries. This allows greater fine-tuning of decisions and implementation to changing circumstances. Even in this regard there are differences, of course, as between the geographically more dispersed and infrastructurally less well-endowed countries such as Sudan, Ethiopia, and Tanzania and the more compact Kenya.

In many African countries improvement of planning and budgeting of rural development programs implies strengthening the very foundations of the governmental administrative structures. This would entail investment in education, training, and infrastructure, improvement in organizational structures and functions, and provision of technical assistance and the necessary equipment for the governmental bureaucracies to facilitate speedy communications. All of this would take a long time to achieve, perhaps from twenty to twenty-five years. Through project experience these systemic constraints are being identified increasingly. And as is illustrated by the recent World Bank financing of agricultural policy planning activities, the project approach when interpreted broadly has been a useful vehicle for developing these national capabilities. Albeit slowly, emphasis has thus begun to shift from providing ad hoc advice to creating national capacity.

The project approach by itself is, however, not adequate to address the broad sectoral and economywide constraints to development. Besides, even through projects the donor community as a whole has a way to go in ameliorating these systemic policy, planning, and budgetary-allocative constraints at the national level which come in the way of realizing objectives at the project level. The emphasis in the international development community on direct alleviation of poverty through target-oriented projects appears to have compounded the problem of inadequate attention to national policy planning constraints. For example, because of their direct accountability to their national political bodies for aid funds, some of the bilateral donor agencies seem to find it difficult to justify such financing because popular domestic perception of development needs does not incorporate an adequate recognition of the need to improve the overall development administration in these countries.

Education. Improving the planning and implementing capacity in African countries would also entail different investment priorities in other sectors. Especially in low-income countries, the emphasis of the international community within the education sector has in recent years been largely on primary education and on short-term basic functional and nonformal education and training. This seems to be the result of a variety of concerns. They include "the need to make education and training systems more responsive to the borrowing country's economic and social needs,"[20] the inefficiency of the existing formal educational systems and the consequently greater number of years of schooling required to create a functionally literate class, the high dropout rate, the concern about increasing the ranks of the educated unemployed in the long run, and the short-run inflationary implications of expansion in budgetary commitments to education.[21] There has also been concern about "the narrow concentration by governments and external assistance agencies upon the improvement of the human resources for the modern economic sector and therefore upon formal educational systems."[22]

The approach of broadening economic opportunities by broadening access to education is based on overwhelmingly strong evidence, particularly from Asian countries, that literate farmers have generally found easier access to agricultural services such as credit, inputs, and extension. There are, however, a number of issues on educational policy that require careful examination of recent experience before firm long-term commitments are made to this strategy.

Contrary to the perceptions in the international community, many countries have expanded investment in education because of the domestic political demands. In countries in which education has been expanded quickly and has been provided free, as in Nigeria, recent efforts have floundered both because of the difficulties of ensuring quality in quick expansion and the budgetary requirements of such expansion. The fact illustrates once again that egalitarianism in education cannot be successfully introduced from abroad without national commitment to that objective. Furthermore, even with such a commitment it is not certain that elitism in

---

20. World Bank, *World Bank Operations: Sectoral Programs and Policies* (Baltimore: Johns Hopkins University Press, 1972), p. 274.

21. In Kenya the recurrent budgetary expenditures on education alone were 28 percent of the total budget. Projections made in early 1970s saw this share rising to 53 percent by 1983/84. Shankar H. Acharya, "Two Studies of Development in Sub-Saharan Africa, World Bank Staff Working Paper No. 300 (Washington, D.C.: World Bank, 1978), p. 50.

22. *World Bank Operations,* p. 258.

education can be avoided entirely, as has been demonstrated in the People's Republic of China and the Eastern European countries. The requirements of formally educated manpower for modernizing the traditional rural sector are also underestimated in much of the recent concern about over investment in education. The extreme difficulties encountered in finding Africans with the necessary formal education for agricultural training demonstrates this point, though in many cases the formal educational requirements have been scaled down or specialized training has been split into many parts to accommodate the limited supply of the formally educated at all levels.

To the extent that official policies toward the rural sector discourage educated Africans from seeking employment there, balancing the supply of formally educated very tightly with the needs of the modern sector only aggrevates the problem. In many Asian countries it is the general oversupply of the formally educated for the modern sector that has eased the problem of their supply to the rural sector. Unless labor allocation is done through nonmarket forces, these considerations will have to be given greater weight in formulating future policies toward expansion of formal education in Africa than appears to be the case by donors at present.

If governments expand formal education gradually and through mobilizing resources for this purpose, the policy is likely to pay off in the long run through producing a greater supply of educated nationals who can be given the appropriate training in specific areas to carry out complex rural development tasks. Charging for education, however, implies unequal access both to education and to employment opportunities. Providing it free may require international assistance of a recurrent budgetary nature—in addition, of course, to technical assistance. This is a dilemma to which there are no easy or clear answers.

Infrastructure. Allocations to feeder roads by international development agencies have increased considerably in recent years. This is partly the result of concern about alleviation of rural poverty and appropriate technology in which low-cost construction and maintenance of feeder roads have received priority. In many countries, however, a net deterioration in the quality of the trunk road system has occurred over time despite the resources allocated by national governments and donors. Where deterioration of trunk roads has occurred, casual observation indicates that it has led to frequent failure of vehicles, increased need for spare parts and replacement of vehicles, spoilage of crops, inaccessibility of rural populations in deficit areas to food supplies in the off-season, and general decline in commercial, personal, and official traffic. It has also frequently led to a reduction in the returns to the feeder-road system.

The inadequacy of infrastructure in the countryside, together with the unwillingness of the educated, qualified staff to take up positions outside the capital city, affects the quality of planning and implementation of governmental services in rural areas.

Even to meet rural development objectives Africa thus needs substantial additional investment in infrastructure, including trunk roads to improve effective communications and exchange of goods and services and to facilitate the efficient working of markets. In contrast to most Asian countries, the low density of population and the present low volume of traffic in many African countries frequently does not suggest high rates of return to investment in trunk roads. The problem of low volume of traffic has been compounded by currency, traffic, and trade restrictions between countries. Any justification for investment in trunk roads would thus require both regional cooperation and imaginative approaches.

The higher rate of disbursements in transport projects compared with agricultural and rural development projects would also suggest that overall rates of investment in African countries can be increased by greater international lending to the development of a transport network.

Technical assistance. Even if investment in education and infrastructure is expanded, technical assistance could in the short run assist in improving governmental planning and implementing procedures. Not all governments are willing to use outside assistance in politically sensitive areas of budgetary and allocative decisions, although use of technical assistance to government departments has increased in purely professional positions such as road engineering or agronomy. Even if technical assistance is accepted, for it to be effective it has to come from countries that are or are seen to be neutral, that have similar administrative systems but whose governments perform at a higher level of efficiency. The individuals involved must have an unusual combination of relevant experience, empathy, candor, and a capacity to work effectively in an alien system. Because of both the sensitivity of the issues and the difficulty of finding such technical assistance, external agencies have generally avoided this important aspect of development, although provisions of technical assistance are usually ample at the project level. There are, of course, individual African countries in which bilateral technical assistance has been utilized, especially from the former metropolitan countries. To some extent such technical assistance simply fills the existing manpower gap. It is difficult to judge whether much of it is geared to improving the governmental procedures that during colonial times were oriented largely to the maintenance of law and order.

The Role of the Public Sector

The role of the public sector is viewed differently among African countries, as, for instance, between Nigeria, Kenya, and Malawi, on the one hand, and Tanzania and Mozambique, on the other, or even in Tanzania as between 1972–74 and 1979. Nevertheless, one factor which is pervasive and thus more limiting in many African countries than elsewhere is the role that the government is expected to play as almost the sole source of services, especially in the traditional rural sector. It would apper that, compared with the countries in which development experience and trained manpower are relatively more abundant (and thus governmental efficiency is probably not as limiting), the need for a more diversified institutional structure would be greater in Africa.

Thus, if parastatals, government departments, or the largely officially instituted cooperatives failed to provide credit and agricultural inputs, to service farm implements, to bring in the much needed food products and other consumer necessities, or to operate health clinics or run schools, these services would be available through other private commercial or communal organizations, albeit at nonsubsidized and even exploitative prices. Over time, competition among governmental, private, and cooperative institutions would, however, have greater positive effect on the quality and the price of services than would a monopoly, even though it might be public. If profitable economic opportunities did exist, there would also be an incentive to exploit them if the productive services and consumer goods and opportunities to invest the earned income were relatively more accessible through institutional diversity.

Again, President Nyerere's observations on Tanzania are most telling of the problem. "Since 1967, Government has been the fastest growing sector of the economy. In 1967 it accounted for 10.9 percent of the National Income; 1975 it was 16 percent... Just now, for example, 80 percent of the recurrent revenue allocated to the Regions is spent on wages and salaries of Government employees. This is absurd. By the end of 1967 we had 64 parastatal organizations; by 1974 we had 139 and the number has increased since... Some costs of Government could be reduced if we helped the people in villages and towns to do more for themselves."[23] Despite a certain increased pragmatism reflected in this statement, few if any effective steps have been taken since this statement was made in the rural areas of Tanzania toward reducing the role of the public sector by greater encouragement of private or cooperative initiative at the local level.

In Tanzania the government's role has increased not only in the provision of services but also in influencing techniques and organization of production. For example, decisions about the amount of fertilizer the farmers should apply and the crops on which they should apply it, whether they should grow single crops rather than planting several crops in one field to minimize risk of crop failures as they have done traditionally, and whether they should cultivate privately or collectively have frequently been influenced by zealous local party and government officials beyond levels justified by the existing technical knowledge or by government and political guidelines—and, most important, beyond the levels of peasant acceptability. In Lesotho fertilizer application has been recommended by senior government officials beyond the levels at which it is known to be technically or economically efficient, simply because of concern about increasing food production.

Where government monopolization of services has been extensive, agricultural growth has not produced any noticeable improvement in distribution. Where a diversified institutional structure has been tolerated, it has led to more rapid growth of the smallholder agricultural sector but not necessarily assured its equitable distribution.

Again, this is an area of policymaking in which ideology and political factors are important; it is not one in which external financing agencies can play a major role. To the extent that external assistance has had any influence, it has been in the direction of increasing the government's role in the service sector (although private smallholder farm production is still preferred by donors), partly because of the potential sensitivity in outsiders' promoting private sector services (especially in the rural sector, in which the political environment is frequently not conducive to its develop-

---

23. Nyerere, *Arusha Declaration,* pp. 37–39. This document, especially, 32 to 48, is the most forthright and insightful recognition of this problem by an African leader.

ment), and partly because it is easier for outside donors to deal with government entities, especially in absence of a well-developed financial or banking system. Donor agencies, including the World Bank, have recently begun to finance small-scale private enterprises through provision of funds to domestic development finance companies. This, however, has been largely in the area of manufacturing rather than the service sector and in the urban rather than rural areas.

Some of the side effects of the extensive role of the public sector is the excessive growth of bureaucracy, the frequent inadequacy of public accountability in the use of public resources, the high cost of services, administrative and political problems in cost recovery, and the consequent need for indiscriminate subsidization of services. Use of scarce government revenues and trained manpower for public services has also resulted in their shortage for other important activities such as construction and maintenance of roads and the effective operation of an educational system, both of which would accelerate the pace of long-run African development.

Recurrent Budgetary Resources

The recurrent resource intensity of many social services and the difficulty of obtaining such resources were the reasons why the earlier study emphasized the need for resource mobilization if integrated projects involving social services were to be successfully implemented. Shortage of local recurrent budgetary resources has since been one of the most pervasive constraints to rural development in most African countries. It limits the operating funds available to utilize the investments already made and causes inadequate maintenance of past investments. Vehicles and equipment financed in rural development projects frequently lie idle for lack of spare parts, repairs, gasoline, and travel allowances for field staff. Schools lack operating funds for salaries of teachers and preparation of teaching materials, and agricultural research stations have difficulty keeping up field trials. Health clinics remain underused for absence of medicines and staff salaries, and roads, stores, and processing facilities suffer from lack of maintenance. This phenomenon explains in part the delays in meeting implementation targets and the slower pace of project benefits. Analysis shows that the return on investment in maintenance is frequently higher than that realized on new investments.

Priorities in resource allocation to defense, industrialization, and maintenance of internal political order explain in part the inadequacy of recurrent budgetary resources for rural development. Failure to recover costs and extensive subsidization are other reasons for shortage of recurrent funds. The earlier discussion of the issues related to education and the role of the public sector have also indicated the effect of government policies on rapidly expanding recurrent budgetary expenditures. The wide fluctuation in the export earnings of primary producing African countries has compounded the problem of predicting resource availability from year to year, especially in view of the countries' limited budgetary capacities.

It is not clear whether the national expenditure patterns are reinforced by the almost simultaneous shift in the emphasis on poverty alleviation by the entire donor community and by the increased aid levels. It is frequently argued by fiscal economists, however, that the problem is aggrevated by the changing mix of projects in favor of those which are more demanding of the recurrent budgetary resources per unit of investment than are projects in heavy industry, ports, or harbors.[24]

There is also a tendency among donors and governments to equate development with investment. International assistance agencies working in the field of highways have typically been prepared to cover three times as high a proportion of the total cost of road construction and reconstruction as of rural maintenance. This in turn creates a bias at the national level against allocation of domestic resources for operating costs and maintenance. One of the reasons for financing investment over maintenance and operating costs by the donor community is the fact that justification for aid has traditionally been made partly because of the exports of goods and services from donor countries that are promoted by the aid. As pointed out by the previous analysis of projects, it is also much easier to achieve visible results by building schools, roads, and stores in the short run than to achieve the institution-building required to ensure maintenance and operation of those investments. The popular pressure for immediate visible results from projects in donor and recipient countries alike and the scrutiny of aid-financed projects by political bodies in donor countries is likely to make the essential long-term institution-building task more difficult in the future than it has been in the past—unless a better understanding of the process of development and the role of the international development agencies is created in the donor community. The recent international debate about direct alleviation of poverty through ensuring basic minimum needs and integrated rural development has not devoted the necessary attention to these fundamental development problems.

Agencies such as the World Bank have gone a considerable way in recognizing the maintenance and institution-building necessary for development. Capital costs for maintenance are increasingly being provided in infrastructure and other development. There is also widespread recognition of the problem of recurrent operating costs. The World Bank has been financing such incremental recurrent costs as salaries and travel allowances during the period in which a project is financed. Graduated government contributions of recurrent funds have been envisaged in other projects, and legal covenants to ensure that governments will provide the necessary recurrent costs to the particular donor-aided project have been required by the Bank and other donors. The donor's reluctance to finance the entire recurrent operating costs itself leads to strengthening financial and administrative discipline and bringing about increased government support for these expenditures.

The various steps outlined above, however, do not as yet address the basic problem, which requires understanding the particular agency's (or department's or ministry's) and sometimes the entire government's existing budgetary and operating procedures to understand and identify the precise nature of constraints before shortfalls in allocations or expen-

---

24. See Peter Heller, "The Underfinancing of Recurrent Development Costs," *Finance and Development,* vol. 16, no. 1 (March 1979), pp. 38-41.

ditures can be corrected. It also requires heavy emphasis on staff development and training. Institution-building is thus slow in disbursement. Because of their limited project focus, most donors thus far have not assessed the availability of resources to implement overall planned expenditures and ways to mobilize revenues adequately. The assumptions about the government revenues expected from projects are frequently overoptimistic in comparison with the actual benefits realized and the government effort to mobilize resources in the public sector. When aggregated at the national level, the higher actual capital-output ratios thus create a budgetary crunch both in the short and the medium run.

To some extent this shortfall could be averted by greater budgetary controls: that is, by elimination of nonessential expenses, reduction in subsidies, and greater effort at cost recovery and taxation. If recurrent resources are not available even after taking these various steps and if projects are to be effective in the future, donors would have to make increased contributions of recurrent funds in their own financing; otherwise, the lending to recurrent cost-oriented projects would have to slow down. This would require detailed analysis of the particular country's priorities and strategies to assess future local recurrent budgetary resources. It would also mean a very different type of technical assistance than is now provided at the project level.

National Manpower Allocation

Many points mentioned with reference to recurrent budgetary resources apply as well to the supply of national manpower to plan and implement projects. Few systematic exercises to assess overall manpower requirements of development activities at the sectoral or national level are carried out either by governments or donors. Manpower required to carry out all developmental activities is, therefore, frequently far in excess of availability, which leads to difficulties in finding staff and explaining the delays experienced in project implementation. The low prestige attached to employment in the rural sector and the shortage of budgetary resources for its development frequently exacerbate the problem of attracting qualified local staff, especially in remote rural areas in which housing, education, roads, and other amenities are scarce. Legal covenants similar to those undertaken to ensure local recurrent resources are required by donors to ensure local staffing.

In a situation of overall shortage even if the donor-aided project achieves full local staffing and realizes project objectives, it is usually at the cost of increasing the number of vacancies in nonproject development activities, including those in parent ministries and departments. The effect of external projects is thus less significant than appears on the surface. An additional consequence of manpower shortages is the frequent transfer of the limited staff, with a resultant lack of continuity in project planning and implementation—which causes delays in achieving results and reduces the benefits of training and experience that can be realized through greater staff continuity. Again, the desire to attract donor resources on the part of recipient countries and the desire to make a visible impact by donors and recipients alike encourages preparation of larger number of large-scale projects than staff availability would justify.

Role of Technical Assistance

The shortage of domestic trained manpower has required extensive use of technical assistance, largely for project implementation. Each staff recruited on international terms and conditions of recruitment costs from US$60,000 to US$100,000 annually. More recently, bilateral technical assistance arrangements have been entered into among developing countries (as between Sudan and Tanzania or the subcontinental countries and Tanzania) in which the technical assistance is available at far lower cost that is, the local government salaries plus certain expatriate allowances. Most of the staff recruited under international terms and conditions work in donor-financed aid projects; most of those provided by developing countries under bilateral agreements work in normal governmental development activities. The resources and support available under the two sets of circumstances are so different that it is difficult to compare the effectiveness of technical assistance based solely on the source of its supply.

The internationally recruited technical assistance plus the large numbers of consultancy firms that prepare feasibility studies have undoubtedly facilitated project formulation and implementation on a scale that would not be possible in their absence. In some cases they have also performed an important training function for the nationals. Nevertheless, there are a number of shortcomings to the development-by-technical-assistance approach. There is the problem of supply of truly technically and otherwise qualified staff available to work in an alien environment. In this regard, the high cost of technical assistance services has not necessarily ensured high quality. There is need to examine the issue of competitive bidding for technical assistance even though the difficulties are greater in assessing benefits when the final product is in the form of a service than they are in the case of goods. The World Bank has been able to go considerably farther in encouraging recipient countries to recruit qualified technical assistance on competitive terms than have bilateral donor agencies, since they frequently follow a policy of tying aid to technical assistance from their own nationals.

There is also the problem of lack of continuity in technical assistance, especially as there are relatively few long-term career prospects for internationally recruited staff in a given country. The lack of continuity means in most cases that by the time expatriates have learned the precise nature of problems and have become acquainted with the work environment, it is usually time for them to depart. The short duration of their recruitment, typically from three to five years, also gives them relatively little motivation to be effective.

The criteria for effectiveness may also be deficient in achieving long-term development objectives. In few cases has effective training of nationals to carry out a job at a similar level of efficiency been explicitly used as a criterion either by donors or recipients. The expatriate has usually expedited the implementation of the more visible investments: construction of roads, schools, and office buildings, distribution of credit, and preparation of accounts. Development of manuals, procedures, systems, and staff have usually been subordinate.

By far the most significant cost of technical assistance lies in the leakage of the learning-by-doing benefit. Millions of dollars expended by the international donor community in project preparation and implementation have not resulted in the nationals' learning from this investment to the extent that it has been possible for many Asian and Latin American countries to be more able to plan and implement their own projects. Nor is there a significant improvement in the quality of information on which the feasibility studies are prepared because of the lack of institutionalization of the information systems. Even after fifteen years of international development assistance to African countries such studies are usually rehashes of the many unreliable, conflicting, and piecemeal data that form the basis of project preparation. This high cost of the alternative approach is by far the strongest argument that can be advanced in favor of expanding formal education sufficiently to liberalize the supply of trained local manpower for modernizing Africa's traditional agriculture.

The extent to which this situation would alter quickly would ultimately depend on the African national expectations. A more appropriate balance is required between institutional development and current investment and approaches to strengthen the institutional capacity, both private and public in Africa.

A Concluding Remark

The assessment of the African rural development problem presented above is based on my personal observation of projects in the field and not on any systematic analysis of the alternative approaches to development. A number of hypotheses have been presented related to realization of immediate short-term results compared with long-term development objectives, the perceived role of international developers and nationals in realizing these development objectives, and the means by which those objectives can most effectively be achieved.

The foregoing discussion is intended to illustrate the extent to which the concept of development projects has already evolved to take into account the complex needs of developing traditional agricultural sectors in Africa. Given the limited capacity to plan and implement rural development projects, African countries do need and will continue to need greater external assistance in the form of project aid than the other more advanced countries. The evolution of the project concept by itself may not, however, be adequate to bring about a better balance between immediate alleviation of poverty and the more economywide institutional development required to improve the supply of trained manpower, economic policies, and budgetary resources available to the rural sector. All of these factors are critical if the alleviation of poverty is to be a national reality over the long run. To this end, at the overall planning level there also needs to be greater attention to issues related to resource mobilization and priorities for their allocation: for example, to education and physical infrastructure. This means that, in addition to project aid, external assistance given by agencies such as the World Bank will have to include greater assistance than before for overall development planning. Also, if this shift in the emphasis to education and infrastructure is reflected in sectoral allocations of agencies such as the World Bank, it will also increase the investment levels and rates of development in African countries in the short and the long run.

There are obviously ways in which international donors and national governments together can bring about the necessary changes in their policies and procedures to realize these objectives. This is too complex a topic to be treated even tangentially in this impressionistic essay; therefore, it is not addressed here. But not all problems outlined above are such to which individuals or even individual donor agencies or recipient countries can find quick and easy solutions. Such an objective would require consideration of a range of issues by the international development community at large.

UMA LELE

July 1979

Bibliography

Entries preceded by an asterisk are considered to be basic sources on rural development.

Background Sources Used

Adelman, Irma, and Morris, Cynthia Taft. "Who Benefits from Economic Development." International Meeting of Directors of Development Research and Training, Belgrade, August 28–30, 1973.

Almy, S.W., and Mbithi, P. "Local Involvement in the SRDP." In *An Overall Evaluation of the Special Rural Development Programme, 1972.* Institute for Development Studies Occasional Paper no. 8. Nairobi: University of Nairobi, 1973.

American University Foreign Area Studies. "Education." In *Area Handbook for Ethiopia.* Washington, D.C.: U.S. Government Printing Office, 1971.

Amogu, O. "Some Notes on Savings in an African Economy." In *Social and Economic Studies,* vol. 5, no. 2, 1959.

Anschel, K.R. "Agricultural Marketing in the Former British West Africa." In *Agricultural Cooperatives and Markets in Developing Countries,* eds. K.R. Anschel, R.H. Brannon, and E.D. Smith. New York: Praeger, 1969.

Anthonio, Q.B.O. "The Marketing of Staple Foodstuffs in Nigeria: A Study of Pricing Efficiency." Ph.D. dissertation, University of London, 1968.

Apthorpe, Raymond J. "Some Problems of Evaluation." In *Cooperatives and Rural Development in East Africa,* ed. C.G. Widstrand. Uppsala: Scandinavian Institute of African Studies, 1970.

Ascroft, J.; Roling, N.; Kariuki, J.; Chege, F. "The Tetu Extension Project: A First Report on a Field Experiment." Paper presented at the East African Universities Social Science Council, Eighth Annual Conference, Nairobi, December 1972.

Baker, Colin. "The Administrative Service of Malawi — A Case Study in Africanisation." In *Journal of Modern African Studies,* vol. 10, no. 4, 1972.

Barlow, Robin. *The Economic Effects of Malaria Eradication.* Ann Arbor: University of Michigan School of Public Health, 1968.

Barnes, C. "Kapanguria SRDP: An Evaluation." In *An Overall Evaluation of the Special Rural Development Programme, 1972.* Institute for Development Studies Occasional Paper no. 8. Nairobi: University of Nairobi, 1973.

————; Heyer, J.; and Almy, S.W. "The Tetu SRDP: The Extension Pilot Project and 4K Club Project." In *An Overall Evaluation of the Special Rural Development Programme, 1972.* Institute for Development Studies Occasional Paper no. 8. Nairobi: University of Nairobi, 1973.

*Bauer, P.T. *West African Trade: A Study of Competition, Oligopoly and Monopoly in a Changing Economy.* Rev. ed. London: Routledge and Kegan Paul, 1963.

Belloncle, Guy. "Total Participation in Public Health Programs: Some Reflections on the Niger Experience." Mimeographed. Paris: Institut de Recherches et d'Applications des Méthodes de Développement, 1973.

————, and Gentil, D. "Pédagogie de l'Implantation du Mouvement Coopératif au Niger." In *Archives Internationales de Sociologie de la Coopération,* no. 23, January–June 1967.

*Belshaw, Deryke, and Chambers, Robert. "PIM: A Practical Management System for Implementing Rural Development Programs and Projects." Institute for Development Studies. Nairobi: University of Nairobi, 1972.

*Berg, Elliot J. "Socialist Ideology and Marketing Policy in Africa." In *Markets and Marketing in Developing Economics,* eds. R. Moyer and S. Hollander. Homewood, Ill.: Richard D. Irwin, 1968.

Bergman, G., and Lindqvist, H. *Credit Situation in Chilalo Awraja.* CADU Minor Research Task no. 3. Asella, Eth.: Chilalo Agricultural Development Unit, July 1969.

Bohadal, M.; Gibbs, N.E.; and Simmons, W.K. "Nutritional Survey and Campaign Against Malnutrition in Kenya, 1964–1968." Report to the Ministry of Health of Kenya on the WHO/FAO/UNICEF–assisted project. Mimeographed, n.d.

*Boserup, Ester. *Women's Role in Economic Development.* New York: St. Martin's Press, 1970.

Capot-Rey, P.; Audebert, D.; and Owerra, R. *Opération Yabassi-Bafang: Enquête Agricole.* Yaoundé, Cam.: Ministère de l'Agriculture, Direction des Statistiques, May–June 1968.

Chabala, H.; Kiiru, D.; Mukuna, S.; and Leonard, D. "An Evaluation of the Programming and Implementing Management (PIM) System." Institute for Development Studies Working Paper no. 89. Nairobi: University of Nairobi, March 1973.

*Chambers, Robert. "Planning for Rural Areas in East Africa: Experience and Prescriptions." In *Rural Administration in Kenya,* ed. David K. Leonard. Nairobi: East African Literature Bureau, 1973.

————, and Belshaw, Deryke. *Managing Rural Development: Lessons and Methods from Eastern Africa.* Institute for Development Studies Discussion Paper no. 15. Brighton, U.K.: University of Sussex, June 1973.

Choldin, Harvey M. "Review of Rural Development in Action." In *Economic Development and Cultural Change,* vol. 20, no. 3, April 1972.

*Cleave, John H. *African Farmers: Labor Use in the Development of Smallholder Agriculture.* New York: Praeger, 1974.

Cliffe, Lionel. "The Policy of Ujamaa Vijijini and the Class Struggle in Tanzania." In *Rural Africana,* no. 13, Winter 1971.

————, and Saul, John S. "The District Development Front." In *Socialism in Tanzania,* vol. 1, eds. Cliffe and Saul. Nairobi: East African Publishing House, 1972.

Cohen, John M. "Effects of Green Revolution Strategies on Tenants and Small-Scale Landowners in the Chilalo Region of Ethiopia." In *Journal of Developing Areas,* vol. 9, no. 3, April 1975.

————. "Ethiopia After Haile Selassie." In *African Affairs,* vol. 72, no. 289, October 1973.

————. "Rural Change in Ethiopia: The Chilalo Agricultural Development Unit." In *Economic Development and Cultural Change,* vol. 22, no. 4, July 1974.

————, and Koehn, Peter H. "Local Government in Ethiopia: Prospects for Reform in the 1970s." Paper presented to the Seventeenth Annual Conference of the African Studies Association, Chicago, October–November 1974.

Collinson, M.P. "Farm Management Survey No. 3, Luguru Ginnery Zone, Maswa District." Unpublished background paper, Ukiriguru, Tanz., 1963.

*Consultative Group on International Agricultural Research. *International Research in Agriculture.* New York: World Bank/FAO/UNDP, 1974.

Cooper, St. George C. *Agricultural Research in Tropical Africa.* Nairobi: East African Literature Bureau, 1970.

Cossins, Noel J. "A Study of People and Their Cattle in the Shire Lowlands." Mimeographed study prepared for the World Bank on behalf of the Ethiopian Livestock and Meat Board, 1973.

Cowan, L.G. *The Cost of Learning: The Politics of Primary Education in Kenya.* New York: Teachers College, Columbia University Press, 1970.

Dell'Amore, Giordano. *The Mobilization of Savings in African Countries.* Milan: Cassa di Risparmio delle Provincie Lombardi, 1971.

*de Wilde, John C. *Experiences with Agricultural Development in Tropical Africa.* 2 vols. Baltimore: Johns Hopkins Press, 1967.

*Dobart, Margarita, and Shields, Nwanganga. "African Women: Security in Tradition, Challenge in Change." In *Africa Report,* vol. 17, no. 7, July–August 1972.

Dryden, Stanley. *Local Administration in Tanzania.* Nairobi: East African Publishing House, 1968.

Ethiopia, government of, Chilalo Agricultural Development Unit. *Cost/Benefit Analysis of CADU for the Period 1967/68–1973/74.* Asella: CADU, 1971.

————, Chilalo Agricultural Development Unit, Evaluation Unit. "An Appraisal of CADU's Experience in Cooperative Promotion." Unpublished report, July 1972.

————, Chilalo Agricultural Development Unit, Marketing Division. "Preliminary Market Data for 1972/73 Annual Report." Mimeographed, January 1974.

————, Economic Research Division, Planning and Program Department. *Findings of a Market Structure Survey and an Analysis of Those Grains that Provide the Basic Subsistence for the People of Ethiopia.* Soddo: Ministry of Agriculture, July 1973.

————, Wolamo Agricultural Development Unit. *Annual Report for Year 2 Programs.* Soddo: Ministry of Agriculture, May 1972.

*Evenson, Robert, and Kislev, Yoav. *Agricultural Research Productivity.* New Haven, Conn.: Yale University Press, 1975.

Food and Agriculture Organization of the United Nations. *FAO Production Yearbook 1971,* vol. 25. Rome: FAO, 1972.

————. *FAO Production Yearbook 1972,* vol. 26. Rome: FAO, 1973.

Galetti, R.; Baldwin, K.D.S.; and Dina, I.O. *Nigerian Cocoa Farmers: An Economic Survey of Yoruba Cocoa Farming Families.* London: Nigerian Cocoa Market Board, 1956.

Ghai, D. "Towards Tax Reform in East Africa." In *Readings on Economic Development and Administration in Tanzania,* ed. H.E. Smith. Institute of Public Administration, University College, Dar es Salaam. London and Nairobi: Oxford University Press, 1966.

Good, C.M. *Rural Markets and Trade in East Africa: A Study of the Functions and Development of Exchange Institutions in Ankole, Uganda.* Research Paper no. 128. Chicago: University of Chicago Department of Geography, 1970.

Hay, F.G., and Heyer, J. "The Vihiga Maize Credit Package." In *An Overall Evaluation of the Special Rural Development Programme, 1972.* Institute for Development Studies Occasional Paper no. 8. Nairobi: University of Nairobi, 1973.

Hedlund, Hans G.G. "The Impact of Group Ranches on a Pastoral Society." Institute for Development Studies Staff Paper no. 100. Nairobi: University of Nairobi, June 1971.

Helleiner, G.K. "The Fiscal Role of the Marketing Boards in Nigerian Economic Development, 1947–1961. In *Economic Journal,* vol. 74, no. 295, September 1964.

*Heyer, J.; Ireri, D.; and Moris, J. *Rural Development in Kenya.* Nairobi: East African Publishing House, 1971.

Hill, Polly. *The Gold Coast Cocoa Farmers: A Preliminary Survey.* London: Oxford University Press, 1956.

————. "Markets in Africa." In *Journal of Modern African Studies,* vol. 1, no. 4, December 1963.

*————. *The Migrant Cocoa Farmers of Southern Ghana: A Study in Rural Capitalism.* Cambridge: Cambridge University Press, 1963.

————. *Rural Hausa: A Village and a Setting.* Cambridge: Cambridge University Press, 1972.

*————. *Studies in Rural Capitalism in West Africa.* Cambridge: Cambridge University Press, 1970.

Hodder, B.W., and Ukwu, N.I. *Markets in West Africa: Studies of Markets and Trade Among the Yoruba and Ibo.* Ibadan: Ibadan University Press, 1969.

Hoffman, H.F.K. "Case Studies of Progressive Farming in Central Malawi: Report on a Socio-Economic Survey Conducted in Selected Areas of the Lilongwe Plateau." n.p.: Government of Malawi, July 1967.

Holmberg, Johan. "The Credit Programme of the Chilalo Agricultural Development Unit (CADU) in Ethiopia." In *AID Small Farmer Credit,* Spring Review, vol. 8, no. 180, February 1973.

Holmquist, Frank W. "Implementing Rural Development Projects." In *Development Administration: The Kenyan Experience,* eds. Goran Hyden, Robert Jackson, and John Okumu. Nairobi: Oxford University Press, 1970.

Hubner, G. "Private Savings in Uganda." In *Financial Aspects of Development in East Africa,* ed. Peter von Marlin. Munich: Weltforum Verlag, 1970.

Hunter, George W.; Frye, W.H.; and Swarzwelder, J.C. *A Manual of Tropical Medicine.* 4th ed. Philadelphia: W.B. Saunders, 1966.

Hyden, Goran. "Basic Civil Service Characteristics." In *Development Administration: The Kenyan Experience,* eds. Goran Hyden, Robert Jackson, and John Okumu. Nairobi: Oxford University Press, 1970.

————. "Government and Cooperatives." In *Development Administration: The Kenyan Experience,* eds. Goran Hyden, Robert Jackson, and John Okumu. Nairobi: Oxford University Press, 1970.

————. "Local Government Reform in Kenya." In *East Africa Journal,* vol. 7, no. 4, April 1970.

Ingle, Clyde R. "From Colonialism to Ujamaa: Case Studies in Tanzania's Search for Independence." Paper delivered at the Conference on the Political Implications of Change at the Local Level in Africa, University of Toronto, January 28–30, 1971.

————. "Compulsion and Rural Development in Tanzania." In *Canadian Journal of African Studies,* vol. 4, no. 1, Winter 1970.

————. "The Ten-House Cell System in Tanzania: A Consideration of an Emerging Village Institution." In *Journal of Developing Areas,* vol. 6, no. 2, January 1972.

*Institute for Development Studies. *An Overall Evaluation of the Special Rural Development Programme, 1972,* Occasional Paper no. 8 (Nairobi: University of Nairobi, 1973).

*International Labour Organisation. *Employment, Incomes and Equality: A Strategy for Increasing Productive Employment in Kenya.* Report of an interagency team financed by the United Nations Development Programme and organized by ILO. Geneva: ILO, 1972.

————. *Report to the Government of the United Republic of Tanzania on Consumers' Cooperatives.* Geneva: ILO, 1970.

*Johnston, Bruce, and Kilby, Peter. *Agriculture and Structural Transformation.* New York: Oxford University Press, 1975.

*Jones, William O. "Economic Man in Africa." In *Food Research Institute Studies,* vol. 1, no. 1, May 1969.

*————. *Marketing Staple Foodstuffs in Tropical Africa.* Ithaca, N.Y.: Cornell University Press, 1972.

Kamarck, A.M. "The Structure of the African Economies." In *Economic Change and Development: Tropical Africa,* ed. J. Oliver Hall. East Lansing: Michigan State University Press, 1969.

Kassapu, Samuel. "Dépenses de Recherche Agricole en Afrique." Unpublished memorandum. Paris: Organisation pour Coopération et Développement Economique, September 14, 1973.

Katorobo, J. *Agricultural Extension in Nyahashenyi.* Mimeographed. Kampala: Makerere University College, 1966.

————. "Agricultural Modernization: Kahoho Parish—Kigezi District." Mimeographed. Kampala: Makerere University College, 1968.

Kenya, government of. *African Socialism and Its Application to Planning in Kenya.* Sessional Paper no. 10. Nairobi: Government Printers Office, 1965.

————. *Development Plan for the Period 1965/66–1969/70.* Nairobi: Government Printers Office, 1966.

————. *Kenya Tea Development Authority Third Tea Project.* Nairobi: Government Printers Office, 1966.

Kenya National Farmers' Union. Unpublished restricted comment on *Employment, Incomes and Equality: A Strategy for Increasing Productive Employment in Kenya.* 1973.

Kifle, Henock. *An Analysis of the CADU Credit Programme 1968/69–1970/71 and Its Impact on Income Distribution.* CADU Publication no. 66. Assella, Eth.: Chilalo Agricultural Development Unit, August 1971.

Kolawole, M.I. "An Economic Study of Tractor Contracting Operations in Western Nigeria." Ph.D. dissertation. Cornell University, 1972.

————. "The Role of Agricultural Labor in Nigerian Rural Development." Paper presented to the Seminar on Rural Development, Ife, Nigeria, November 1973.

Korte, R. "The Nutritional and Health Status of the People Living on the Mwea-Tebere Irrigation Settlement." In *Investigations into Health and Nutrition in East Africa,* eds. H. Kraut and H.D. Cremer. Afrika-Studien no. 42. Munich: Weltforum Verlag, 1969.

Kreisal, H.C. *Cocoa Marketing in Nigeria.* Consortium for the Study of Nigerian Rural Development Paper no. 21. East Lansing: Michigan State University Press, May 1969.

Kreysler, J., and Schlage, C. "The Nutrition Situation in the Pangani Basin." In *Investigations into Health and Nutrition in East Africa,* eds. H. Kraut and H.D. Cremer. Afrika-Studien no. 42. Munich: Weltforum Verlag, 1969.

Lele, Uma J. "Role of Credit and Marketing in Agricultural Development." In *Agricultural Policy in Developing Countries,* ed. Nural Islam. London: Macmillan, 1974.

————, and Mellor, John W. "Jobs, Poverty, and the 'Green Revolution'." In *International Affairs,* vol. 48, no. 1, January 1972.

Leonard, David K. "The Administration of Kenyan Agricultural Extension Services." Institute for Development Studies. Nairobi: University of Nairobi, 1972.

————. "Communication and Deconcentration." In *Development Administration: The Kenyan Experience,* eds. Goran Hyden, Robert Jackson, and John Okumu. Nairobi: Oxford University Press, 1970.

————. "Organizational Structures for Productivity in Kenyan Agricultural Extension." In *Rural Administration in Kenya,* ed. David K. Leonard. Nairobi: East African Literature Bureau, 1973.

————. "Some Hypotheses Concerning the Impact of Kenya Government Agricultural Extension on Small Farmers." Institute for Development Studies Staff Paper no. 71. Nairobi: University of Nairobi, 1970.

————. "Some Hypotheses Concerning the Organization of Communication in Agricultural Extension." Institute for Development Studies Staff Paper no. 72. Nairobi: University of Nairobi, 1970.

————. "Why Do Kenya's Agricultural Extension Services Favor the Rich Farmers?" Paper read at the Sixteenth Annual Meeting of the African Studies Association, Syracuse, N.Y., October–November 1973.

————, Opindi, W.; Lucheme, E.A.; and Tumwa, J.K. "The Work Performance of Junior Agricultural Extension Staff in Western Province, Basic Tables." Institute for Development Studies Discussion Paper no. 109. Nairobi: University of Nairobi, 1971.

Leys, Colin. "Kenya's Second Development Plan: Political and Administrative Aspects." In *East Africa Journal,* vol. 7, no. 3, March 1970.

Livingstone, I. "Production, Prices and Marketing Policy for Staple Foodstuffs in Tanzania." In *Agricultural Policy Issues in East Africa,* ed. V.F. Amann. Kampala: Makerere University, May 1973.

————. "Some Requirements for Agricultural Planning in Tanzania." In *Agricultural Policy Issues in East Africa,* ed. V.F. Amann. Kampala: Makerere University, May 1973.

Luttrell, William L. "Villagization, Cooperative Production, and Rural Cadres: Strategies and Tactics in Tanzanian Socialist Rural Development." Economic Research Bureau Paper 71.11. Dar es Salaam: University of Dar es Salaam, 1971.

MacArthur, J.D. *The Development of Policy and Planning for Land Resettlement in Ethiopia.* Mimeographed. Bradford, U.K.: Project Planning Centre, University of Bradford, September 1972.

McHenry, Dean E. "Policy Implementation in Rural Africa: The Case of Ujamaa Villages in Tanzania." Paper read at the Sixteenth Annual Meeting of the African Studies Association, Syracuse, N.Y., October–November 1973.

McLoughlin, Peter F.M. "The Farmer, the Politician and the Bureaucrat: Local Government and Agricultural Development in Independent Africa." Notes and papers in *Development* no. 4. Fredericton, New Brunswick: Peter McLoughlin Associates, n.d.

*McNamara, Robert S. *Address to the Board of Governors,* Nairobi, September 24, 1973. Washington, D.C.: World Bank, 1973.

Malawi, government of. *Economic Report, 1972.* Budget Document no. 4. n.p.: Office of the President and Cabinet, Economic Planning Division, n.d.

————, Capital City Development Corporation. *Industrial Lilongwe.* n.p., n.d.

————, Department of Census and Statistics. *Malawi Population Census, 1966.* n.p., n.d.

————, Lilongwe Land Development Program. *Quarterly Report.* n.p., January–March 1974.

————, Lilongwe Land Development Program, Credit Section. *Monthly Report.* Various issues. n.p., 1970.

————, Lilongwe Land Development Program, Credit Section. *Report for the Year 1970.* n.p., n.d.

Manig, W. *Marketing of Selected Agricultural Commodities in Bako Area, Ethiopia.* Occasional Paper no. 66. Ithaca, N.Y.: Cornell University Department of Agricultural Economics, December 1973.

Marticou, H. *Les Structures Agricoles dans le Centre Cameroun.* Yaoundé: Ministre de l'Agriculture, Direction des Statistiques, 1961.

Massell, Benton F. "Consistent Estimation of Expenditure Elasticities from Cross-Section Data on Households Producing Partly for Subsistence. In *The Review of Economics and Statistics,* vol. 51, no. 2, May 1969.

Mellor, John W. "Agricultural Price Policy and Income Distribution." Unpublished paper prepared for the World Bank, December 1974.

————. "The Use and Productivity of Farm Family Labor in Early Stages of Agricultural Development." In *Journal of Farm Economics,* vol. 45, no. 3, August 1973.

————, and Lele, Uma J. "Growth Linkages of the New Foodgrain Technologies." In *Indian Journal of Agricultural Economics,* vol. 28, no. 1, January–March 1973.

Miracle, Marvin P. "Market Structure in Commodity Trade and Capital Accumulation in West Africa." In *Agricultural Cooperatives and Markets in Developing Countries,* eds. R. Moyer and S. Hollander. New York: Praeger, 1969.

————. "Market Structures in the Tribal Economies of West Africa." In *Agricultural Cooperatives and Markets in Developing Countries,* eds. K.R. Anschel, R.H. Brannon, and E.D. Smith. New York: Praeger, 1969.

Moris, Jon. "Agriculture in the Schools: The East African Experience." Mimeographed, n.d. Its earlier draft was presented as a paper at the Annual Symposium of the East African Academy, Dar es Salaam, 1972.

————. "Farmer Training as a Strategy of Rural Development." In *Education, Employment and Rural Development: The Proceedings of a Conference Held at Kericho, Kenya, in September 1966,* ed. J.R. Sheffield. Nairobi: East African Publishing House, 1967.

Mulusa, Thomas. "Central Government and Local Authorities." In *Development Administration: The Kenyan Experience,* eds. Goran Hyden, Robert Jackson, and John Okumu. Nairobi: Oxford University Press, 1970.

Nekby, Bengt. *CADU: An Ethiopian Experiment in Developing Peasant Farming.* Stockholm: Prisma Publishers, 1971.

Nellis, J.R. "The Administration of Rural Development in Kenya." In *East Africa Journal,* vol. 9, no. 3, March 1972.

Ngeze, P.B. "Some Aspects of Agricultural Development in Ujamaa Villages." Paper presented to the East African Agricultural Economics Society Conference, Dar es Salaam, 1973.

*Norman, D.W. "Inter-disciplinary Research on Rural Development: The Reru Experience." Paper prepared for a Development from Below Workshop, organized by the Overseas Liaison Committee of the American Council on Education and the Association for the Advancement of Agricultural Sciences in Africa, Addis Ababa, October 12–20, 1973.

————. "The Organisational Consequences of Social and Economic Constraints and Policies in Dry-Land Areas." Paper presented to the Second International Seminar on Change in Agriculture, Reading, U.K., September 9–19, 1974.

Nyangira, Nicholas. "Relative Modernization and Public Resource Allocation in Kenya." Paper presented to the East African Universities Social Science Council, Eighth Annual Conference, Nairobi, December 19–23, 1972.

*Nyerere, Julius K. *Freedom and Socialism.* Dar es Salaam: Oxford University Press, 1968.

*————. *Freedom and Unity.* Dar es Salaam: Oxford University Press, 1966.

*———. *Socialism and Rural Development.* Dar es Salaam: Government Printers Office, 1967.

Ogunsheye, A. "Marketing Boards and Domestic Stabilization in Nigeria." In *Review of Economics and Statistics,* vol. 48, no. 1, February 1966.

Okai, M. "The Adequacy of the Technical Base for the Agricultural Extension Service in Uganda: A Case Study in Lango District." Rural Development Research Paper no. 6. Kampala: Makerere University College Department of Agriculture, 1965.

———. "Field Administration and Agricultural Development." Mimeographed. Kampala: Makerere University College, 1966.

Othieno, T.M., and Belshaw, D.G.R. "Technical Innovation in Two Systems of Peasant Agriculture in Bukedi District: Uganda." Paper presented at the East African Institute of Social Research Conference. Kampala: Makerere University College, 1965.

Oyugi, W.O. "Participation in Planning at the Local Level." In *Rural Administration in Kenya,* ed. David K. Leonard. Nairobi: East African Literature Bureau, 1973.

Phieps, B.A. "Evaluating Development Schemes: Problems and Implications, A Malawi Case Study." Mimeographed. Dar es Salaam: East African Universities Social Science Council, Sixth Annual Conference, December 1970.

Raikes, P.L.; Lawrence, P.R.; and Saylor, L.G.; Warner, D. "Regional Planning in Tanzania: An Economic View from the Field." Economic Research Bureau Paper 68:8. Dar es Salaam: University College, 1968.

Raper, Arthur R., et al. *Rural Development in Action: The Comprehensive Experiment at Comilla, East Pakistan.* Ithaca, N.Y.: Cornell University Press, 1970.

Roberts, R.A.J. "The Role of Money in the Development of Farming in the Mumbawa and Katete Area of Zambia." Ph.D. dissertation, University of Nottingham, 1972.

Ruthenberg, Hans. "Adaptation of Extension Projects to Changing Circumstances." Paper delivered at the International Seminar on Extension and Other Services Supporting the Small Farmer in Asia by the German Foundation for Developing Countries, Berlin, October 31–November 21, 1972.

———. *African Agricultural Development Policy in Kenya, 1952–1965.* Berlin: Springer-Verlag, 1966.

———. *Agricultural Development in Tanganyika.* Berlin: Springer-Verlag, 1964.

*———. *Farming Systems in the Tropics.* Oxford: Clarendon Press, 1971.

———. "Types of Organisation in Agricultural Production Development." In *Zeitschrift für Auslandische Landwirtschaft,* Jahragang 12, Heft 3/4. July–December 1973.

Saylor, R.G. "The Administration of Innovations." Economic Research Bureau Paper. Dar es Salaam: University College, 1969.

———. "An Economic Evaluation of Agricultural Extension in Tanzania." Economic Research Bureau Paper. Dar es Salaam: University of Dar es Salaam, n.d.

———. "A Social/Benefit Analysis of the Agricultural Extension and Research Services in Selected Cotton Growing Areas of Western Tanzania." Economic Research Bureau Service Paper 70.2. Dar es Salaam: University of Dar es Salaam, 1970.

————. "Studies on the Cost/Benefit Analysis of the Agricultural Research Services in Selected Cotton and Coffee Growing Areas of Tanzania." Economic Research Bureau Paper. Dar es Salaam: University of Dar es Salaam, n.d.

————. "Variations in Sukumaland Cotton Yields and the Extension Service." Economic Research Bureau Paper 70.5. Dar es Salaam: University of Dar es Salaam, 1970.

Scheffler, W. *Baüerliche Produktion unter Aufsicht am Beispiel des Tabakanbaus in Tanzania, Eine Social-Ökonomische Studie.* Afrika-Studien no. 27. Munich: Weltforum Verlag, 1968.

*————. "Tobacco Schemes in the Central Region." In *Smallholder Farming and Smallholder Development in Tanzania,* ed. Hans Ruthenberg. Afrika-Studien no. 24. Munich: Weltforum Verlag, 1968.

Seibel, Hans, and Massing, Andreas. *Traditional Organizations and Economic Development: Studies of Indigenous Cooperatives in Liberia.* New York: Praeger, 1974.

Singer, H.W., and Doss, A.C. "Technical Assistance in Kenya: Some Thoughts on Flows and Programming." In *Eastern Africa Economic Review,* vol. 1, no. 1, June 1969.

Soo, G., and Mollet, A. *Esquisse d'une Problématique pour les EPL de Mengueme, N'goulemakong, et Zoetele.* Yaoundé, Cam.: Direction des ZAPI du Centre Sud, 1970.

Stamp, Lawrence Dudley, and Morgan, W.T.W. *Africa: A Study in Tropical Development,* 3rd ed. New York: Wiley, 1972.

Tanganyika African National Union. *TANU Guidelines, 1971.* Dar es Salaam: Government Printers Office, 1971.

Tanzania, government of. *Annual Manpower Report to the President.* Dar es Salaam: Ministry of Economic Affairs and Development Planning, 1971.

————. *The Economic Survey, 1970–71.* Dar es Salaam: Government Printers Office, 1971.

————. "Preliminary Report of the Sukumaland Interdisciplinary Research Project." BRALUP Report no. 40. Bureau of Resource Assessment and Land Use Planning, June 1970.

————. *Recorded Population Changes, 1948–1967.* Dar es Salaam: Central Statistical Bureau, n.d.

————. *Report of the Presidential Special Committee of Enquiry into the Cooperative Movement and Marketing Boards.* Dar es Salaam: Government Printers Office, 1966.

————. "Rural Water Supply in East Africa." In *Proceedings of the Workshop on Rural Water Supply,* ed. Dennis Warner. BRALUP/Economic Land Use Paper no. 11. Dar es Salaam: University College, May 1970.

————. *Second Five Year Plan, July 1969–June 1974,* vol. 1, General Analysis. Dar es Salaam: Government Printers Office, 1969.

————. "Urambo Annual Report for 1962–63." Tanganyika Agricultural Corporation, n.d.

————. "Urambo Production Report." Unpublished, Ministry of Agriculture and Cooperatives, 1970.

————. "Water Development—Tanzania, A Critical Review of Research." BRALUP Planning Paper no. 12. Dar es Salaam: University College, April 1970.

Thoday, A.R. *Marketing of Grains and Pulses in Ethiopia.* Stanford, Calif.: Stanford Research Institute, April 1969.

Toborn, Johan. *The Innovation-Diffusion Process in the Gonde Area.* CADU Special Study no. 3. Asella, Eth.: Chilalo Agricultural Development Unit, March 1971.

*United Nations Economic Commission for Africa. "Women and National Development in African Countries." Position paper prepared by the Human Resources Development Division, Women's Programme Unit. Mimeographed. February 1973.

*————, Human Resources Development Division. "Women: The Neglected Human Resources for African Development." In *Canadian Journal of African Studies,* vol. 6, no. 2, 1972.

————; Food and Agriculture Organization of the United Nations; and the Netherlands, government of. *Report: 5 Workshops for Trainers in Home Economics and Other Family Oriented Fields, Eastern and Southern Africa.* Mimeographed, 1973.

USAID, Statistics and Reports Division. "Central Government Finances: Kenya." In *AID Economic Data Book for Africa,* revision no. 286. Washington, D.C.: U.S. Government Printing Office, October 1972.

————. *AID Economic Data Book for Africa.* Washington, D.C.: U.S. Government Printing Office, annual, 1970–74.

Vail, David J. "Technology for Socialist Development in Rural Tanzania." Mimeographed, n.d. Background paper for the Sixteenth Annual Meeting of the African Studies Association, Chicago, November 1974.

von Rotenhan, D. "Cotton Farming in Sukumaland." In *Smallholder Farming and Smallholder Development in Tanzania,* ed. Hans Ruthenberg. Afrika-Studien no. 24. Munich: Weltforum Verlag, 1968.

Wallerstein, I. "The Range of Choice: Constraints on the Policies of Governments of Contemporary African Independent States." In *The State of the Nations: Constraints on Development in Independent Africa,* ed. M.F. Lofchie. Berkeley: University of California Press, 1971.

Watts, E.R. "Agricultural Extension in Embu District of Kenya." In *East African Journal of Rural Development,* vol. 2, no. 1, 1969.

Weitz, Raanan, ed. "Problem of Peasant Women." In *Rural Planning in Developing Countries.* Report on the Second Rehovoth Conference, Rehovoth, Israel, August 1963. Cleveland: Western Reserve University Press, 1966.

Williams, S.K. Taiwo. "The Confluence of Extension Education, Agricultural Extension and Community Development." In *Bulletin of Rural Economics and Sociology,* vol. 2, no. 3, 1967.

World Bank. *Lilongwe Land Development Project, Malawi.* Appraisal report no. TO-610a (restricted circulation). Washington, D.C., January 1968.

————. *World Bank Atlas.* Washington, D.C., 1973.

Yirgou, D.; Hunter, G.; Bekure, S.; and Ryden, H. *Final Report on the Appraisal of CADU and EPID.* Addis Ababa: Government of Ethiopia and the Swedish International Development Authority, May 1974.

Young, M. Crawford. "Agricultural Policy in Uganda: Capability and Choice." In *The State of the Nations: Constraints on Development in Independent Africa,* ed. M.F. Lofchie. Berkeley: University of California Press, 1971.

Additional Basic Readings

*Berg, Alan, with Muscat, Robert J. *The Nutrition Factor: Its Role in National Development.* Washington, D.C.: Brookings Institution, 1973.

*Chambers, Robert. *Managing Rural Development: Ideas and Experiences from East Africa.* Uppsala: Scandinavian Institute of African Studies, 1974.

*Collinson, M.P. *Farm Management in Peasant Agriculture, A Handbook for Rural Development Planning in Africa.* New York: Praeger, 1972.

*Eicher, Carl K. *Research on Agricultural Development in Five English-speaking Countries in West Africa.* New York: Agricultural Development Council, 1970.

*————, and Liedholm, Carl, eds. *Growth and Development of the Nigerian Economy.* East Lansing: Michigan State University Press, 1970.

*————, and Witt, Lawrence, eds. *Agriculture in Economic Development.* New York: McGraw-Hill, 1964.

*Hayami, Yujiro, and Ruttan, Vernon W. *Agricultural Development: An International Perspective.* Baltimore: Johns Hopkins University Press, 1971.

*Hunter, Guy. *Modernizing Peasant Societies: A Comparative Study in Asia and Africa.* London: Oxford University Press, 1969.

*Hyden, Goran; Jackson, Robert; and Okumu, John. *Development Administration: The Kenyan Experience.* Nairobi: Oxford University Press, 1970.

*Leonard, David K., ed. *Rural Administration in Kenya.* Nairobi: East African Literature Bureau, 1973.

*McLoughlin, Peter F.M. *African Food Production Systems.* Baltimore: Johns Hopkins Press, 1970.

*————. *Agriculture in East and Central Africa.* London: Longman, 1970.

*Mellor, John W. *The Economics of Agricultural Development.* Ithaca, N.Y.: Cornell University Press, 1966.

*Sheffield, J.R., ed. *Education, Employment and Rural Development: The Proceedings of a Conference Held at Kericho, Kenya, in September 1966.* Nairobi: East African Publishing House, 1967.

*Southworth, H.D., and Johnston, Bruce F., eds. *Agricultural Development and Economic Growth.* Ithaca, N.Y.: Cornell University Press, 1967.

*Widstrand, C.G., ed. *Cooperatives and Rural Development in East Africa.* Uppsala: Scandinavian Institute of African Studies, 1970.

Index

Agencies, programs, and projects generally referred to by acronym (for which see the Glossary, pages 193–96) are listed here under their full names. Material in the author's "Postscript to the Third Printing" is not included.

A

Abraham, Paulos, 11, 134
Administration. *See* Program administration; Project administration
African Rural Development Study, 3, 14–17, 116, 118, 121, 153, 189–94; aims of, 6–7, 19; findings of, 189–92
Agarwal, M., 11
Agency for International Development, U.S. *See* Aid, external (—by USAID)
Agricultural credit, 81–99, 129n, 168n, 199, 200, 216, 221, 223, 225; default on, 93–96, 97; eligibility for, 85–87, 92–93, 184; interest rates, 18, 84n, 184; to large-scale farmers, 81, 88–89, 93; policies, 15, 17–18, 81, 83, 184–85; repayments, 93–96, 97; and savings, 82, 83, 97, 98; and Small Industry Credit Schemes, 9, 165–66, 219, 221; to small-scale farmers, 17–18, 81, 82, 85–87, 88–89, 178, 206, 208, 209; and World Bank, 17, 218–19, 223, 225. *See also* Kenya Livestock Development Program (loans); Vihiga Maize Credit Program
Agricultural Finance Corporation, 8–9, 81, 204, 206, 207–08; aid to, 208–09; aims of, 8, 17, 176, 208; and British Land Transfer Program, 208; costs, 9, 204, 206; and default, 94n; demography of, 9, 206, 208; interest rates, 18, 84n,

206; loans, 81, 206, 208; small-holder credit programs, 17–18, 81, 206, 208, 209
Agricultural implements, 33–38, 159n
Agriculture, Department of, U.S.: dairy cow project, 28
Agriculture, ministries of: Ethiopian, 18, 174, 202; Kenyan, 133; Malawian, 139
Agriculture, subsistence-level, 25–26, 28n, 32–34, 36; crops, 24, 29, 32; and food, 27–33; incentives, 25–26, 29; and labor shortages, 23, 33–34, 36, 37; patterns, 23–27, 31–32, 33n, 119
Agriculture and Industrial Development Bank: loan policies, 81
Agriculture Development and Marketing Corporation, 31; and fertilizer inputs, 102; and maize, 105–06, 107, 108n, 114, 115, 135; as monopoly, 102n, 103n, 105–06, 181–82; profits, 181–82
Aid, external: to Cameroon, 9, 171n; to Ethiopia, 9, 18, 100n, 136–37, 171–72, 179n, 203; to Kenya, 8, 9, 28, 55, 145–46, 148–50, 155, 171n, 204, 206, 208–09, 212; to Malawi, 9, 15, 130, 214; to Mali, 9, 219; to Nigeria, 9, 165–66, 219, 221; to Tanzania, 8, 9, 17, 112, 138, 156, 223, 225
—by British Land Transfer Program, 8, 9, 203, 208, 212
—by FAO, 9, 149
—by Federal Republic of Germany, 8, 9, 171, 208, 209

—by IDA, 8, 9, 15, 17, 24, 28, 100n, 130, 138, 156, 203, 204, 208, 214, 219, 223, 225
—by Sweden, 17, 18, 112, 136–37, 149, 171, 172, 179n, 203, 204, 218–19
—by USAID, 9, 11, 55, 145, 146n, 155, 165–66, 212, 219, 221
—by the World Bank, 9, 11, 17–19, 53n, 57, 81
Aid, internal. *See* Agricultural credit
Almy, S.W., 125, 163
Anderson, W., 11, 37n
Arusha Declaration of 1967, 17, 181, 184, 225

B
_____

Banda, H., 128n
Barley, 103
Barnes, C., 11, 40, 51, 52
Bedi, N., 11
Belloncle, G., 8, 9, 30, 52, 72, 79–80, 99, 110, 126, 164, 170, 171n, 173
British American Tobacco Company, 8, 9, 13, 137, 222
British Land Transfer Program. *See* Aid, external (—by British Land Transfer Program)
Bureau pour le Développement de Production Agricole. *See* Opération Arachide

C
_____

Cacao. *See* Cocoa
Cameroon, 8–9, 15, 16, 26, 121, 168n, 197, 200; and Local Progress Enterprise, 197–99; self-help in, 125, 126. *See also* Société de Développement du Nkam; Zones d'Action Prioritaires Intégrées
Cash income, 9, 13, 14, 28, 185, 222
Cattle. *See* Livestock
Chambers, Robert, 142–43
Chilalo Agricultural Development Unit, 8–9, 46, 75, 85, 103, 110–11, 132, 136–37, 164, 165, 172, 179; administration, 67, 133, 136–37; aid to, 136–37, 171–72; aims of, 8, 15, 202; costs, 9, 106–07, 202; and credit, 83–89, 93–94, 178; demography of, 9, 15, 47, 202, 203; and

loans, 15, 83, 94–95; and model farmers, 75; training, 166–67; yields, 46–47, 103
Cleave, John H., 23, 24
Cliffe, Lionel, 157
Cocoa, 15, 16, 199, 200
Coffee, 199
Cohen, John M., 42, 47, 93n, 94n, 109n
Collinson, M., 11, 29, 31, 38n, 40, 109n
Comilla, 136
Commodity programs, 12–14
Communal plots. *See* Ujàmaa
Community Development, Ministry of, Malawi, 139–40
Commonwealth Development Corporation, 9
Compagnie d'Etudes Industrielles et d'Aménagement du Territoire, 15, 197
Compagnie Française pour le Développement des Fibres et Textiles, 10–11, 13, 14, 31, 216–19; aims of, 10, 216, 218; costs, 11; and Opération Fana, 218; yields, 218
Company for the Development of the Yabassi-Bafang Region, 200
Construction, civil: in LLDP, 15, 216
Cooperatives, 109–10, 111, 225. *See also Ujàmaa*
Corn. *See* Maize
Costs, 9, 11; of agricultural development, 69n; in AFC, 204, 206; in CADU, 202; of extension services, 68–69, 166–67, 172, 214; in KLDP, 69, 204, 206; in MPP, 203; of ox-drawn implements, 36–38; of Tanzanian social services, 122, 124; in WADU, 43, 203; in ZAPI, 199
Cotton: development in Sukumaland, 7, 12, 13, 23, 29, 30n, 34–35, 39, 109, 156, 223, 225; in CFDT, 8, 13, 31, 218; in Mali, 12, 13, 31; market prices, 14, 223; in SRDP, 148, 212; in Tanzania, 14, 17n, 29, 35–36, 39n, 40
Cows. *See* Livestock
Credit. *See* Agricultural credit
Crops, 5, 24, 29–30, 31, 37, 46, 52, 101, 103, 156; diversification, 37, 46, 50–53; export, 12–14, 27, 28, 31–32, 64–65, 109, 180; yields, 48–49, 63, 69, 71, 102, 113. *See also* specific crops

D

Development constraints, 6, 17, 189, 192
Development programs: by type, 12
De Wilde, John C., 53

E

Ethiopia, 8-9, 16, 58n, 101-04, 106-08, 113-14, 127-30, 134, 203; and agricultural credit, 81, 83-90, 93-96, 178; agricultural development in, 14, 101; and cooperatives, 109-11; and land, 42-43; tenancy in, 42-43, 85, 107, 108, 178-79. *See also* Aid, external (to Ethiopia); Chilalo Agricultural Development Unit; Minimum Package Program; Wolamo Agricultural Development Unit
European Development Fund, 9, 216
Evaluation surveys. *See* Institute for Development Studies
Expatriates, 16, 127-28, 132-33, 135-38, 148, 171-72
Export crops. *See* Crops
Extension and Project Implementation Department, 202
Extension service, 14, 15, 51, 52, 64-76, 102, 151, 168-69, 212; autonomy, 66; costs, 68-69, 166-67, 172, 214; effectiveness, 51-53, 63, 69, 70-73, 75, 169, 172, 202; improvements, 63-66, 68, 71-72, 78-80; and model farmers, 75-76, 168; staff training, 67-68, 170-71, 182-84, 192; women in, 76-78, 167-68
—agents, 14, 65, 67, 68, 70, 71-72, 76; ratio to farmers, 14, 62-63, 66-69, 70-71, 73, 199, 203, 222
External aid. *See* Aid, external

F

Farm families: in Cameroon, 15, 16, 200; in Kenya, 14, 204, 206, 214
Farm income: in Kenya, 41n; in Tanzania, 25
Farm production systems, 22, 25, 33n, 34, 36, 37
Farmers, 70, 102, 138, 155-57, 179,

197; as leaders, 75-76, 173; training of, 15, 166-67, 168-69, 197. *See also* Agricultural credit (to large-scale farmers; to small-scale farmers); Extension service agents (ratio to farmers)
Field staff: inadequacies of in SODENKAM, 69, 170; training of, 67-68, 170-71, 182-84, 192
Finance and Economic Planning, Ministry of, Kenya, 144-45
Flax, 103
Fonds d'Aide et de Coopération, 216, 218
Food and Agriculture Organization of the United Nations. *See* Aid, external (—by FAO)
Food supply, domestic, 27, 56, 118, 181; government policy on, 31-32; shortages, 30-32, 44, 180; versus export supply, 27, 31-32, 180
Foreign aid. *See* Aid, external
Functional programs, 17

G

Gentil, D., 8, 9, 30, 52, 72, 79, 80, 99, 110, 126, 164, 170, 171n, 173
Germany, Federal Republic of. *See* Aid, external (—by Federal Republic of Germany)
Grain, 103, 104, 107-08, 110, 113, 156n
Groundnuts, 50-51; and Malawi, 49, 50-51, 57, 71, 216; and Mali, 8, 12, 13, 31, 37, 38, 70, 135, 218

H

Harambee, 125, 126, 148
Health, 117-19, 140; services, 16, 117, 119, 121, 126
Holmquist, Frank W., 135

I

Implements, agricultural, 33-38, 159n
Income. *See* Farm income; Lilongwe Land Development Program (income in)
Income distribution, 122-23, 185n

Industrial Development Centers:
aims of, 8, 18, 166, 219; costs, 9;
loans, 18, 165, 221; and USAID, 9,
165–66, 219, 221
Industry, Federal Ministry of,
Nigeria: budget of, 219, 221
Institute for Development Studies:
evaluation surveys in Kenya, 145,
146n, 147, 148n, 169
Institutional development. See Program administration
Interest rates: in Ethiopia, 83–84; in
Kenya, 204. See also Agricultural
credit; Agricultural Finance Corporation
International Bank for Reconstruction and Development. See World
Bank
International Development Agency.
See Aid, external (—by IDA)

J

Jahnke, H., 8, 9

K

Kenya, 3, 5, 7, 8–11, 12, 25, 51, 55,
67, 69, 76, 83, 117, 118n, 133, 135,
150, 162, 168–69, 204; credit
systems of, 208; economy of, 5,
213; farmers in, 14, 41n, 204, 206,
214; government expenditures, 14,
51, 124, 145–46, 208, 210, 214; and
land, 40–41; loan volume of, 41n,
204, 208; Million Acre Scheme,
214; population distribution, 3,
40–41, 45; self-help in, 125; and
squatters, 7, 19, 41–42, 51, 117,
119, 213, 214. See also Agricultural
Finance Corporation; Aid, external
(to Kenya); Finance and Economic
Planning, Ministry of; Institute for
Development Studies; Kenya Livestock Development Project; Kenya
Tea Development Authority; National Rural Development Committee; Special Crops Development
Authority; Special Rural Development Program; Vihiga Maize Credit Program
Kenya Livestock Development Project, 8–9, 18, 28, 59; aid to, 204,
206, 208, 212; aims of, 8, 204;
costs, 9, 69, 204, 206; demography
of, 9, 206; investments, 18, 204,
206; and Livestock Marketing Project, 212; loans, 18, 204, 206;
ranches, 18, 60, 204, 206
Kenya Tea Development Authority,
8–9, 28, 64n, 133, 210; aims of, 8,
209; demography of, 9, 12, 27, 73,
138, 209, 210; extension services,
14, 65, 67, 69, 76; and incomes, 9,
13, 28, 185; production, 12, 73,
138, 209, 210; return, 12
Kericho conference, 144, 210
Khan, Akhter Hameed, 136
Kinsey, B.H., 11, 49

L

Labor, 24, 27, 119; allocation, 23–27,
31–32, 33, 119; bottlenecks, 23,
33–34, 36, 37, 38; migration,
38–45; sexual division of, 25–27;
shortage, 23, 33–34, 36, 37; smallholder, 23–27; surplus, 23
Land, 5, 40–43, 190. See also Project
area
Leonard, David K., 72
Lilongwe Land Development Program, 10–11, 15, 44, 50–51, 54, 57,
66–67, 70–71, 90–95, 97–99, 108,
113, 120, 129n, 214, 216; administration, 131, 139, 140; Africanization of, 130, 172; aims of, 10, 214,
216; costs, 11, 68, 129n, 130,
166–67, 214; and credit, 15, 57,
90–93, 98–99, 129n, 216; demography of, 9, 15, 44, 48, 214; and
groundnuts, 50–51, 57, 71, 216; income in, 53, 54–55, 57–58, 216;
and livestock, 57–59, 216; and
maize, 32, 49–50, 70, 105–06,
113–15, 135, 182; training in, 15,
70–71, 166–68, 216; yields, 48–49,
216
Linsenmeyer, D., 11
Lint and Seed Marketing Board, 110,
225
Literacy, 164
Livestock, 56–59, 216. See also Kenya
Livestock Development Project
Loans. See Agricultural credit
Local participation, 89–90, 99, 124,

162–64, 184; in Ethiopia, 136, 164, 179; in Kenya, 147–48, 150, 162–63; in Tanzania, 162, 179
Local Progress Enterprise, 197, 199

M

McLoughlin, Peter F.M., 65
Maize, 29–30, 105, 119n; in Ethiopia, 47–48, 203; prices, 48–49, 105–06; return on, 181; in Tanzania, 29. See also Agriculture Development and Marketing Corporation (and maize); Lilongwe Land Development Program (and maize); Vihiga Maize Credit Program
Malaria, 39, 117
Malawi, 44, 49, 56–57, 66, 69n, 120, 182; Master Farmer Program, 81; program structure of, 16, 127, 130, 131, 139; Salima project in, 102n. See also Agriculture Development and Marketing Corporation; Aid, external (to Malawi); Lilongwe Land Development Program
Mali, 3, 31–32, 37–38, 45, 70, 135, 165; and cotton, 12, 13, 31; and groundnuts, 12, 31, 38, 70, 135. See also Aid, external (to Mali); Compagnie Française pour le Développement des Fibres et Textiles; Opération Arachide
Manpower shortage, 177–78, 182–84, 191–92
Marketing: in Cameroon, 199–200; channels, 31–33, 101, 108, 113, 181; of coffee, 200; cooperatives, 109–11; costs, 106–07, 108; in Ethiopia, 101–04, 106–08, 113–14; improvements, 32–33, 103, 112–13, 181–82; paternalism in, 110–11; and purchasing component, 101–03, 106, 191–92; return, 102
Marticou, H., 56
Masai cattle production, 59
Master Farmers Scheme, 16, 149, 212
Mbithi, P., 11, 40, 51, 52, 125, 163
Mechanization, 33–38, 159n
Migration: intra-rural, 38–45
Minimum Package Program, 8–9, 85, 100n, 203–04; aid to, 18, 203; aims of, 8, 18–19, 33, 203; cost, 9, 203;

and credit, 84–85, 87–89; demography of, 9, 203; return, 203; yields, 203
Ministry. See specific ministry
Mwongozo, 155

N

Nairobi: population growth, 5
National Rural Development Committee, 145–46
Nekby, Bengt, 135–36, 137n, 170n
Netherlands: aid to Kenya, 9, 212
Niger: health project, 126; literacy program, 164
Nigeria, 24, 26n, 219. See also Aid, external (to Nigeria); Industrial Development Centers; Industry, Federal Ministry of
Nkondjok, 121
Nomads, 3
Norman, D.W., 23–24
Norwegian Agency for International Development: aid to Kenya, 9, 145
Nutrition, 117–18
Nuts. See Groundnuts
Nyerere, Julius, 151, 156, 223, 225

O

Office des Produits Agricoles du Mali: as cereal supplier, 31–32
Opération Arachide, 13, 31–32, 37–38, 76, 218–19; aims of, 9, 218; costs of, 9; demography of, 9, 218; extension agents, 70, 76; and groundnuts, 8, 13, 37, 70, 218; and World Bank aid, 218–19; yields, 218
Opération Fana, 218
Organization for Economic Cooperation and Development, 28n
Ox-drawn implements, 36–38

P

Paddy: in Tanzania, 29
Participation. See Local participation
pH soil factor: of groundnuts, 51
Population, 4, 5, 42n, 44; distribution in Kenya, 3, 19, 40–41, 45, 213, 214; migration, 38–45; rural percentage, 4; totals by country, 4

—, program or project: in AFC, 9, 204, 206; in CADU, 9, 203; in CFDT, 9; in KLDP, 9, 206; in KTDA, 9, 209; in MPP, 9, 203; in Opération Arachide, 9, 218; in SCDA, 9; in SODENKAM, 9, 121, 200; in SRDP, 9; in Sukumaland, 9; in *ujàmaa* system, 9; in WADU, 9, 202; in ZAPI, 9, 197
Production, Ministry of, Mali, 32, 135
Program administration, 14–17, 143–44, 186–87, 191; aims of, 17, 19–20, 142, 149, 154–55; and implementation, 142, 190–91; planning, 146–50, 188, 190–91; priorities, 142, 192. *See also Ujàmaa*
Project administration, 16, 127–30, 132, 134, 135, 139–41; Africanization of, 128, 130–35; decentralization of, 16, 187–88; expatriates in, 16, 127–28, 132–33, 135, 136–37, 148; and local administration, 129–30, 134–35, 138–40; salaries, 131, 133–34; staff training, 16, 17, 127–30, 133, 138, 189, 192
Project area, 9, 11; in Kenya, 9, 12, 15, 47, 73, 138, 202, 206, 209, 210; in Malawi, 15, 48, 214; in Mali, 218; in Tanzania, 14, 29, 30n, 35
Projects, 53, 186, 189, 190; aims of, 3, 6, 19–20, 53, 132n, 176; and collectives, 179; defined, 20; effectiveness, 176–77; evaluation, 175, 182, 189; focus, 190; implementation, 190–91; and land tenure, 176, 178–79; and low-income participation, 20, 53, 175–78, 184, 186, 192; manpower, 177–78, 182–84, 191–92; self-sustenance, 20, 176. *See also* Project administration; Training for rural development; specific projects
Public Works, Ministry of, Malawi, 139

R

Rainfall, 3, 40n
Regional Development Fund, 155
Research: in CADU, 46; deficiencies, 50–52, 56; effects on crops, 46, 50, 52–53; expenditures, 28n; needs, 173–74

Roads: in Malawi, 113, 139, 216
Robinson, F., 11
Rural sector surveys. *See* World Bank (report on Kenya; report on Malawi; report on Tanzania)
Ruthenberg, H., 8, 9, 40n, 64

S

Salary scales, 131, 133–34
Salima project, 102n
Savings, 82, 83, 97, 98
Self-help, 20, 55, 125, 126, 148
Sequential Implementation Program, Kenya, 163, 212; implications of, 190, 192, 193–94; second stage of, 190
Sexual division of labor, 25, 26–27
Shah, M., 11
Shire Lowlands, 58n
Small businesses: aid to, 9, 165–66, 219, 221
Smallholder sector: 12, 13, 17, 23–27, 51–52. *See also* Agricultural Finance Corporation
Small Industry Credit Schemes. *See* Agricultural credit
Social services: "bottom up" administration, 121–22, 124, 152, 186; costs, 122, 124; defined, 117; and income distribution, 122–23, 185; local participation in, 124; resources, 116, 120, 121n, 122–24, 186; in SODENKAM, 200; "top down" administration, 120–21; in *ujàmaa* system, 122, 159. *See also* Health; Water supply
Société Centrale pour les Etudes du Territoire–Coopération: as planner, 200
Société de Développement du Nkam, 8–9, 15, 16, 111, 171n, 200; aim of, 8; and coffee, 200; costs, 9; demography of, 9, 15, 16, 121, 200; extension programs, 52; and health services, 16, 121; productivity in, 30; and social services, 200; staff, 69, 170
Société d'Etudes du Développement Economique et Social, 70
Sorghum production, 29
Special Crops Development Authority, 12; aims of, 8; costs, 9; demography of, 9

Special Rural Development Program, 10–11, 145–48, 168, 212; administration, 16, 17, 143–44, 147, 149–50, 173–74, 187–88; aid to, 9, 145–46, 148–50; aims of, 8, 9, 144, 210, 212; costs, 9; and cotton block scheme, 148, 212; demography of, 9; funding, 145–46; and *harambee,* 148; and local participation, 147–48, 150, 162–63; Master Farmers Scheme, 16, 149, 212; planning, 143, 146–48, 149–50, 162

Squatters. *See* Kenya (and squatters)

Staggered planting, 29–30

Storage needs, 118

Sukumaland, 10–11, 25, 29, 36, 67, 223; aims in, 10; costs, 11; and cotton, 7, 12, 13, 23, 29, 30n, 34–35, 39, 109, 156, 223, 225; demography of, 9, 39, 223; migration, 39; time-use pattern in, 25–26; tractor use in, 34–35

Sulfur dust, 51

Sullivan, D., 8, 9

Sweden. *See* Aid, external (— by Sweden)

Swedish International Development Authroity. *See* Aid, external (— by Sweden)

T

Tabora Tobacco Growers Cooperative, 13, 137, 222

Tanganyika African National Union, 155, 226; and *ujàmaa,* 17, 151–53, 155, 226

Tanganyika Agricultural Corporation, 13, 30, 133

Tanzania, 7, 26–27, 67, 118, 121, 153, 159, 160, 162, 179, 188–89; and cooperatives, 109–10, 111, 225; and cotton, 35–36, 39n, 40; and food production, 29, 156; government expenditures, 121–22, 124, 188; incomes, 13, 14, 222; and land, 40n, 156–57, 223; Lint and Seed Marketing Board, 110, 225; and maize, 29–30; migration in, 39–40; social services, 122, 124; and tobacco, 8, 9, 13, 17n, 30, 67, 133, 137, 156, 222; tractor use in, 34–36, 158. *See also* Aid, external (to Tanzania); Cooperatives; Tanganyika African National Union; Tanganyika Agricultural Corporation; *Ujàmaa;* Urambo Farmers Cooperative Society; Urambo Settlement Scheme

Tanzania Agricultural Machinery Testing Unit, 37

Tanzania Rural Development Bank, 17

Tanzania Tobacco Authority, 133

Tea. *See* Kenya Tea Development Authority

Technology for small farms, 37, 180. *See also* Mechanization

Tecle, T., 8, 9, 114, 134

Teff, 203

Tenants, 42–43, 85, 107, 108, 178–79

Thim, H., 8, 9

Time-use pattern, 23–27, 31–32, 33n, 119

Tobacco, 8, 9, 11, 13, 17n, 24n, 30, 54, 65n, 67, 133, 137, 138, 156, 181, 222, 223

Tomatoes, 24n

Tontines, 83, 168n

Tractors, 33–35

Training for rural development, 65, 165–67, 171–74; administration, 172–74; Africanization of, 171; budget, 172; effectiveness, 171–72; of farmers, 168–69; and literacy, 164; and local participation, 162–64, 184; of staff, 170–71, 182–84; and women, 167–68. *See also* Extension service; Farmers (training of); Field staff; Project administration

Trypanosomiasis, 39

Tsetse, 29, 139, 225

Tumbi Tobacco Scheme, 10–11, 13, 137, 222

Turner, H., 11

U

Uganda: farmer's work day in, 24

Ujàmaa, 7n, 10–11, 12, 111n, 151–61, 179, 225–26; administration, 16, 17, 35–36, 151–53, 155, 157–58, 159, 160, 188–89; aid to, 223, 225; communal plots, 74–75, 151, 154, 156, 179, 223; costs in, 9;

demography of, 9, 17, 151–52, 154, 226; extension services, 74, 151; future needs of, 157–58, 160, 179; philosophy, 8, 17, 151, 153, 154, 155–56, 160, 225; and social services, 122, 159; and TANU, 17, 151–53, 155, 226; taxing power, 153; and tobacco, 138, 156, 223; tractor incentives, 36, 159n; and villagization, 152, 157, 158, 179, 225–26

United Kingdom. *See* Aid, external (— by British Land Transfer Program)

Urambo Farmers Cooperative Society, 13, 29, 30n, 67

Urambo Settlement Scheme, 10–11, 137

Urambo Tobacco Scheme, 10–11, 30n, 67, 137, 222

USAID. *See* Aid, external (— by USAID)

V

Vail, David J., 157, 158n, 159, 160

Vihiga Maize Credit Program, 55–56, 71–72, 96, 146n, 212

Villagization: defined, 152n. *See also* *Ujàmaa*

Von Pischke, J. D., 8, 9, 40n, 83, 94n

Von Rotenhan, D., 30, 31, 36

W

Water supply, 27, 119, 123

Weeding, 33n, 34, 36

Wheat, 40, 103–04, 202

Wolamo Agricultural Development Unit, 8–9, 67, 78–79, 94, 135, 203; administration, 131–32, 134, 135; aid to, 203; aims of, 8, 15, 203; costs, 9, 43, 203; and credit, 84, 87–90, 94; crops, 48, 104, 107–08, 110; demography of, 9, 15, 48, 202; and land, 9, 43; loans, 15, 84; staff training, 164; yields, 47–48, 203

Women: training programs for, 76–78, 167–68. *See also* Sexual division of labor

World Bank, 3, 6, 7n, 132n; report on Kenya, 5, 7, 118; report on Malawi, 49; report on Tanzania, 7, 118, 121, 153. *See also* Aid, external (—by World Bank)

World Food Program, 9, 203

Y

Yields: of crops, 48–49, 222; with ox-drawn implements, 37

Z

Zambia: and maize, 106n, 119n

Zones d'Action Prioritaires Intégrées, 8–9, 75–76, 117, 173, 199, 200; aims of, 8, 15; cooperatives, 110; costs, 9, 199; crops, 78, 199; demography of, 9, 197; extension services, 15, 69–70; loans, 15, 199, 200; and women, 167n